SAUCER COUNTRY
THE RETICULAN CANDIDATE

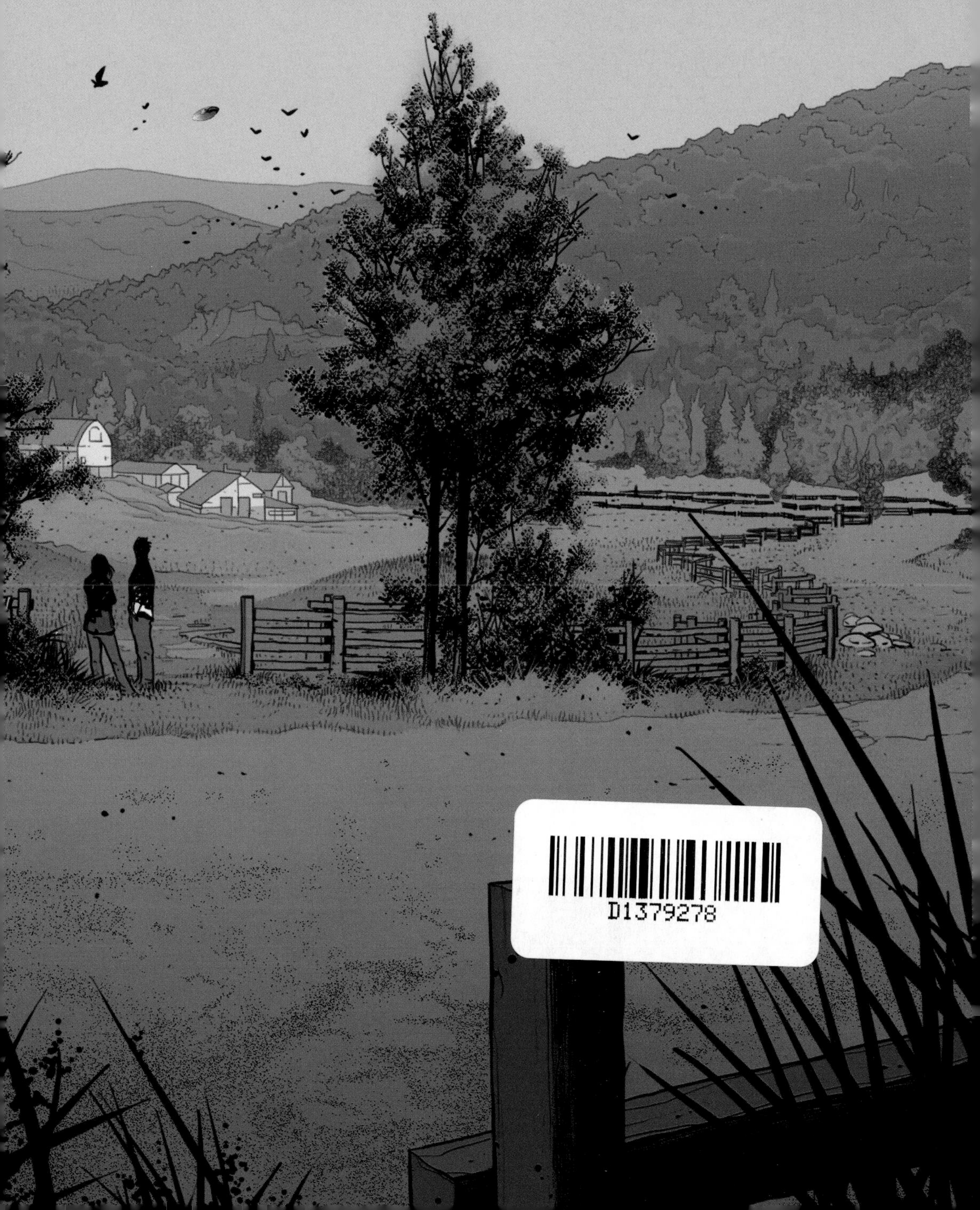

SAUCER
COUNTRY

THE RETICULAN CANDIDATE

PAUL CORNELL
WRITER

RYAN KELLY
DAVID LAPHAM PGS. 7-26
MIRKO COLAK & ANDREA MUTTI PGS. 93-112
ARTISTS

GIULIA BRUSCO
LEE LOUGHRIDGE
COLORISTS

SAL CIPRIANO
LETTERER

RYAN KELLY
SERIES & COLLECTION COVER ARTIST

SAUCER COUNTRY CREATED BY **CORNELL & KELLY**

WILL DENNIS   EDITOR - ORIGINAL SERIES
MARK DOYLE   ASSOCIATE EDITOR - ORIGINAL SERIES
SARA MILLER   ASSISTANT EDITOR - ORIGINAL SERIES
ROWENA YOW   EDITOR
ROBBIN BROSTERMAN   DESIGN DIRECTOR - BOOKS

HANK KANALZ   SENIOR VP - VERTIGO & INTEGRATED PUBLISHING

DIANE NELSON   PRESIDENT
DAN DIDIO AND JIM LEE   CO-PUBLISHERS
GEOFF JOHNS   CHIEF CREATIVE OFFICER
JOHN ROOD   EXECUTIVE VP - SALES, MARKETING
      AND BUSINESS DEVELOPMENT
AMY GENKINS   SENIOR VP - BUSINESS AND LEGAL AFFAIRS
NAIRI GARDINER   SENIOR VP - FINANCE
JEFF BOISON   VP - PUBLISHING PLANNING
MARK CHIARELLO   VP - ART DIRECTION AND DESIGN
JOHN CUNNINGHAM   VP - MARKETING
TERRI CUNNINGHAM   VP - EDITORIAL ADMINISTRATION
ALISON GILL   SENIOR VP - MANUFACTURING AND OPERATIONS
JAY KOGAN   VP - BUSINESS AND LEGAL AFFAIRS, PUBLISHING
JACK MAHAN   VP - BUSINESS AFFAIRS, TALENT
NICK NAPOLITANO   VP - MANUFACTURING ADMINISTRATION
SUE POHJA   VP - BOOK SALES
COURTNEY SIMMONS   SENIOR VP - PUBLICITY
BOB WAYNE   SENIOR VP - SALES

SAUCER COUNTRY VOLUME 2: THE RETICULAN CANDIDATE
PUBLISHED BY DC COMICS. COVER AND COMPILATION COPYRIGHT © 2013
PAUL CORNELL AND RYAN KELLY. ALL RIGHTS RESERVED.
ORIGINALLY PUBLISHED IN SINGLE MAGAZINE FORM IN SAUCER COUNTRY
#7-14 COPYRIGHT © 2012, 2013 PAUL CORNELL AND RYAN KELLY. ALL
RIGHTS RESERVED. VERTIGO IS A TRADEMARK OF DC COMICS. ALL
CHARACTERS, THEIR DISTINCTIVE LIKENESSES AND RELATED ELEMENTS
FEATURED IN THIS PUBLICATION ARE TRADEMARKS OF DC COMICS. THE
STORIES, CHARACTERS AND INCIDENTS FEATURED IN THIS PUBLICATION
ARE ENTIRELY FICTIONAL. DC COMICS DOES NOT READ OR ACCEPT
UNSOLICITED IDEAS, STORIES OR ARTWORK.

DC COMICS, 1700 BROADWAY, NEW YORK, NY 10019
A WARNER BROS. ENTERTAINMENT COMPANY.
PRINTED IN THE USA. 7/03/13. FIRST PRINTING.
ISBN: 978-1-4012-4047-9

LIBRARY OF CONGRESS CATALOGING-IN-PUBLICATION DATA

CORNELL, PAUL, AUTHOR.
  SAUCER COUNTRY. VOLUME 2, THE RETICULAN CANDIDATE / PAUL CORNELL,
DAVID LAPHAM.
      PAGES CM
  "ORIGINALLY PUBLISHED IN SINGLE MAGAZINE FORM IN SAUCER COUNTRY
7-14."
  ISBN 978-1-4012-4047-9
  1. GRAPHIC NOVELS. I. BROXTON, JIMMY, ILLUSTRATOR. II. LAPHAM,
DAVID, ILLUSTRATOR. III. TITLE. IV. TITLE: RETICULAN CANDIDATE.
  PN6728.S28C68 2013
  741.5'973—DC23
                                          2012050775

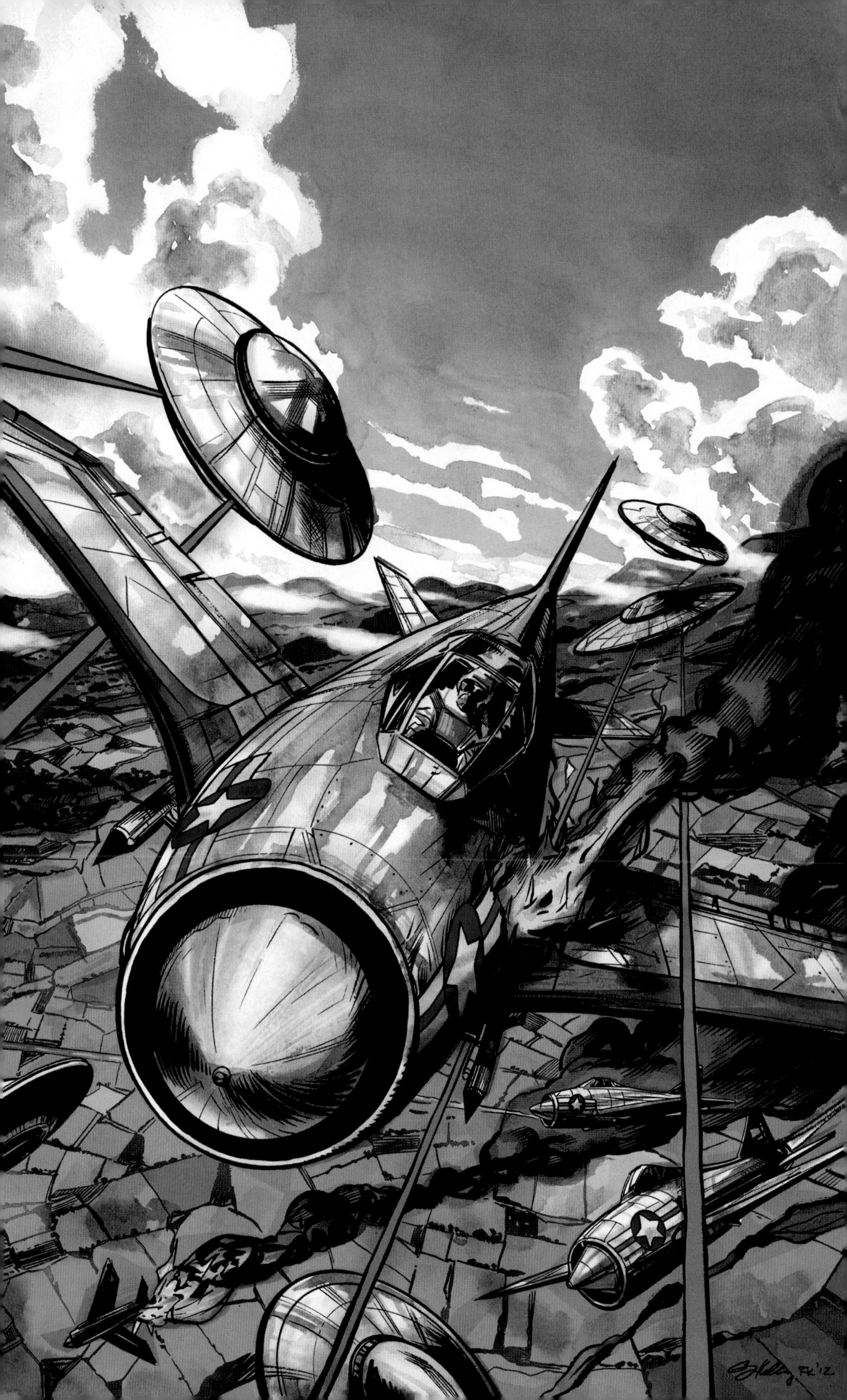

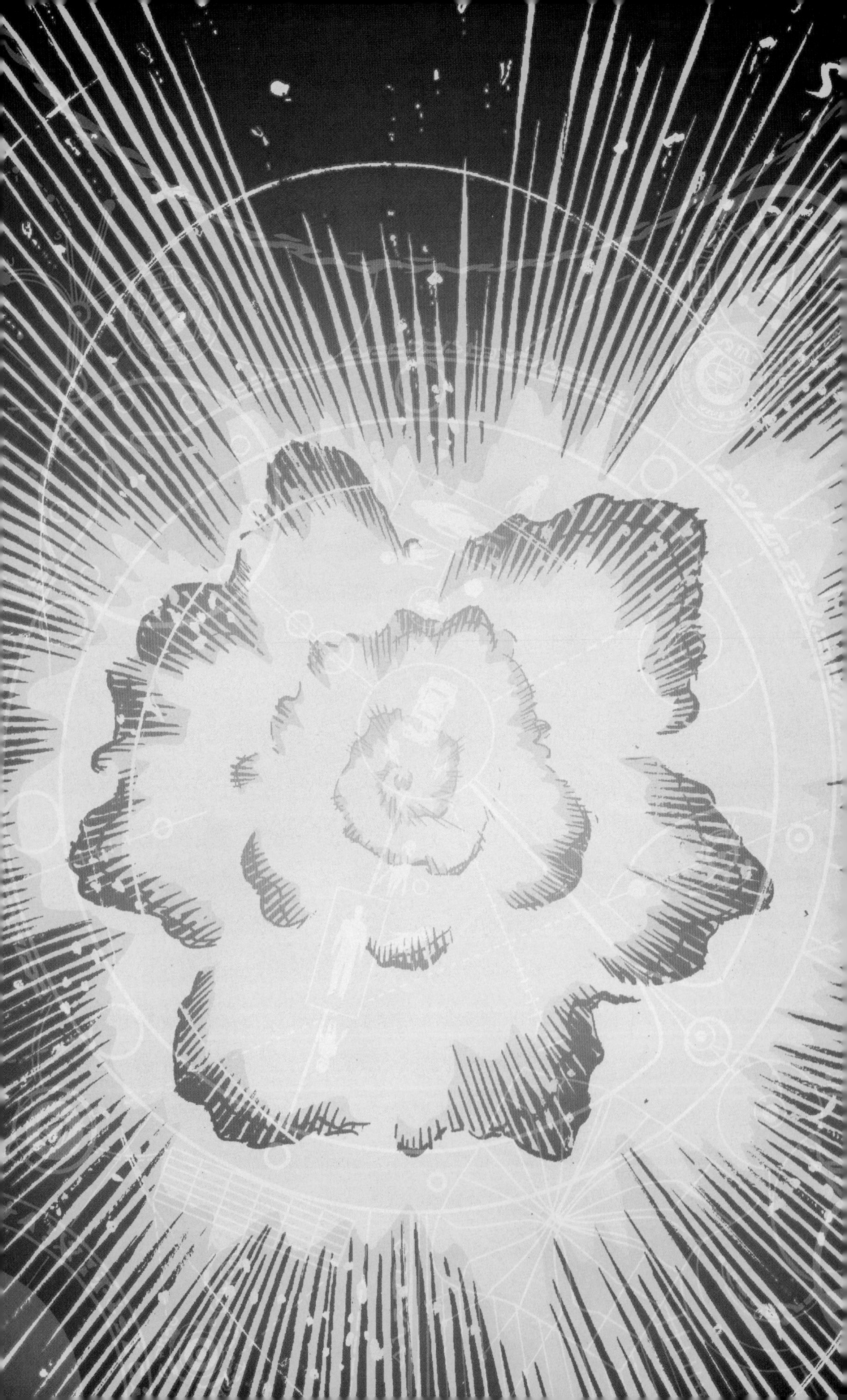

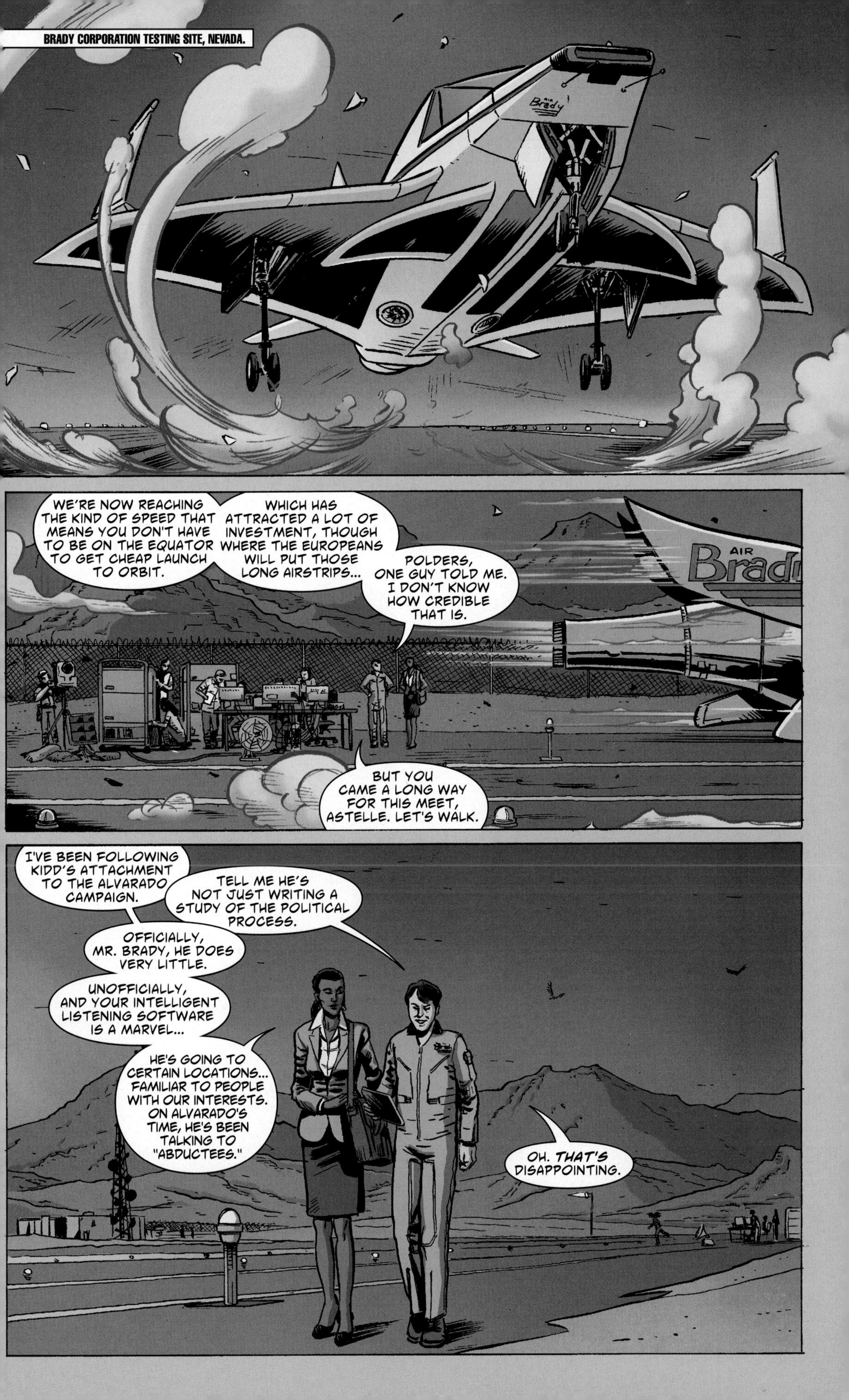
BRADY CORPORATION TESTING SITE, NEVADA.
AIR Brady
WE'RE NOW REACHING THE KIND OF SPEED THAT MEANS YOU DON'T HAVE TO BE ON THE EQUATOR TO GET CHEAP LAUNCH TO ORBIT.
WHICH HAS ATTRACTED A LOT OF INVESTMENT, THOUGH WHERE THE EUROPEANS WILL PUT THOSE LONG AIRSTRIPS...
POLDERS, ONE GUY TOLD ME. I DON'T KNOW HOW CREDIBLE THAT IS.
BUT YOU CAME A LONG WAY FOR THIS MEET, ASTELLE. LET'S WALK.
I'VE BEEN FOLLOWING KIDD'S ATTACHMENT TO THE ALVARADO CAMPAIGN.
TELL ME HE'S NOT JUST WRITING A STUDY OF THE POLITICAL PROCESS.
OFFICIALLY, MR. BRADY, HE DOES VERY LITTLE.
UNOFFICIALLY, AND YOUR INTELLIGENT LISTENING SOFTWARE IS A MARVEL...
HE'S GOING TO CERTAIN LOCATIONS... FAMILIAR TO PEOPLE WITH OUR INTERESTS. ON ALVARADO'S TIME, HE'S BEEN TALKING TO "ABDUCTEES."
OH. *THAT'S* DISAPPOINTING.

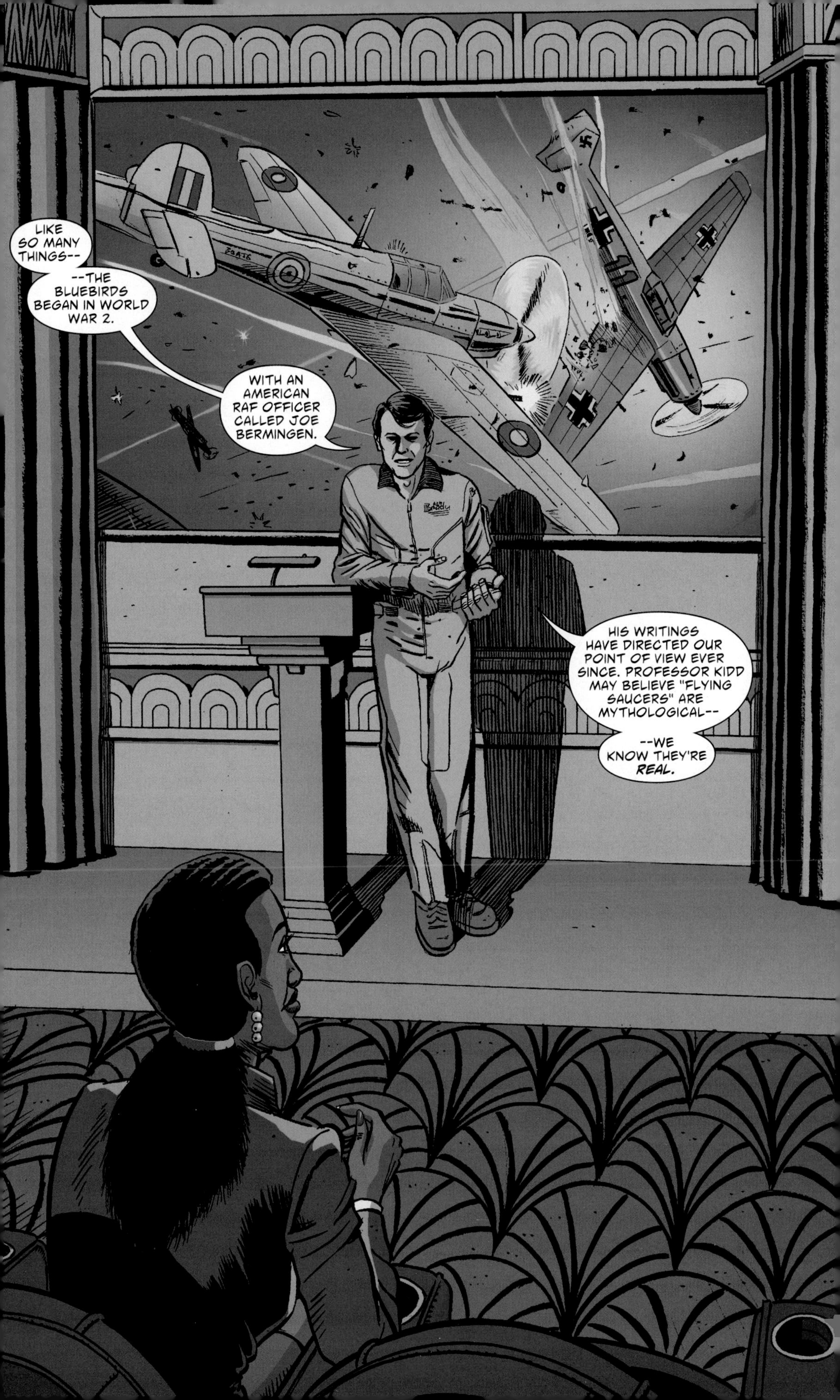
LIKE SO MANY THINGS--
--THE BLUEBIRDS BEGAN IN WORLD WAR 2.
WITH AN AMERICAN RAF OFFICER CALLED JOE BERMINGEN.
HIS WRITINGS HAVE DIRECTED OUR POINT OF VIEW EVER SINCE. PROFESSOR KIDD MAY BELIEVE "FLYING SAUCERS" ARE MYTHOLOGICAL--
--WE KNOW THEY'RE *REAL*.

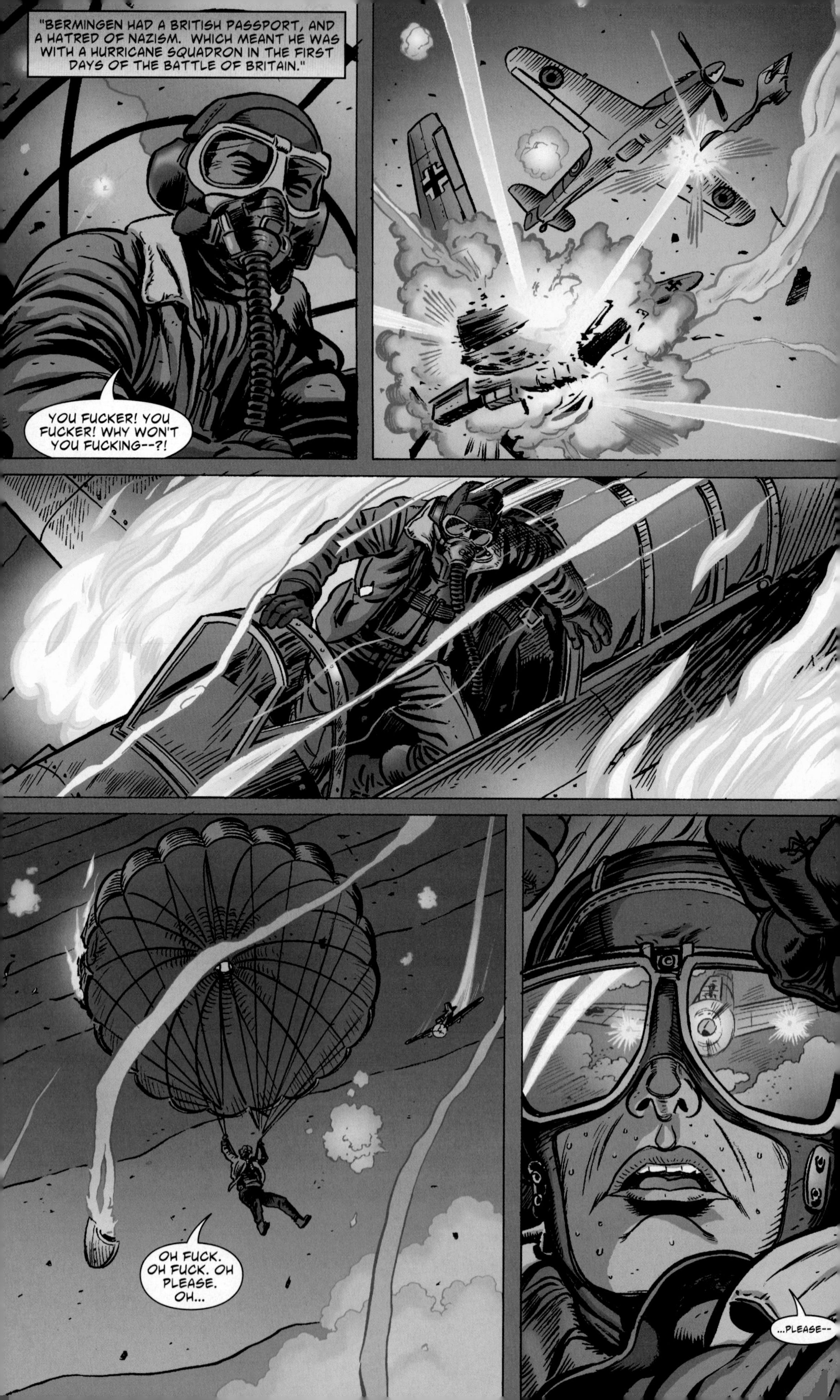
"BERMINGEN HAD A BRITISH PASSPORT, AND A HATRED OF NAZISM. WHICH MEANT HE WAS WITH A HURRICANE SQUADRON IN THE FIRST DAYS OF THE BATTLE OF BRITAIN."
YOU FUCKER! YOU FUCKER! WHY WON'T YOU FUCKING--?!
OH FUCK. OH FUCK. OH PLEASE. OH...
...PLEASE--

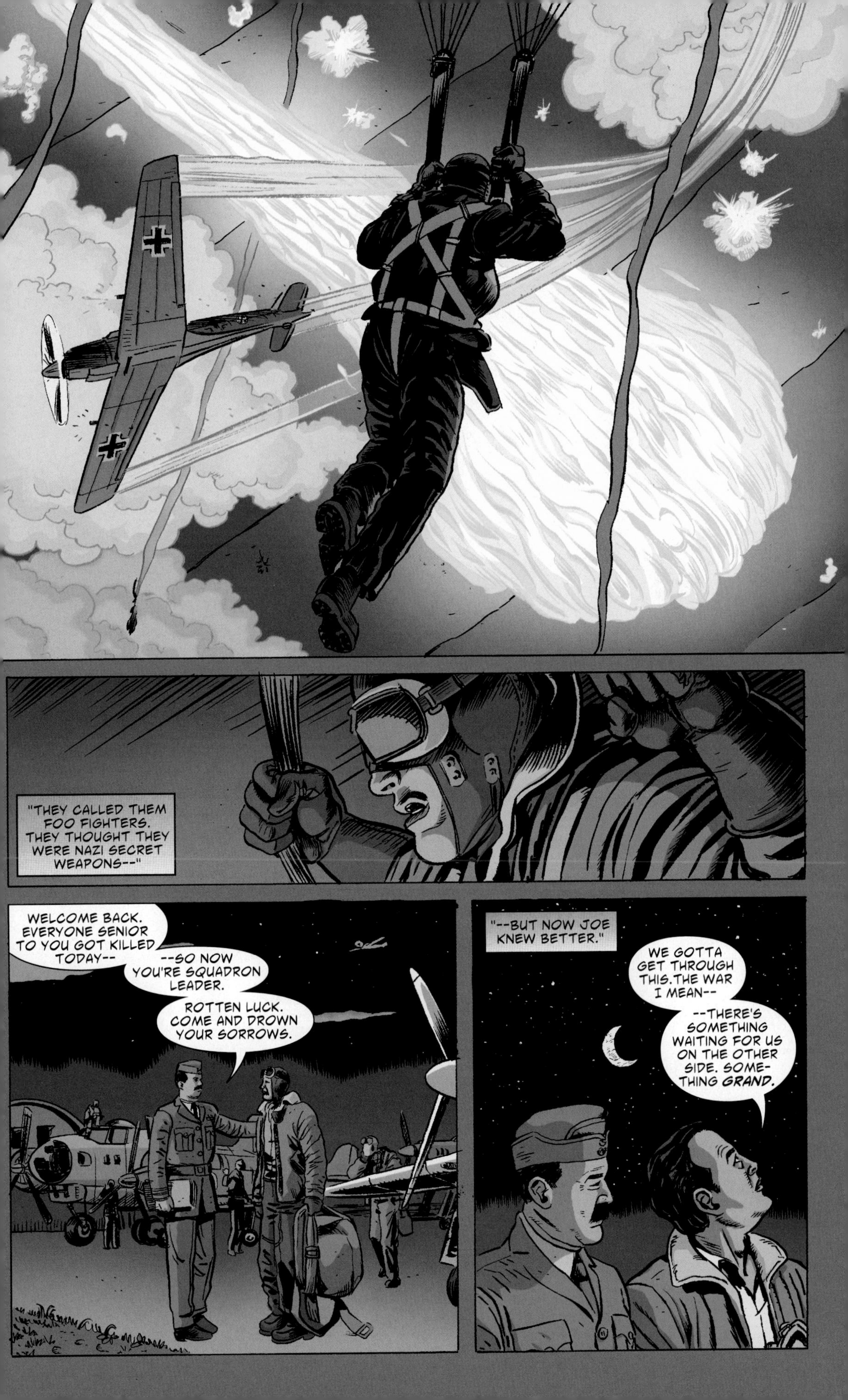
"THEY CALLED THEM FOO FIGHTERS. THEY THOUGHT THEY WERE NAZI SECRET WEAPONS--"
WELCOME BACK. EVERYONE SENIOR TO YOU GOT KILLED TODAY--
--SO NOW YOU'RE SQUADRON LEADER.
ROTTEN LUCK. COME AND DROWN YOUR SORROWS.
"--BUT NOW JOE KNEW BETTER."
WE GOTTA GET THROUGH THIS. THE WAR I MEAN--
--THERE'S SOMETHING WAITING FOR US ON THE OTHER SIDE. SOMETHING *GRAND*.

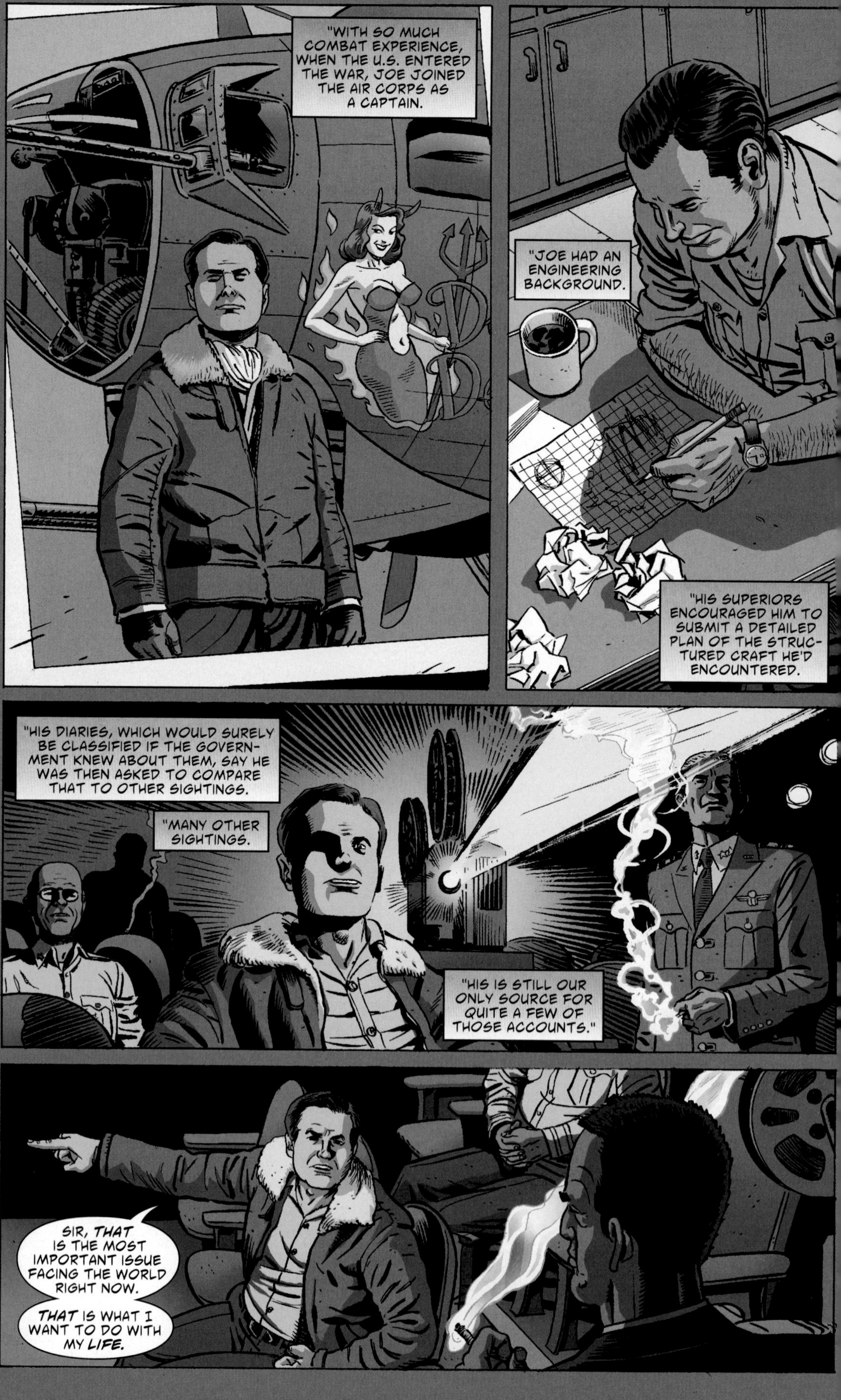
"WITH SO MUCH COMBAT EXPERIENCE, WHEN THE U.S. ENTERED THE WAR, JOE JOINED THE AIR CORPS AS A CAPTAIN.
"JOE HAD AN ENGINEERING BACKGROUND.
"HIS SUPERIORS ENCOURAGED HIM TO SUBMIT A DETAILED PLAN OF THE STRUCTURED CRAFT HE'D ENCOUNTERED.
"HIS DIARIES, WHICH WOULD SURELY BE CLASSIFIED IF THE GOVERNMENT KNEW ABOUT THEM, SAY HE WAS THEN ASKED TO COMPARE THAT TO OTHER SIGHTINGS.
"MANY OTHER SIGHTINGS.
"HIS IS STILL OUR ONLY SOURCE FOR QUITE A FEW OF THOSE ACCOUNTS."
SIR, *THAT* IS THE MOST IMPORTANT ISSUE FACING THE WORLD RIGHT NOW.
THAT IS WHAT I WANT TO DO WITH MY *LIFE*.

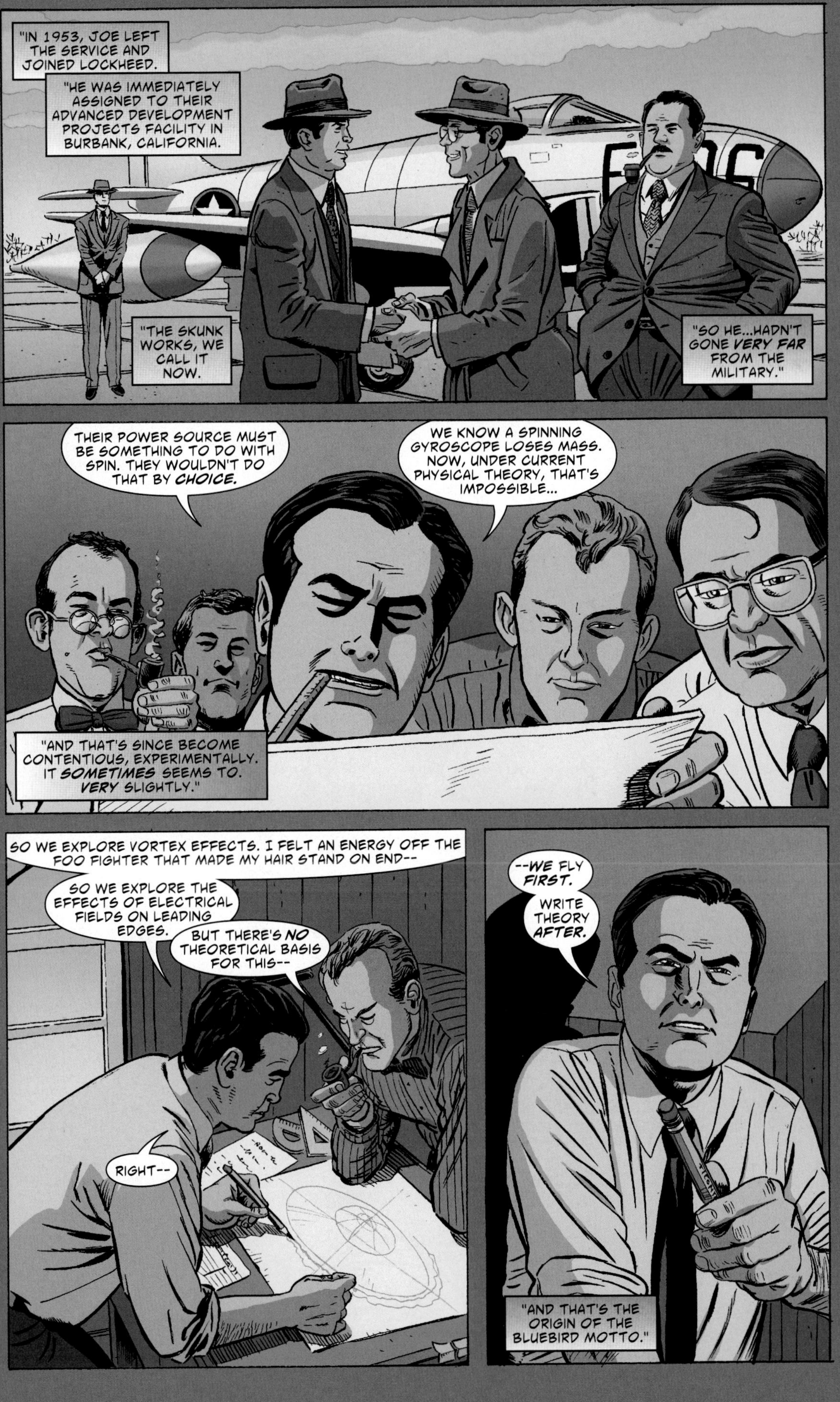
"IN 1953, JOE LEFT THE SERVICE AND JOINED LOCKHEED.
"HE WAS IMMEDIATELY ASSIGNED TO THEIR ADVANCED DEVELOPMENT PROJECTS FACILITY IN BURBANK, CALIFORNIA.
"THE SKUNK WORKS, WE CALL IT NOW.
"SO HE...HADN'T GONE VERY FAR FROM THE MILITARY."
THEIR POWER SOURCE MUST BE SOMETHING TO DO WITH SPIN. THEY WOULDN'T DO THAT BY CHOICE.
WE KNOW A SPINNING GYROSCOPE LOSES MASS. NOW, UNDER CURRENT PHYSICAL THEORY, THAT'S IMPOSSIBLE...
"AND THAT'S SINCE BECOME CONTENTIOUS, EXPERIMENTALLY. IT SOMETIMES SEEMS TO. VERY SLIGHTLY."
SO WE EXPLORE VORTEX EFFECTS. I FELT AN ENERGY OFF THE FOO FIGHTER THAT MADE MY HAIR STAND ON END--
SO WE EXPLORE THE EFFECTS OF ELECTRICAL FIELDS ON LEADING EDGES.
BUT THERE'S NO THEORETICAL BASIS FOR THIS--
RIGHT--
--WE FLY FIRST.
WRITE THEORY AFTER.
"AND THAT'S THE ORIGIN OF THE BLUEBIRD MOTTO."

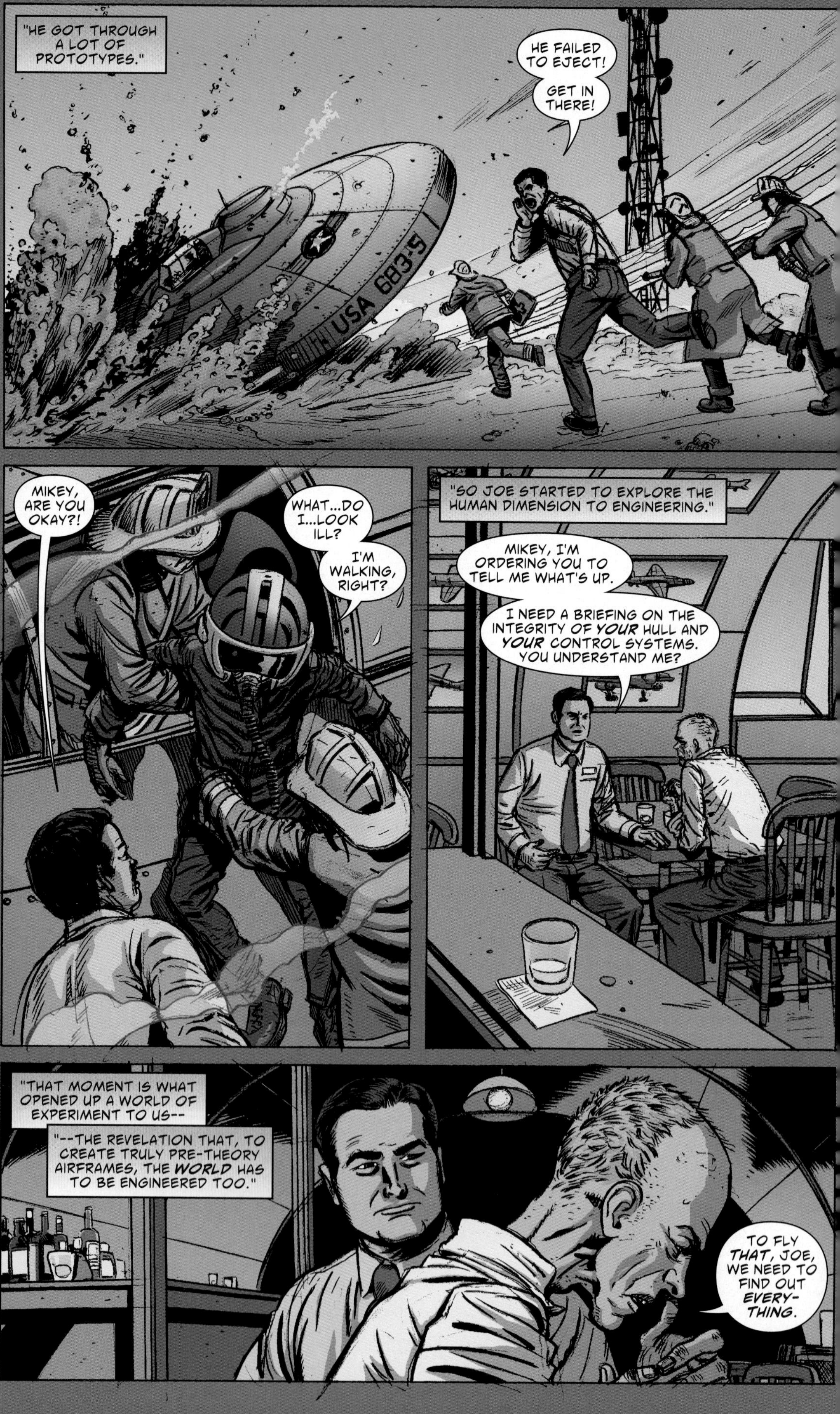
"HE GOT THROUGH A LOT OF PROTOTYPES."
HE FAILED TO EJECT!
GET IN THERE!
USA 683-5
MIKEY, ARE YOU OKAY?!
WHAT...DO I...LOOK ILL?
I'M WALKING, RIGHT?
"SO JOE STARTED TO EXPLORE THE HUMAN DIMENSION TO ENGINEERING."
MIKEY, I'M ORDERING YOU TO TELL ME WHAT'S UP.
I NEED A BRIEFING ON THE INTEGRITY OF YOUR HULL AND YOUR CONTROL SYSTEMS. YOU UNDERSTAND ME?
"THAT MOMENT IS WHAT OPENED UP A WORLD OF EXPERIMENT TO US--
"--THE REVELATION THAT, TO CREATE TRULY PRE-THEORY AIRFRAMES, THE WORLD HAS TO BE ENGINEERED TOO."
TO FLY THAT, JOE, WE NEED TO FIND OUT EVERYTHING.

"JOE WAS KIND OF A HERMIT. HE NEVER MARRIED. HE DEVOTED HIMSELF TO HIS CAUSE.

"SOME OF US INSIST WHAT HE WROTE IN THIS PHASE *IS* THEORY--

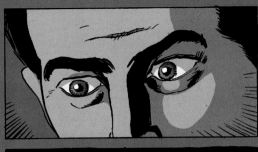

"--I PREFER TO CALL IT *POETRY.*

"READING BETWEEN THE LINES, HE SEEMS TO FORESEE IDEAS CONCERNING SPIN...THE QUALITY LABELED AS SUCH IN QUANTUM MECHANICS, WHICH MAY OR MAY NOT HAVE ANYTHING TO DO WITH EVERYDAY SPIN...

"HE SEEMS TO SEE THAT AS WHAT WE'D NOW CALL THE DARK ENERGY PUSHING THE UNIVERSE --

"--THE MATRIX THAT CONVEYED INFORMATION FROM *ANOTHER* COSMOS--

"--WHICH GAVE BIRTH TO OURS THROUGH A BLACK HOLE.

SKTCH
SKITCH

"BUT IT'S SOMETIMES HARD TO DISCERN *WHAT JOE MEANT.*

"BY THEN, HE HAD STARTED TO *DRINK.*"

"IN 1961, KENNEDY TOLD CONGRESS WE WERE GOING TO THE MOON.

"JOE FLEW OFF THE HANDLE.

"THEN AS NOW, FEDERAL GOVERNMENT LOOKS MONOLITHIC. BUT REALLY IT'S A BUNCH OF COMPETING FIEFDOMS."

YOUR TWO-YEAR-OLD BULLSHIT "SPACE AGENCY" IS GOING TO THE *MOON*?!

YOU FUCKING *NAZIS* ARE GOING TO THE *MOON*?!

NOT IF I GET THERE *FIRST*!

"BECAUSE ALL THIS 'NAZI SAUCER' CRAP IS JUST POST-WAR PROPAGANDA.

"THE THIRD REICH HAD *NO CLUE* ABOUT OUR FIELD OF INTEREST."

YOUR PROMOTION OF *ALTERNATIVES* ISN'T *HELPING* THE LUNAR PROJECT, MR. BERMINGEN.

I'M HAPPY FOR YOU TO TAKE A *POST* AT NASA. I CAN MAKE THEM ACCEPT YOU--

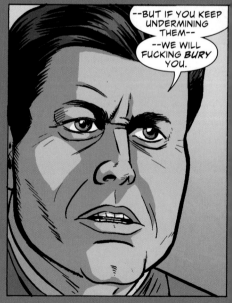

--BUT IF YOU KEEP UNDERMINING THEM--

--WE WILL FUCKING *BURY* YOU.

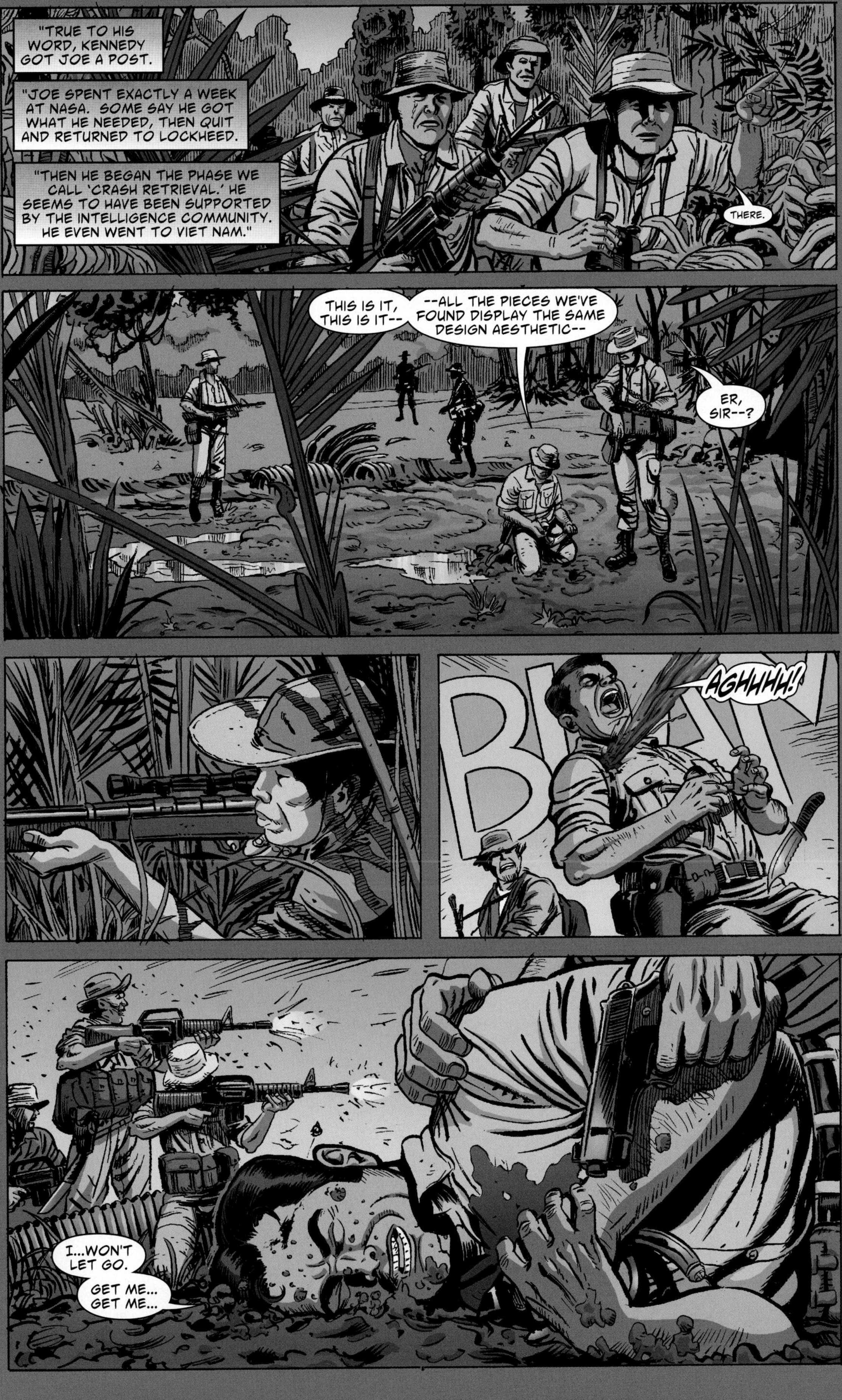
"TRUE TO HIS WORD, KENNEDY GOT JOE A POST.
"JOE SPENT EXACTLY A WEEK AT NASA. SOME SAY HE GOT WHAT HE NEEDED, THEN QUIT AND RETURNED TO LOCKHEED.
"THEN HE BEGAN THE PHASE WE CALL 'CRASH RETRIEVAL.' HE SEEMS TO HAVE BEEN SUPPORTED BY THE INTELLIGENCE COMMUNITY. HE EVEN WENT TO VIET NAM."
THERE.
THIS IS IT, THIS IS IT--
--ALL THE PIECES WE'VE FOUND DISPLAY THE SAME DESIGN AESTHETIC--
ER, SIR--?
AGHHHH!
I...WON'T LET GO.
GET ME... GET ME...

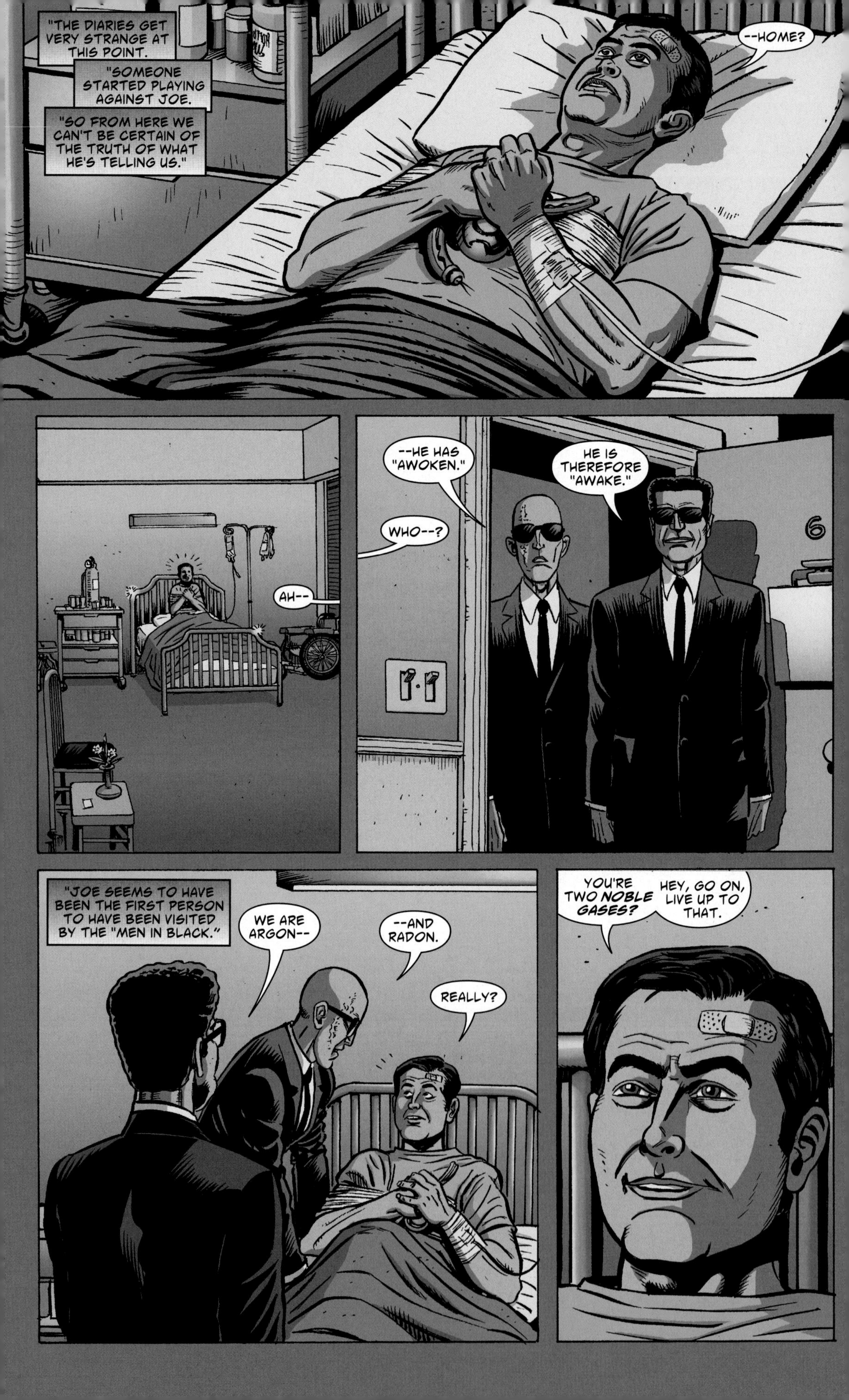
"THE DIARIES GET VERY STRANGE AT THIS POINT.
"SOMEONE STARTED PLAYING AGAINST JOE.
"SO FROM HERE WE CAN'T BE CERTAIN OF THE TRUTH OF WHAT HE'S TELLING US."
--HOME?
AH--
WHO--?
--HE HAS "AWOKEN."
HE IS THEREFORE "AWAKE."
6
"JOE SEEMS TO HAVE BEEN THE FIRST PERSON TO HAVE BEEN VISITED BY THE "MEN IN BLACK."
WE ARE ARGON--
--AND RADON.
REALLY?
YOU'RE TWO *NOBLE GASES?*
HEY, GO ON, LIVE UP TO THAT.

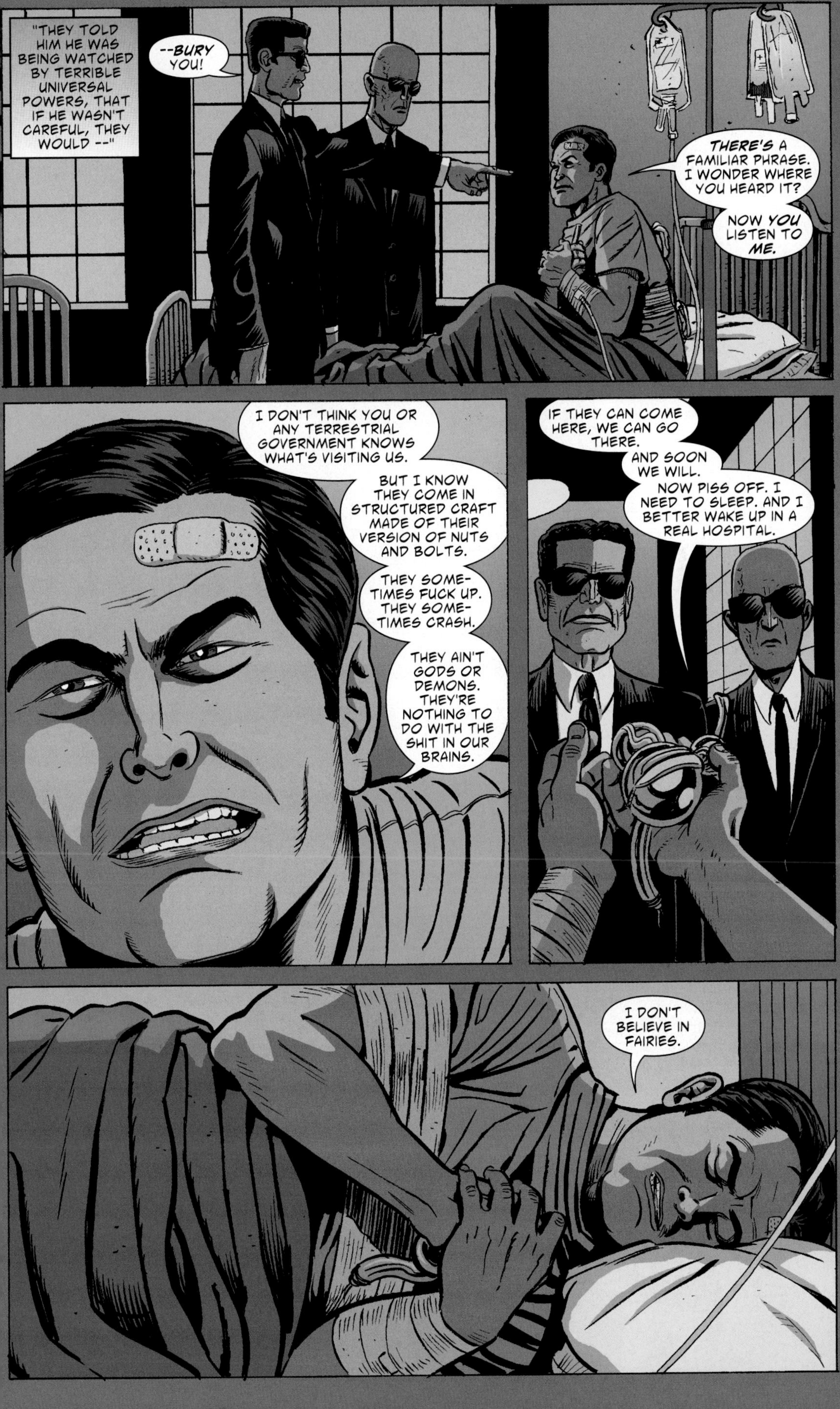
"THEY TOLD HIM HE WAS BEING WATCHED BY TERRIBLE UNIVERSAL POWERS, THAT IF HE WASN'T CAREFUL, THEY WOULD --"
--BURY YOU!
THERE'S A FAMILIAR PHRASE. I WONDER WHERE YOU HEARD IT?
NOW YOU LISTEN TO ME.
I DON'T THINK YOU OR ANY TERRESTRIAL GOVERNMENT KNOWS WHAT'S VISITING US.
BUT I KNOW THEY COME IN STRUCTURED CRAFT MADE OF THEIR VERSION OF NUTS AND BOLTS.
THEY SOME-TIMES FUCK UP. THEY SOME-TIMES CRASH.
THEY AIN'T GODS OR DEMONS. THEY'RE NOTHING TO DO WITH THE SHIT IN OUR BRAINS.
IF THEY CAN COME HERE, WE CAN GO THERE.
AND SOON WE WILL.
NOW PISS OFF. I NEED TO SLEEP. AND I BETTER WAKE UP IN A REAL HOSPITAL.
I DON'T BELIEVE IN FAIRIES.

"IN 1969, APOLLO 11 LIFTED OFF FOR THE MOON."

"JOE'S DIARIES INDICATE HE WAS WORKING DAY AND NIGHT ON SOME SECRET PROJECT OF HIS OWN."

"NO REAL ENGINEER HAS TIME FOR THAT 'WE DIDN'T GO TO THE MOON' CRAP--"

"--BUT THERE ARE SECRET DATA LOGS THAT NASA HAS NEVER MADE PUBLIC--"

"--RECORDS OF A PRIVATE COMMUNICATIONS CHANNEL, THAT SOMETIMES INCLUDES AUDIO."

HOUSTON, THIS IS TRANQUILITY BASE ON AZURE--

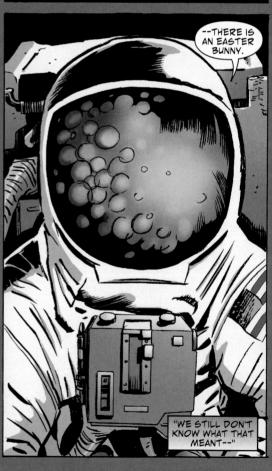

--THERE IS AN EASTER BUNNY.

"WE STILL DON'T KNOW WHAT THAT MEANT--"

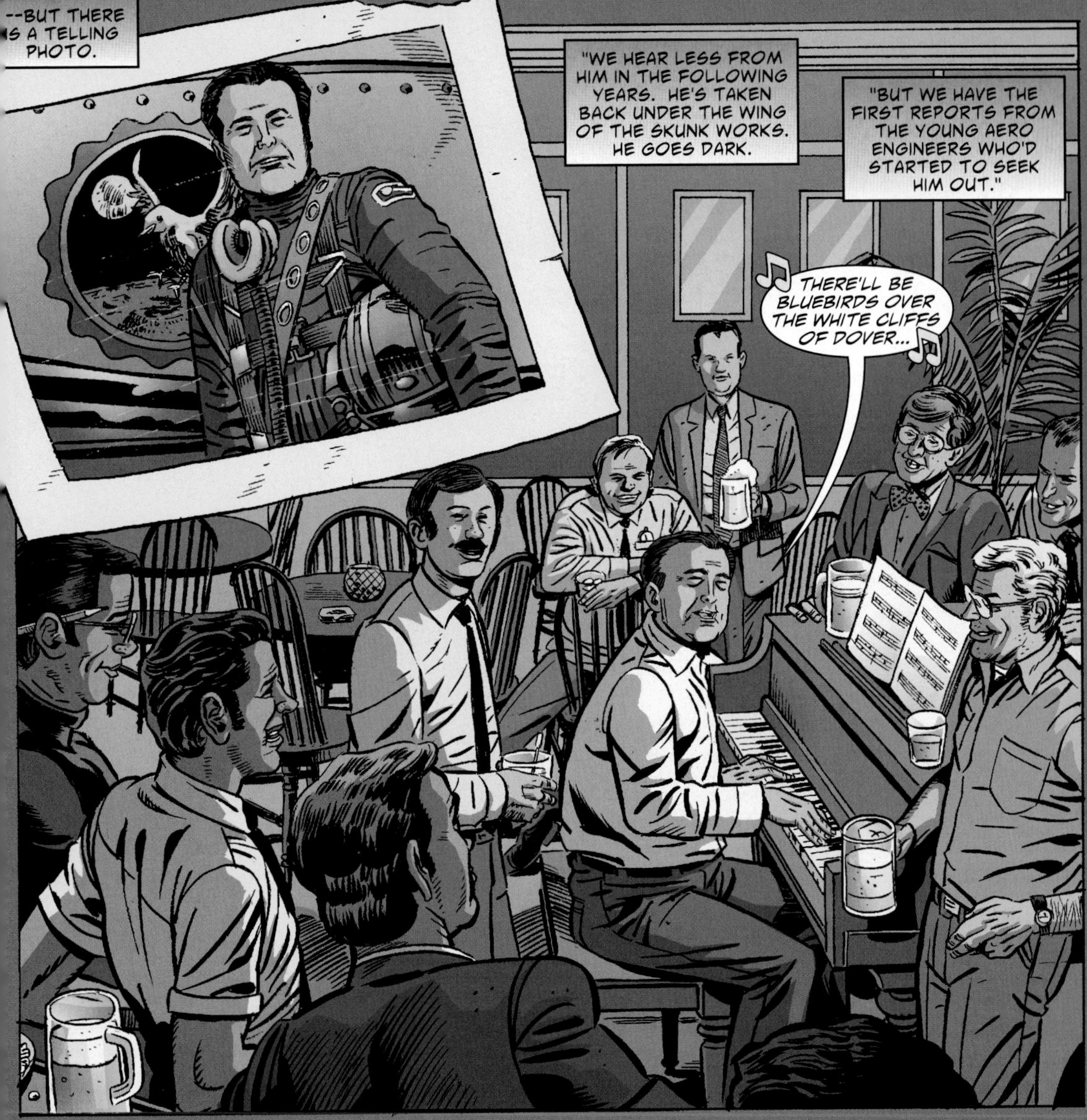
--BUT THERE IS A TELLING PHOTO.
"WE HEAR LESS FROM HIM IN THE FOLLOWING YEARS. HE'S TAKEN BACK UNDER THE WING OF THE SKUNK WORKS. HE GOES DARK.
"BUT WE HAVE THE FIRST REPORTS FROM THE YOUNG AERO ENGINEERS WHO'D STARTED TO SEEK HIM OUT."
THERE'LL BE BLUEBIRDS OVER THE WHITE CLIFFS OF DOVER...

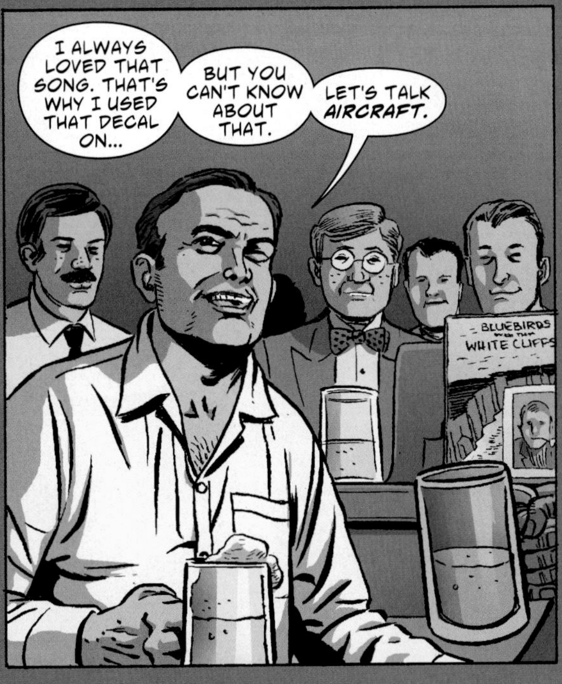
I ALWAYS LOVED THAT SONG. THAT'S WHY I USED THAT DECAL ON...
BUT YOU CAN'T KNOW ABOUT THAT.
LET'S TALK *AIRCRAFT.*
BLUEBIRDS
WHITE CLIFFS

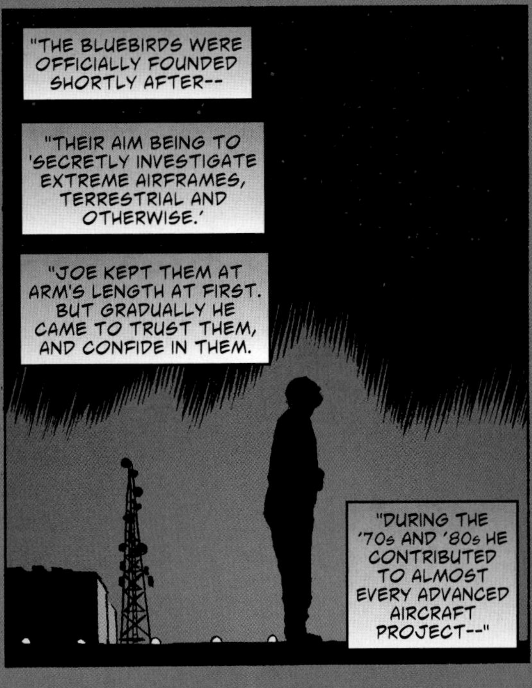
"THE BLUEBIRDS WERE OFFICIALLY FOUNDED SHORTLY AFTER--
"THEIR AIM BEING TO 'SECRETLY INVESTIGATE EXTREME AIRFRAMES, TERRESTRIAL AND OTHERWISE.'
"JOE KEPT THEM AT ARM'S LENGTH AT FIRST. BUT GRADUALLY HE CAME TO TRUST THEM, AND CONFIDE IN THEM.
"DURING THE '70s AND '80s HE CONTRIBUTED TO ALMOST EVERY ADVANCED AIRCRAFT PROJECT--"

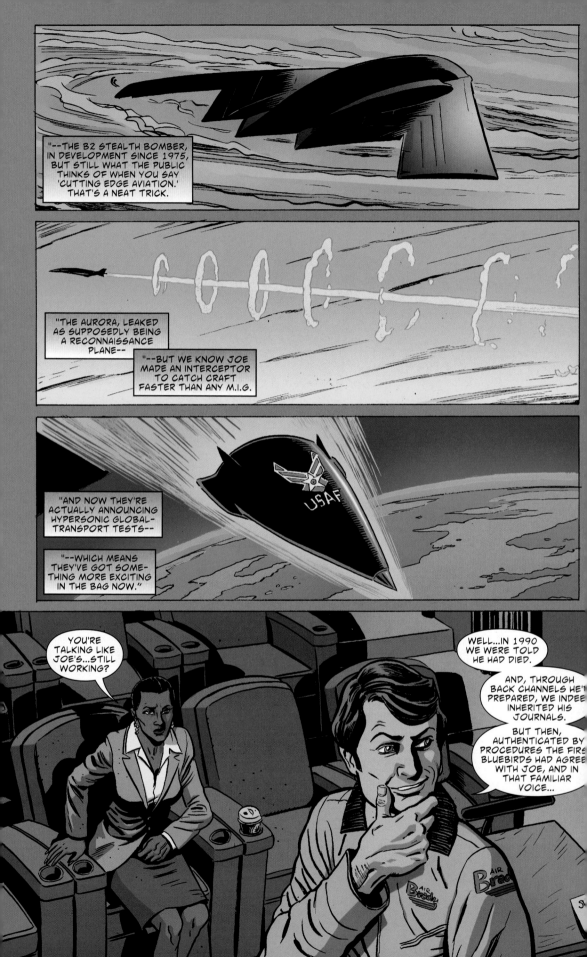

"--THE B2 STEALTH BOMBER, IN DEVELOPMENT SINCE 1975, BUT STILL WHAT THE PUBLIC THINKS OF WHEN YOU SAY 'CUTTING EDGE AVIATION.' THAT'S A NEAT TRICK.

"THE AURORA, LEAKED AS SUPPOSEDLY BEING A RECONNAISSANCE PLANE--

"--BUT WE KNOW JOE MADE AN INTERCEPTOR TO CATCH CRAFT FASTER THAN ANY M.I.G.

"AND NOW THEY'RE ACTUALLY ANNOUNCING HYPERSONIC GLOBAL-TRANSPORT TESTS--

"--WHICH MEANS THEY'VE GOT SOME-THING MORE EXCITING IN THE BAG NOW."

YOU'RE TALKING LIKE JOE'S...STILL WORKING?

WELL...IN 1990 WE WERE TOLD HE HAD DIED.

AND, THROUGH BACK CHANNELS HE'D PREPARED, WE INDEED INHERITED HIS JOURNALS.

BUT THEN, AUTHENTICATED BY PROCEDURES THE FIRST BLUEBIRDS HAD AGREED WITH JOE, AND IN THAT FAMILIAR VOICE...

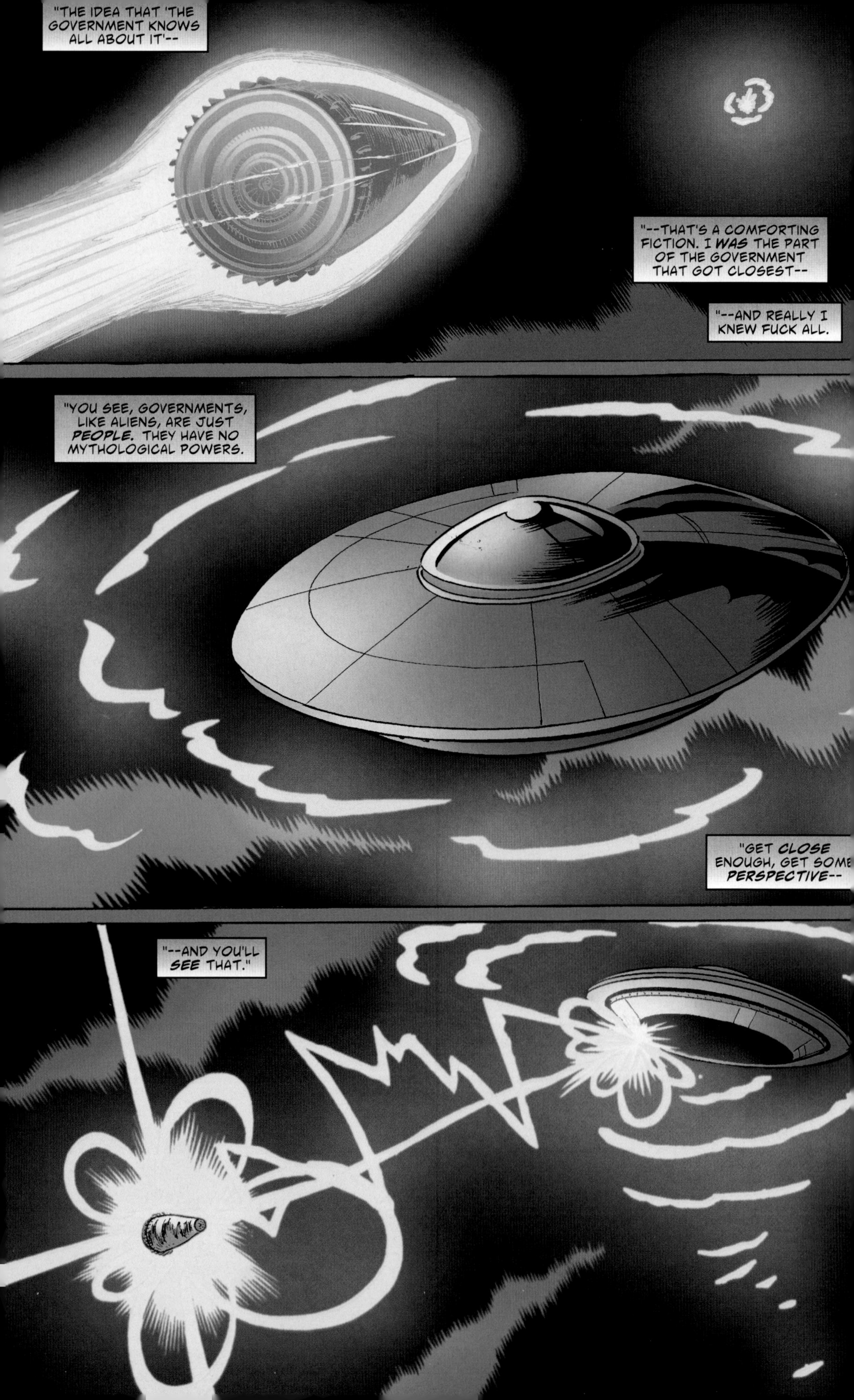
"THE IDEA THAT 'THE GOVERNMENT KNOWS ALL ABOUT IT'--
"--THAT'S A COMFORTING FICTION. I *WAS* THE PART OF THE GOVERNMENT THAT GOT CLOSEST--
"--AND REALLY I KNEW FUCK ALL.
"YOU SEE, GOVERNMENTS, LIKE ALIENS, ARE JUST *PEOPLE.* THEY HAVE NO MYTHOLOGICAL POWERS.
"GET *CLOSE* ENOUGH, GET SOME *PERSPECTIVE*--
"--AND YOU'LL *SEE* THAT."

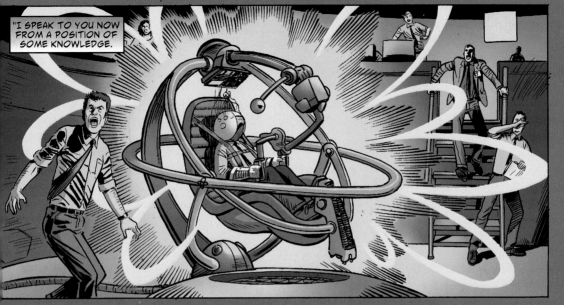

"I SPEAK TO YOU NOW FROM A POSITION OF SOME KNOWLEDGE.

"I'M TOLD I'LL BE ABLE TO CONTINUE SENDING YOU THESE JOURNALS--

"--BUT I'LL HAVE TO BE CAREFUL WITH WHAT I SAY.

"CARRY ON IN THE SPIRIT OF THE BLUEBIRDS. IT'S THE RIGHT WAY TO GO.

"'FLYING SAUCERS ARE REAL.

"AND ONLY THAT."

YOU DON'T BELIEVE--?

NOT ALL OF IT.

THERE'S CONTINUAL DEBATE ABOUT THE INFORMATION WE STILL RECEIVE.

WE KNOW OTHERS ARE BEING PLAYED.

IT'S POSSIBLE WE ARE TOO.

BUT WE WERE SENT SOMETHING--

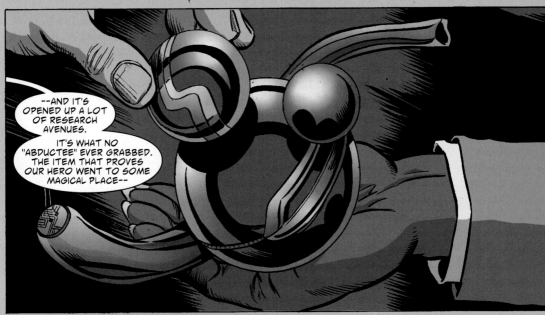

--AND IT'S OPENED UP A LOT OF RESEARCH AVENUES.

IT'S WHAT NO "ABDUCTEE" EVER GRABBED. THE ITEM THAT PROVES OUR HERO WENT TO SOME MAGICAL PLACE--

--LIKE IN ALL THE BEST STORIES.

NOW, LET'S GET SOME COFFEE--

--AND I'LL TELL YOU WHAT WE'RE GOING TO DO TO PROFESSOR KIDD.

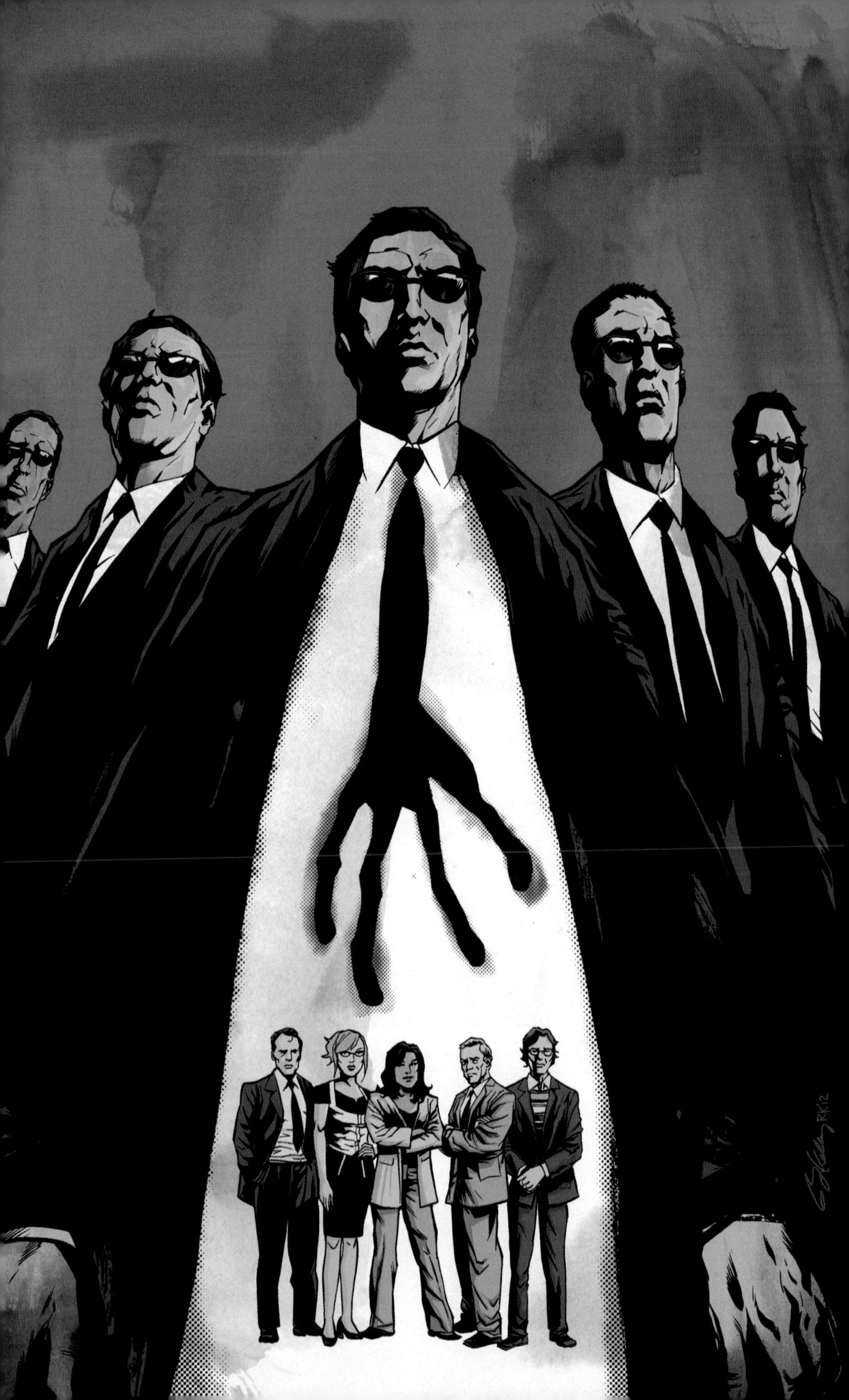

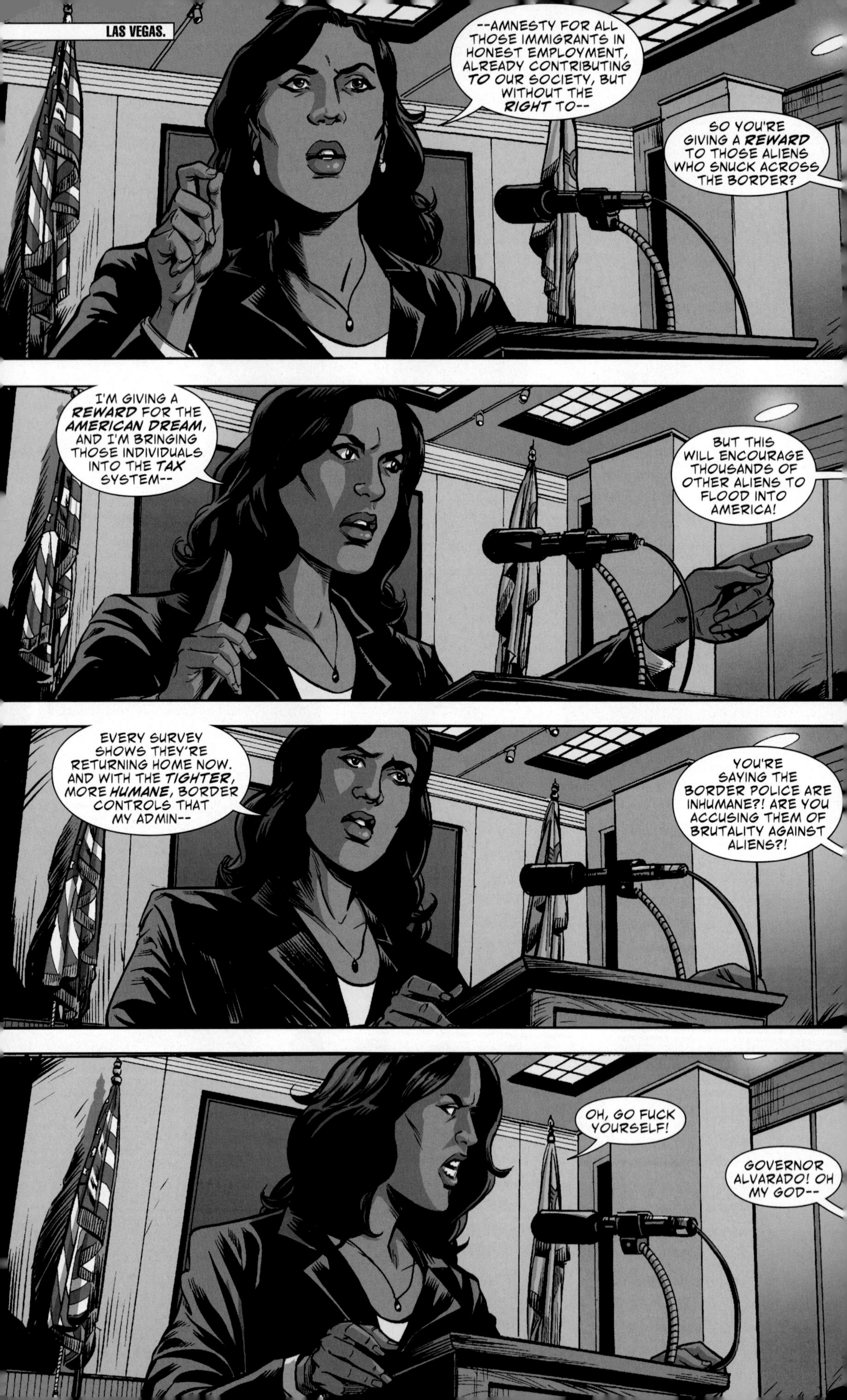
LAS VEGAS.
--AMNESTY FOR ALL THOSE IMMIGRANTS IN HONEST EMPLOYMENT, ALREADY CONTRIBUTING TO OUR SOCIETY, BUT WITHOUT THE RIGHT TO--
SO YOU'RE GIVING A REWARD TO THOSE ALIENS WHO SNUCK ACROSS THE BORDER?
I'M GIVING A REWARD FOR THE AMERICAN DREAM, AND I'M BRINGING THOSE INDIVIDUALS INTO THE TAX SYSTEM--
BUT THIS WILL ENCOURAGE THOUSANDS OF OTHER ALIENS TO FLOOD INTO AMERICA!
EVERY SURVEY SHOWS THEY'RE RETURNING HOME NOW. AND WITH THE TIGHTER, MORE HUMANE, BORDER CONTROLS THAT MY ADMIN--
YOU'RE SAYING THE BORDER POLICE ARE INHUMANE?! ARE YOU ACCUSING THEM OF BRUTALITY AGAINST ALIENS?!
OH, GO FUCK YOURSELF!
GOVERNOR ALVARADO! OH MY GOD--

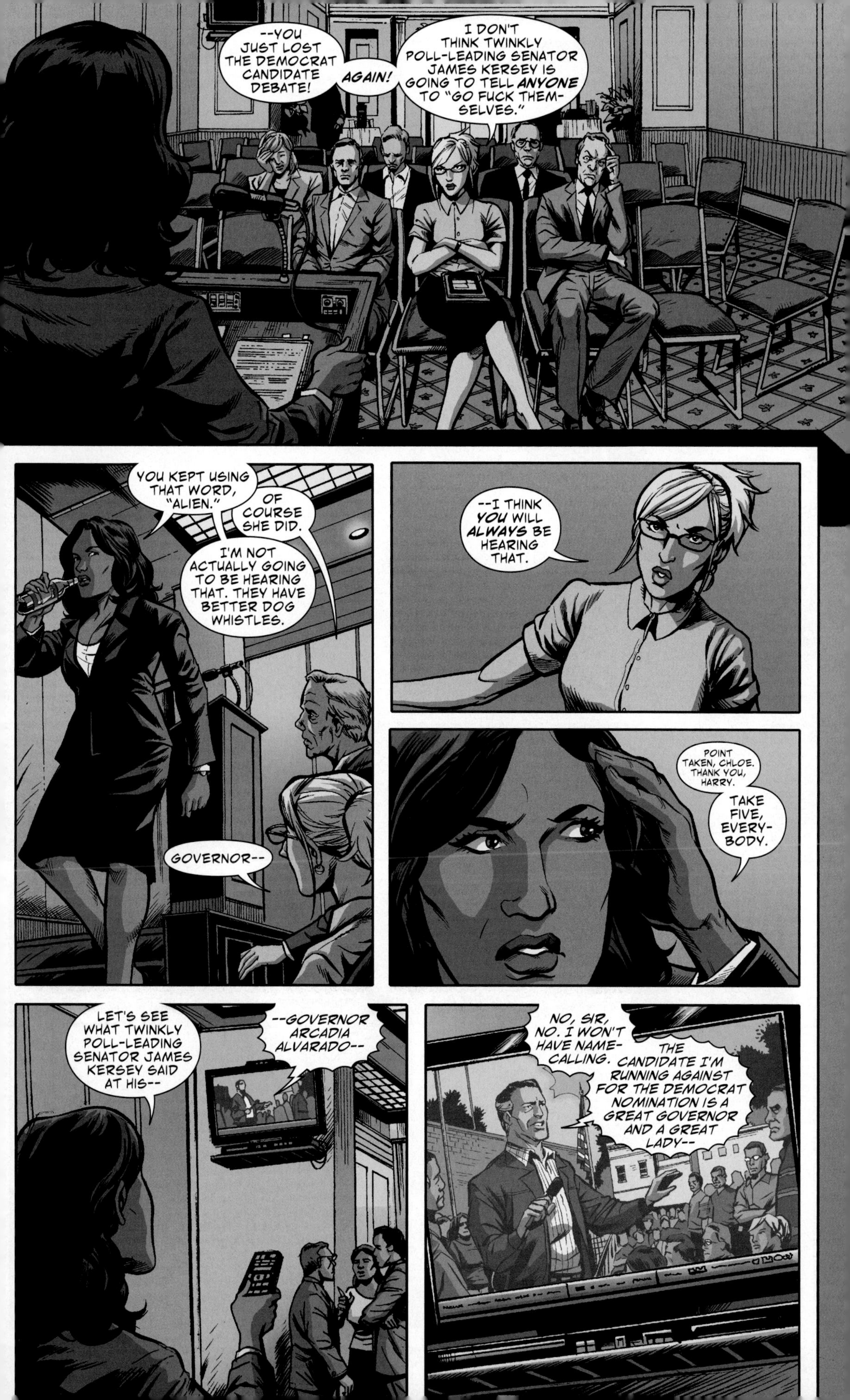
--YOU JUST LOST THE DEMOCRAT CANDIDATE DEBATE!
AGAIN!
I DON'T THINK TWINKLY POLL-LEADING SENATOR JAMES KERSEY IS GOING TO TELL ANYONE TO "GO FUCK THEMSELVES."
YOU KEPT USING THAT WORD, "ALIEN."
OF COURSE SHE DID.
I'M NOT ACTUALLY GOING TO BE HEARING THAT. THEY HAVE BETTER DOG WHISTLES.
GOVERNOR--
--I THINK YOU WILL ALWAYS BE HEARING THAT.
POINT TAKEN, CHLOE. THANK YOU, HARRY.
TAKE FIVE, EVERYBODY.
LET'S SEE WHAT TWINKLY POLL-LEADING SENATOR JAMES KERSEY SAID AT HIS--
--GOVERNOR ARCADIA ALVARADO--
NO, SIR, NO. I WON'T HAVE NAME-CALLING.
THE CANDIDATE I'M RUNNING AGAINST FOR THE DEMOCRAT NOMINATION IS A GREAT GOVERNOR AND A GREAT LADY--

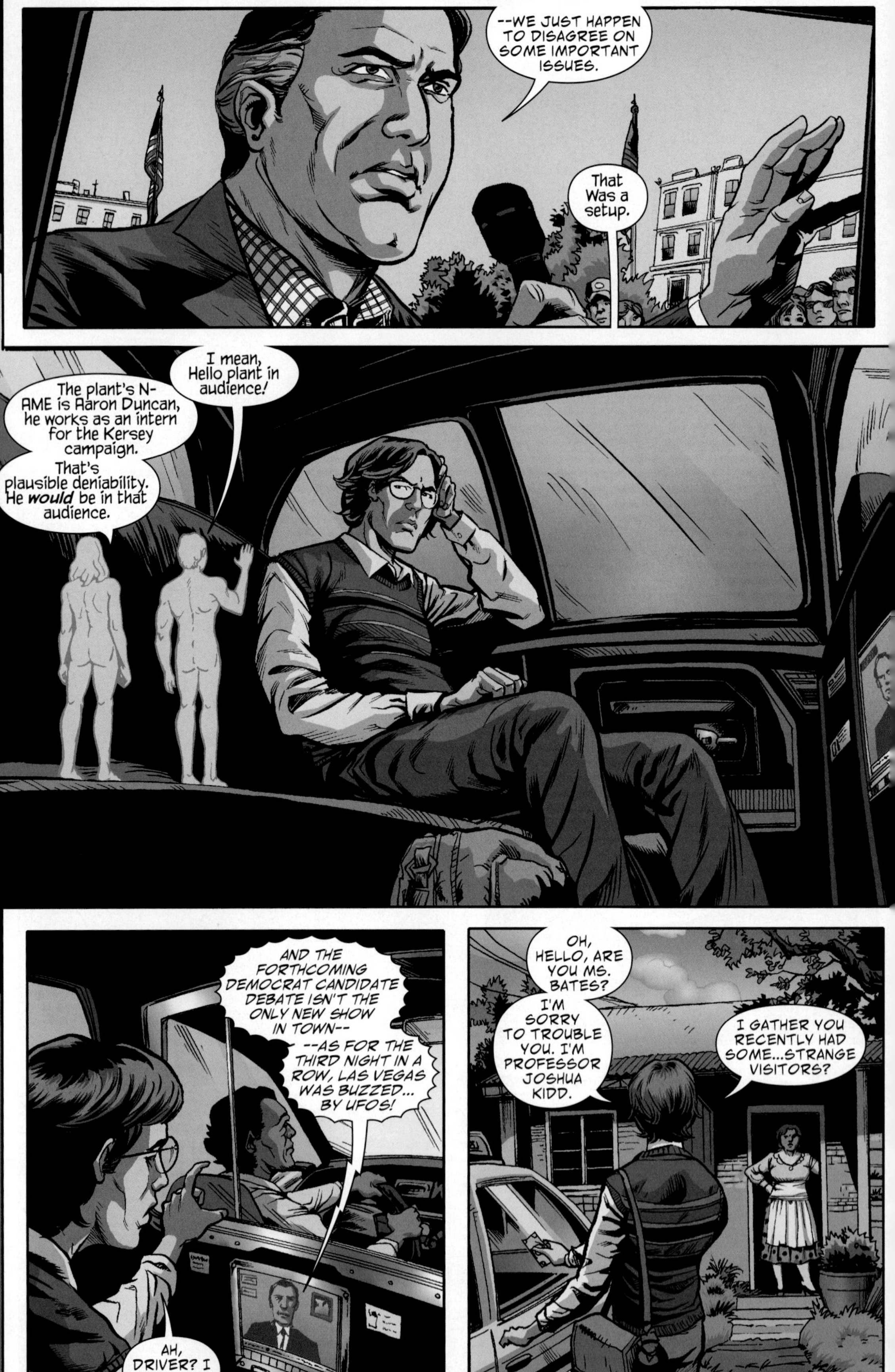
--WE JUST HAPPEN TO DISAGREE ON SOME IMPORTANT ISSUES.
That Was a setup.
I mean, Hello plant in audience!
The plant's N-AME is Aaron Duncan, he works as an intern for the Kersey campaign.
That's plausible deniability. He *would* be in that audience.
AND THE FORTHCOMING DEMOCRAT CANDIDATE DEBATE ISN'T THE ONLY NEW SHOW IN TOWN--
--AS FOR THE THIRD NIGHT IN A ROW, LAS VEGAS WAS BUZZED... BY UFOS!
AH, DRIVER? I THINK THIS IS *IT*.
OH, HELLO, ARE YOU MS. BATES?
I'M SORRY TO TROUBLE YOU. I'M PROFESSOR JOSHUA KIDD.
I GATHER YOU RECENTLY HAD SOME...STRANGE VISITORS?

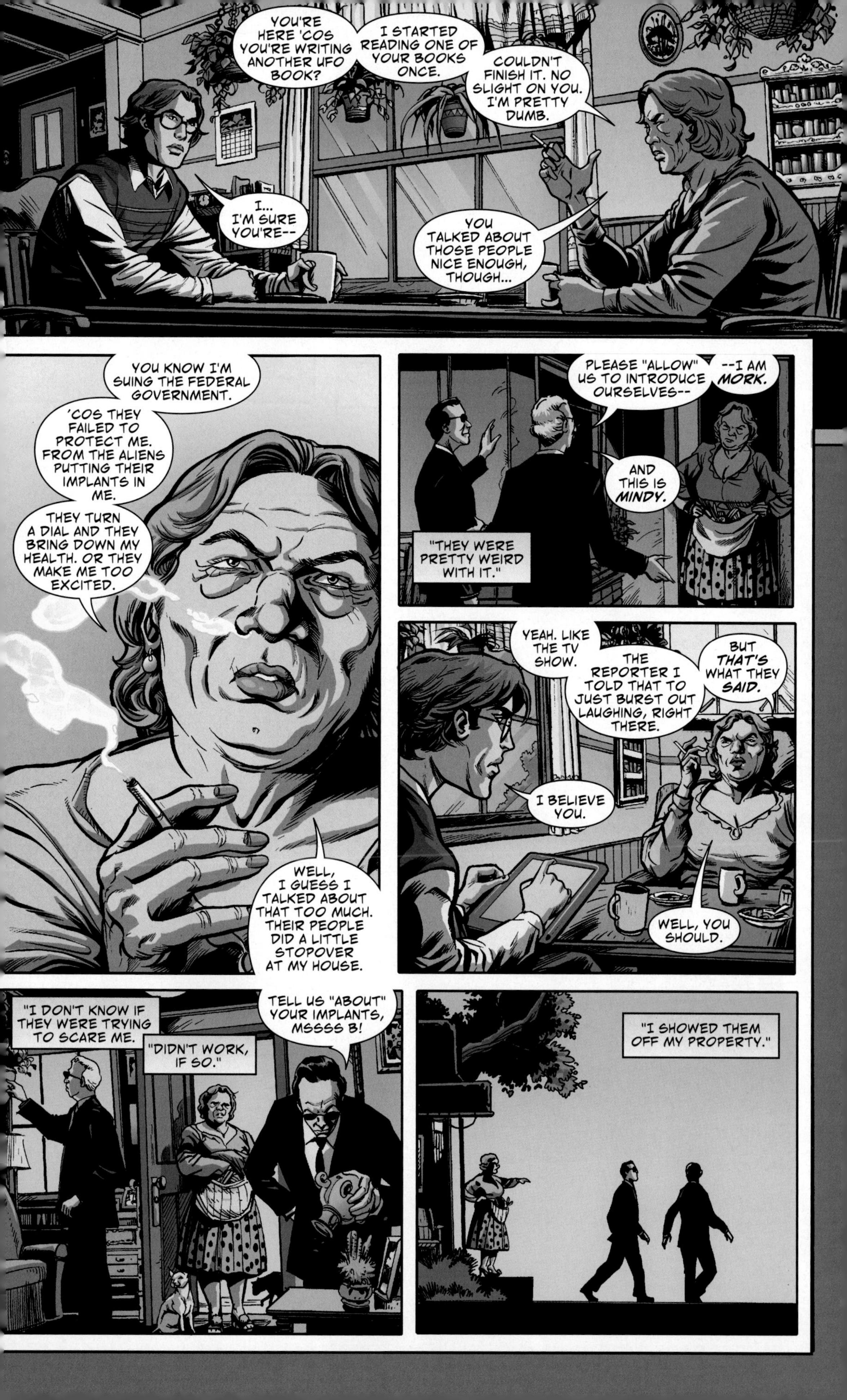
YOU'RE HERE 'COS YOU'RE WRITING ANOTHER UFO BOOK?
I STARTED READING ONE OF YOUR BOOKS ONCE.
COULDN'T FINISH IT. NO SLIGHT ON YOU. I'M PRETTY DUMB.
I... I'M SURE YOU'RE--
YOU TALKED ABOUT THOSE PEOPLE NICE ENOUGH, THOUGH...
YOU KNOW I'M SUING THE FEDERAL GOVERNMENT.
'COS THEY FAILED TO PROTECT ME. FROM THE ALIENS PUTTING THEIR IMPLANTS IN ME.
THEY TURN A DIAL AND THEY BRING DOWN MY HEALTH. OR THEY MAKE ME TOO EXCITED.
WELL, I GUESS I TALKED ABOUT THAT TOO MUCH. THEIR PEOPLE DID A LITTLE STOPOVER AT MY HOUSE.
PLEASE "ALLOW" US TO INTRODUCE OURSELVES--
--I AM MORK.
AND THIS IS MINDY.
"THEY WERE PRETTY WEIRD WITH IT."
YEAH. LIKE THE TV SHOW.
THE REPORTER I TOLD THAT TO JUST BURST OUT LAUGHING, RIGHT THERE.
BUT THAT'S WHAT THEY SAID.
I BELIEVE YOU.
WELL, YOU SHOULD.
"I DON'T KNOW IF THEY WERE TRYING TO SCARE ME.
"DIDN'T WORK, IF SO."
TELL US "ABOUT" YOUR IMPLANTS, MSSSS B!
"I SHOWED THEM OFF MY PROPERTY."

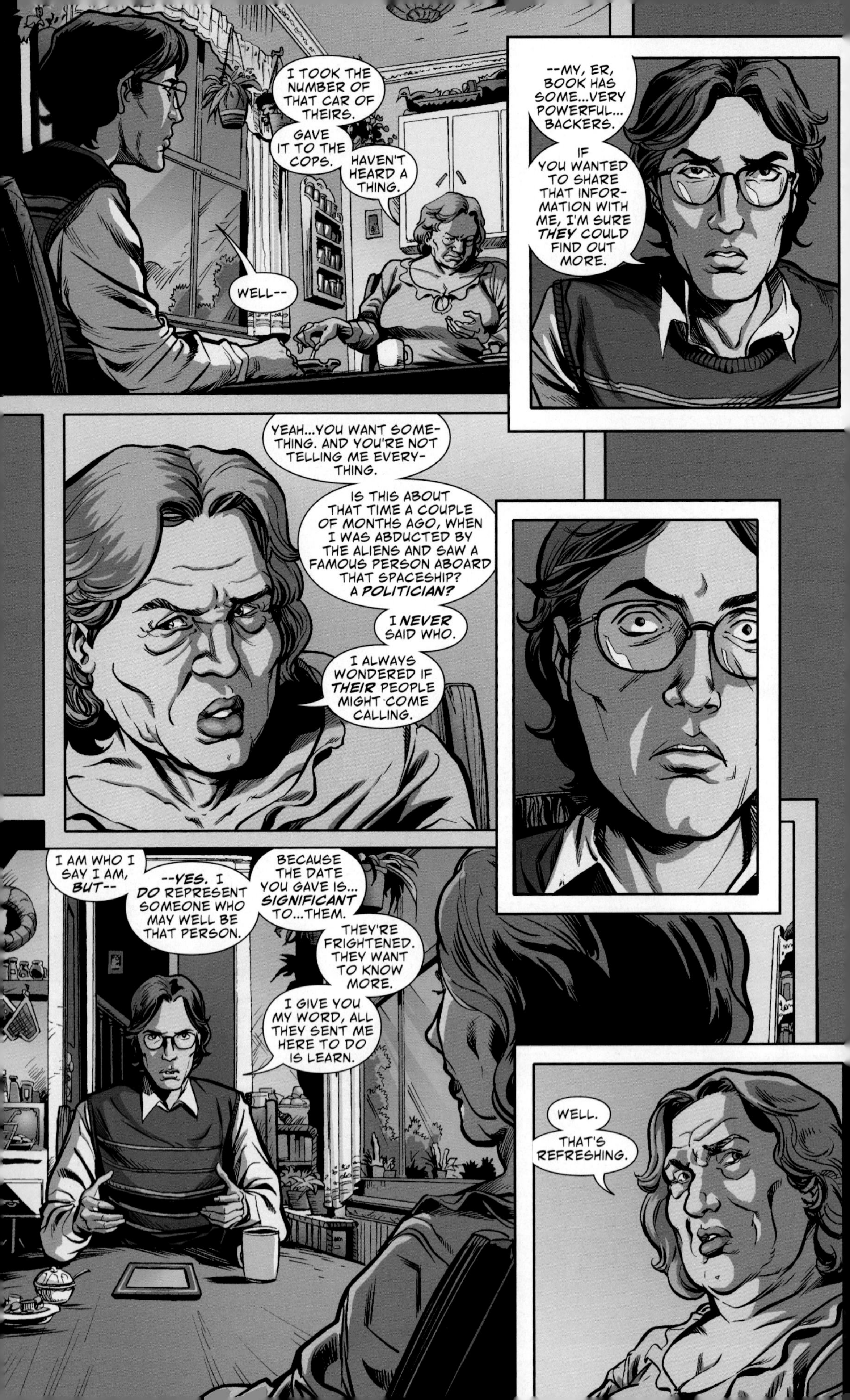
I TOOK THE NUMBER OF THAT CAR OF THEIRS.
GAVE IT TO THE COPS.
HAVEN'T HEARD A THING.
WELL--
--MY, ER, BOOK HAS SOME...VERY POWERFUL... BACKERS.
IF YOU WANTED TO SHARE THAT INFORMATION WITH ME, I'M SURE THEY COULD FIND OUT MORE.
YEAH...YOU WANT SOMETHING. AND YOU'RE NOT TELLING ME EVERYTHING.
IS THIS ABOUT THAT TIME A COUPLE OF MONTHS AGO, WHEN I WAS ABDUCTED BY THE ALIENS AND SAW A FAMOUS PERSON ABOARD THAT SPACESHIP? A POLITICIAN?
I NEVER SAID WHO.
I ALWAYS WONDERED IF THEIR PEOPLE MIGHT COME CALLING.
I AM WHO I SAY I AM, BUT--
--YES. I DO REPRESENT SOMEONE WHO MAY WELL BE THAT PERSON.
BECAUSE THE DATE YOU GAVE IS... SIGNIFICANT TO...THEM.
THEY'RE FRIGHTENED. THEY WANT TO KNOW MORE.
I GIVE YOU MY WORD, ALL THEY SENT ME HERE TO DO IS LEARN.
WELL.
THAT'S REFRESHING.

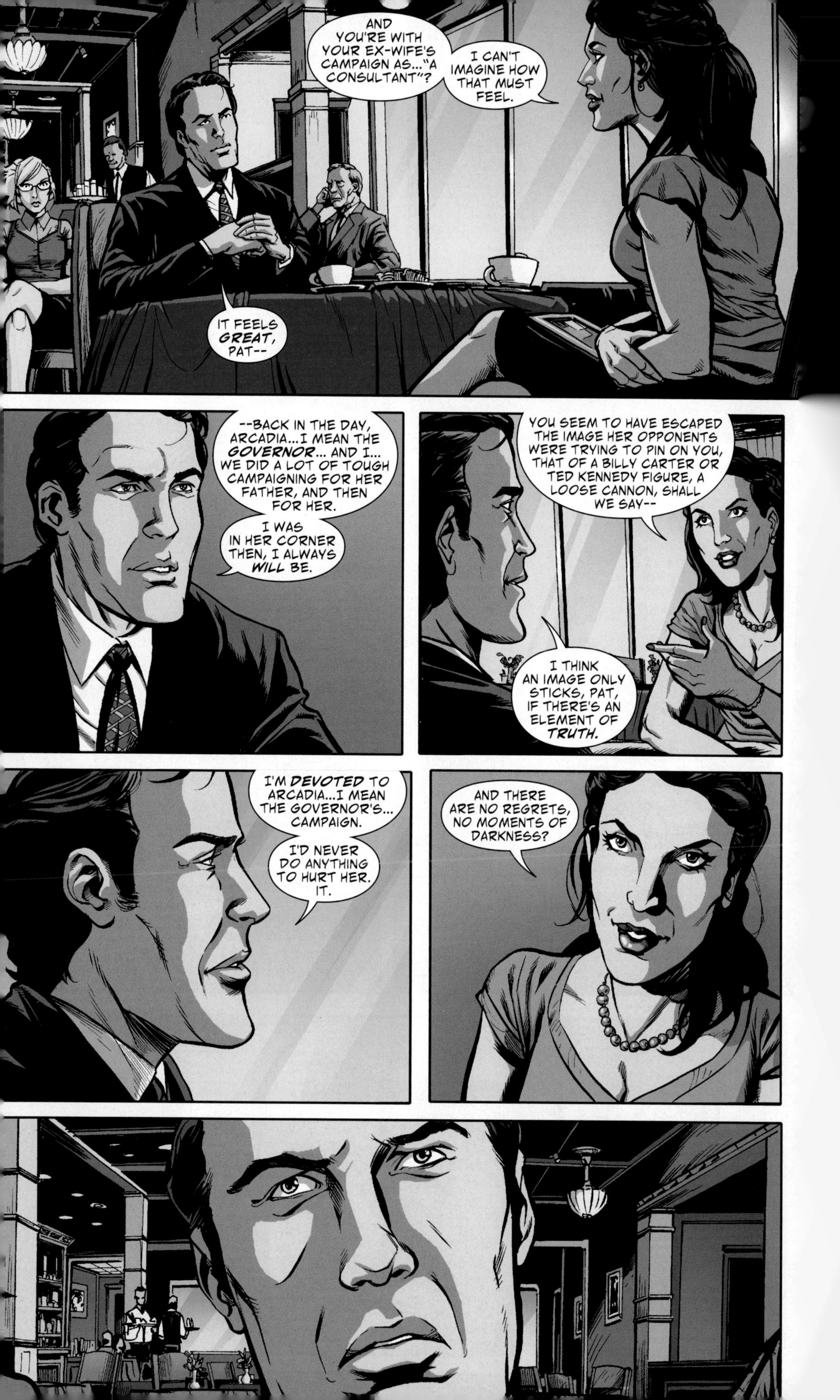

AND YOU'RE WITH YOUR EX-WIFE'S CAMPAIGN AS..."A CONSULTANT"?
I CAN'T IMAGINE HOW THAT MUST FEEL.
IT FEELS GREAT, PAT--
--BACK IN THE DAY, ARCADIA...I MEAN THE GOVERNOR... AND I... WE DID A LOT OF TOUGH CAMPAIGNING FOR HER FATHER, AND THEN FOR HER.
I WAS IN HER CORNER THEN, I ALWAYS WILL BE.
YOU SEEM TO HAVE ESCAPED THE IMAGE HER OPPONENTS WERE TRYING TO PIN ON YOU, THAT OF A BILLY CARTER OR TED KENNEDY FIGURE, A LOOSE CANNON, SHALL WE SAY--
I THINK AN IMAGE ONLY STICKS, PAT, IF THERE'S AN ELEMENT OF TRUTH.
I'M DEVOTED TO ARCADIA...I MEAN THE GOVERNOR'S... CAMPAIGN.
I'D NEVER DO ANYTHING TO HURT HER. IT.
AND THERE ARE NO REGRETS, NO MOMENTS OF DARKNESS?

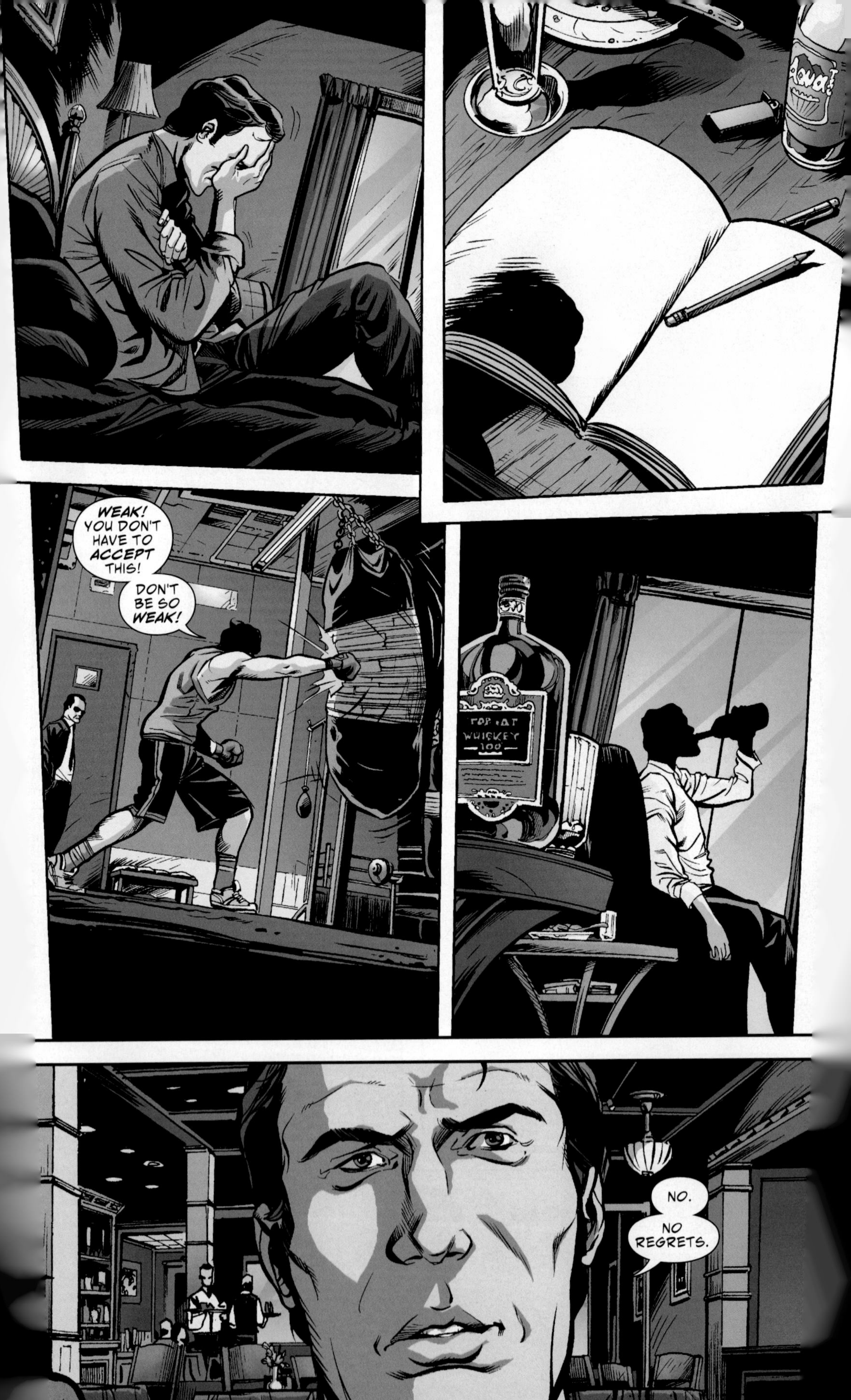
WEAK! YOU DON'T HAVE TO ACCEPT THIS!
DON'T BE SO WEAK!
TOP KAT WHISKEY 100
NO.
NO REGRETS.

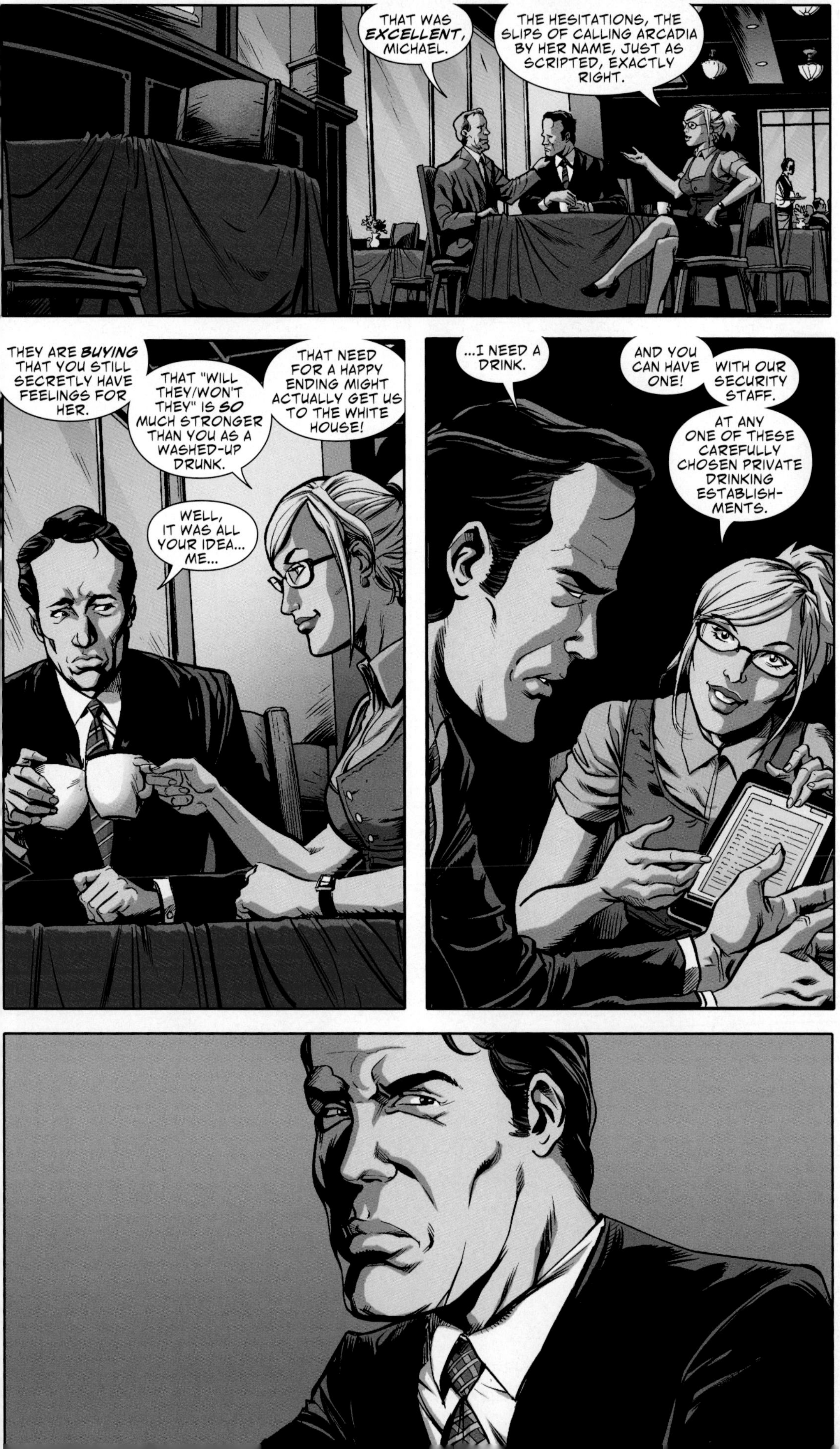

THAT WAS EXCELLENT, MICHAEL.
THE HESITATIONS, THE SLIPS OF CALLING ARCADIA BY HER NAME, JUST AS SCRIPTED, EXACTLY RIGHT.
THEY ARE BUYING THAT YOU STILL SECRETLY HAVE FEELINGS FOR HER.
THAT "WILL THEY/WON'T THEY" IS SO MUCH STRONGER THAN YOU AS A WASHED-UP DRUNK.
THAT NEED FOR A HAPPY ENDING MIGHT ACTUALLY GET US TO THE WHITE HOUSE!
WELL, IT WAS ALL YOUR IDEA... ME...
...I NEED A DRINK.
AND YOU CAN HAVE ONE!
WITH OUR SECURITY STAFF.
AT ANY ONE OF THESE CAREFULLY CHOSEN PRIVATE DRINKING ESTABLISH-MENTS.

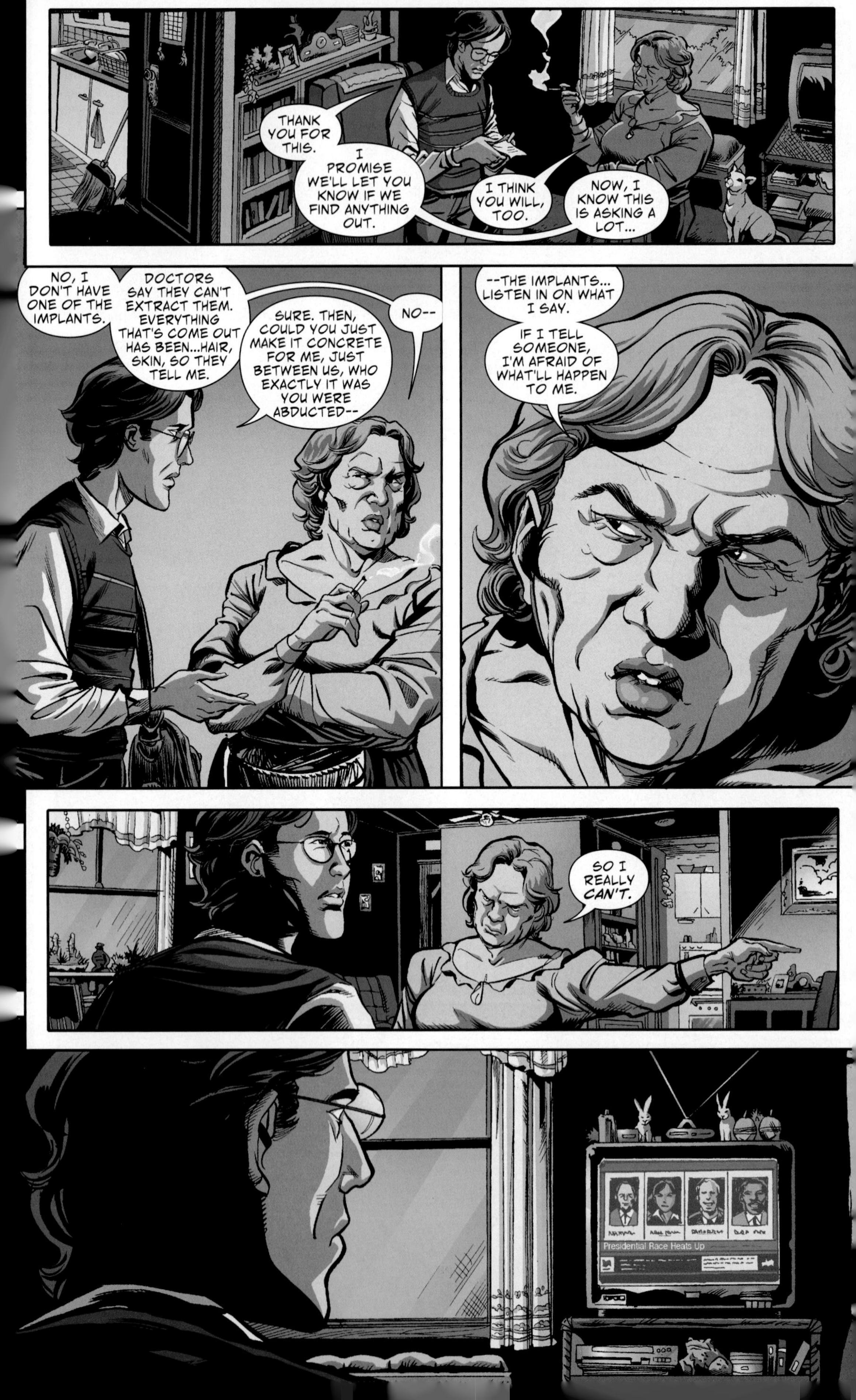
THANK YOU FOR THIS.
I PROMISE WE'LL LET YOU KNOW IF WE FIND ANYTHING OUT.
I THINK YOU WILL, TOO.
NOW, I KNOW THIS IS ASKING A LOT...
NO, I DON'T HAVE ONE OF THE IMPLANTS.
DOCTORS SAY THEY CAN'T EXTRACT THEM. EVERYTHING THAT'S COME OUT HAS BEEN...HAIR, SKIN, SO THEY TELL ME.
SURE. THEN, COULD YOU JUST MAKE IT CONCRETE FOR ME, JUST BETWEEN US, WHO EXACTLY IT WAS YOU WERE ABDUCTED--
NO--
--THE IMPLANTS... LISTEN IN ON WHAT I SAY.
IF I TELL SOMEONE, I'M AFRAID OF WHAT'LL HAPPEN TO ME.
SO I REALLY *CAN'T.*
Presidential Race Heats Up

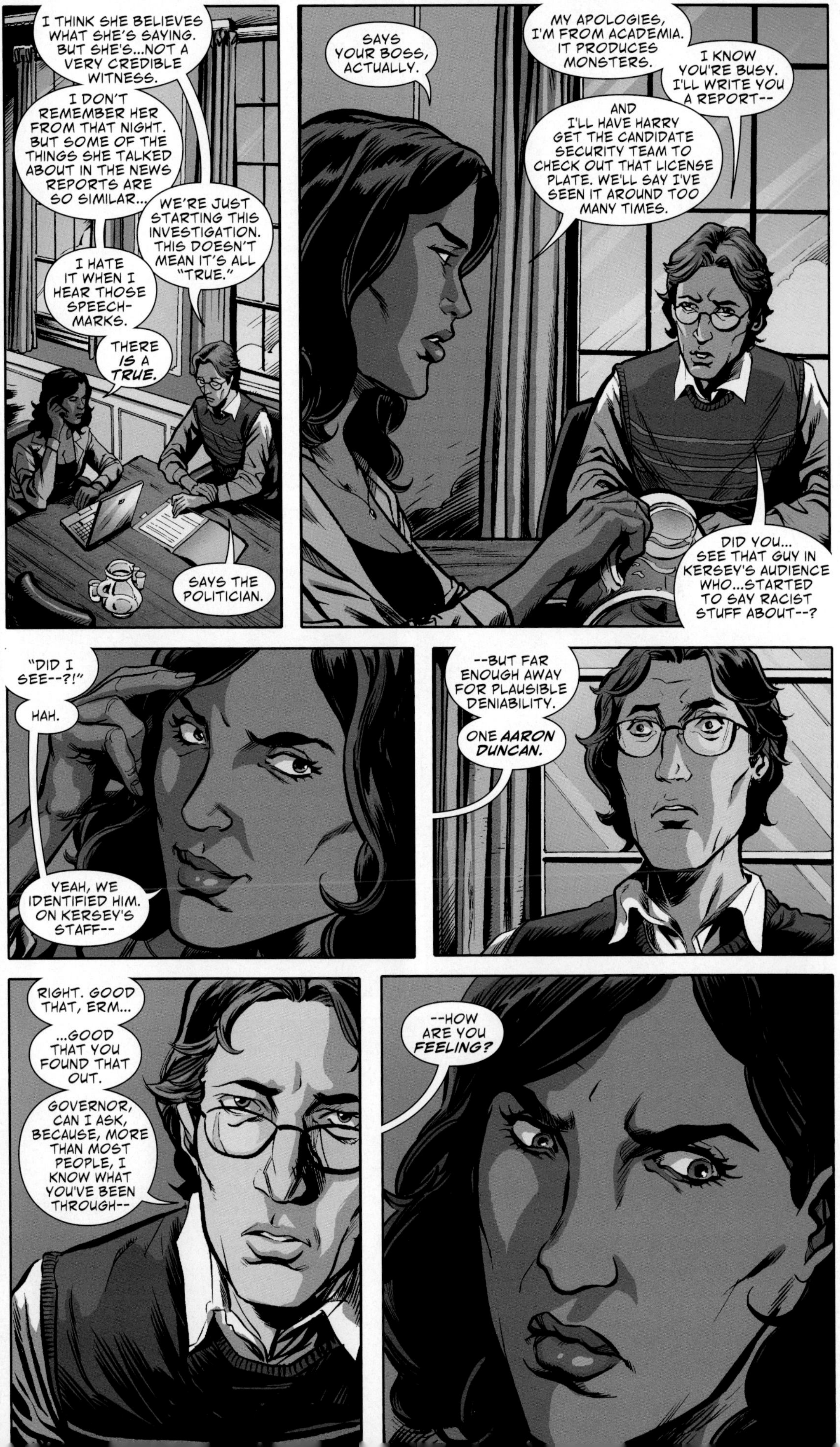
I THINK SHE BELIEVES WHAT SHE'S SAYING. BUT SHE'S...NOT A VERY CREDIBLE WITNESS.
I DON'T REMEMBER HER FROM THAT NIGHT. BUT SOME OF THE THINGS SHE TALKED ABOUT IN THE NEWS REPORTS ARE SO SIMILAR...
WE'RE JUST STARTING THIS INVESTIGATION. THIS DOESN'T MEAN IT'S ALL "TRUE."
I HATE IT WHEN I HEAR THOSE SPEECH-MARKS.
THERE *IS* A ***TRUE.***
SAYS THE POLITICIAN.
SAYS YOUR BOSS, ACTUALLY.
MY APOLOGIES, I'M FROM ACADEMIA. IT PRODUCES MONSTERS.
I KNOW YOU'RE BUSY. I'LL WRITE YOU A REPORT--
AND I'LL HAVE HARRY GET THE CANDIDATE SECURITY TEAM TO CHECK OUT THAT LICENSE PLATE. WE'LL SAY I'VE SEEN IT AROUND TOO MANY TIMES.
DID YOU... SEE THAT GUY IN KERSEY'S AUDIENCE WHO...STARTED TO SAY RACIST STUFF ABOUT--?
"DID I SEE--?!"
HAH.
YEAH, WE IDENTIFIED HIM. ON KERSEY'S STAFF--
--BUT FAR ENOUGH AWAY FOR PLAUSIBLE DENIABILITY.
ONE ***AARON DUNCAN.***
RIGHT. GOOD THAT, ERM...
...GOOD THAT YOU FOUND THAT OUT.
GOVERNOR, CAN I ASK, BECAUSE, MORE THAN MOST PEOPLE, I KNOW WHAT YOU'VE BEEN THROUGH--
--HOW ARE YOU ***FEELING?***

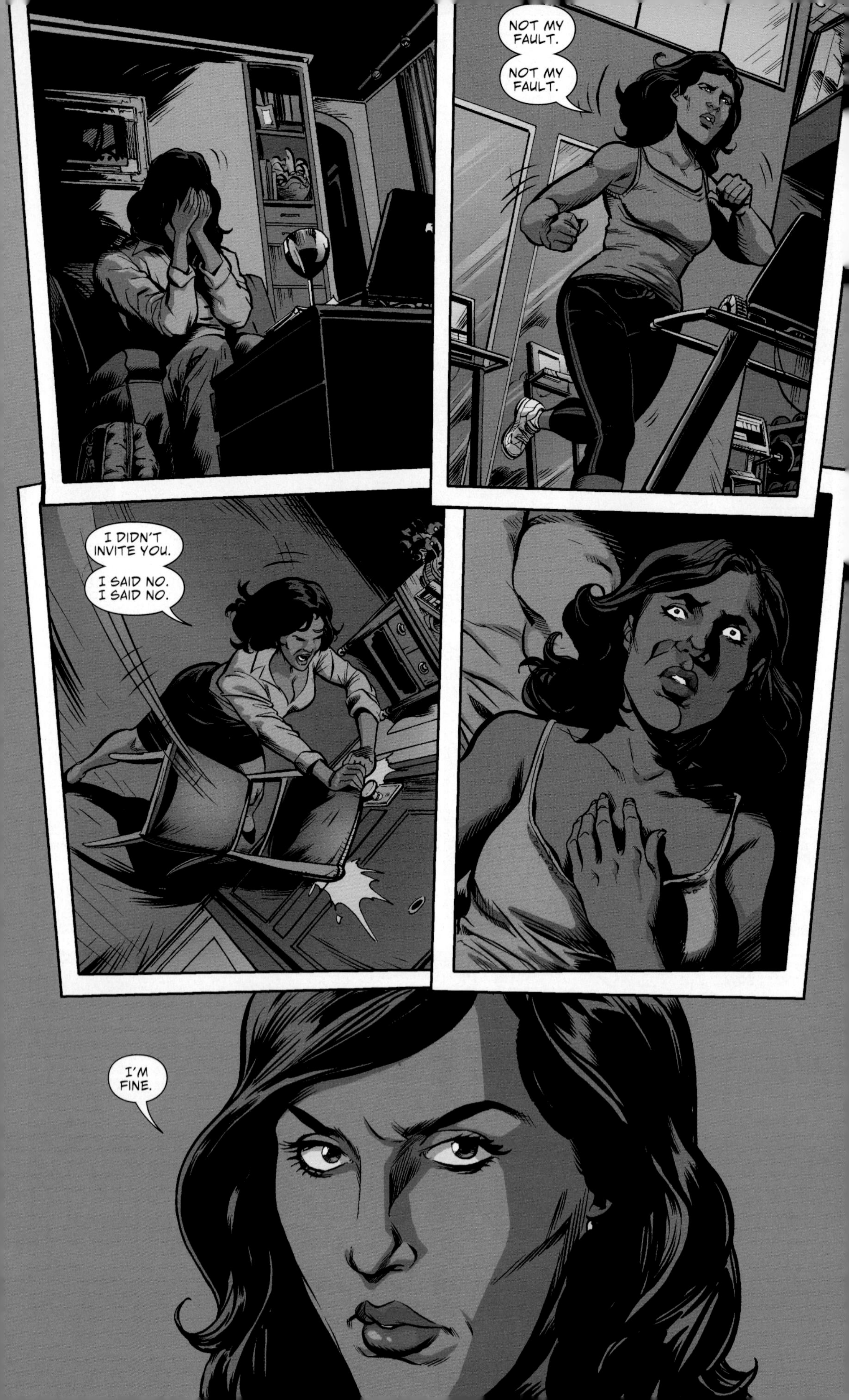
NOT MY FAULT.
NOT MY FAULT.
I DIDN'T INVITE YOU.
I SAID NO. I SAID NO.
I'M FINE.

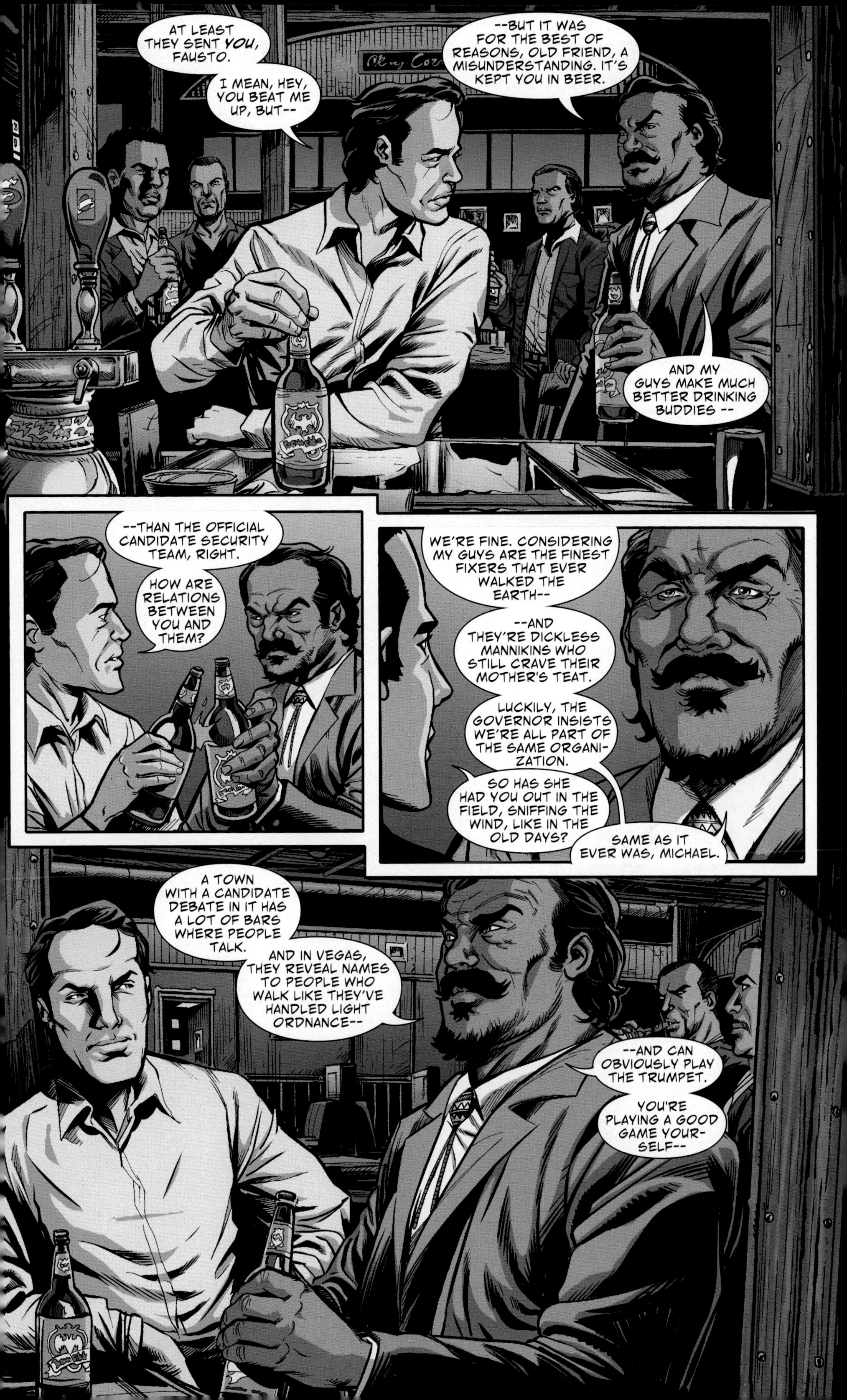
AT LEAST THEY SENT *YOU*, FAUSTO.
I MEAN, HEY, YOU BEAT ME UP, BUT--
--BUT IT WAS FOR THE BEST OF REASONS, OLD FRIEND, A MISUNDERSTANDING. IT'S KEPT YOU IN BEER.
AND MY GUYS MAKE MUCH BETTER DRINKING BUDDIES --
--THAN THE OFFICIAL CANDIDATE SECURITY TEAM, RIGHT.
HOW ARE RELATIONS BETWEEN YOU AND THEM?
WE'RE FINE. CONSIDERING MY GUYS ARE THE FINEST FIXERS THAT EVER WALKED THE EARTH--
--AND THEY'RE DICKLESS MANNIKINS WHO STILL CRAVE THEIR MOTHER'S TEAT.
LUCKILY, THE GOVERNOR INSISTS WE'RE ALL PART OF THE SAME ORGANI-ZATION.
SO HAS SHE HAD YOU OUT IN THE FIELD, SNIFFING THE WIND, LIKE IN THE OLD DAYS?
SAME AS IT EVER WAS, MICHAEL.
A TOWN WITH A CANDIDATE DEBATE IN IT HAS A LOT OF BARS WHERE PEOPLE TALK.
AND IN VEGAS, THEY REVEAL NAMES TO PEOPLE WHO WALK LIKE THEY'VE HANDLED LIGHT ORDNANCE--
--AND CAN OBVIOUSLY PLAY THE TRUMPET.
YOU'RE PLAYING A GOOD GAME YOUR-SELF--

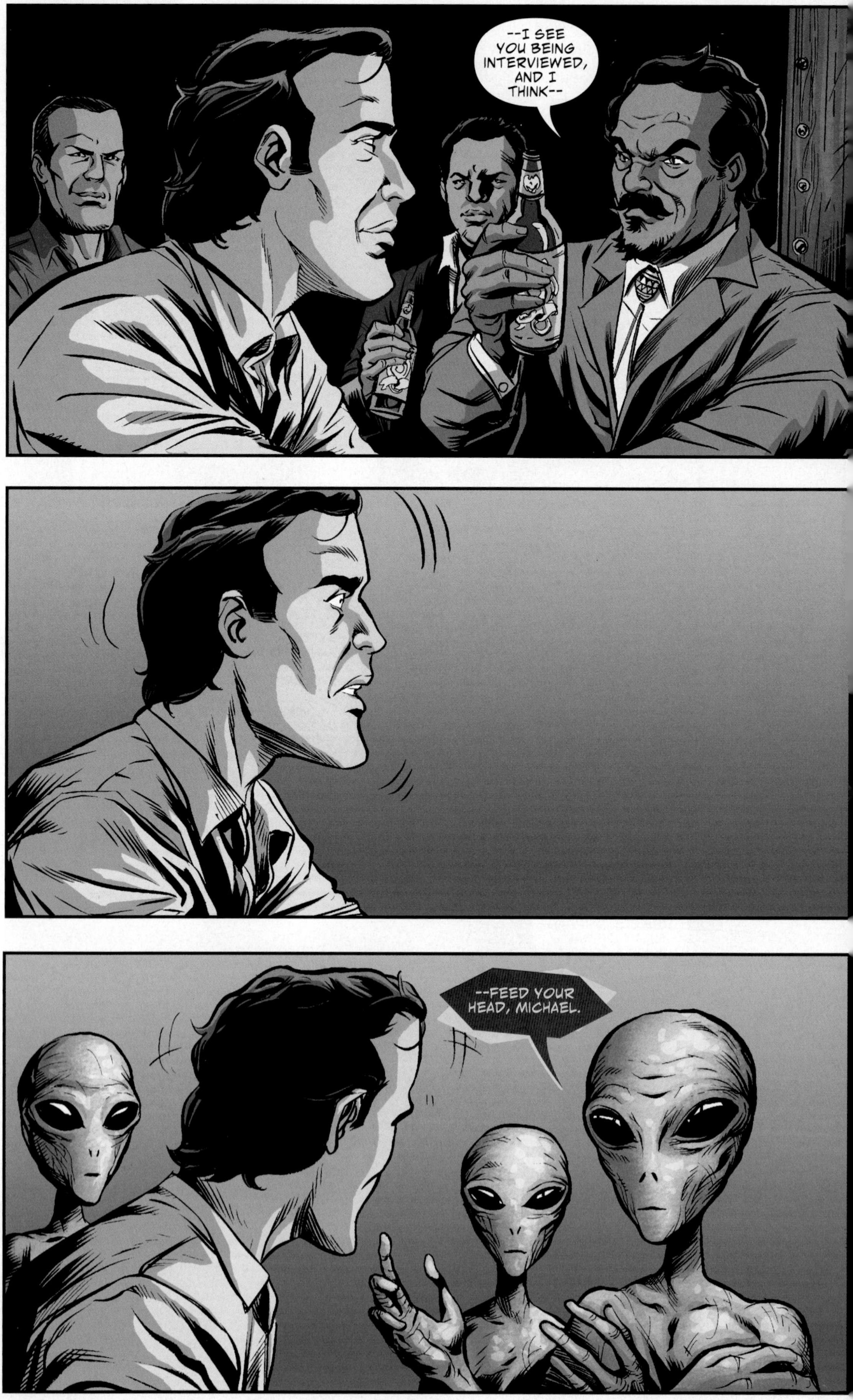
--I SEE YOU BEING INTERVIEWED, AND I THINK--
--FEED YOUR HEAD, MICHAEL.

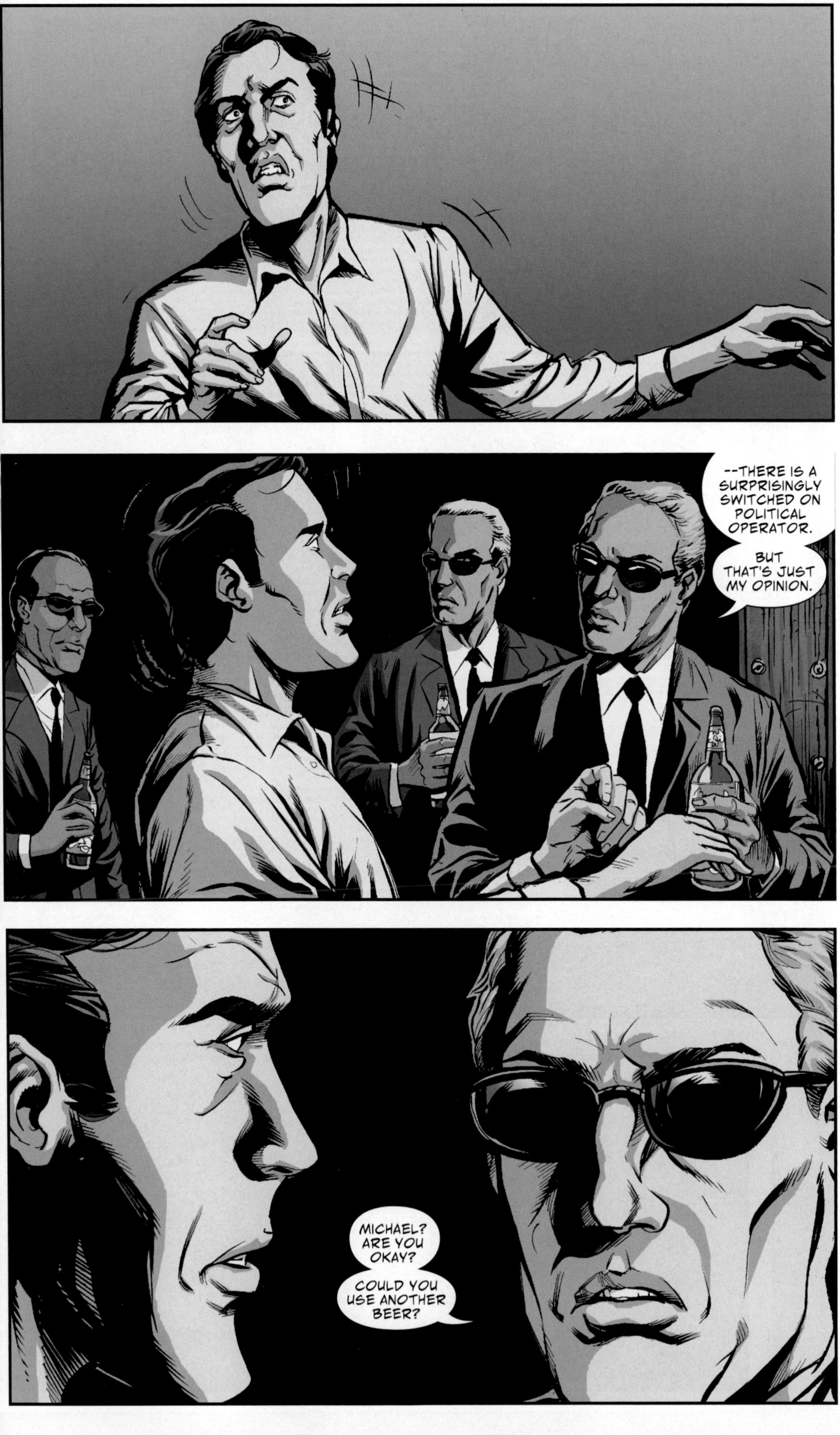
--THERE IS A SURPRISINGLY SWITCHED ON POLITICAL OPERATOR.
BUT THAT'S JUST MY OPINION.
MICHAEL? ARE YOU OKAY?
COULD YOU USE ANOTHER BEER?

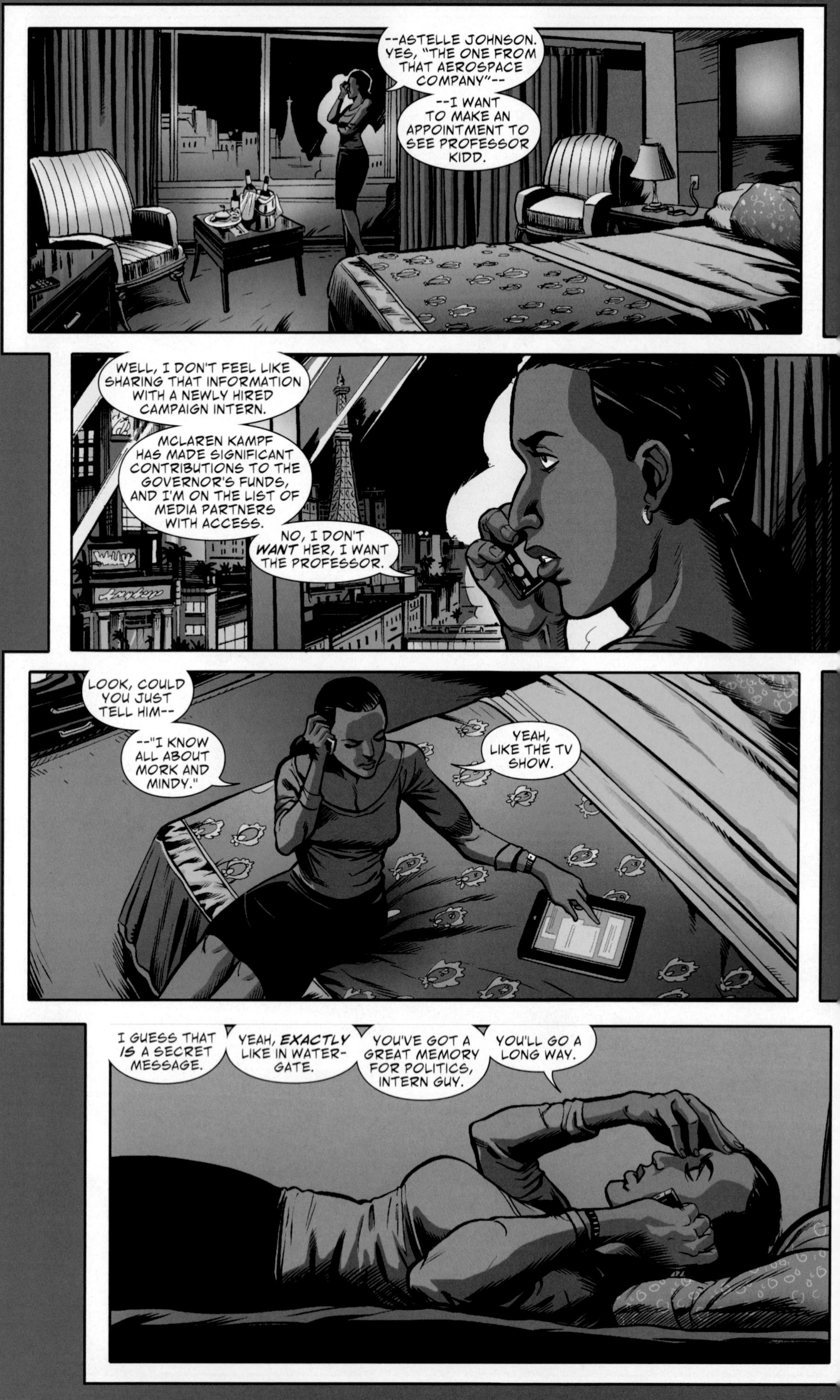
--ASTELLE JOHNSON. YES, "THE ONE FROM THAT AEROSPACE COMPANY"--
--I WANT TO MAKE AN APPOINTMENT TO SEE PROFESSOR KIDD.
WELL, I DON'T FEEL LIKE SHARING THAT INFORMATION WITH A NEWLY HIRED CAMPAIGN INTERN.
MCLAREN KAMPF HAS MADE SIGNIFICANT CONTRIBUTIONS TO THE GOVERNOR'S FUNDS, AND I'M ON THE LIST OF MEDIA PARTNERS WITH ACCESS.
NO, I DON'T *WANT* HER, I WANT THE PROFESSOR.
LOOK, COULD YOU JUST TELL HIM--
--"I KNOW ALL ABOUT MORK AND MINDY."
YEAH, LIKE THE TV SHOW.
I GUESS THAT *IS* A SECRET MESSAGE.
YEAH, *EXACTLY* LIKE IN WATER-GATE.
YOU'VE GOT A GREAT MEMORY FOR POLITICS, INTERN GUY.
YOU'LL GO A LONG WAY.

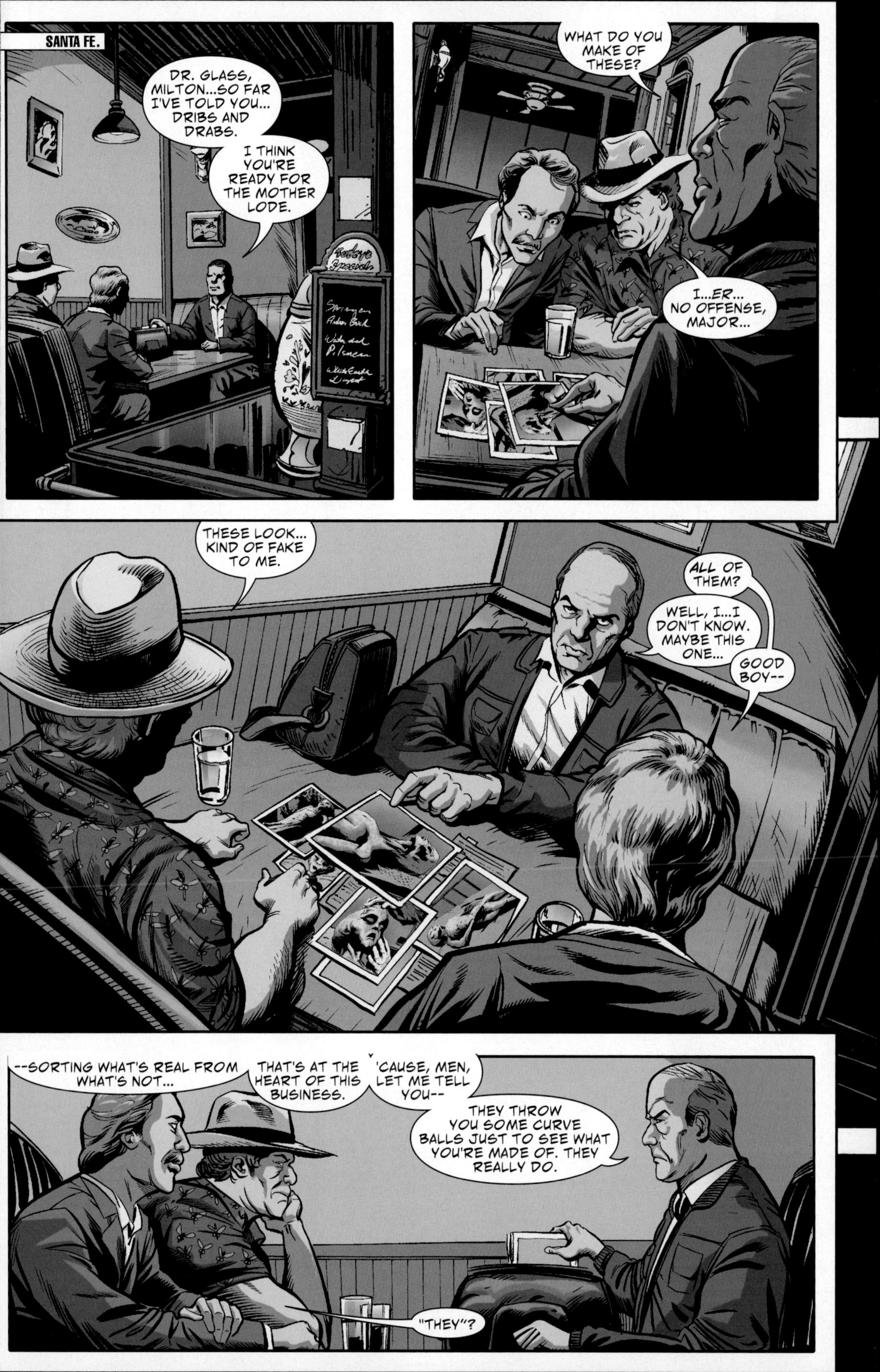
SANTA FE.
DR. GLASS, MILTON...SO FAR I'VE TOLD YOU... DRIBS AND DRABS.
I THINK YOU'RE READY FOR THE MOTHER LODE.
WHAT DO YOU MAKE OF THESE?
I...ER... NO OFFENSE, MAJOR...
THESE LOOK... KIND OF FAKE TO ME.
ALL OF THEM?
WELL, I...I DON'T KNOW. MAYBE THIS ONE...
GOOD BOY--
--SORTING WHAT'S REAL FROM WHAT'S NOT...
THAT'S AT THE HEART OF THIS BUSINESS.
'CAUSE, MEN, LET ME TELL YOU--
THEY THROW YOU SOME CURVE BALLS JUST TO SEE WHAT YOU'RE MADE OF. THEY REALLY DO.
"THEY"?

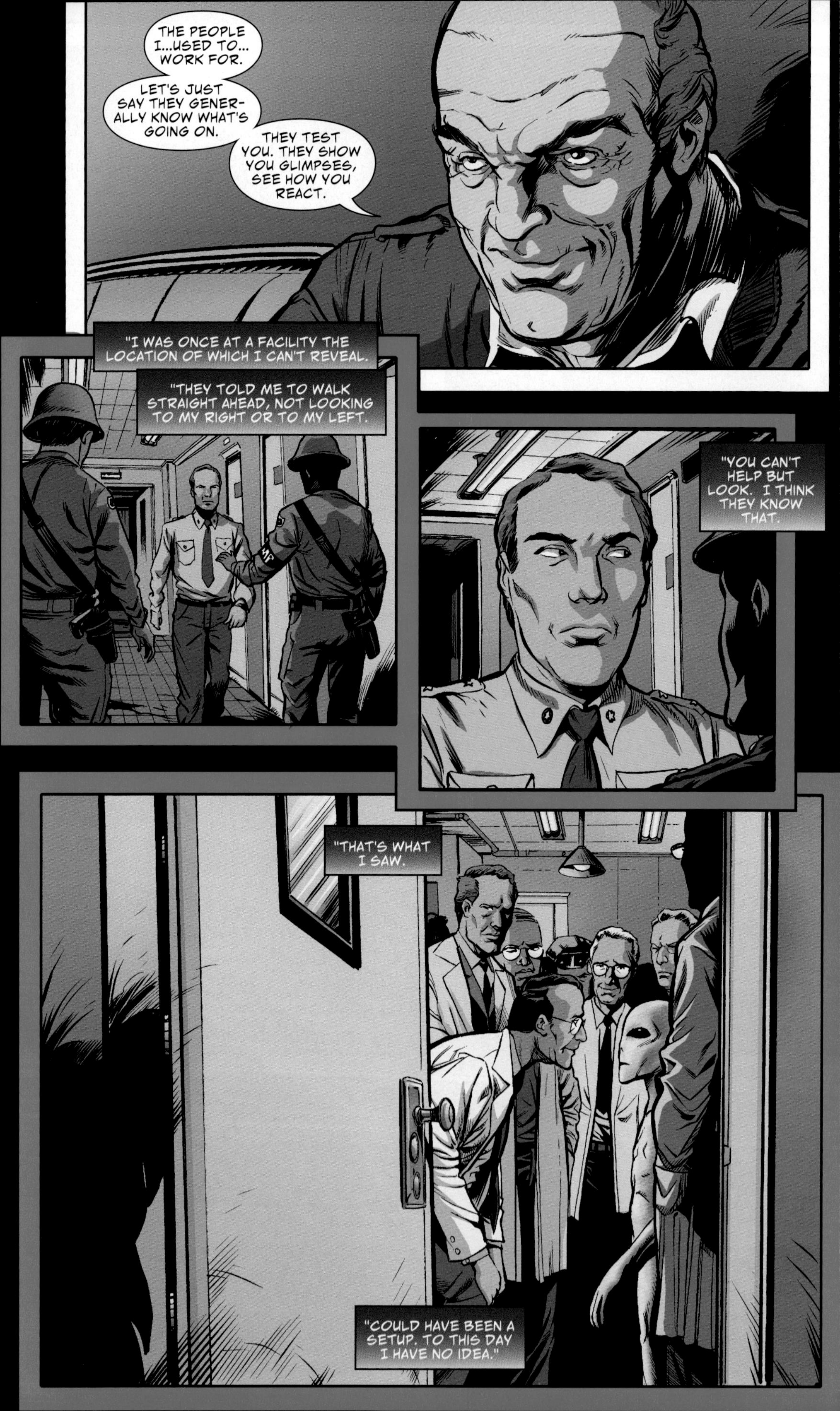
THE PEOPLE I...USED TO... WORK FOR.
LET'S JUST SAY THEY GENERALLY KNOW WHAT'S GOING ON.
THEY TEST YOU. THEY SHOW YOU GLIMPSES, SEE HOW YOU REACT.
"I WAS ONCE AT A FACILITY THE LOCATION OF WHICH I CAN'T REVEAL.
"THEY TOLD ME TO WALK STRAIGHT AHEAD, NOT LOOKING TO MY RIGHT OR TO MY LEFT.
"YOU CAN'T HELP BUT LOOK. I THINK THEY KNOW THAT.
"THAT'S WHAT I SAW.
"COULD HAVE BEEN A SETUP. TO THIS DAY I HAVE NO IDEA."

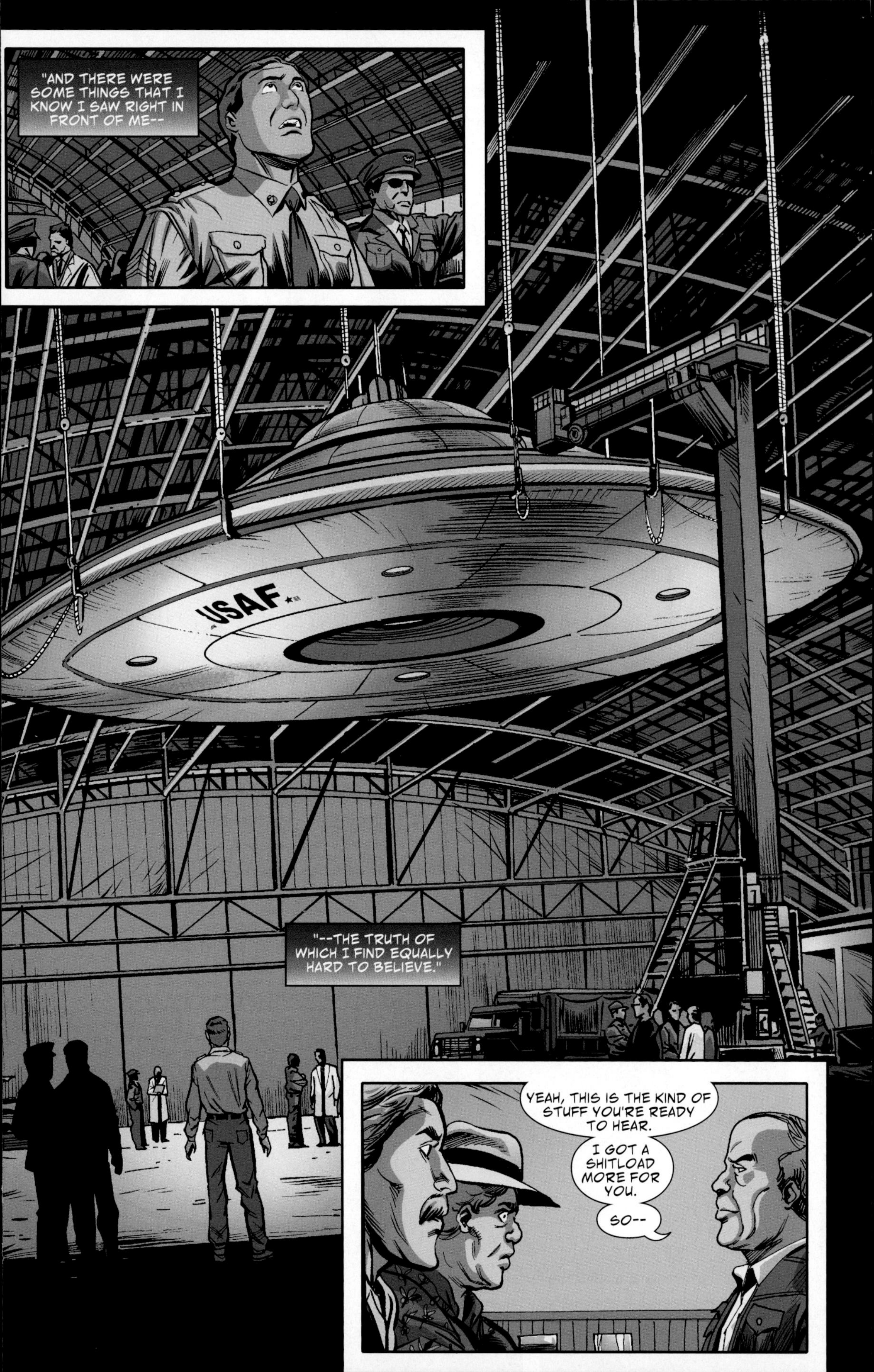
"AND THERE WERE SOME THINGS THAT I KNOW I SAW RIGHT IN FRONT OF ME--
USAF
"--THE TRUTH OF WHICH I FIND EQUALLY HARD TO BELIEVE."
YEAH, THIS IS THE KIND OF STUFF YOU'RE READY TO HEAR.
I GOT A SHITLOAD MORE FOR YOU.
SO--

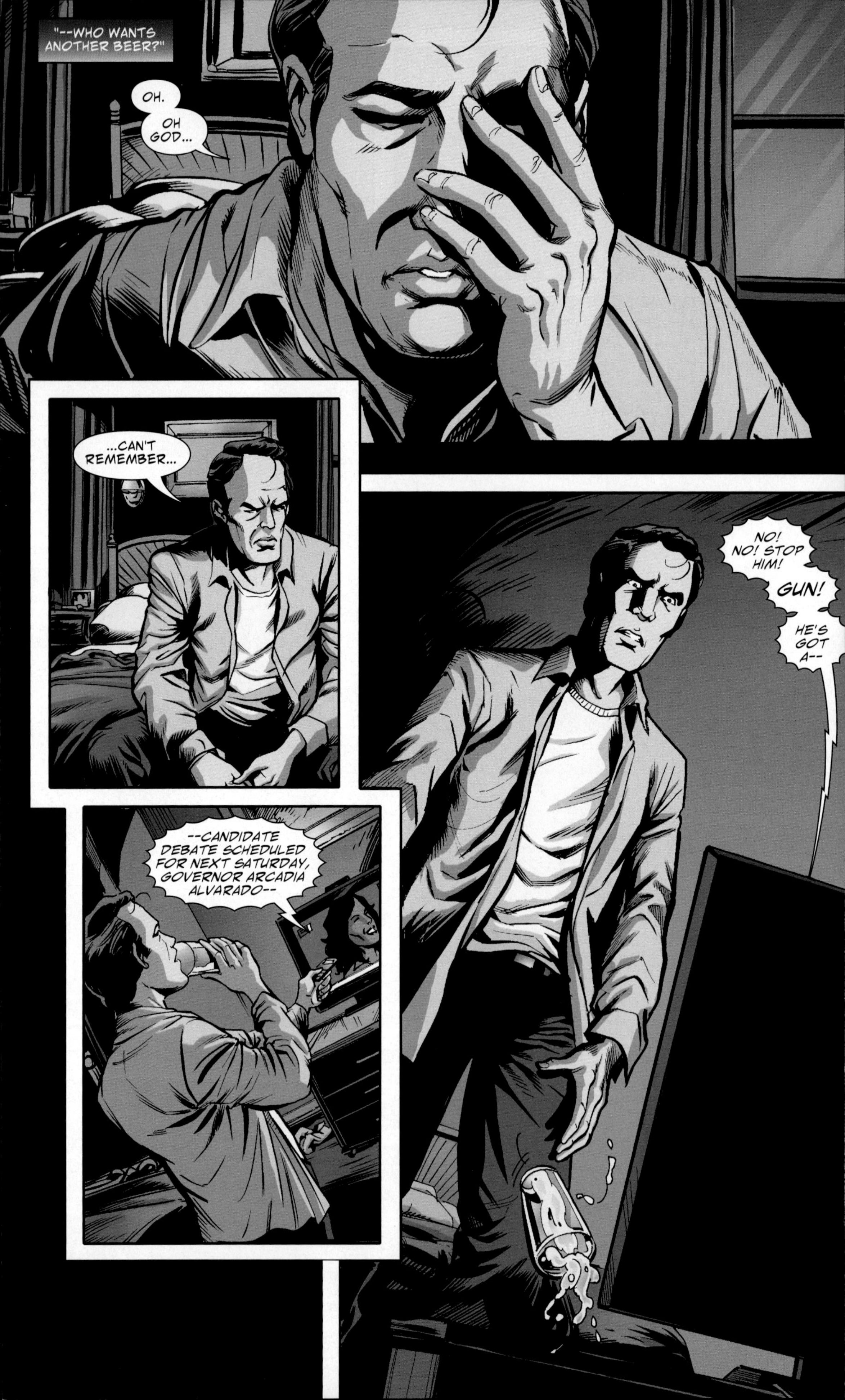
"--WHO WANTS ANOTHER BEER?"
OH.
OH GOD...
...CAN'T REMEMBER...
--CANDIDATE DEBATE SCHEDULED FOR NEXT SATURDAY, GOVERNOR ARCADIA ALVARADO--
NO! NO! STOP HIM!
GUN!
HE'S GOT A--

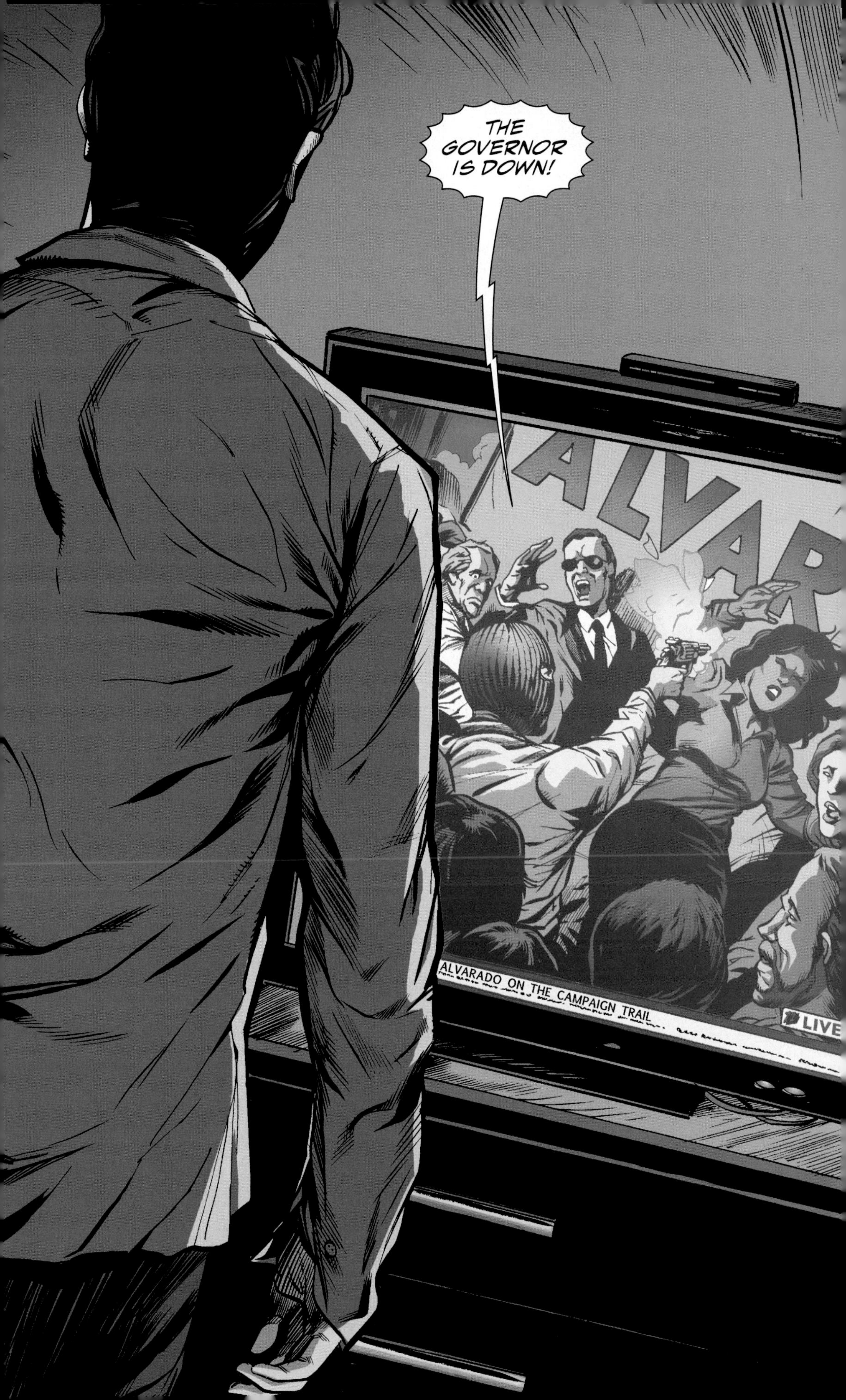
THE GOVERNOR IS DOWN!
ALVAR
ALVARADO ON THE CAMPAIGN TRAIL
LIVE

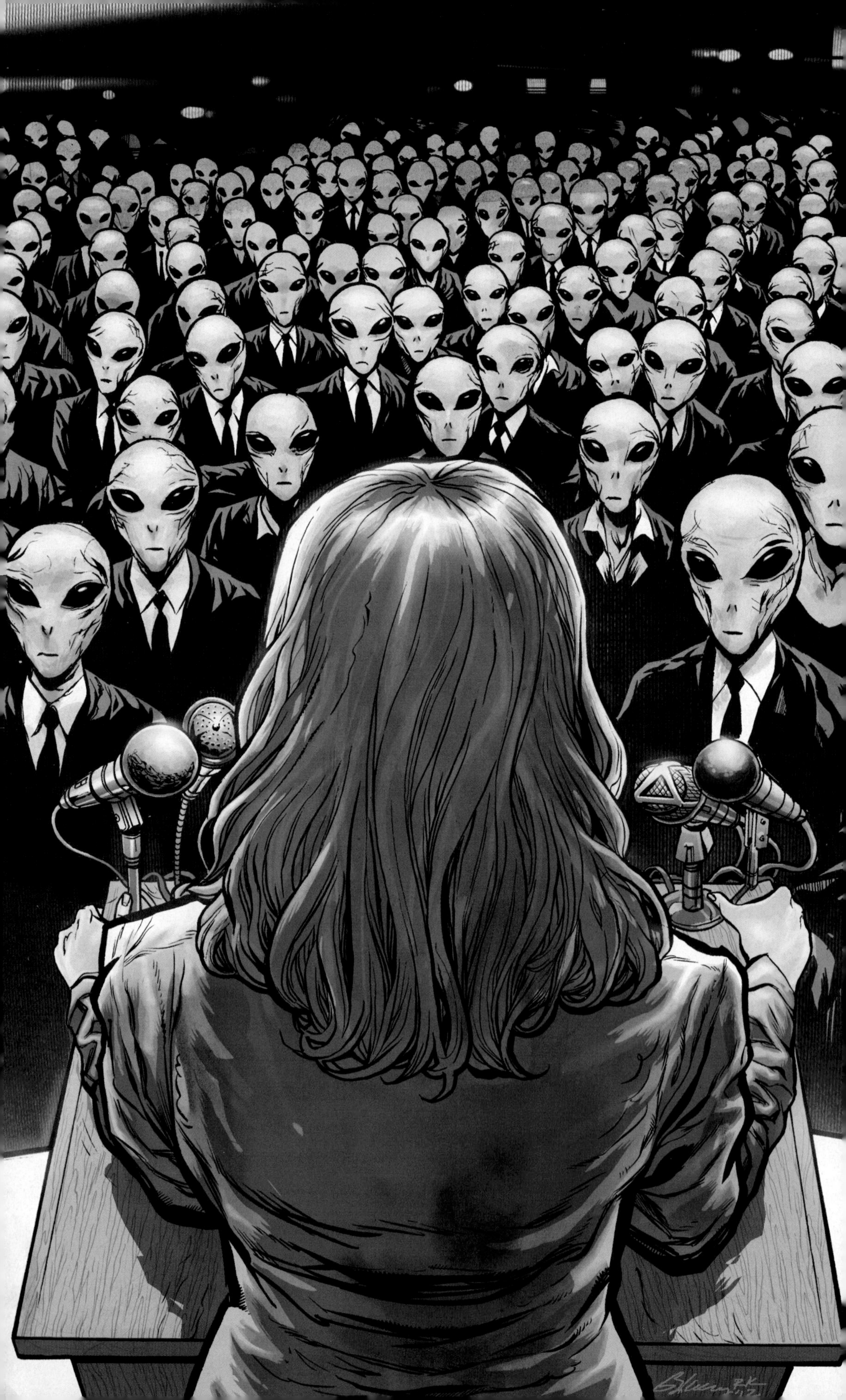

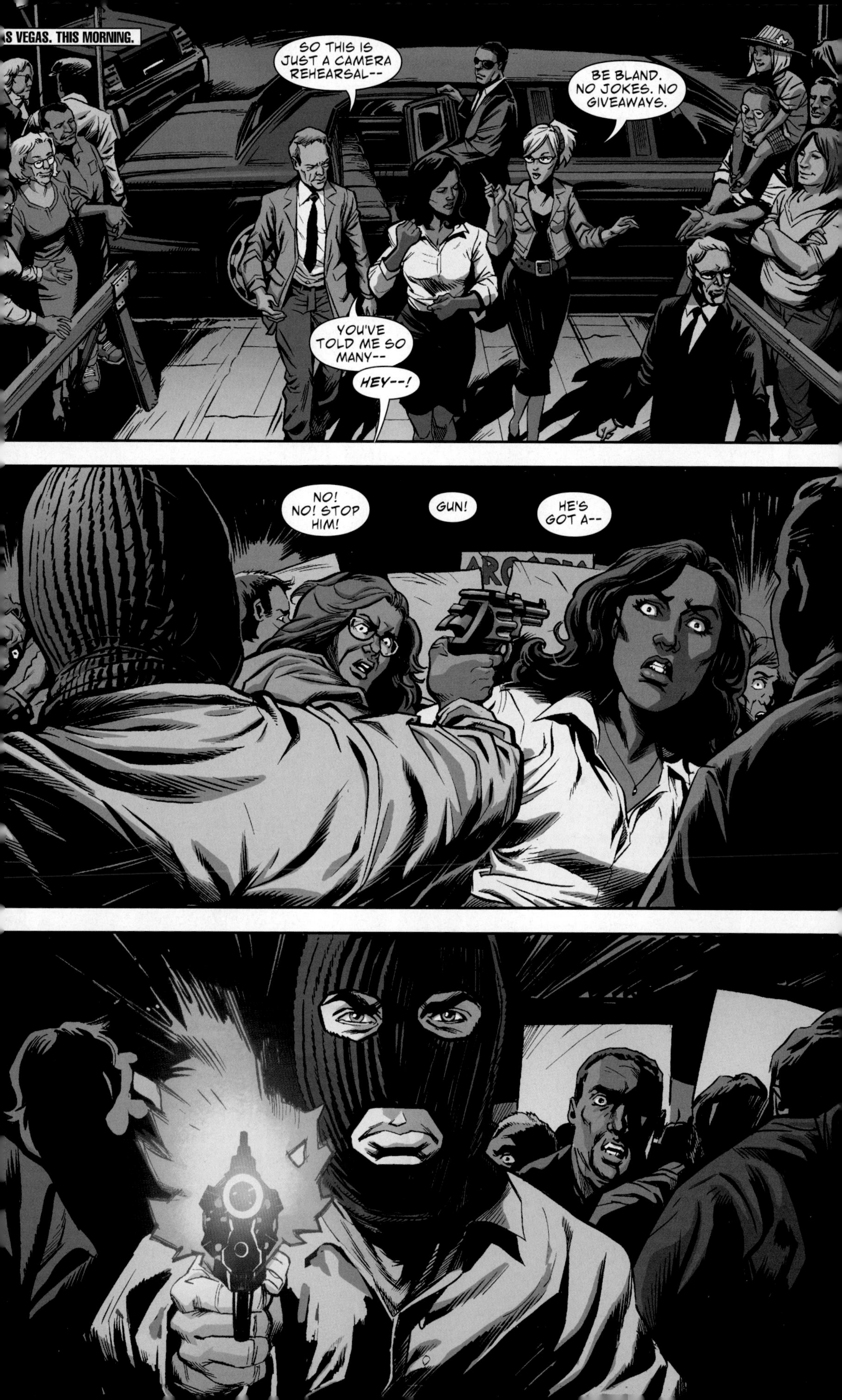

S VEGAS. THIS MORNING.
SO THIS IS JUST A CAMERA REHEARSAL--
BE BLAND. NO JOKES. NO GIVEAWAYS.
YOU'VE TOLD ME SO MANY--
HEY--!
NO! NO! STOP HIM!
GUN!
HE'S GOT A--

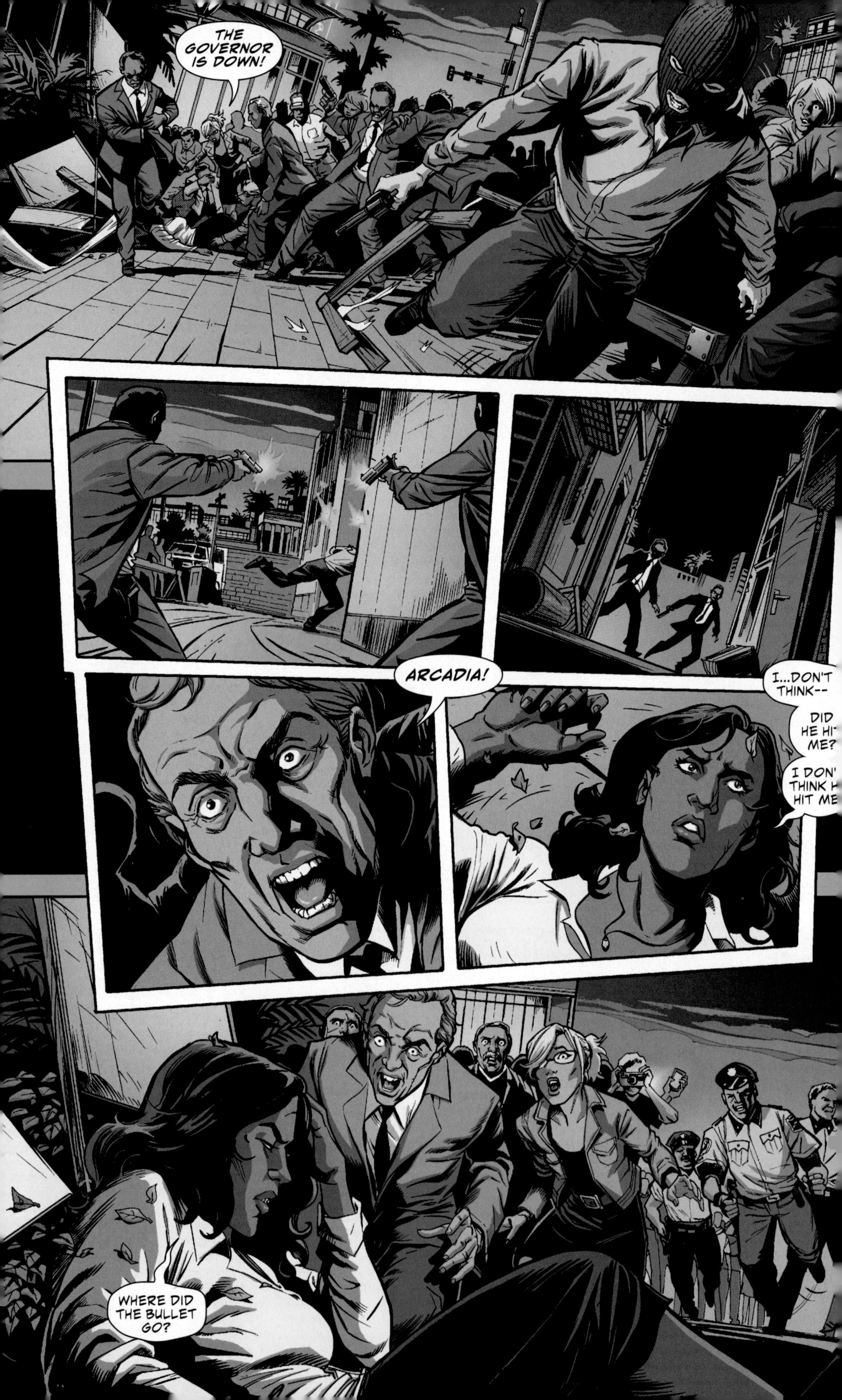

THE GOVERNOR IS DOWN!
ARCADIA!
I...DON'T THINK--
DID HE HI ME?
I DON' THINK H HIT ME
WHERE DID THE BULLET GO?

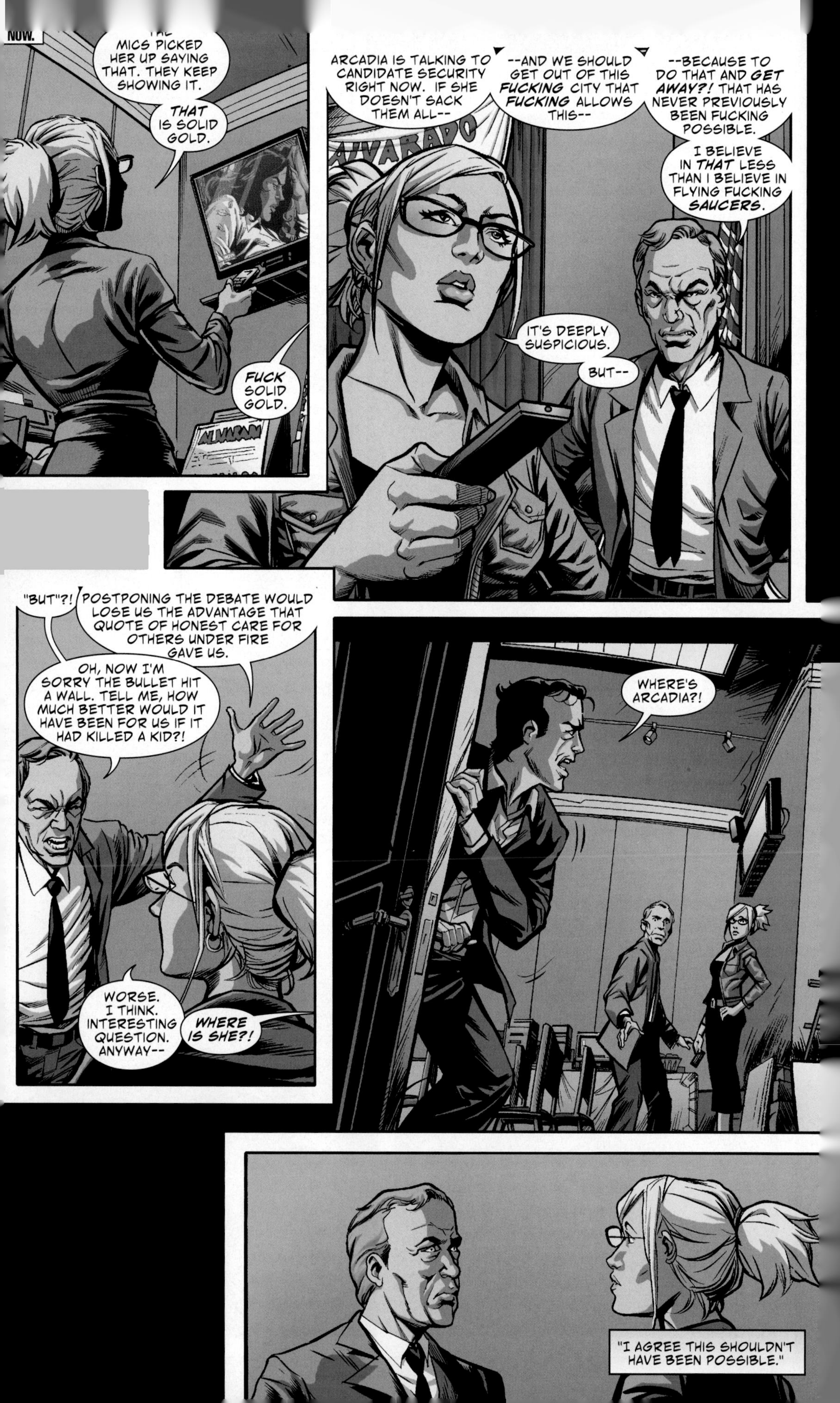
NOW.
MICS PICKED HER UP SAYING THAT. THEY KEEP SHOWING IT.
THAT IS SOLID GOLD.
FUCK SOLID GOLD.
ARCADIA IS TALKING TO CANDIDATE SECURITY RIGHT NOW. IF SHE DOESN'T SACK THEM ALL--
--AND WE SHOULD GET OUT OF THIS FUCKING CITY THAT FUCKING ALLOWS THIS--
--BECAUSE TO DO THAT AND GET AWAY?! THAT HAS NEVER PREVIOUSLY BEEN FUCKING POSSIBLE.
I BELIEVE IN THAT LESS THAN I BELIEVE IN FLYING FUCKING SAUCERS.
IT'S DEEPLY SUSPICIOUS.
BUT--
"BUT"?!
POSTPONING THE DEBATE WOULD LOSE US THE ADVANTAGE THAT QUOTE OF HONEST CARE FOR OTHERS UNDER FIRE GAVE US.
OH, NOW I'M SORRY THE BULLET HIT A WALL. TELL ME, HOW MUCH BETTER WOULD IT HAVE BEEN FOR US IF IT HAD KILLED A KID?!
WORSE. I THINK. INTERESTING QUESTION. ANYWAY--
WHERE IS SHE?!
WHERE'S ARCADIA?!
"I AGREE THIS SHOULDN'T HAVE BEEN POSSIBLE."

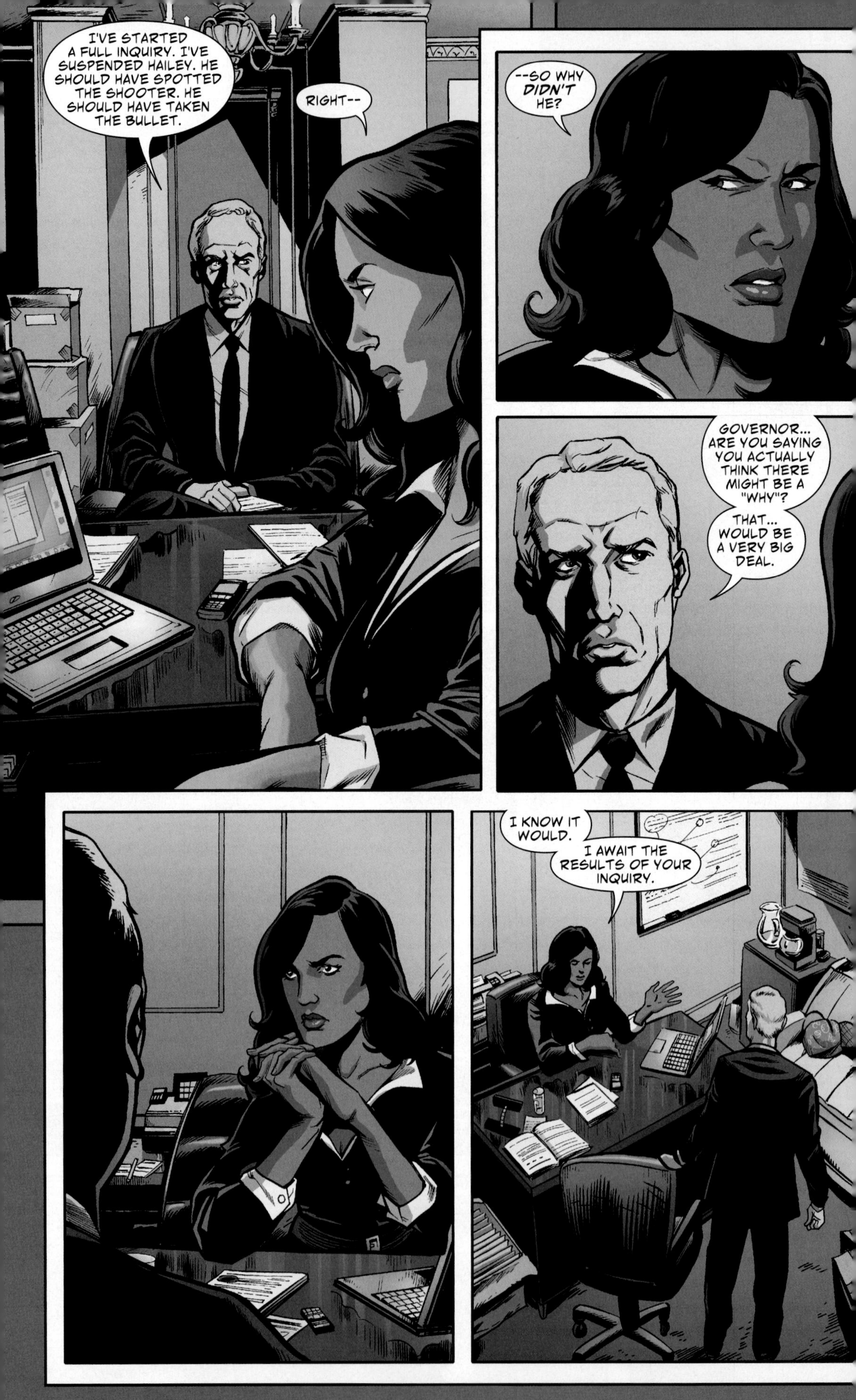

I'VE STARTED A FULL INQUIRY. I'VE SUSPENDED HAILEY. HE SHOULD HAVE SPOTTED THE SHOOTER. HE SHOULD HAVE TAKEN THE BULLET.
RIGHT--
--SO WHY *DIDN'T* HE?
GOVERNOR... ARE YOU SAYING YOU ACTUALLY THINK THERE MIGHT BE A "WHY"?
THAT... WOULD BE A VERY BIG DEAL.
I KNOW IT WOULD.
I AWAIT THE RESULTS OF YOUR INQUIRY.

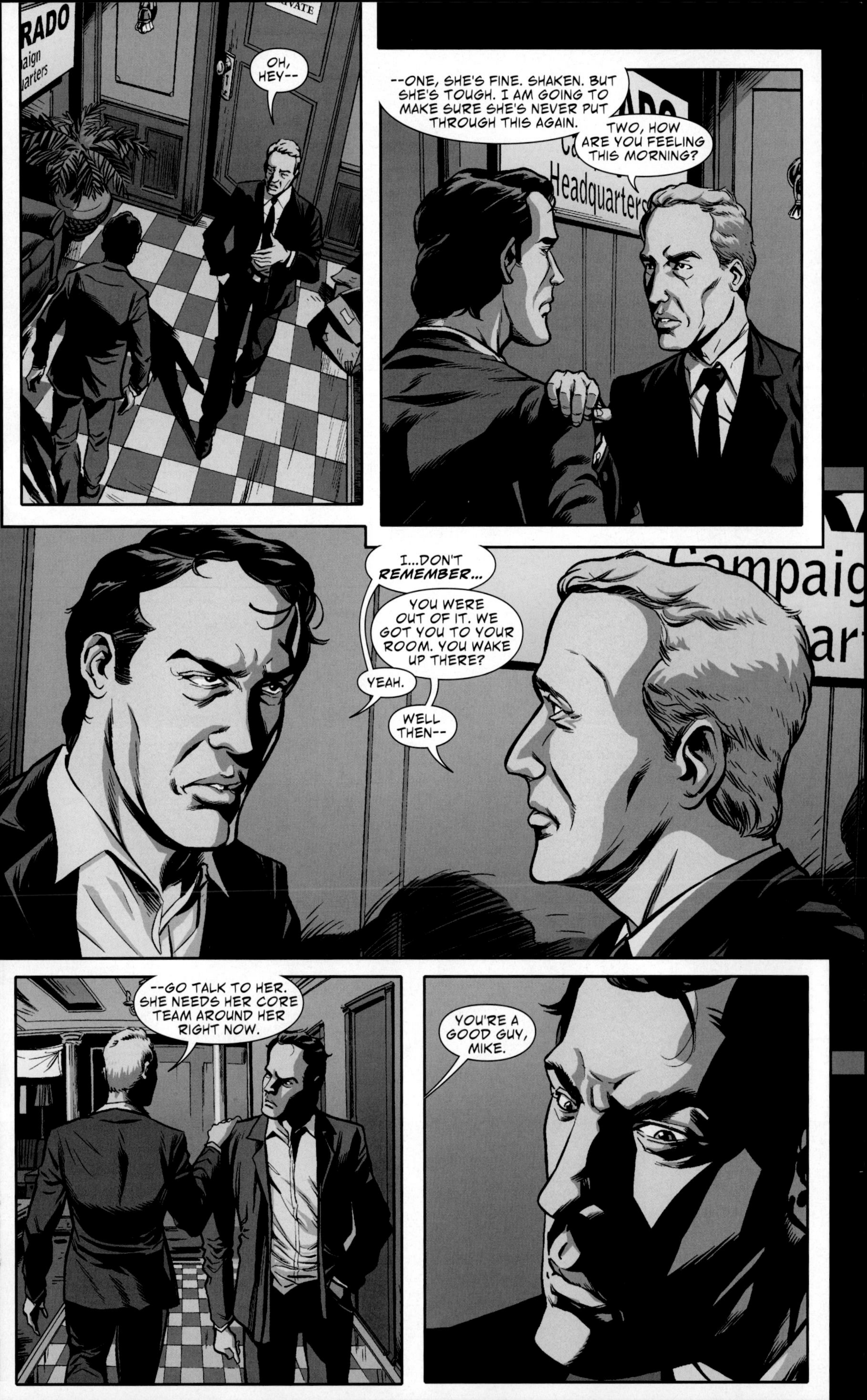
RADO
aign
quarters
PRIVATE
OH, HEY--
--ONE, SHE'S FINE. SHAKEN. BUT SHE'S TOUGH. I AM GOING TO MAKE SURE SHE'S NEVER PUT THROUGH THIS AGAIN.
TWO, HOW ARE YOU FEELING THIS MORNING?
Headquarters
I...DON'T REMEMBER...
YOU WERE OUT OF IT. WE GOT YOU TO YOUR ROOM. YOU WAKE UP THERE?
YEAH.
WELL THEN--
--GO TALK TO HER. SHE NEEDS HER CORE TEAM AROUND HER RIGHT NOW.
YOU'RE A GOOD GUY, MIKE.

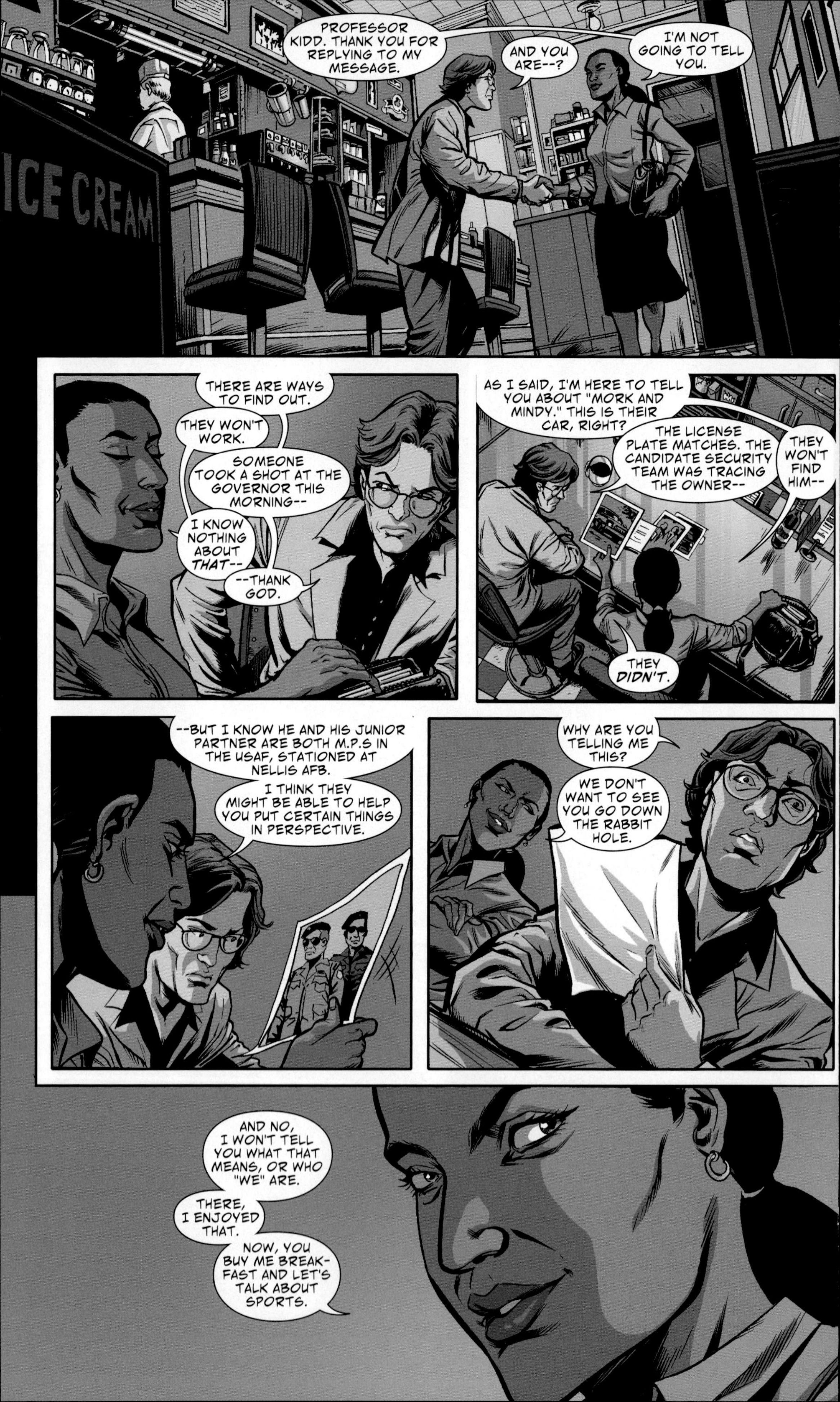
ICE CREAM
PROFESSOR KIDD. THANK YOU FOR REPLYING TO MY MESSAGE.
AND YOU ARE--?
I'M NOT GOING TO TELL YOU.
THERE ARE WAYS TO FIND OUT.
THEY WON'T WORK.
SOMEONE TOOK A SHOT AT THE GOVERNOR THIS MORNING--
I KNOW NOTHING ABOUT *THAT*--
--THANK GOD.
AS I SAID, I'M HERE TO TELL YOU ABOUT "MORK AND MINDY." THIS IS THEIR CAR, RIGHT?
THE LICENSE PLATE MATCHES. THE CANDIDATE SECURITY TEAM WAS TRACING THE OWNER--
THEY WON'T FIND HIM--
THEY *DIDN'T*.
--BUT I KNOW HE AND HIS JUNIOR PARTNER ARE BOTH M.P.S IN THE USAF, STATIONED AT NELLIS AFB.
I THINK THEY MIGHT BE ABLE TO HELP YOU PUT CERTAIN THINGS IN PERSPECTIVE.
WHY ARE YOU TELLING ME THIS?
WE DON'T WANT TO SEE YOU GO DOWN THE RABBIT HOLE.
AND NO, I WON'T TELL YOU WHAT THAT MEANS, OR WHO "WE" ARE.
THERE, I ENJOYED THAT.
NOW, YOU BUY ME BREAK-FAST AND LET'S TALK ABOUT SPORTS.

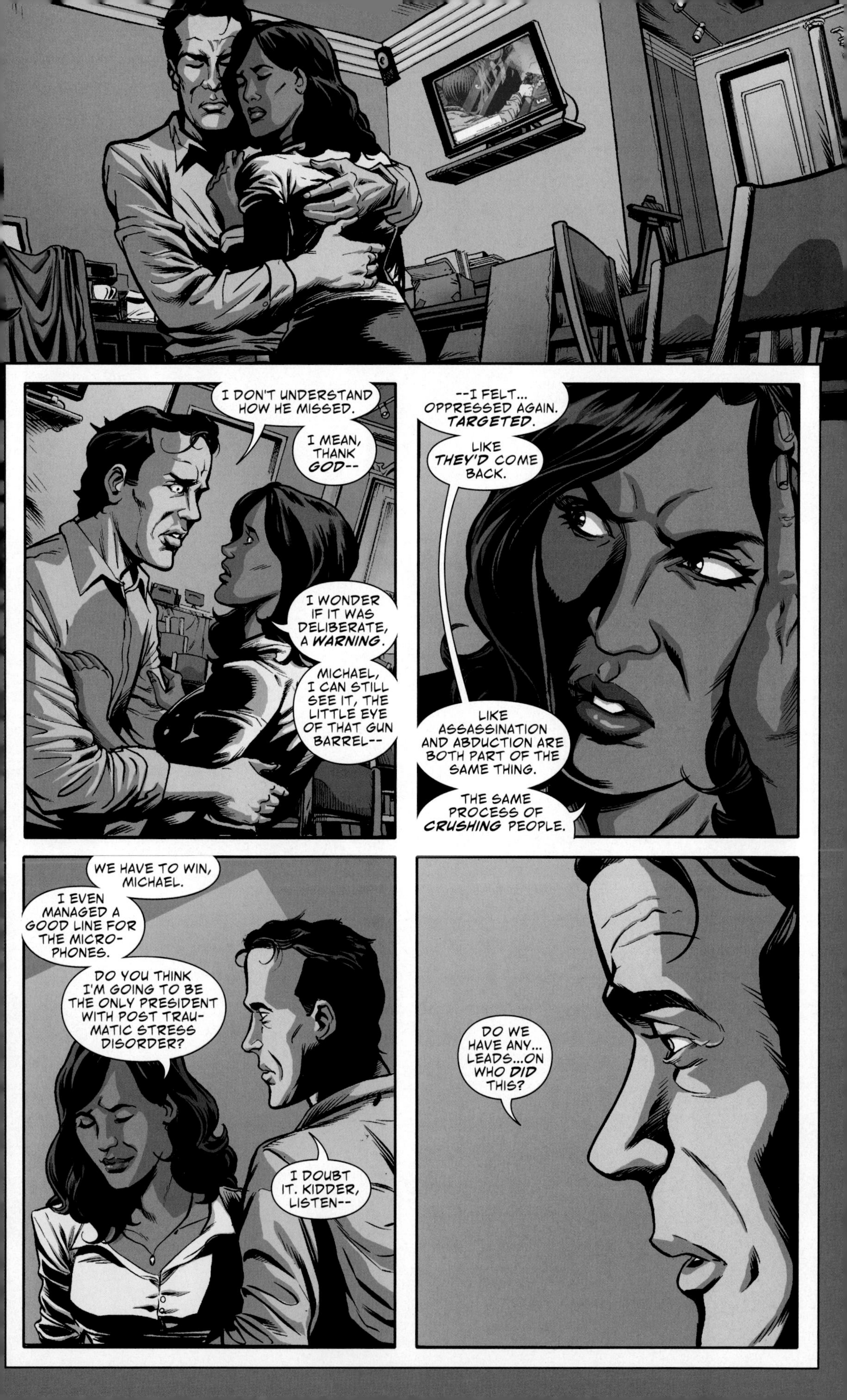

I DON'T UNDERSTAND HOW HE MISSED.
I MEAN, THANK GOD--
I WONDER IF IT WAS DELIBERATE, A WARNING.
MICHAEL, I CAN STILL SEE IT, THE LITTLE EYE OF THAT GUN BARREL--
--I FELT... OPPRESSED AGAIN. TARGETED.
LIKE THEY'D COME BACK.
LIKE ASSASSINATION AND ABDUCTION ARE BOTH PART OF THE SAME THING.
THE SAME PROCESS OF CRUSHING PEOPLE.
WE HAVE TO WIN, MICHAEL.
I EVEN MANAGED A GOOD LINE FOR THE MICRO-PHONES.
DO YOU THINK I'M GOING TO BE THE ONLY PRESIDENT WITH POST TRAU-MATIC STRESS DISORDER?
I DOUBT IT. KIDDER, LISTEN--
DO WE HAVE ANY... LEADS...ON WHO DID THIS?

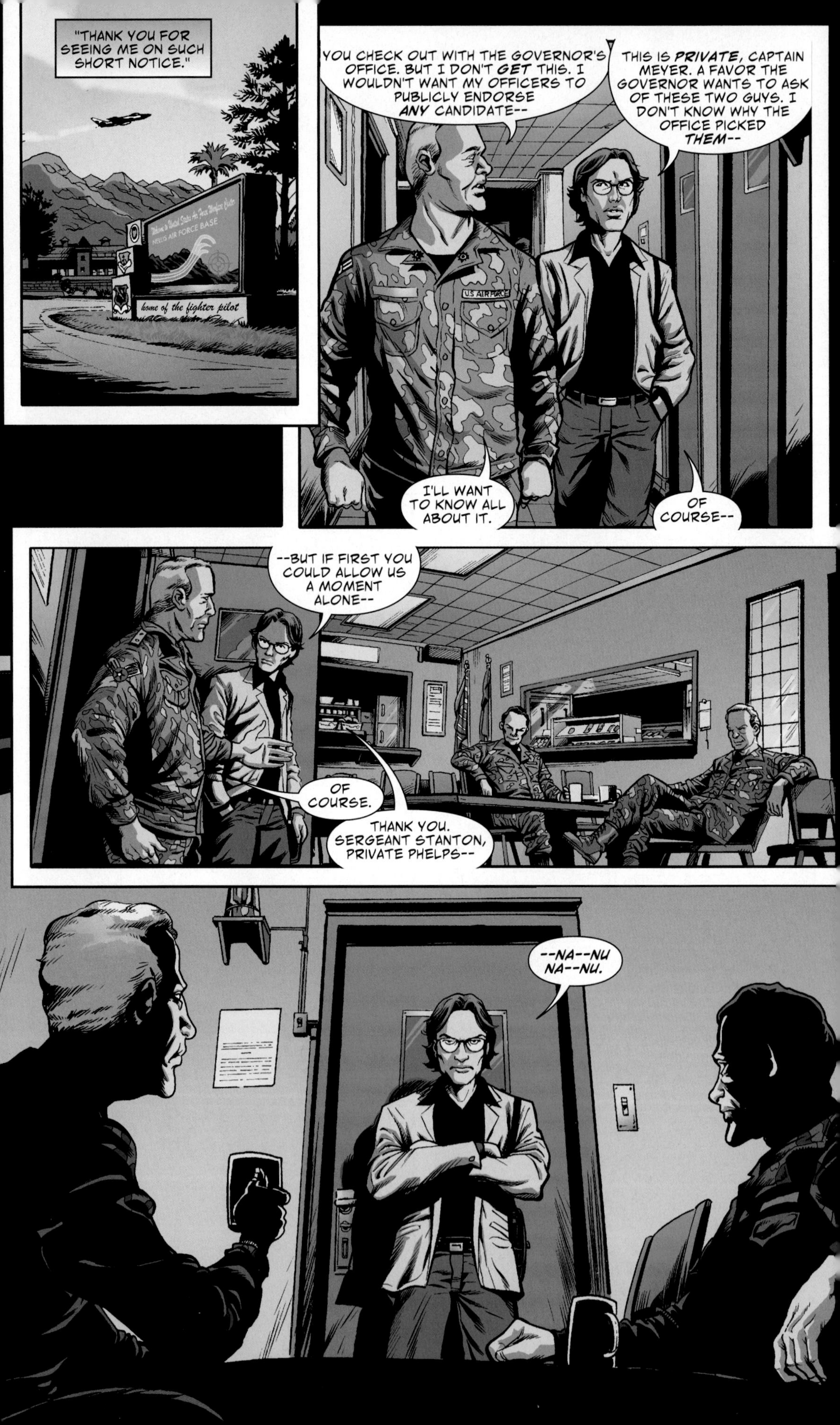
"THANK YOU FOR SEEING ME ON SUCH SHORT NOTICE."
NELLIS AIR FORCE BASE
home of the fighter pilot
YOU CHECK OUT WITH THE GOVERNOR'S OFFICE. BUT I DON'T GET THIS. I WOULDN'T WANT MY OFFICERS TO PUBLICLY ENDORSE ANY CANDIDATE--
THIS IS PRIVATE, CAPTAIN MEYER. A FAVOR THE GOVERNOR WANTS TO ASK OF THESE TWO GUYS. I DON'T KNOW WHY THE OFFICE PICKED THEM--
U.S. AIR FORCE
I'LL WANT TO KNOW ALL ABOUT IT.
OF COURSE--
--BUT IF FIRST YOU COULD ALLOW US A MOMENT ALONE--
OF COURSE.
THANK YOU. SERGEANT STANTON, PRIVATE PHELPS--
--NA--NU NA--NU.

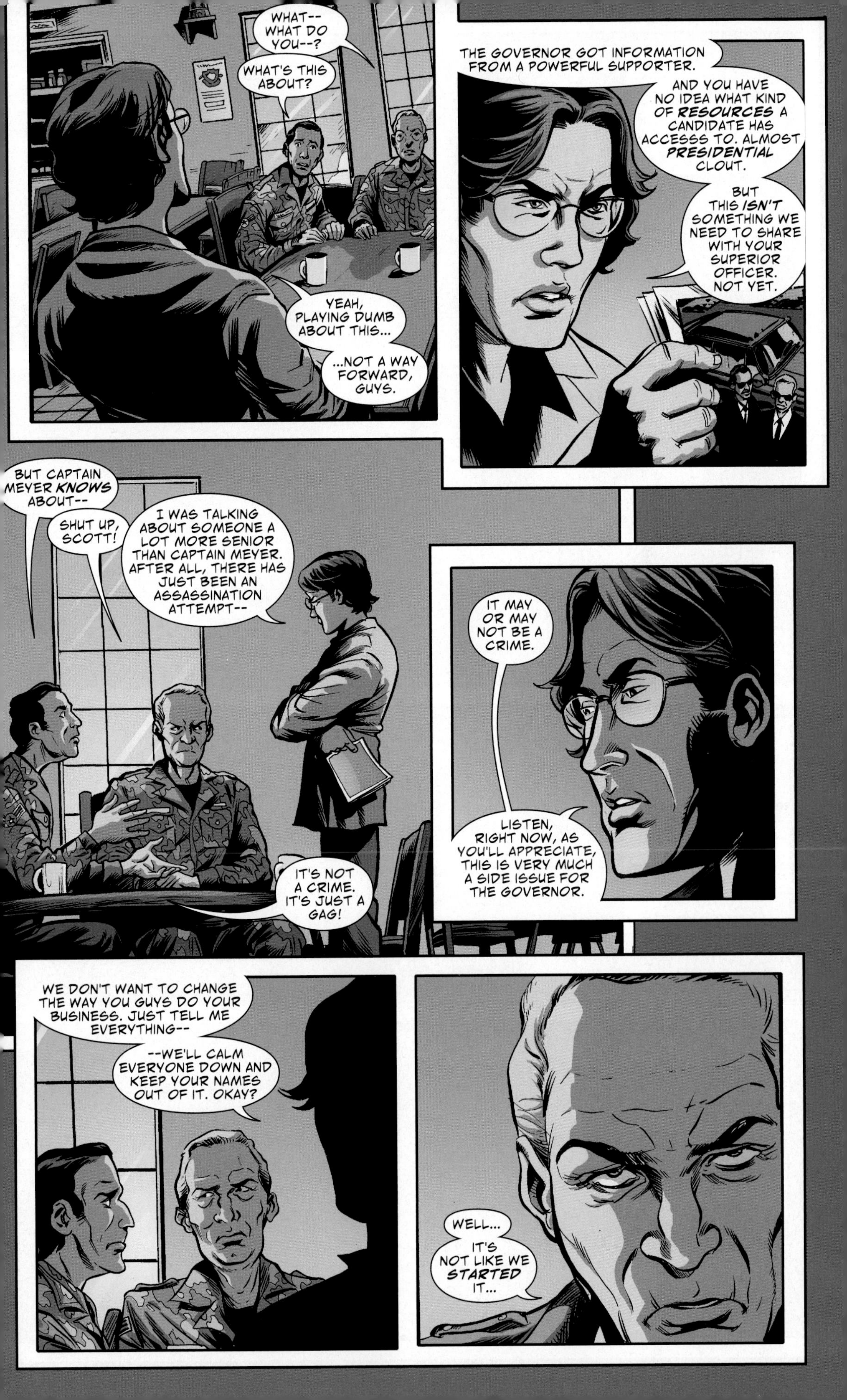
WHAT-- WHAT DO YOU--?
WHAT'S THIS ABOUT?
YEAH, PLAYING DUMB ABOUT THIS...
...NOT A WAY FORWARD, GUYS.
THE GOVERNOR GOT INFORMATION FROM A POWERFUL SUPPORTER.
AND YOU HAVE NO IDEA WHAT KIND OF RESOURCES A CANDIDATE HAS ACCESSS TO. ALMOST PRESIDENTIAL CLOUT.
BUT THIS ISN'T SOMETHING WE NEED TO SHARE WITH YOUR SUPERIOR OFFICER. NOT YET.
BUT CAPTAIN MEYER KNOWS ABOUT--
SHUT UP, SCOTT!
I WAS TALKING ABOUT SOMEONE A LOT MORE SENIOR THAN CAPTAIN MEYER. AFTER ALL, THERE HAS JUST BEEN AN ASSASSINATION ATTEMPT--
IT'S NOT A CRIME. IT'S JUST A GAG!
IT MAY OR MAY NOT BE A CRIME.
LISTEN, RIGHT NOW, AS YOU'LL APPRECIATE, THIS IS VERY MUCH A SIDE ISSUE FOR THE GOVERNOR.
WE DON'T WANT TO CHANGE THE WAY YOU GUYS DO YOUR BUSINESS. JUST TELL ME EVERYTHING--
--WE'LL CALM EVERYONE DOWN AND KEEP YOUR NAMES OUT OF IT. OKAY?
WELL...
IT'S NOT LIKE WE STARTED IT...

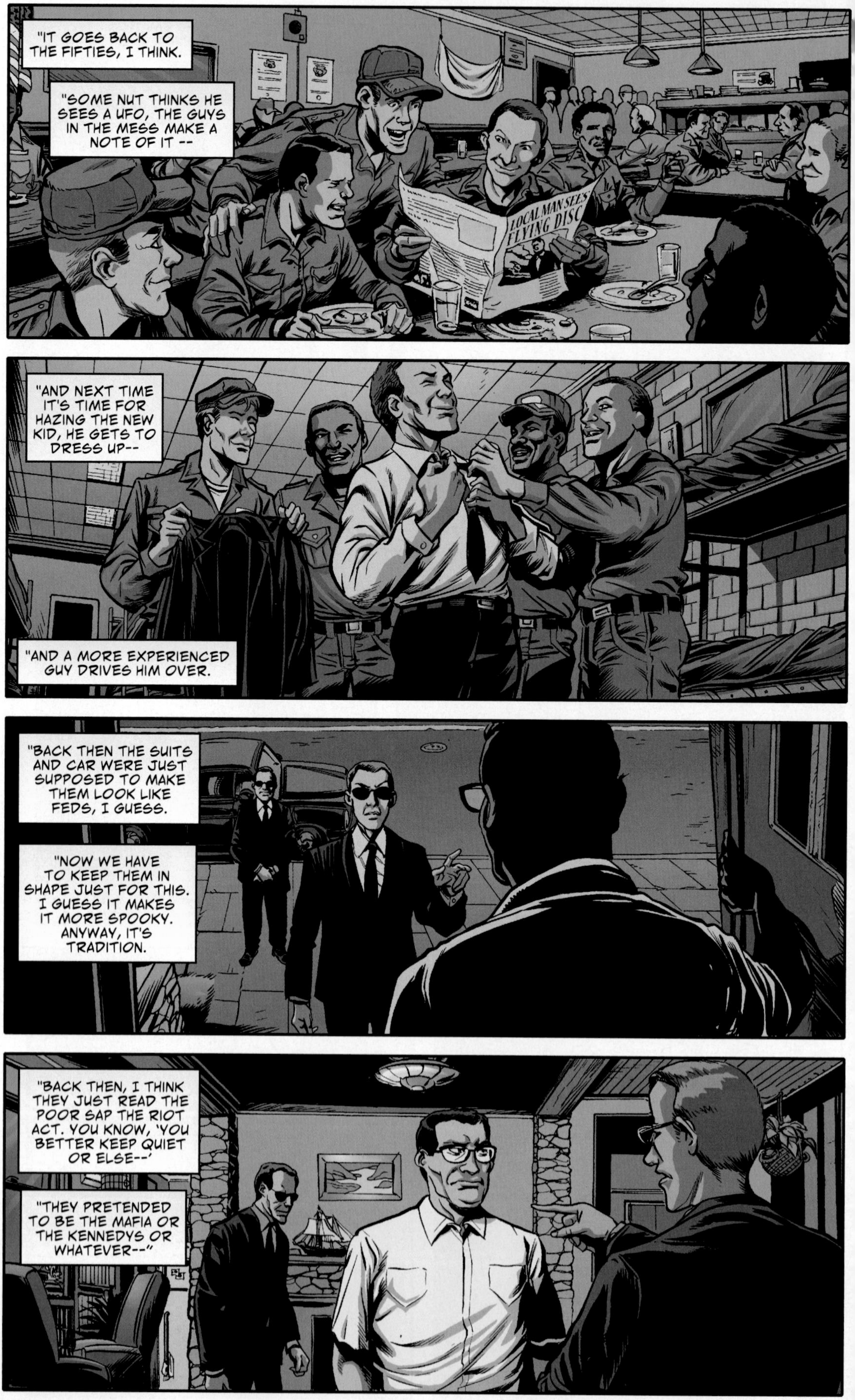
"IT GOES BACK TO THE FIFTIES, I THINK.
"SOME NUT THINKS HE SEES A UFO, THE GUYS IN THE MESS MAKE A NOTE OF IT --
LOCAL MAN SEES FLYING DISC
"AND NEXT TIME IT'S TIME FOR HAZING THE NEW KID, HE GETS TO DRESS UP--
"AND A MORE EXPERIENCED GUY DRIVES HIM OVER.
"BACK THEN THE SUITS AND CAR WERE JUST SUPPOSED TO MAKE THEM LOOK LIKE FEDS, I GUESS.
"NOW WE HAVE TO KEEP THEM IN SHAPE JUST FOR THIS. I GUESS IT MAKES IT MORE SPOOKY. ANYWAY, IT'S TRADITION.
"BACK THEN, I THINK THEY JUST READ THE POOR SAP THE RIOT ACT. YOU KNOW, 'YOU BETTER KEEP QUIET OR ELSE--'
"THEY PRETENDED TO BE THE MAFIA OR THE KENNEDYS OR WHATEVER--"

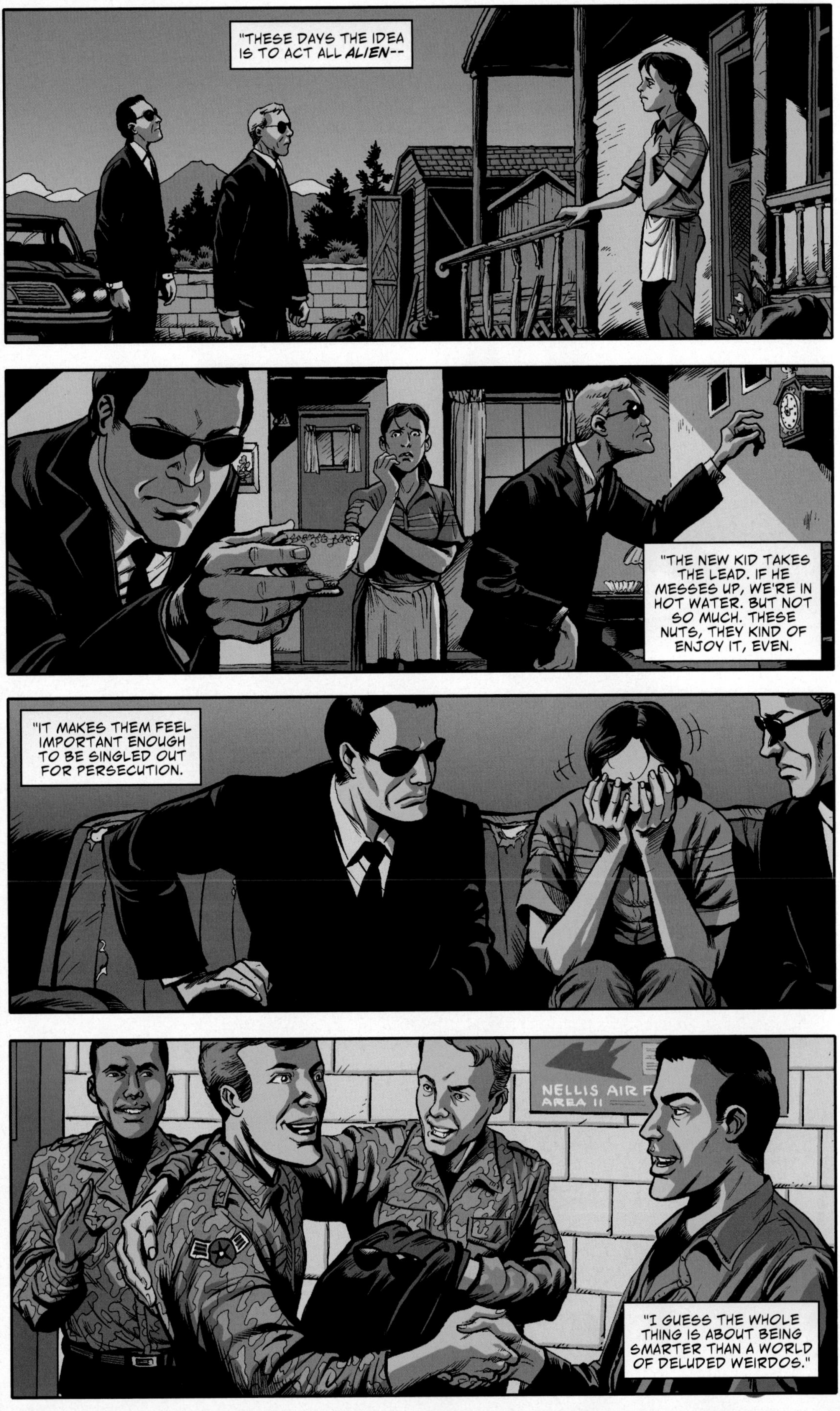
"THESE DAYS THE IDEA IS TO ACT ALL *ALIEN*--
"THE NEW KID TAKES THE LEAD. IF HE MESSES UP, WE'RE IN HOT WATER. BUT NOT SO MUCH. THESE NUTS, THEY KIND OF ENJOY IT, EVEN.
"IT MAKES THEM FEEL IMPORTANT ENOUGH TO BE SINGLED OUT FOR PERSECUTION.
NELLIS AIR F
AREA 11
"I GUESS THE WHOLE THING IS ABOUT BEING SMARTER THAN A WORLD OF DELUDED WEIRDOS."

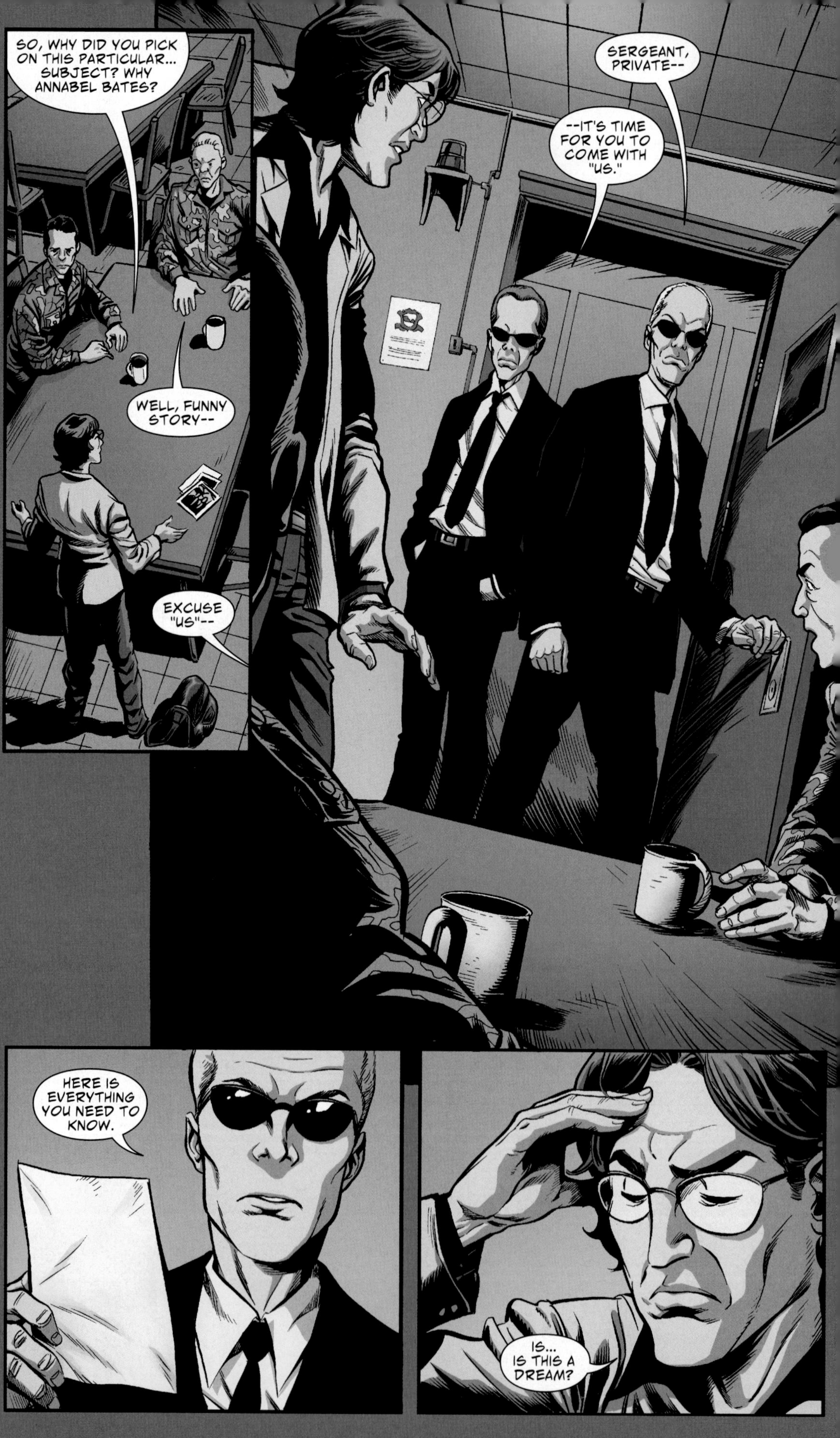
SO, WHY DID YOU PICK ON THIS PARTICULAR... SUBJECT? WHY ANNABEL BATES?
WELL, FUNNY STORY--
EXCUSE "US"--
SERGEANT, PRIVATE--
--IT'S TIME FOR YOU TO COME WITH "US."
HERE IS EVERYTHING YOU NEED TO KNOW.
IS... IS THIS A DREAM?

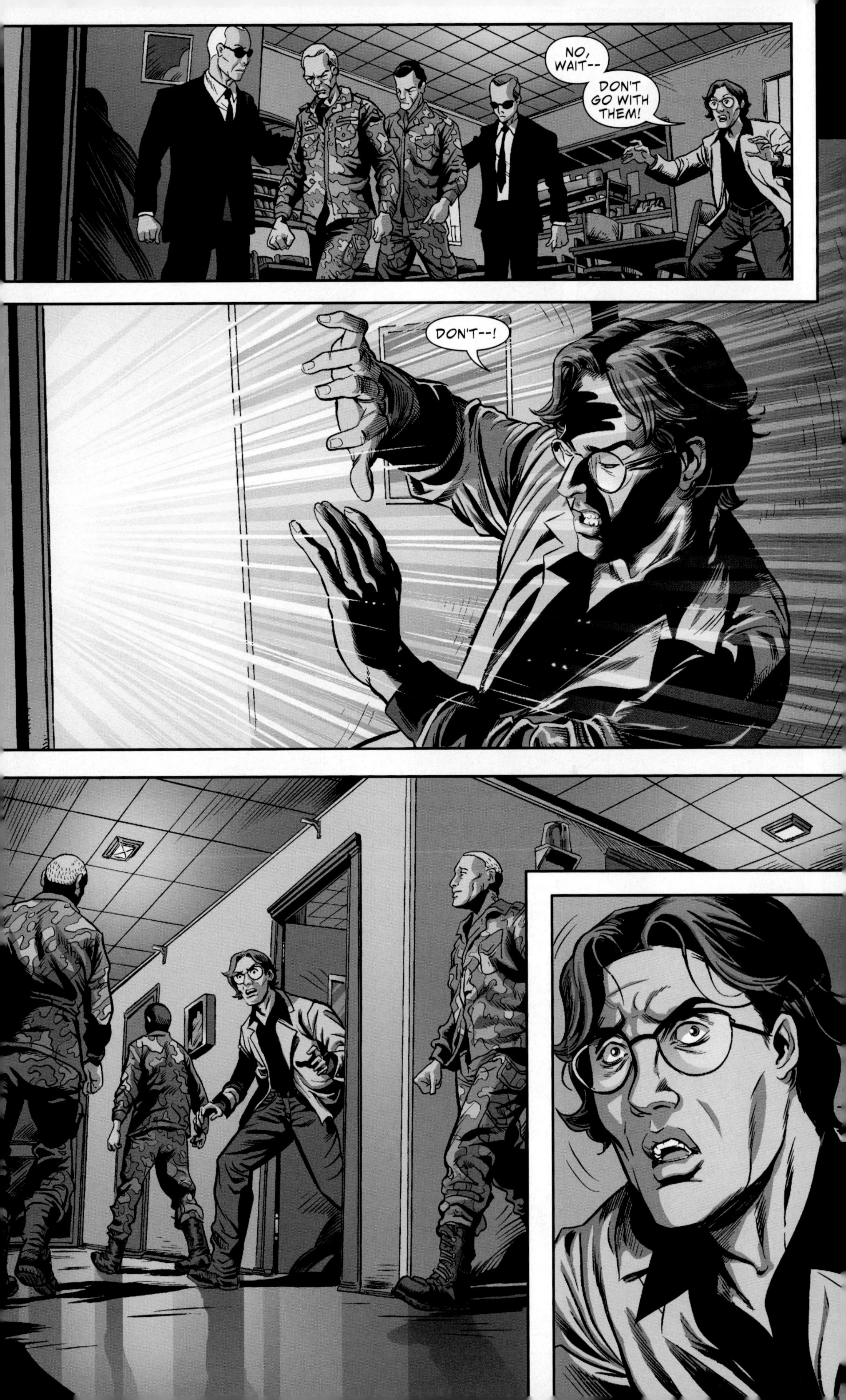
NO, WAIT--
DON'T GO WITH THEM!
DON'T--!

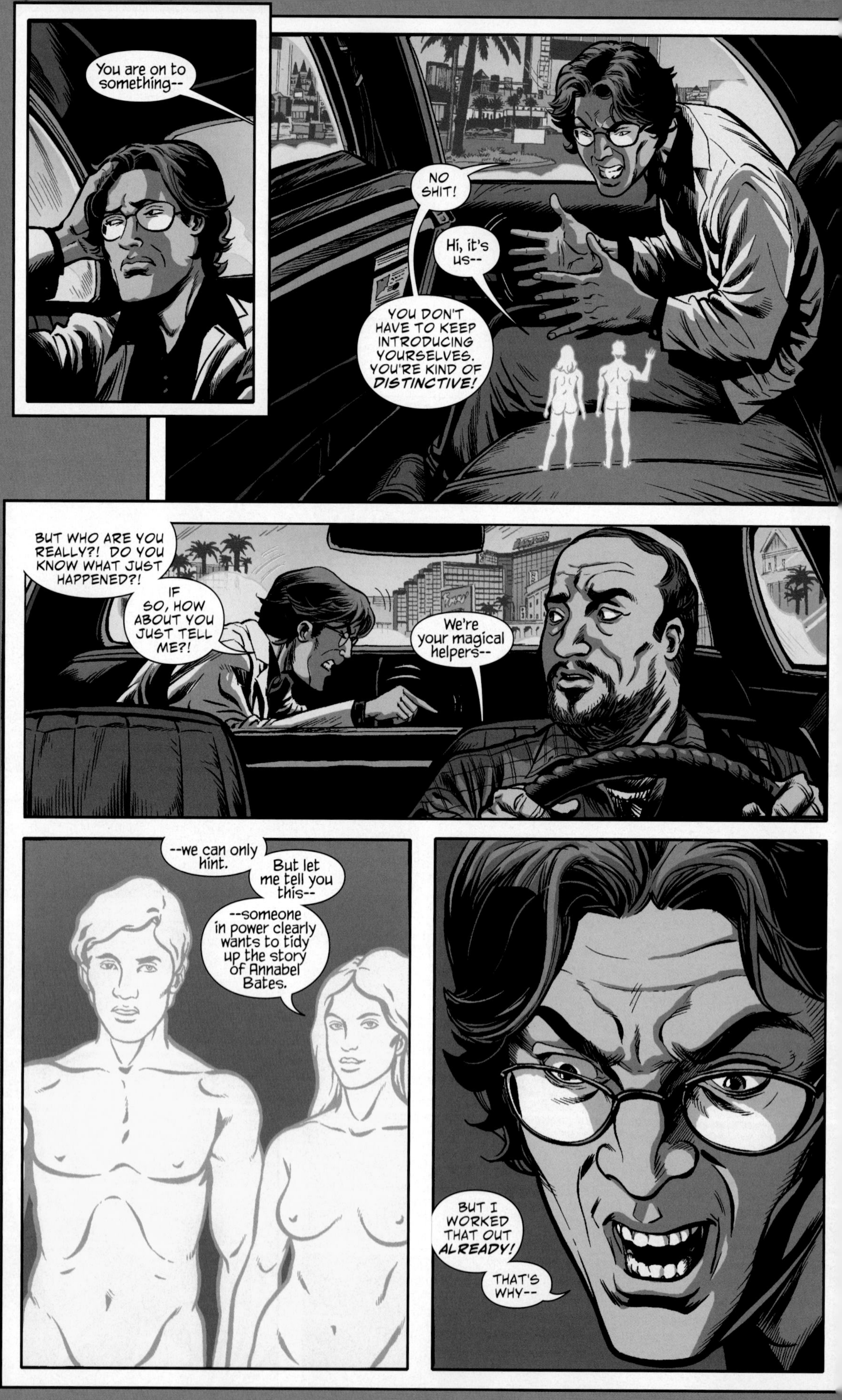
You are on to something--
NO SHIT!
Hi, it's us--
YOU DON'T HAVE TO KEEP INTRODUCING YOURSELVES. YOU'RE KIND OF DISTINCTIVE!
BUT WHO ARE YOU REALLY?! DO YOU KNOW WHAT JUST HAPPENED?!
IF SO, HOW ABOUT YOU JUST TELL ME?!
We're your magical helpers--
--we can only hint.
But let me tell you this--
--someone in power clearly wants to tidy up the story of Annabel Bates.
BUT I WORKED THAT OUT ALREADY!
THAT'S WHY--

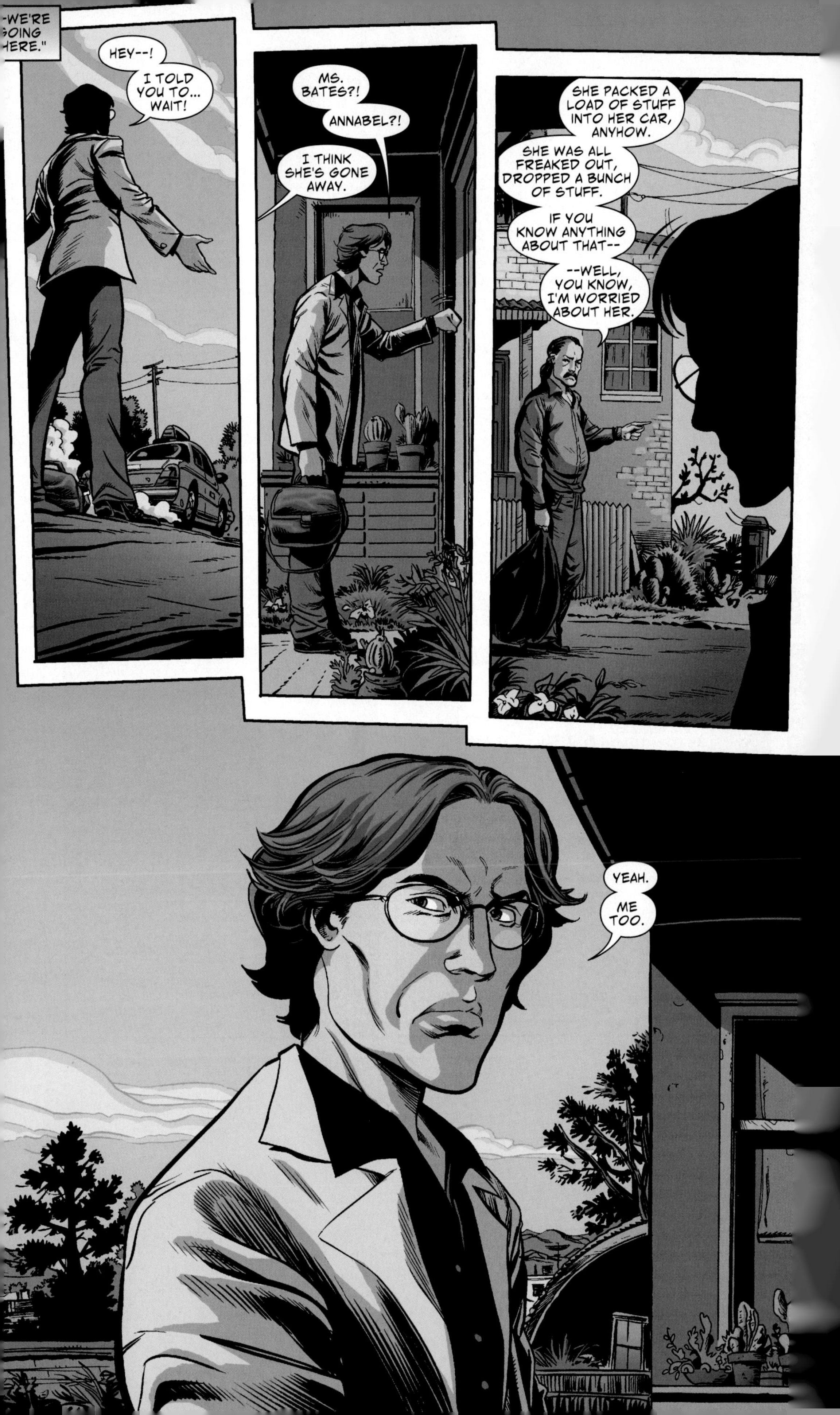
-WE'RE GOING HERE."
HEY--!
I TOLD YOU TO... WAIT!
MS. BATES?!
ANNABEL?!
I THINK SHE'S GONE AWAY.
SHE PACKED A LOAD OF STUFF INTO HER CAR, ANYHOW.
SHE WAS ALL FREAKED OUT, DROPPED A BUNCH OF STUFF.
IF YOU KNOW ANYTHING ABOUT THAT--
--WELL, YOU KNOW, I'M WORRIED ABOUT HER.
YEAH.
ME TOO.

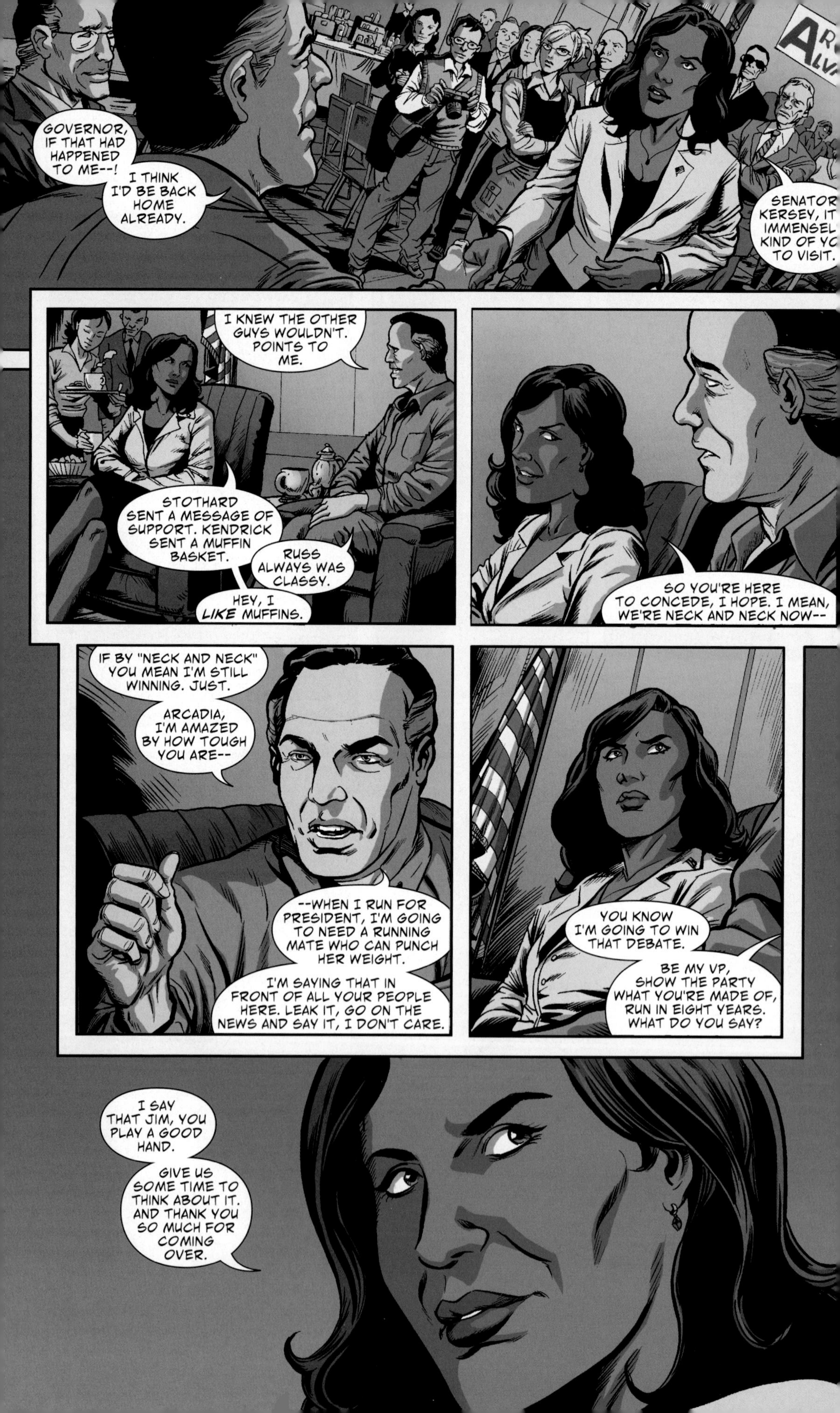
GOVERNOR, IF THAT HAD HAPPENED TO ME--!
I THINK I'D BE BACK HOME ALREADY.
SENATOR KERSEY, IT IMMENSEL KIND OF YO TO VISIT.
I KNEW THE OTHER GUYS WOULDN'T. POINTS TO ME.
STOTHARD SENT A MESSAGE OF SUPPORT. KENDRICK SENT A MUFFIN BASKET.
RUSS ALWAYS WAS CLASSY.
HEY, I LIKE MUFFINS.
SO YOU'RE HERE TO CONCEDE, I HOPE. I MEAN, WE'RE NECK AND NECK NOW--
IF BY "NECK AND NECK" YOU MEAN I'M STILL WINNING. JUST.
ARCADIA, I'M AMAZED BY HOW TOUGH YOU ARE--
--WHEN I RUN FOR PRESIDENT, I'M GOING TO NEED A RUNNING MATE WHO CAN PUNCH HER WEIGHT.
I'M SAYING THAT IN FRONT OF ALL YOUR PEOPLE HERE. LEAK IT, GO ON THE NEWS AND SAY IT, I DON'T CARE.
YOU KNOW I'M GOING TO WIN THAT DEBATE.
BE MY VP, SHOW THE PARTY WHAT YOU'RE MADE OF, RUN IN EIGHT YEARS. WHAT DO YOU SAY?
I SAY THAT JIM, YOU PLAY A GOOD HAND.
GIVE US SOME TIME TO THINK ABOUT IT. AND THANK YOU SO MUCH FOR COMING OVER.

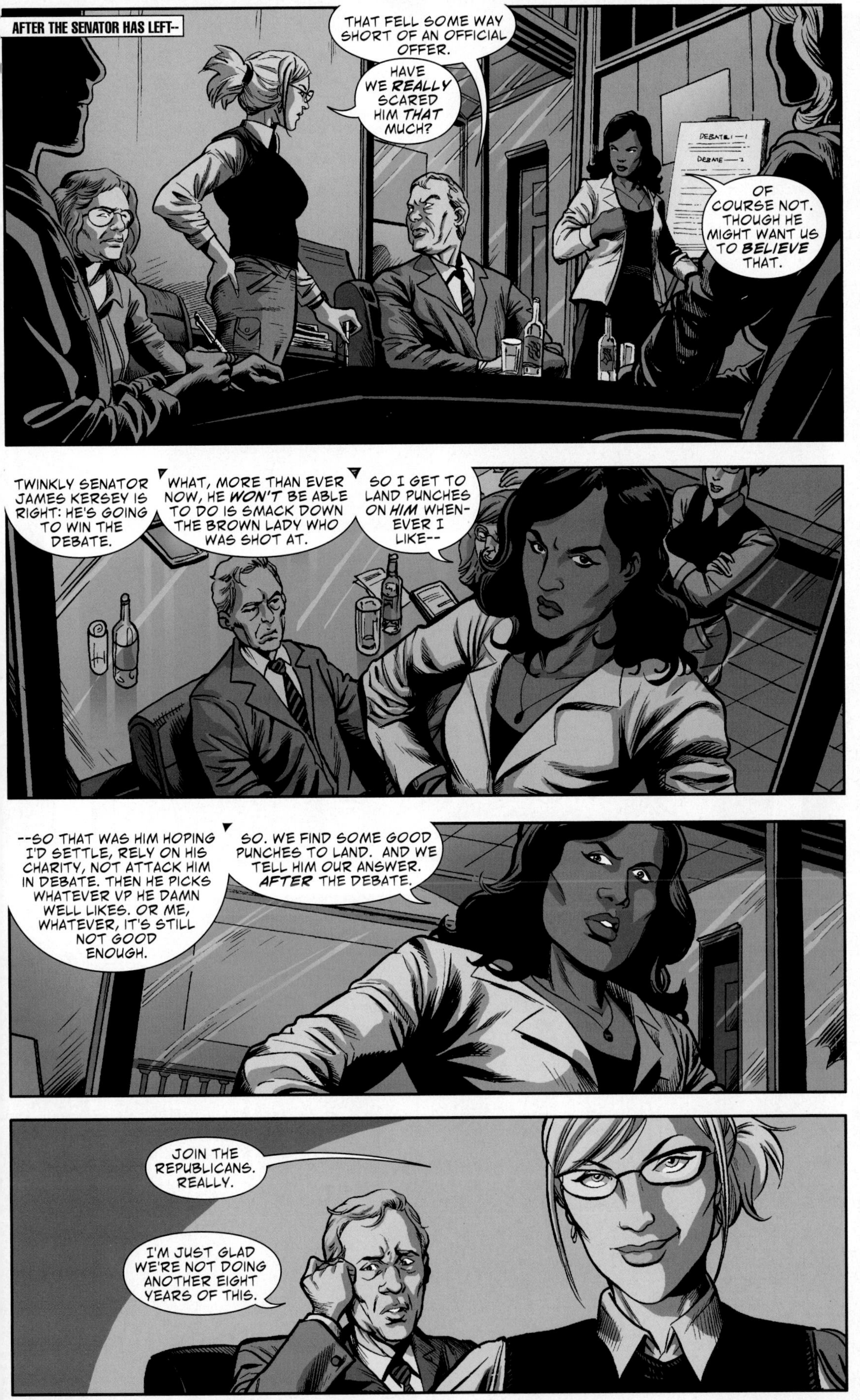
AFTER THE SENATOR HAS LEFT--
THAT FELL SOME WAY SHORT OF AN OFFICIAL OFFER.
HAVE WE REALLY SCARED HIM THAT MUCH?
OF COURSE NOT. THOUGH HE MIGHT WANT US TO BELIEVE THAT.
TWINKLY SENATOR JAMES KERSEY IS RIGHT: HE'S GOING TO WIN THE DEBATE.
WHAT, MORE THAN EVER NOW, HE WON'T BE ABLE TO DO IS SMACK DOWN THE BROWN LADY WHO WAS SHOT AT.
SO I GET TO LAND PUNCHES ON HIM WHENEVER I LIKE--
--SO THAT WAS HIM HOPING I'D SETTLE, RELY ON HIS CHARITY, NOT ATTACK HIM IN DEBATE. THEN HE PICKS WHATEVER VP HE DAMN WELL LIKES. OR ME, WHATEVER, IT'S STILL NOT GOOD ENOUGH.
SO. WE FIND SOME GOOD PUNCHES TO LAND. AND WE TELL HIM OUR ANSWER. AFTER THE DEBATE.
JOIN THE REPUBLICANS. REALLY.
I'M JUST GLAD WE'RE NOT DOING ANOTHER EIGHT YEARS OF THIS.

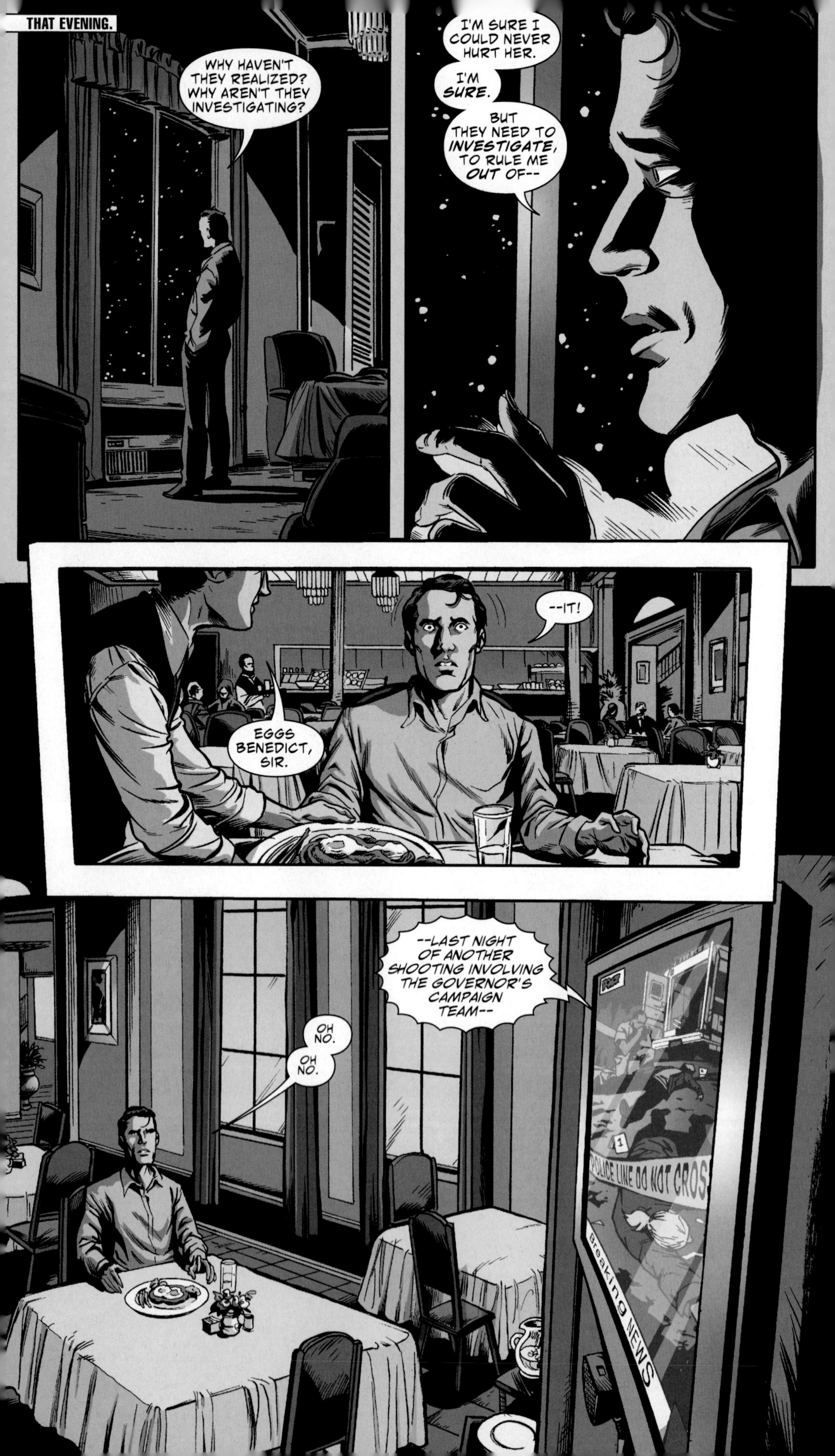
THAT EVENING.
WHY HAVEN'T THEY REALIZED? WHY AREN'T THEY INVESTIGATING?
I'M SURE I COULD NEVER HURT HER.
I'M *SURE*.
BUT THEY NEED TO *INVESTIGATE*, TO RULE ME *OUT* OF--
--IT!
EGGS BENEDICT, SIR.
--LAST NIGHT OF ANOTHER SHOOTING INVOLVING THE GOVERNOR'S CAMPAIGN TEAM--
OH NO.
OH NO.
POLICE LINE DO NOT CROS
Breaking NEWS

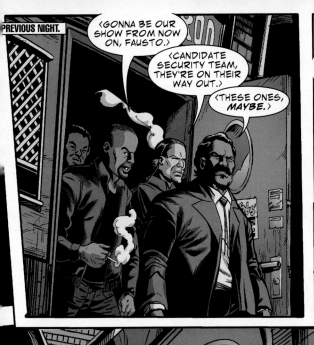

<GONNA BE OUR SHOW FROM NOW ON, FAUSTO.>

<CANDIDATE SECURITY TEAM, THEY'RE ON THEIR WAY OUT.>

<THESE ONES, MAYBE.>

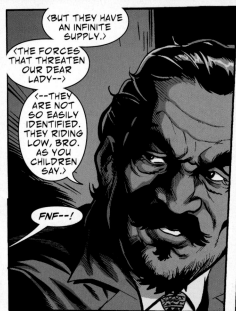

<BUT THEY HAVE AN INFINITE SUPPLY.>

<THE FORCES THAT THREATEN OUR DEAR LADY--->

<--THEY ARE NOT SO EASILY IDENTIFIED. THEY RIDING LOW, BRO. AS YOU CHILDREN SAY.>

FNF--!

FNF! FNF!

--!

FLAUGGGHHH--!

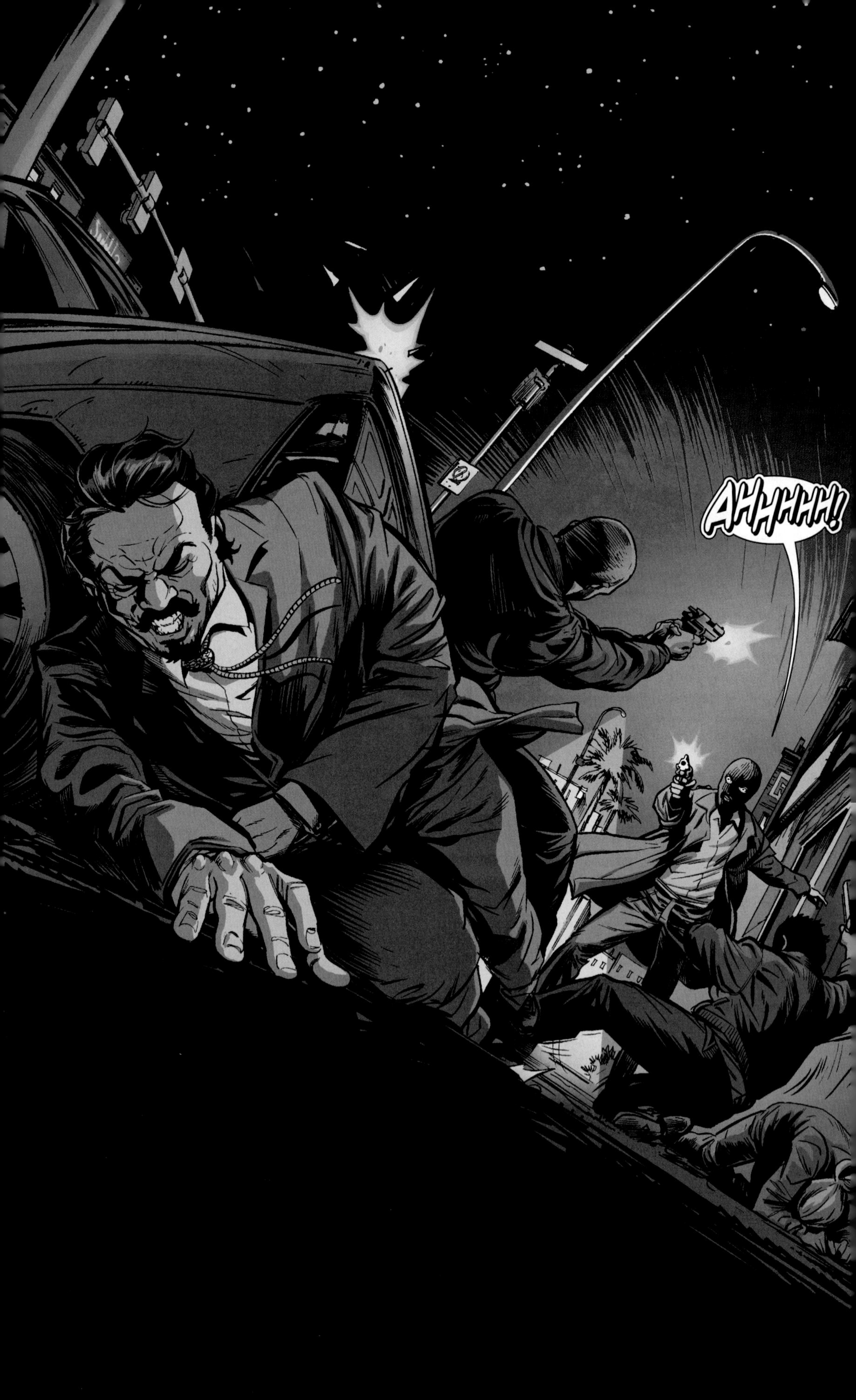
AHHHHH!

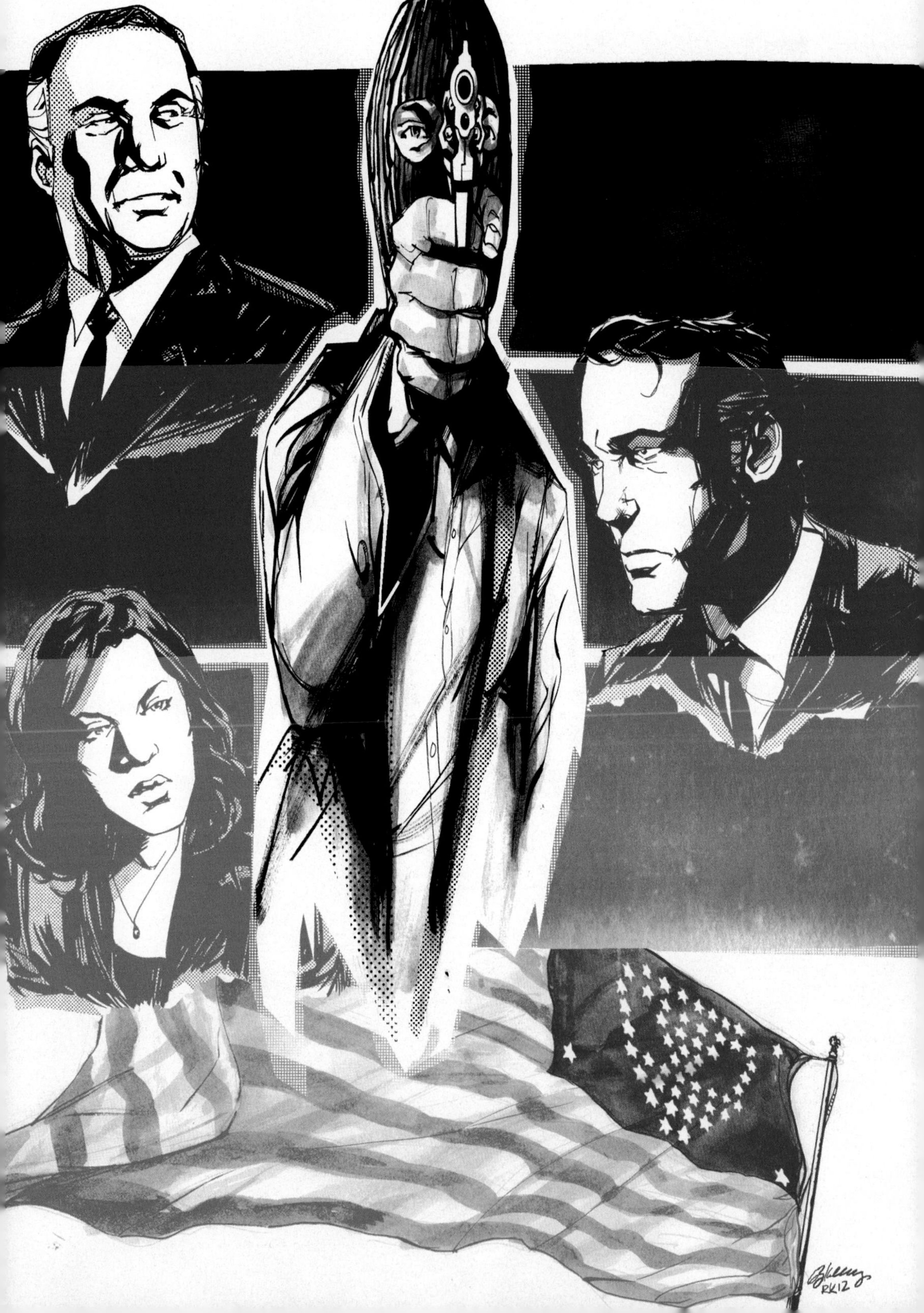

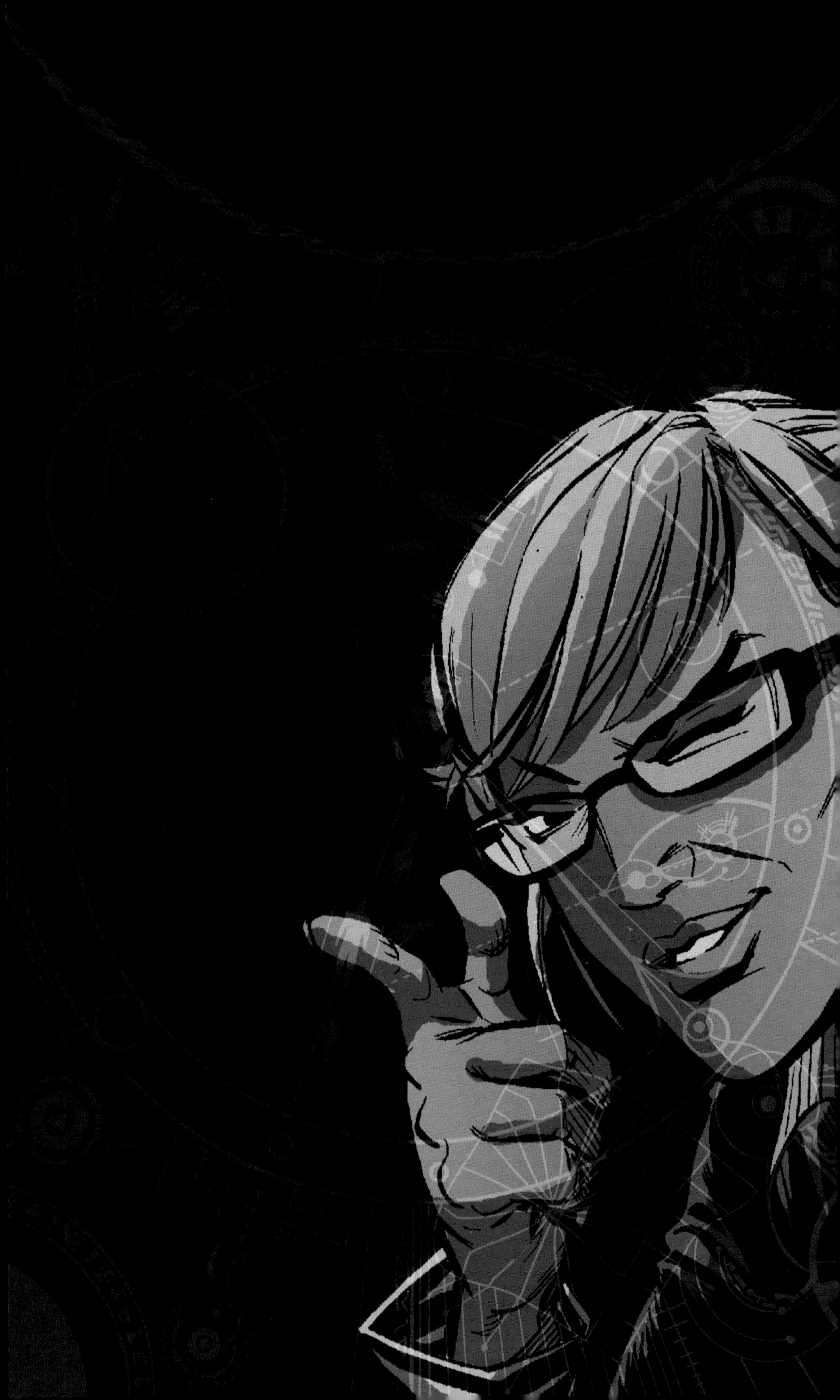

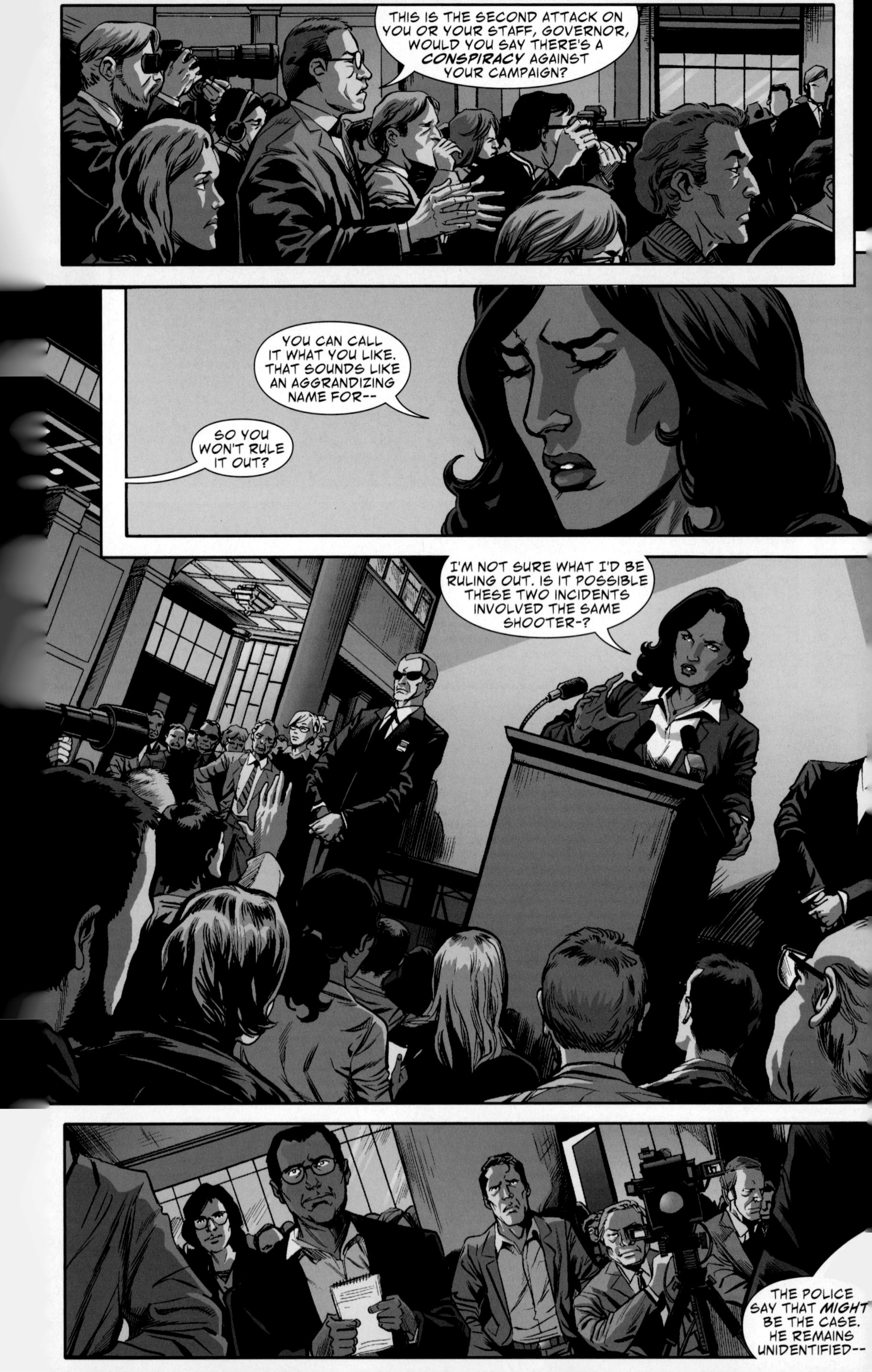
THIS IS THE SECOND ATTACK ON YOU OR YOUR STAFF, GOVERNOR, WOULD YOU SAY THERE'S A *CONSPIRACY* AGAINST YOUR CAMPAIGN?
YOU CAN CALL IT WHAT YOU LIKE. THAT SOUNDS LIKE AN AGGRANDIZING NAME FOR--
SO YOU WON'T RULE IT OUT?
I'M NOT SURE WHAT I'D BE RULING OUT. IS IT POSSIBLE THESE TWO INCIDENTS INVOLVED THE SAME SHOOTER-?
THE POLICE SAY THAT *MIGHT* BE THE CASE. HE REMAINS UNIDENTIFIED--

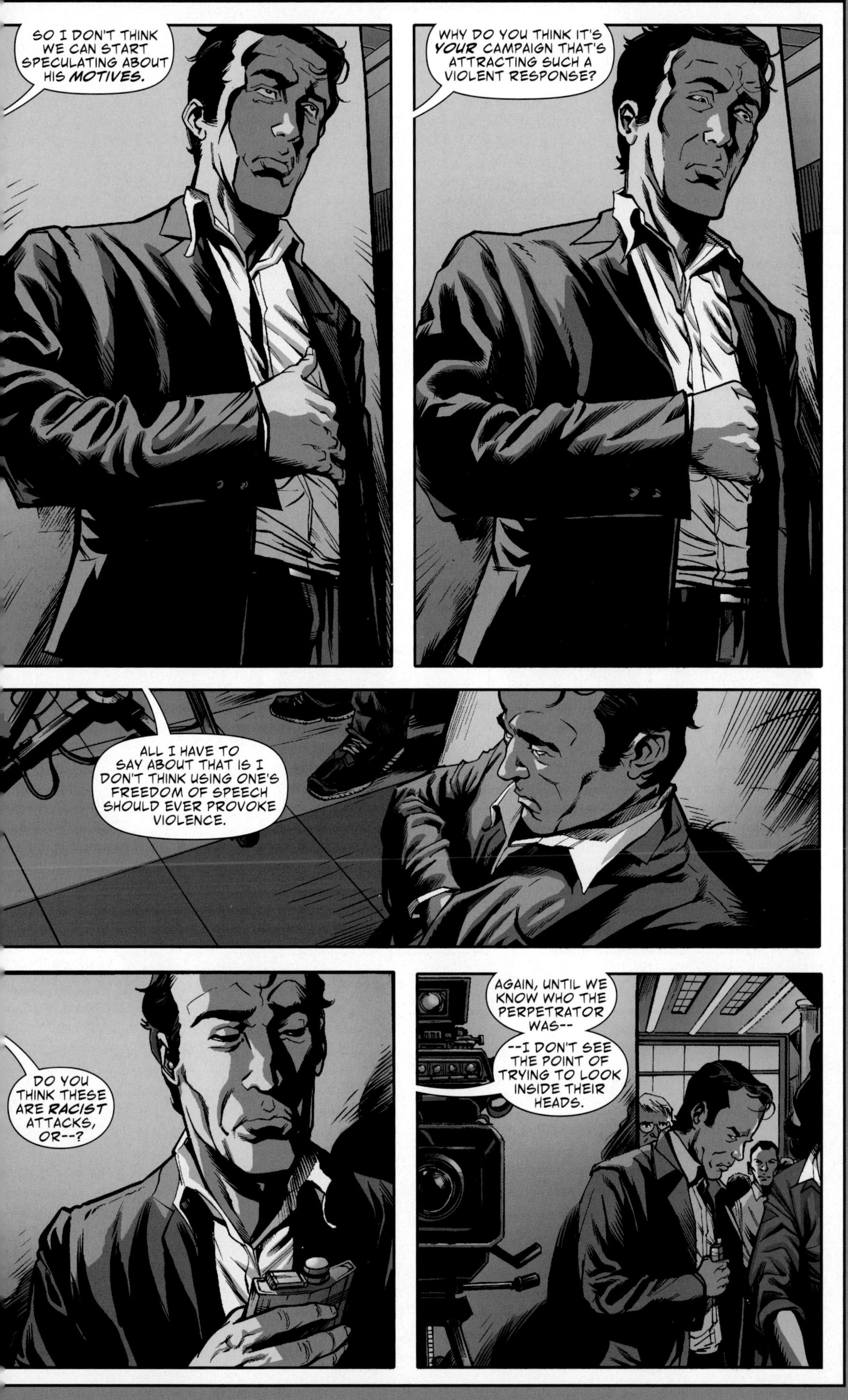

SO I DON'T THINK WE CAN START SPECULATING ABOUT HIS *MOTIVES.*
WHY DO YOU THINK IT'S *YOUR* CAMPAIGN THAT'S ATTRACTING SUCH A VIOLENT RESPONSE?
ALL I HAVE TO SAY ABOUT THAT IS I DON'T THINK USING ONE'S FREEDOM OF SPEECH SHOULD EVER PROVOKE VIOLENCE.
DO YOU THINK THESE ARE *RACIST* ATTACKS, OR--?
AGAIN, UNTIL WE KNOW WHO THE PERPETRATOR WAS--
--I DON'T SEE THE POINT OF TRYING TO LOOK INSIDE THEIR HEADS.

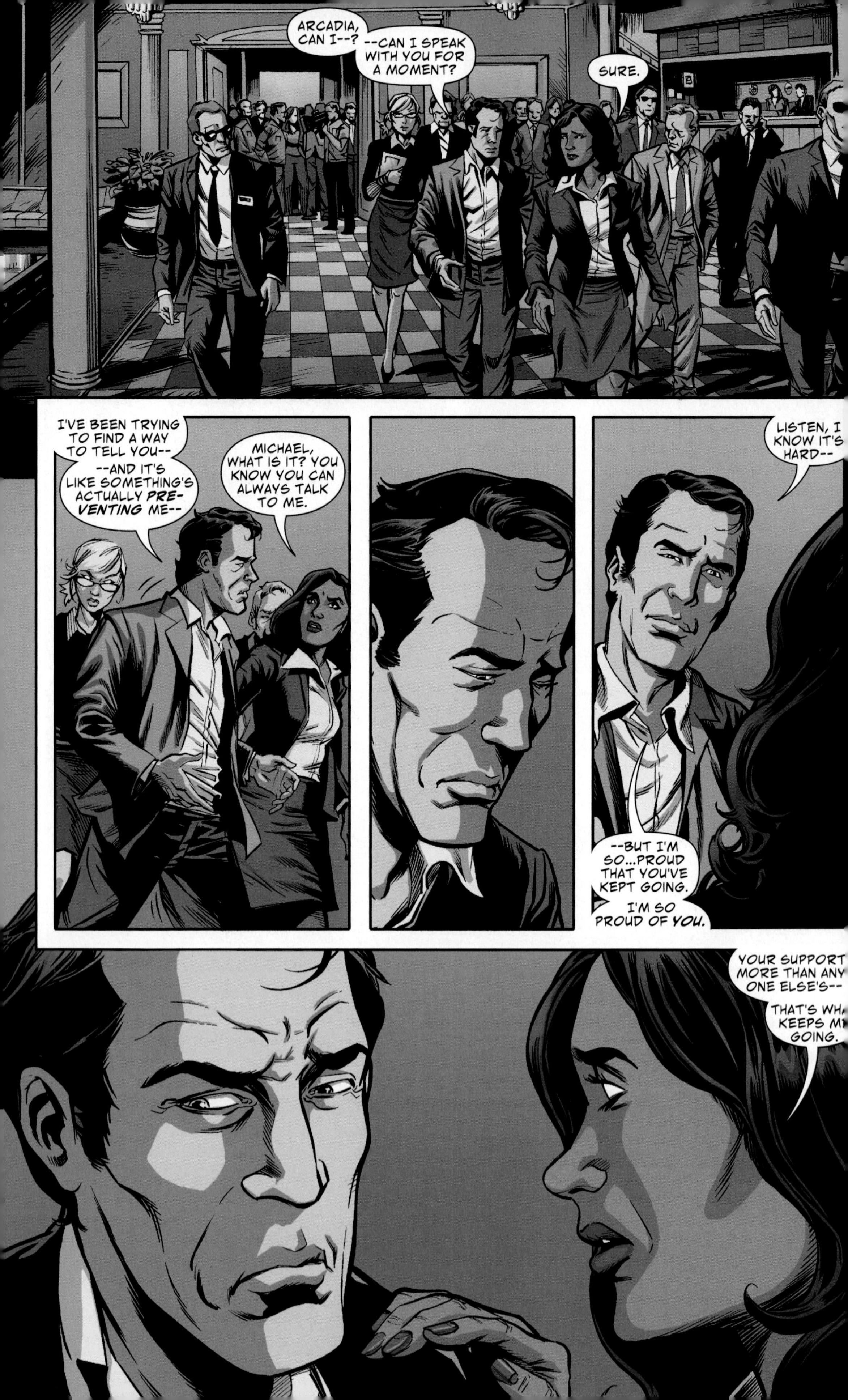
ARCADIA, CAN I--?
--CAN I SPEAK WITH YOU FOR A MOMENT?
SURE.
I'VE BEEN TRYING TO FIND A WAY TO TELL YOU--
--AND IT'S LIKE SOMETHING'S ACTUALLY *PRE-VENTING* ME--
MICHAEL, WHAT IS IT? YOU KNOW YOU CAN ALWAYS TALK TO ME.
LISTEN, I KNOW IT'S HARD--
--BUT I'M SO...PROUD THAT YOU'VE KEPT GOING.
I'M SO PROUD OF *YOU.*
YOUR SUPPORT MORE THAN ANY ONE ELSE'S--
THAT'S WHA KEEPS M GOING.

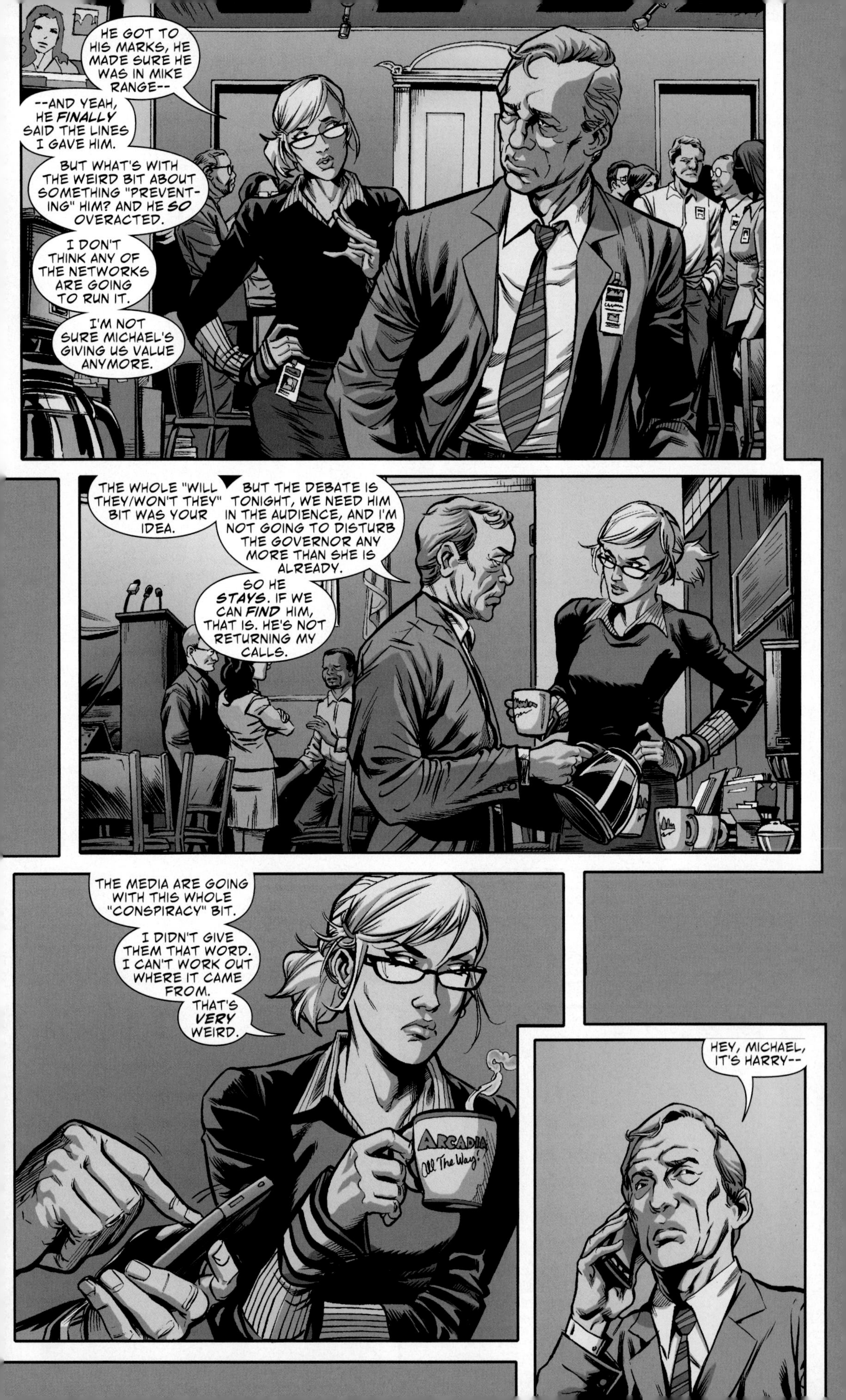
HE GOT TO HIS MARKS, HE MADE SURE HE WAS IN MIKE RANGE--
--AND YEAH, HE *FINALLY* SAID THE LINES I GAVE HIM.
BUT WHAT'S WITH THE WEIRD BIT ABOUT SOMETHING "PREVENTING" HIM? AND HE *SO* OVERACTED.
I DON'T THINK ANY OF THE NETWORKS ARE GOING TO RUN IT.
I'M NOT SURE MICHAEL'S GIVING US VALUE ANYMORE.
THE WHOLE "WILL THEY/WON'T THEY" BIT WAS YOUR IDEA.
BUT THE DEBATE IS TONIGHT, WE NEED HIM IN THE AUDIENCE, AND I'M NOT GOING TO DISTURB THE GOVERNOR ANY MORE THAN SHE IS ALREADY.
SO HE *STAYS*. IF WE CAN *FIND* HIM, THAT IS. HE'S NOT RETURNING MY CALLS.
THE MEDIA ARE GOING WITH THIS WHOLE "CONSPIRACY" BIT.
I DIDN'T GIVE THEM THAT WORD. I CAN'T WORK OUT WHERE IT CAME FROM.
THAT'S *VERY* WEIRD.
ARCADIA
All The Way!
HEY, MICHAEL, IT'S HARRY--

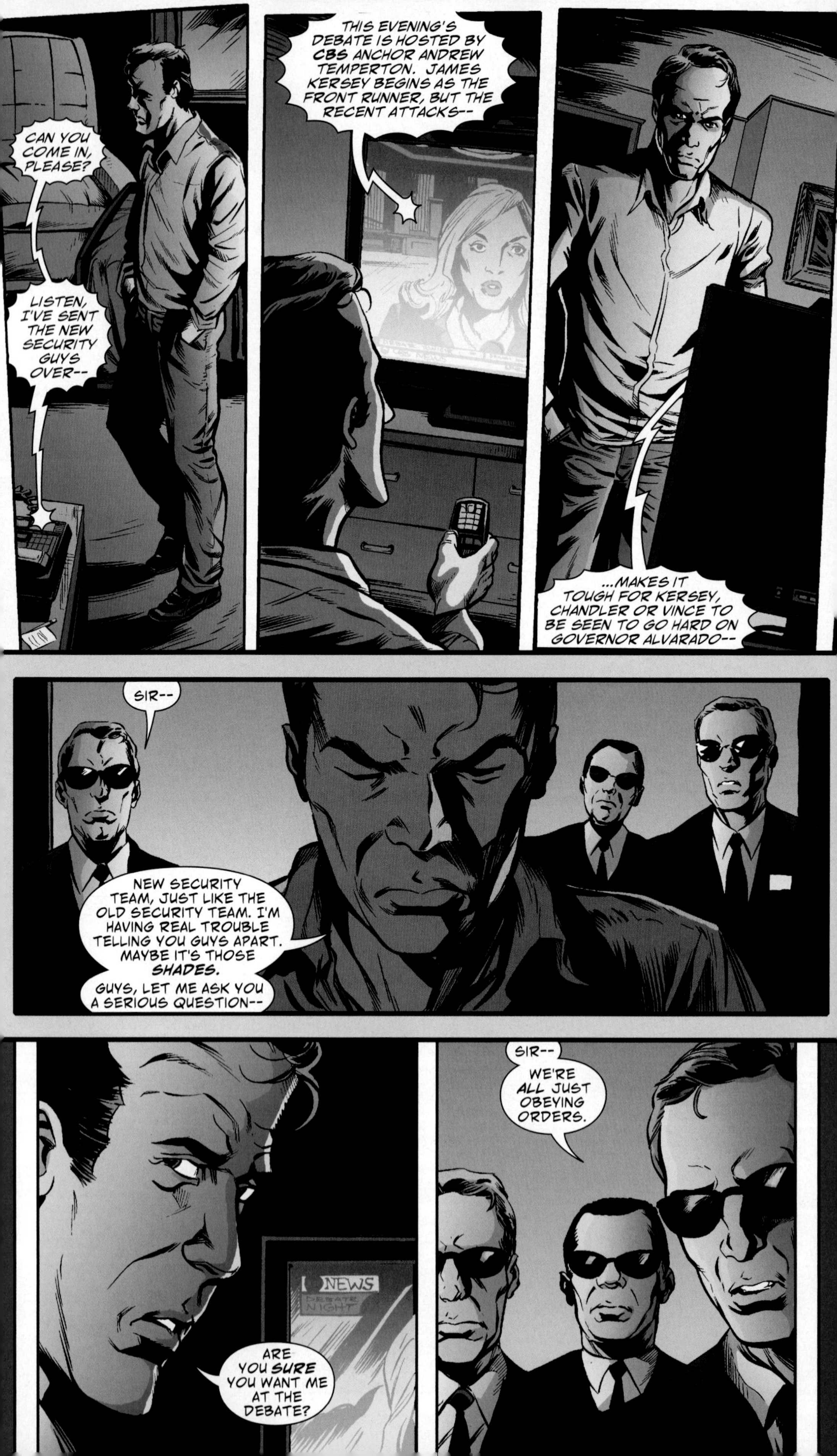
CAN YOU COME IN, PLEASE?
LISTEN, I'VE SENT THE NEW SECURITY GUYS OVER--
THIS EVENING'S DEBATE IS HOSTED BY CBS ANCHOR ANDREW TEMPERTON. JAMES KERSEY BEGINS AS THE FRONT RUNNER, BUT THE RECENT ATTACKS--
...MAKES IT TOUGH FOR KERSEY, CHANDLER OR VINCE TO BE SEEN TO GO HARD ON GOVERNOR ALVARADO--
SIR--
NEW SECURITY TEAM, JUST LIKE THE OLD SECURITY TEAM. I'M HAVING REAL TROUBLE TELLING YOU GUYS APART. MAYBE IT'S THOSE SHADES.
GUYS, LET ME ASK YOU A SERIOUS QUESTION--
NEWS
DEBATE NIGHT
ARE YOU SURE YOU WANT ME AT THE DEBATE?
SIR--
WE'RE ALL JUST OBEYING ORDERS.

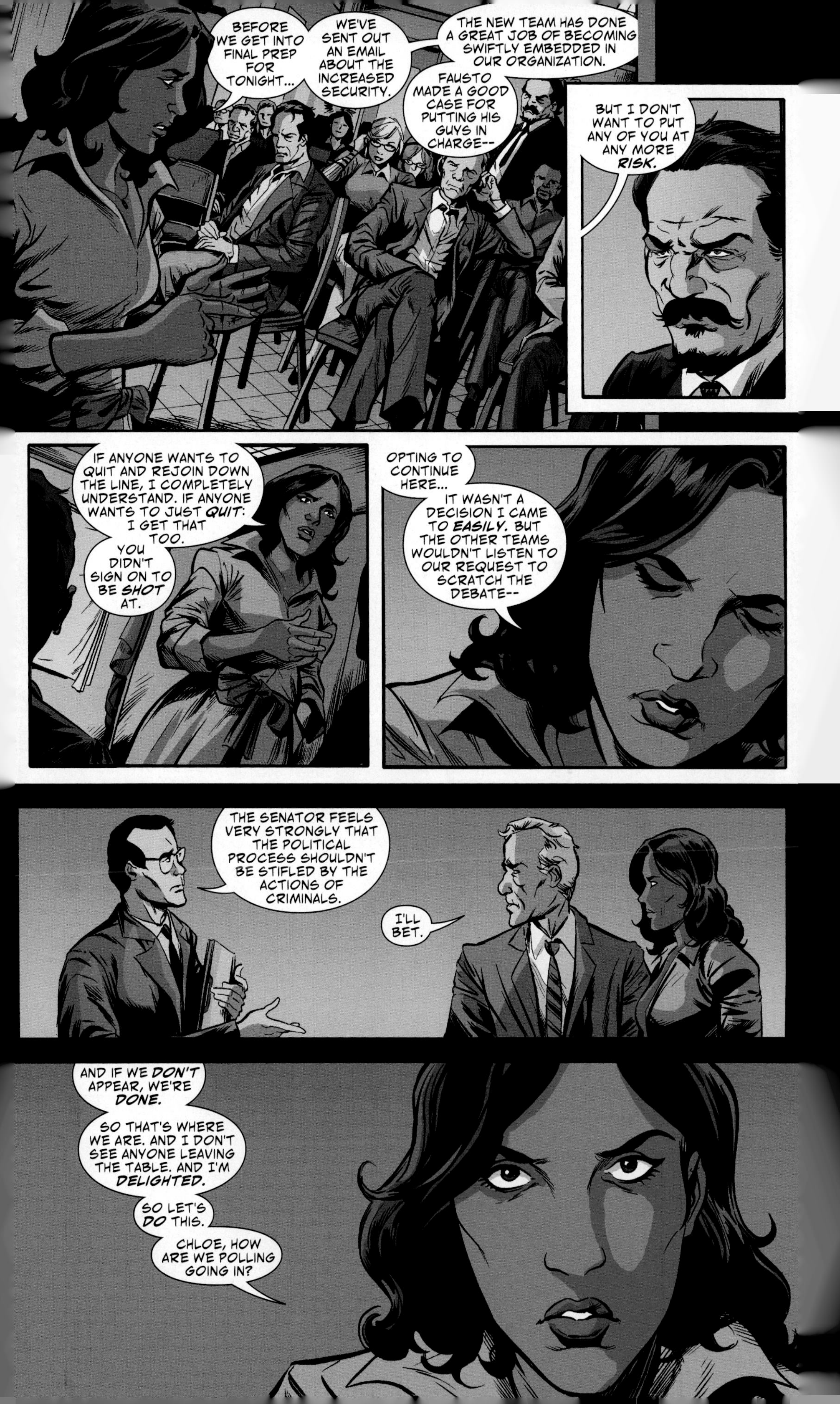
BEFORE WE GET INTO FINAL PREP FOR TONIGHT...
WE'VE SENT OUT AN EMAIL ABOUT THE INCREASED SECURITY.
THE NEW TEAM HAS DONE A GREAT JOB OF BECOMING SWIFTLY EMBEDDED IN OUR ORGANIZATION.
FAUSTO MADE A GOOD CASE FOR PUTTING HIS GUYS IN CHARGE--
BUT I DON'T WANT TO PUT ANY OF YOU AT ANY MORE RISK.
IF ANYONE WANTS TO QUIT AND REJOIN DOWN THE LINE, I COMPLETELY UNDERSTAND. IF ANYONE WANTS TO JUST QUIT: I GET THAT TOO.
YOU DIDN'T SIGN ON TO BE SHOT AT.
OPTING TO CONTINUE HERE...
IT WASN'T A DECISION I CAME TO EASILY. BUT THE OTHER TEAMS WOULDN'T LISTEN TO OUR REQUEST TO SCRATCH THE DEBATE--
THE SENATOR FEELS VERY STRONGLY THAT THE POLITICAL PROCESS SHOULDN'T BE STIFLED BY THE ACTIONS OF CRIMINALS.
I'LL BET.
AND IF WE DON'T APPEAR, WE'RE DONE.
SO THAT'S WHERE WE ARE. AND I DON'T SEE ANYONE LEAVING THE TABLE. AND I'M DELIGHTED.
SO LET'S DO THIS.
CHLOE, HOW ARE WE POLLING GOING IN?

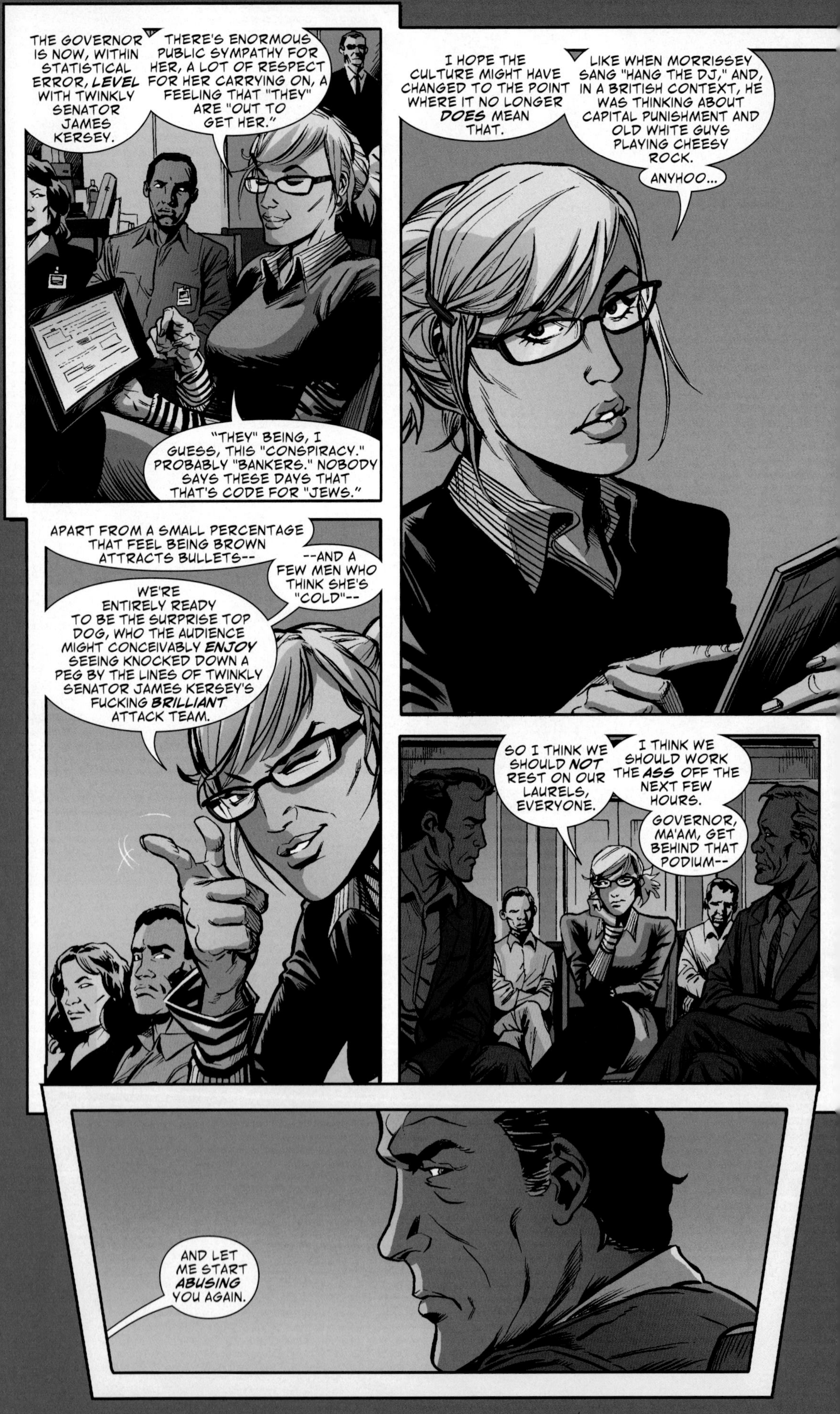
THE GOVERNOR IS NOW, WITHIN STATISTICAL ERROR, **LEVEL** WITH TWINKLY SENATOR JAMES KERSEY.
THERE'S ENORMOUS PUBLIC SYMPATHY FOR HER, A LOT OF RESPECT FOR HER CARRYING ON, A FEELING THAT "THEY" ARE "OUT TO GET HER."
"THEY" BEING, I GUESS, THIS "CONSPIRACY." PROBABLY "BANKERS." NOBODY SAYS THESE DAYS THAT THAT'S CODE FOR "JEWS."
I HOPE THE CULTURE MIGHT HAVE CHANGED TO THE POINT WHERE IT NO LONGER **DOES** MEAN THAT.
LIKE WHEN MORRISSEY SANG "HANG THE DJ," AND, IN A BRITISH CONTEXT, HE WAS THINKING ABOUT CAPITAL PUNISHMENT AND OLD WHITE GUYS PLAYING CHEESY ROCK.
ANYHOO...
APART FROM A SMALL PERCENTAGE THAT FEEL BEING BROWN ATTRACTS BULLETS--
--AND A FEW MEN WHO THINK SHE'S "COLD"--
WE'RE ENTIRELY READY TO BE THE SURPRISE TOP DOG, WHO THE AUDIENCE MIGHT CONCEIVABLY **ENJOY** SEEING KNOCKED DOWN A PEG BY THE LINES OF TWINKLY SENATOR JAMES KERSEY'S FUCKING **BRILLIANT** ATTACK TEAM.
SO I THINK WE SHOULD **NOT** REST ON OUR LAURELS, EVERYONE.
I THINK WE SHOULD WORK THE **ASS** OFF THE NEXT FEW HOURS.
GOVERNOR, MA'AM, GET BEHIND THAT PODIUM--
AND LET ME START **ABUSING** YOU AGAIN.

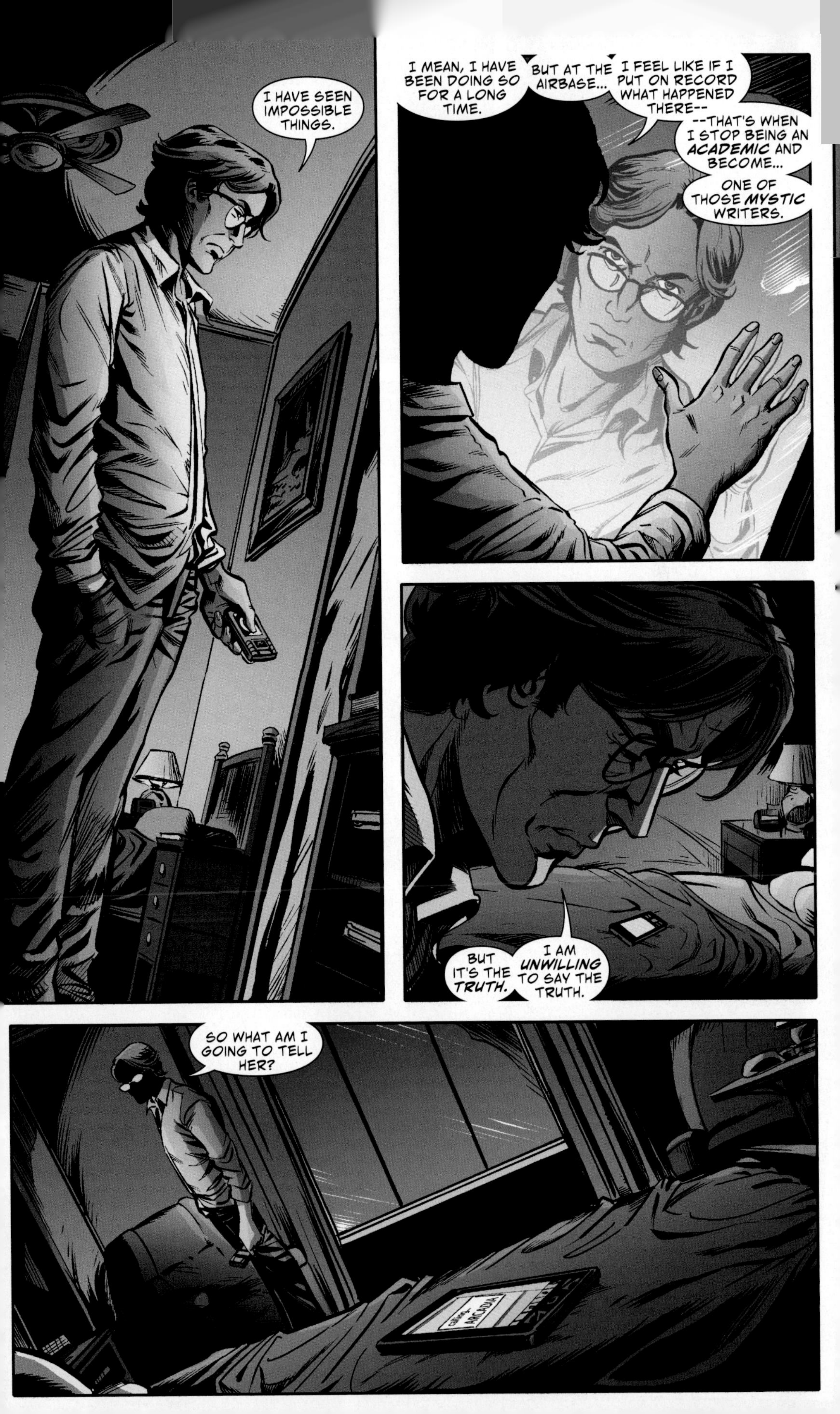
I HAVE SEEN IMPOSSIBLE THINGS.
I MEAN, I HAVE BEEN DOING SO FOR A LONG TIME.
BUT AT THE AIRBASE...
I FEEL LIKE IF I PUT ON RECORD WHAT HAPPENED THERE--
--THAT'S WHEN I STOP BEING AN *ACADEMIC* AND BECOME...
ONE OF THOSE *MYSTIC* WRITERS.
I AM *UNWILLING* TO SAY THE TRUTH.
BUT IT'S THE *TRUTH.*
SO WHAT AM I GOING TO TELL HER?

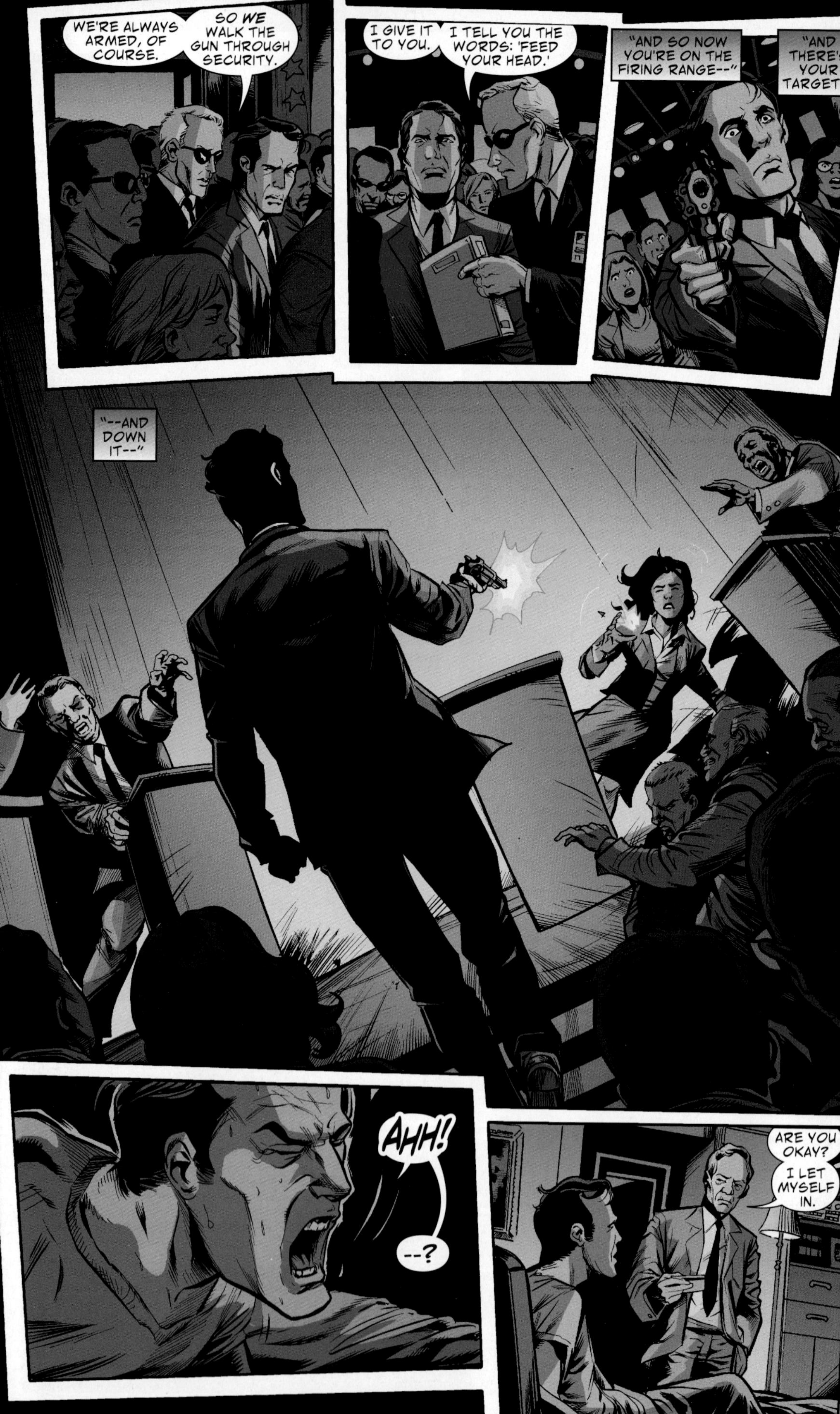
WE'RE ALWAYS ARMED, OF COURSE.
SO WE WALK THE GUN THROUGH SECURITY.
I GIVE IT TO YOU.
I TELL YOU THE WORDS: 'FEED YOUR HEAD.'
"AND SO NOW YOU'RE ON THE FIRING RANGE--"
"AND THERE'S YOUR TARGET
"--AND DOWN IT--"
AHH!
--?
ARE YOU OKAY?
I LET MYSELF IN.

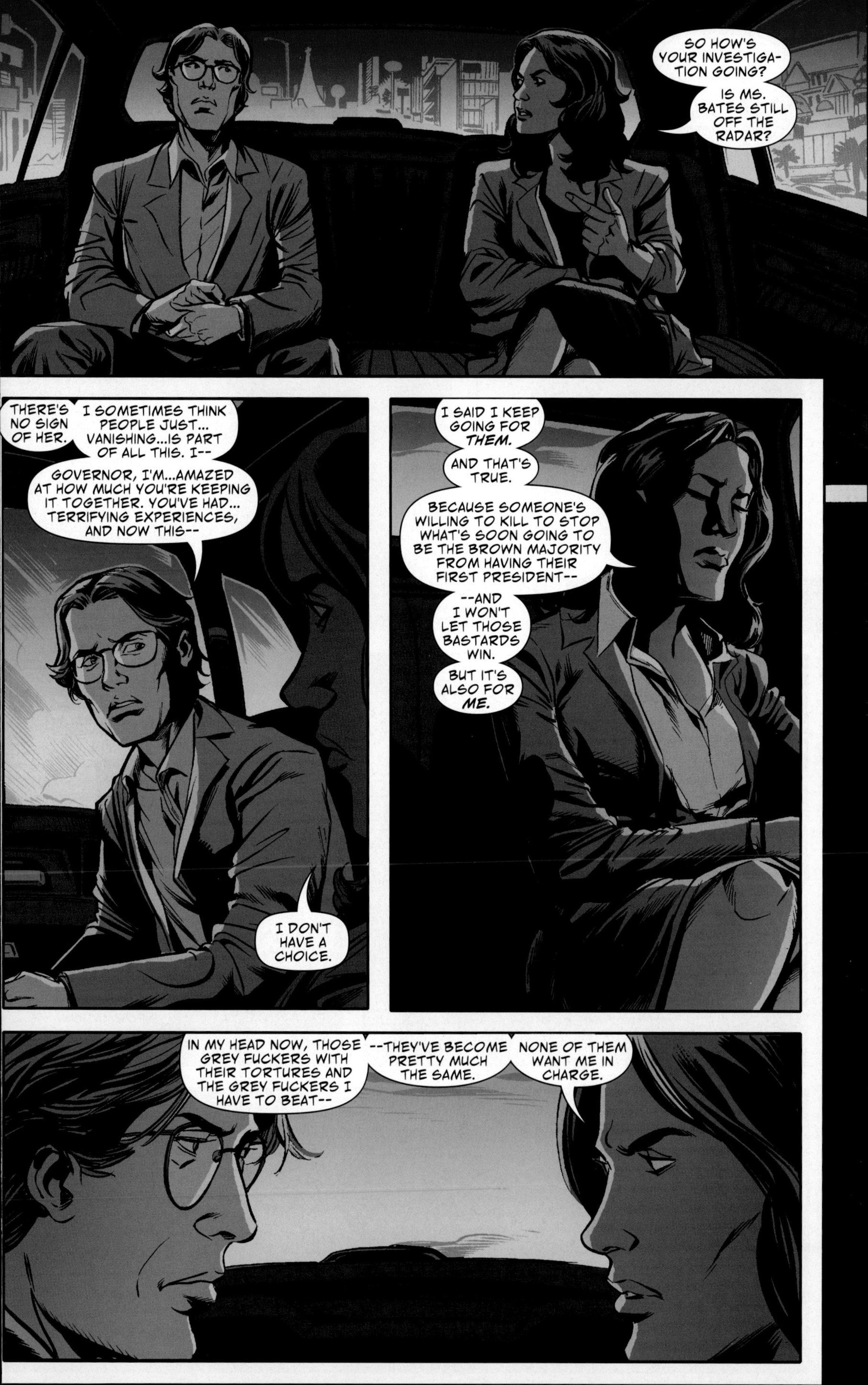
SO HOW'S YOUR INVESTIGATION GOING?
IS MS. BATES STILL OFF THE RADAR?
THERE'S NO SIGN OF HER.
I SOMETIMES THINK PEOPLE JUST... VANISHING...IS PART OF ALL THIS. I--
GOVERNOR, I'M...AMAZED AT HOW MUCH YOU'RE KEEPING IT TOGETHER. YOU'VE HAD... TERRIFYING EXPERIENCES, AND NOW THIS--
I DON'T HAVE A CHOICE.
I SAID I KEEP GOING FOR *THEM.*
AND THAT'S TRUE.
BECAUSE SOMEONE'S WILLING TO KILL TO STOP WHAT'S SOON GOING TO BE THE BROWN MAJORITY FROM HAVING THEIR FIRST PRESIDENT--
--AND I WON'T LET THOSE BASTARDS WIN.
BUT IT'S ALSO FOR *ME.*
IN MY HEAD NOW, THOSE GREY FUCKERS WITH THEIR TORTURES AND THE GREY FUCKERS I HAVE TO BEAT--
--THEY'VE BECOME PRETTY MUCH THE SAME.
NONE OF THEM WANT ME IN CHARGE.

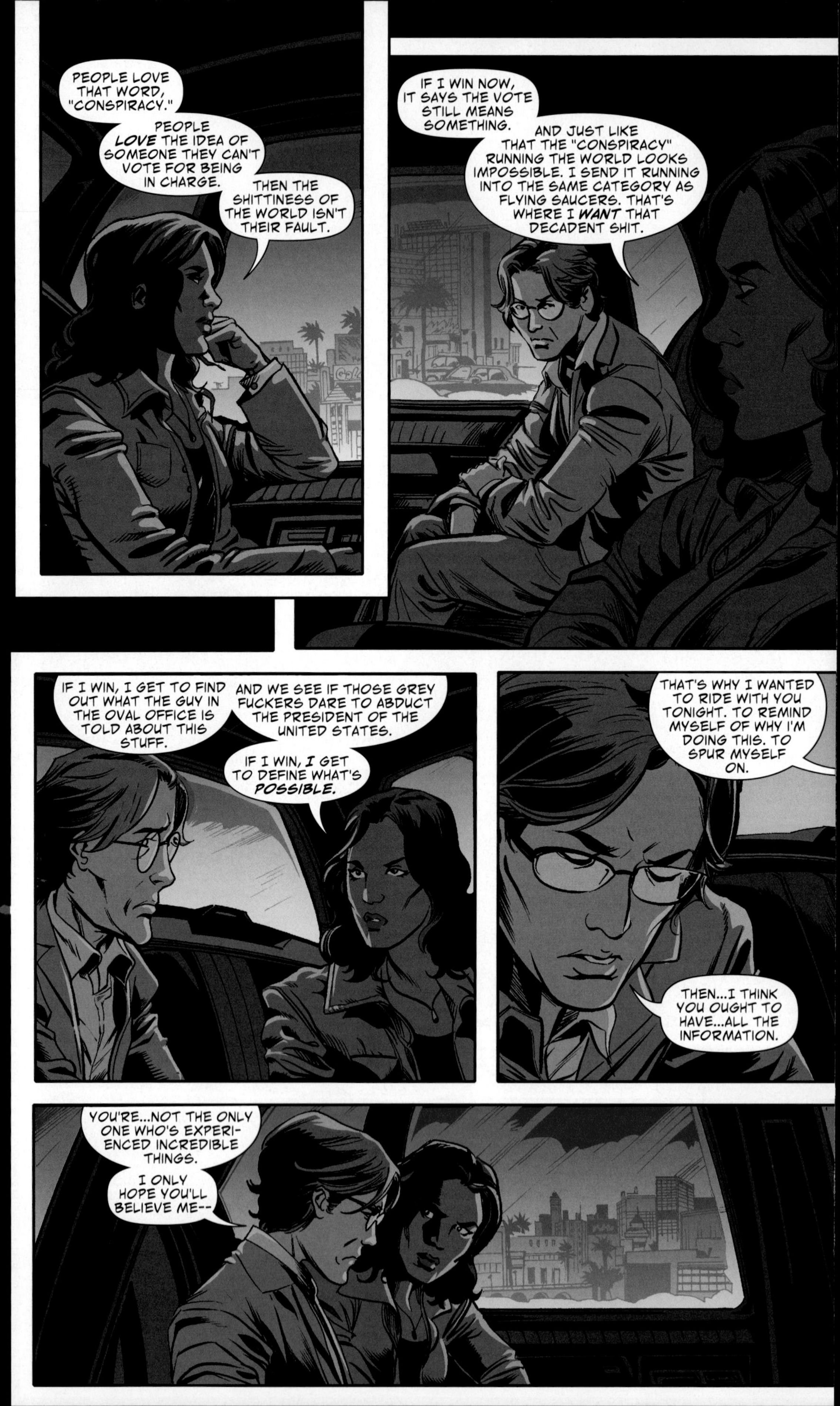
PEOPLE LOVE THAT WORD, "CONSPIRACY."
PEOPLE LOVE THE IDEA OF SOMEONE THEY CAN'T VOTE FOR BEING IN CHARGE.
THEN THE SHITTINESS OF THE WORLD ISN'T THEIR FAULT.
IF I WIN NOW, IT SAYS THE VOTE STILL MEANS SOMETHING.
AND JUST LIKE THAT THE "CONSPIRACY" RUNNING THE WORLD LOOKS IMPOSSIBLE. I SEND IT RUNNING INTO THE SAME CATEGORY AS FLYING SAUCERS. THAT'S WHERE I WANT THAT DECADENT SHIT.
IF I WIN, I GET TO FIND OUT WHAT THE GUY IN THE OVAL OFFICE IS TOLD ABOUT THIS STUFF.
AND WE SEE IF THOSE GREY FUCKERS DARE TO ABDUCT THE PRESIDENT OF THE UNITED STATES.
IF I WIN, I GET TO DEFINE WHAT'S POSSIBLE.
THAT'S WHY I WANTED TO RIDE WITH YOU TONIGHT. TO REMIND MYSELF OF WHY I'M DOING THIS. TO SPUR MYSELF ON.
THEN...I THINK YOU OUGHT TO HAVE...ALL THE INFORMATION.
YOU'RE...NOT THE ONLY ONE WHO'S EXPERI-ENCED INCREDIBLE THINGS.
I ONLY HOPE YOU'LL BELIEVE ME--

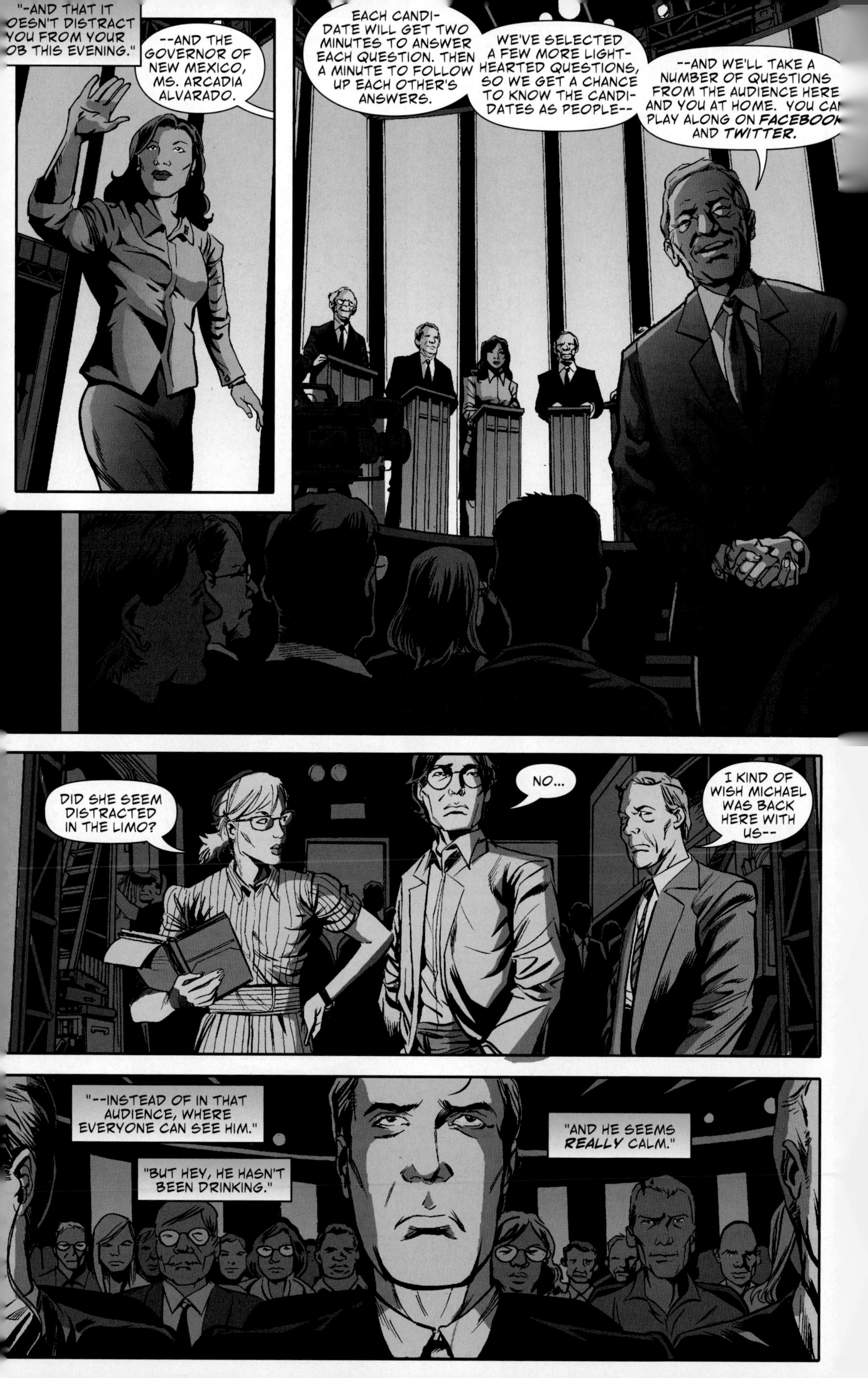
"-AND THAT IT OESN'T DISTRACT YOU FROM YOUR OB THIS EVENING."
--AND THE GOVERNOR OF NEW MEXICO, MS. ARCADIA ALVARADO.
EACH CANDIDATE WILL GET TWO MINUTES TO ANSWER EACH QUESTION. THEN A MINUTE TO FOLLOW UP EACH OTHER'S ANSWERS.
WE'VE SELECTED A FEW MORE LIGHT-HEARTED QUESTIONS, SO WE GET A CHANCE TO KNOW THE CANDIDATES AS PEOPLE--
--AND WE'LL TAKE A NUMBER OF QUESTIONS FROM THE AUDIENCE HERE AND YOU AT HOME. YOU CA PLAY ALONG ON FACEBOO AND TWITTER.
DID SHE SEEM DISTRACTED IN THE LIMO?
NO...
I KIND OF WISH MICHAEL WAS BACK HERE WITH US--
"--INSTEAD OF IN THAT AUDIENCE, WHERE EVERYONE CAN SEE HIM."
"BUT HEY, HE HASN'T BEEN DRINKING."
"AND HE SEEMS REALLY CALM."

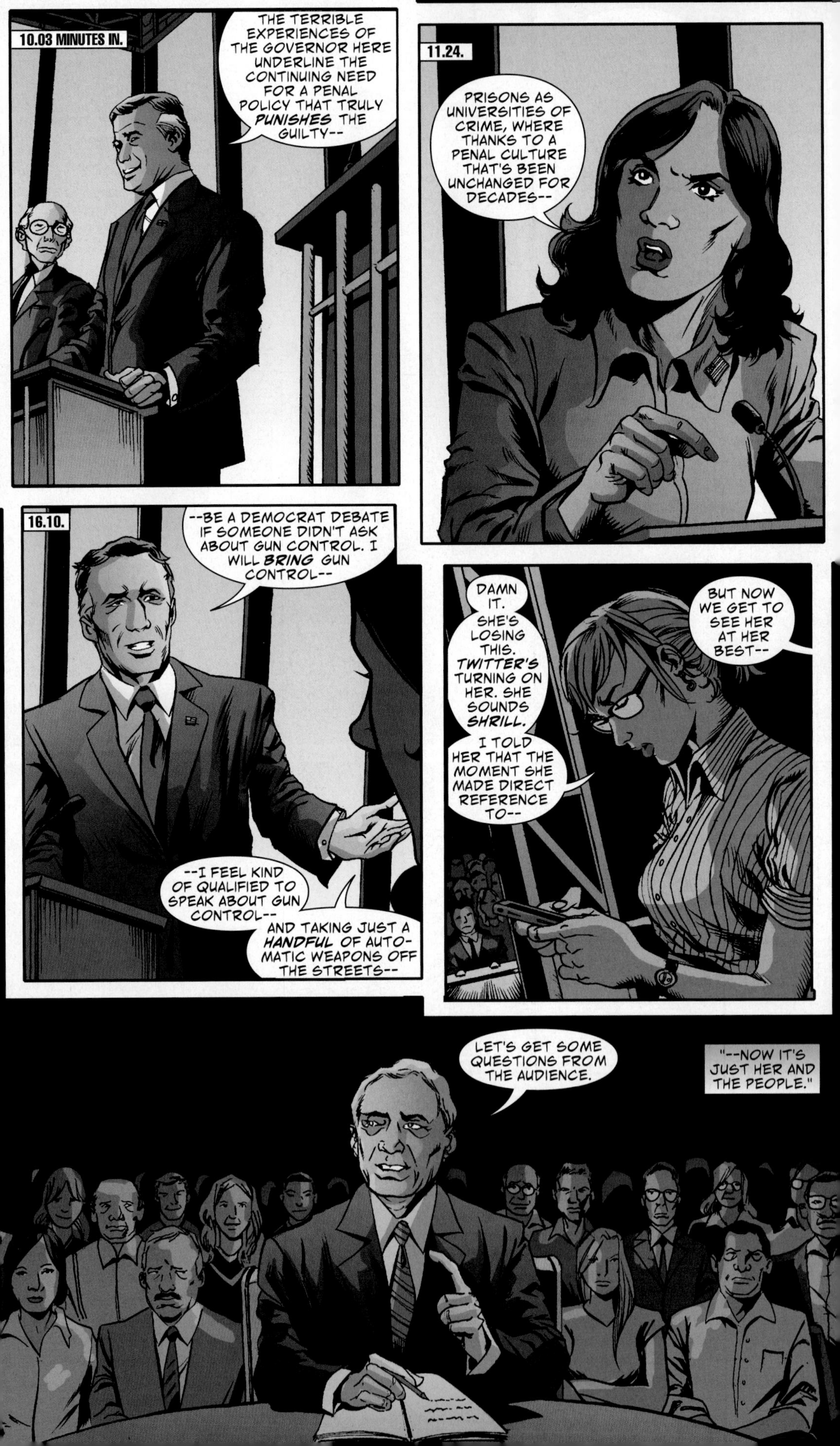
10.03 MINUTES IN.
THE TERRIBLE EXPERIENCES OF THE GOVERNOR HERE UNDERLINE THE CONTINUING NEED FOR A PENAL POLICY THAT TRULY PUNISHES THE GUILTY--
11.24.
PRISONS AS UNIVERSITIES OF CRIME, WHERE THANKS TO A PENAL CULTURE THAT'S BEEN UNCHANGED FOR DECADES--
16.10.
--BE A DEMOCRAT DEBATE IF SOMEONE DIDN'T ASK ABOUT GUN CONTROL. I WILL BRING GUN CONTROL--
--I FEEL KIND OF QUALIFIED TO SPEAK ABOUT GUN CONTROL--
AND TAKING JUST A HANDFUL OF AUTO-MATIC WEAPONS OFF THE STREETS--
DAMN IT. SHE'S LOSING THIS. TWITTER'S TURNING ON HER. SHE SOUNDS SHRILL.
I TOLD HER THAT THE MOMENT SHE MADE DIRECT REFERENCE TO--
BUT NOW WE GET TO SEE HER AT HER BEST--
LET'S GET SOME QUESTIONS FROM THE AUDIENCE.
"--NOW IT'S JUST HER AND THE PEOPLE."

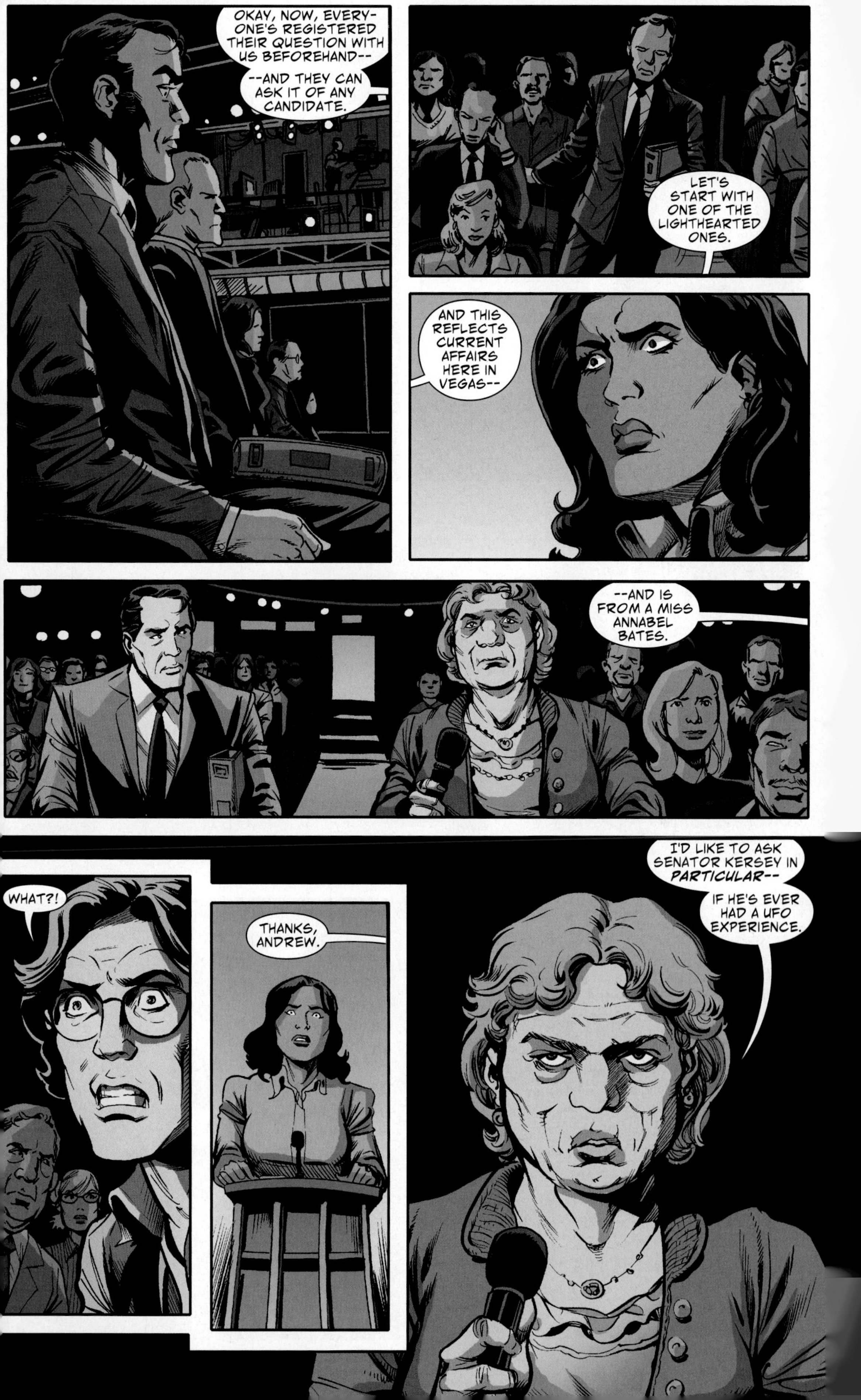
OKAY, NOW, EVERYONE'S REGISTERED THEIR QUESTION WITH US BEFOREHAND--
--AND THEY CAN ASK IT OF ANY CANDIDATE.
LET'S START WITH ONE OF THE LIGHTHEARTED ONES.
AND THIS REFLECTS CURRENT AFFAIRS HERE IN VEGAS--
--AND IS FROM A MISS ANNABEL BATES.
I'D LIKE TO ASK SENATOR KERSEY IN PARTICULAR--
IF HE'S EVER HAD A UFO EXPERIENCE.
WHAT?!
THANKS, ANDREW.

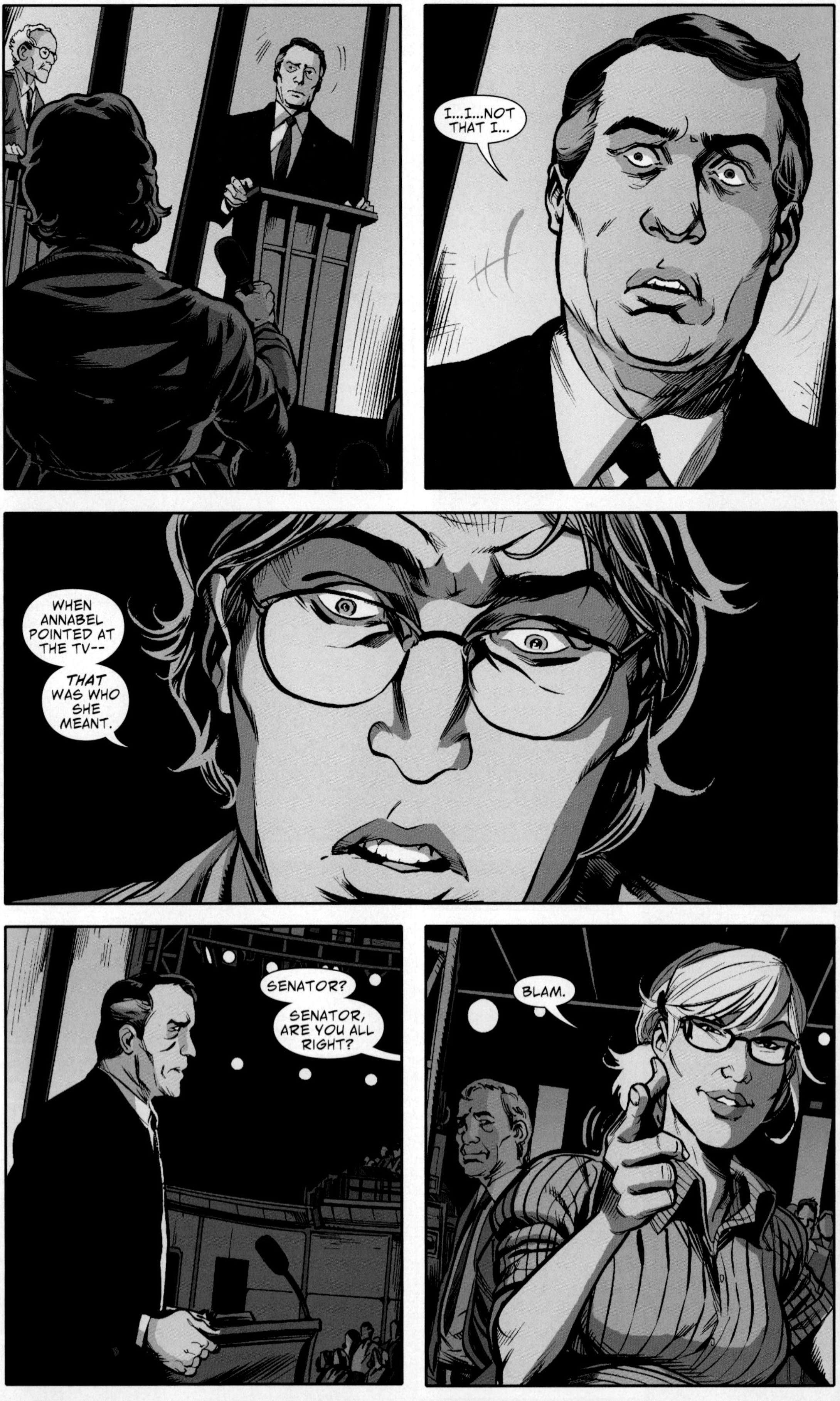
I...I...NOT THAT I...
WHEN ANNABEL POINTED AT THE TV--
THAT WAS WHO SHE MEANT.
SENATOR?
SENATOR, ARE YOU ALL RIGHT?
BLAM.

LET'S, ER, LET'S MOVE ON TO THE NEXT QUESTION.

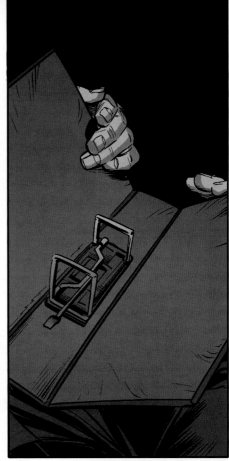

THE WORLD IS WONDERING WHAT THE HELL THAT WAS.

FROM NOW ON, EVERY QUESTION HE'S ASKED WILL BE ABOUT UFOS. IRONY: IT'S MY FAVORITE THING.

YEAH. HARRY, YOU KNOW, THIS *IS* TERRIBLE.

WHAT?

EVERYTHING THAT'S HAPPENED IN THIS CITY HAS TURNED OUT WELL FOR US.

AND WE DID HARDLY ANY OF IT.

IT'S LIKE THERE *IS* A CONSPIRACY--

--AND IT'S ON *OUR* SIDE.

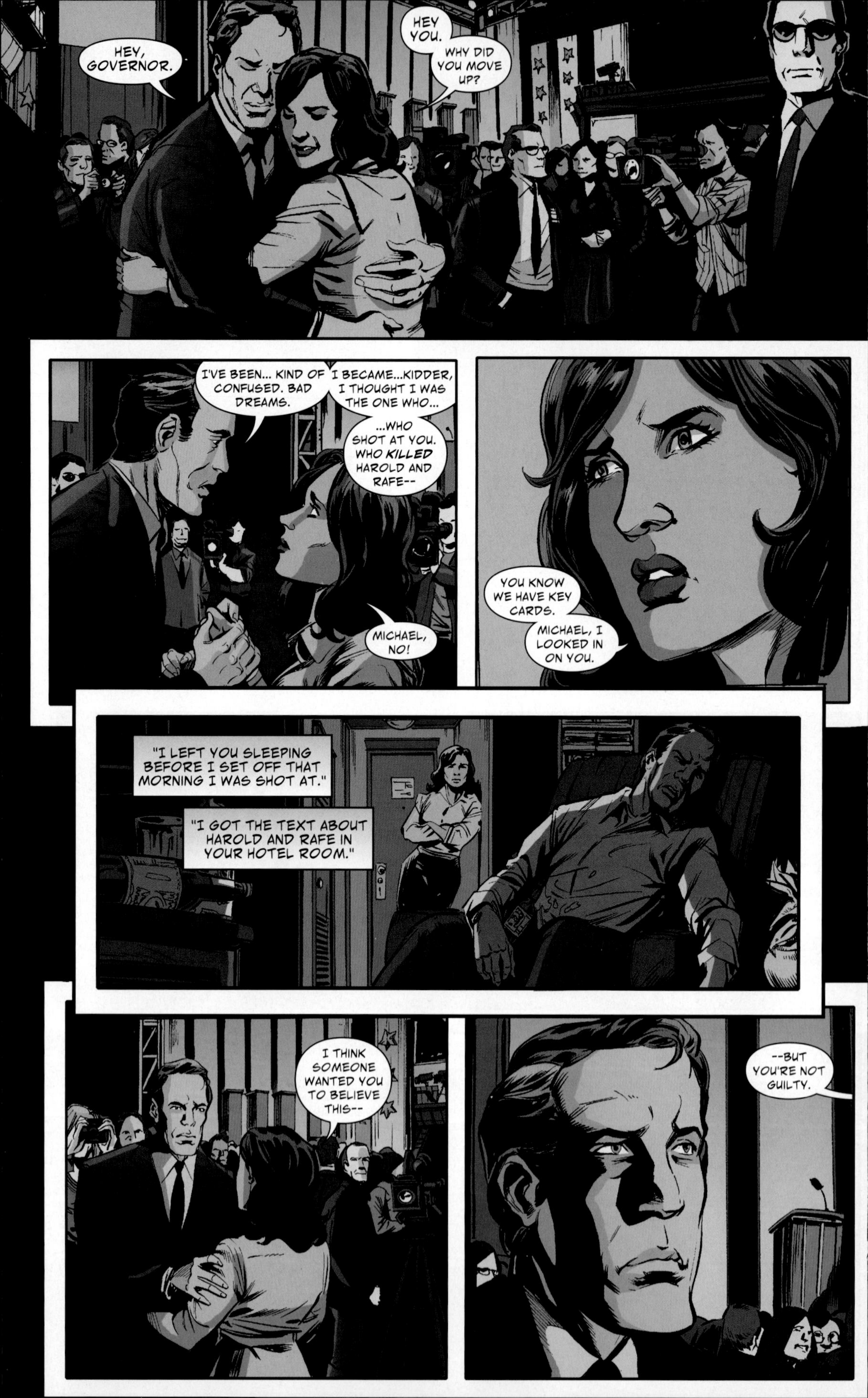
HEY, GOVERNOR.
HEY YOU.
WHY DID YOU MOVE UP?
I'VE BEEN... KIND OF CONFUSED. BAD DREAMS.
I BECAME...KIDDER, I THOUGHT I WAS THE ONE WHO...
...WHO SHOT AT YOU. WHO KILLED HAROLD AND RAFE--
MICHAEL, NO!
YOU KNOW WE HAVE KEY CARDS.
MICHAEL, I LOOKED IN ON YOU.
"I LEFT YOU SLEEPING BEFORE I SET OFF THAT MORNING I WAS SHOT AT."
"I GOT THE TEXT ABOUT HAROLD AND RAFE IN YOUR HOTEL ROOM."
I THINK SOMEONE WANTED YOU TO BELIEVE THIS--
--BUT YOU'RE NOT GUILTY.

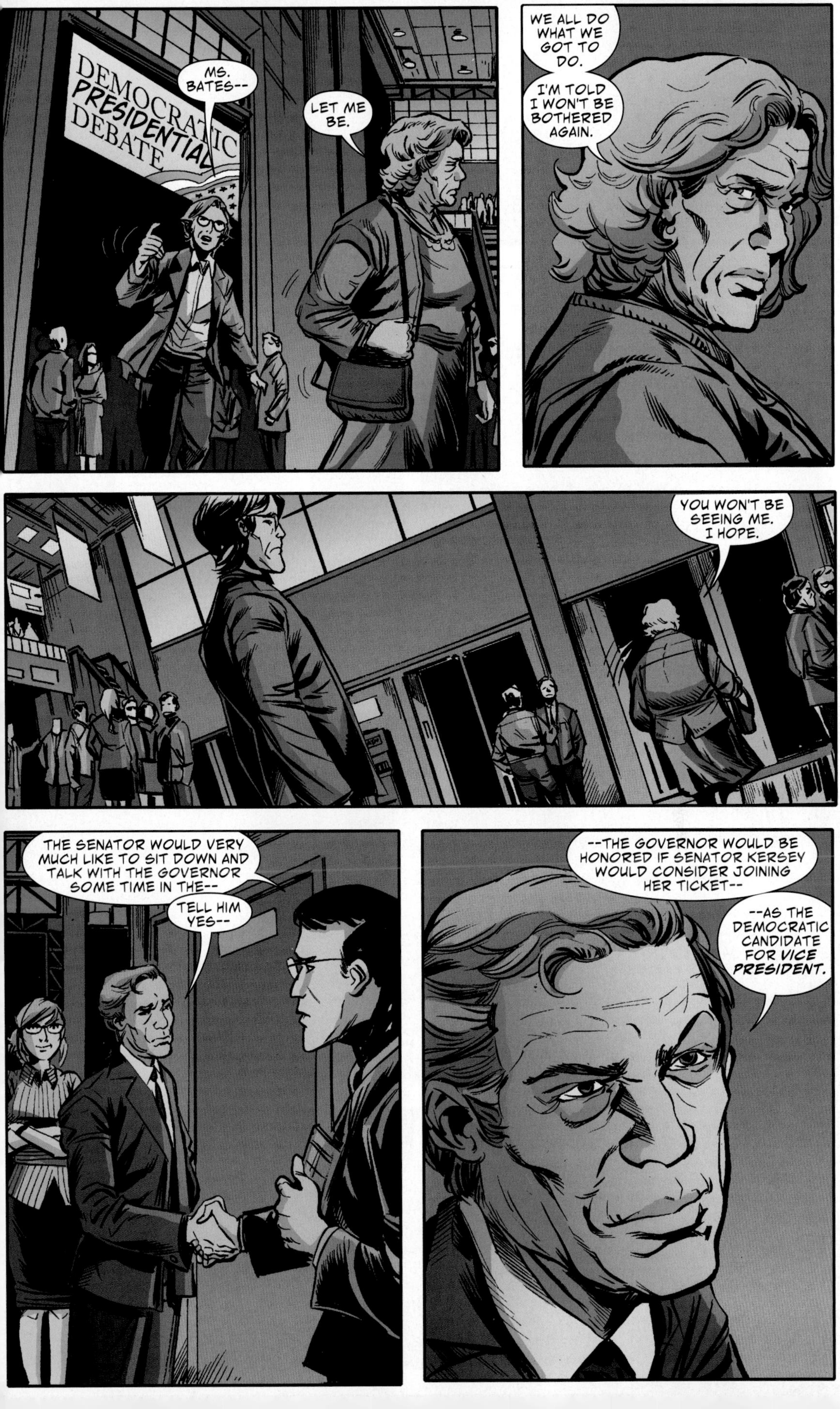
DEMOCRATIC PRESIDENTIAL DEBATE
MS. BATES--
LET ME BE.
WE ALL DO WHAT WE GOT TO DO.
I'M TOLD I WON'T BE BOTHERED AGAIN.
YOU WON'T BE SEEING ME. I HOPE.
THE SENATOR WOULD VERY MUCH LIKE TO SIT DOWN AND TALK WITH THE GOVERNOR SOME TIME IN THE--
TELL HIM YES--
--THE GOVERNOR WOULD BE HONORED IF SENATOR KERSEY WOULD CONSIDER JOINING HER TICKET--
--AS THE DEMOCRATIC CANDIDATE FOR *VICE PRESIDENT*.

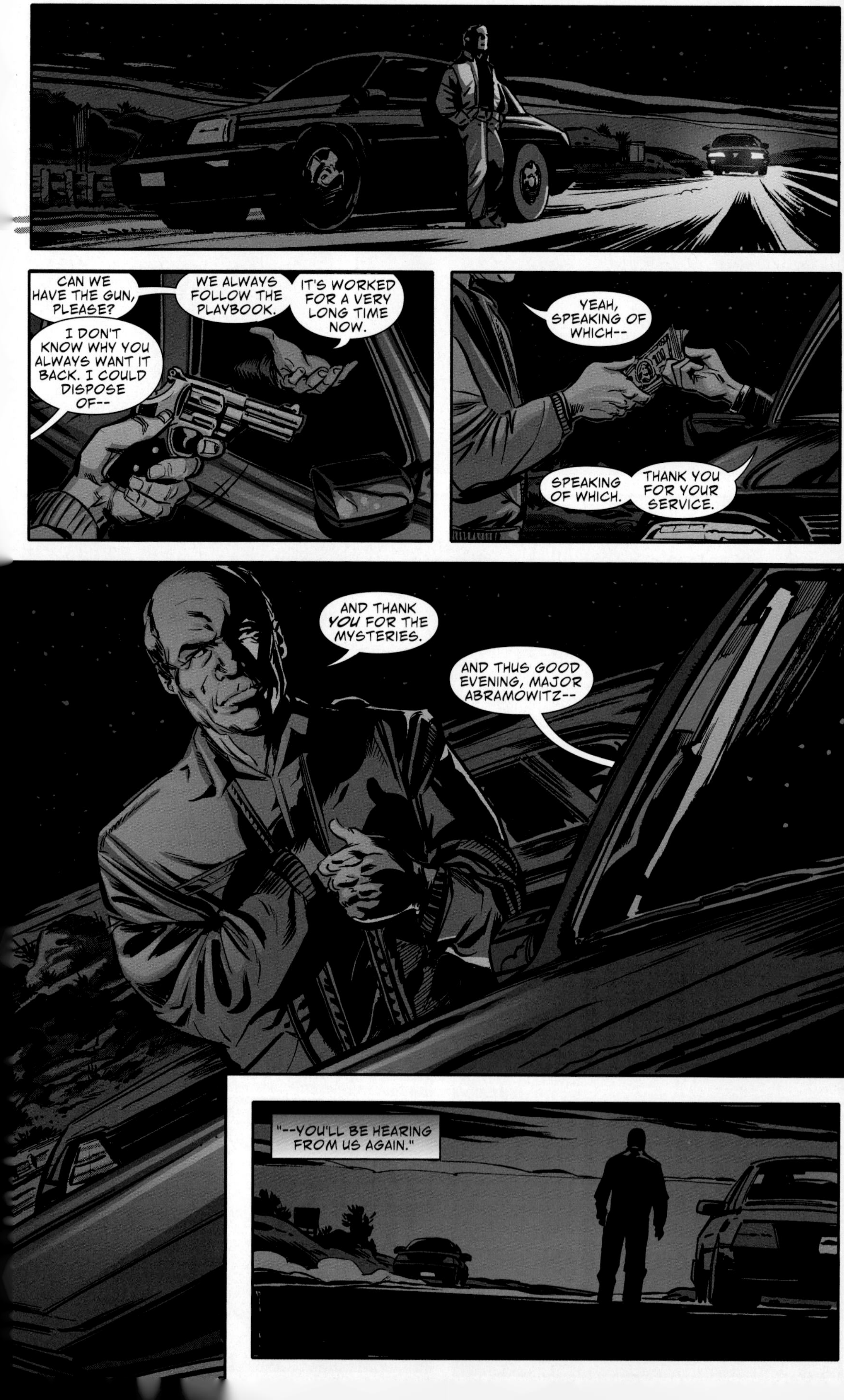
CAN WE HAVE THE GUN, PLEASE?
WE ALWAYS FOLLOW THE PLAYBOOK.
IT'S WORKED FOR A VERY LONG TIME NOW.
I DON'T KNOW WHY YOU ALWAYS WANT IT BACK. I COULD DISPOSE OF--
YEAH, SPEAKING OF WHICH--
SPEAKING OF WHICH.
THANK YOU FOR YOUR SERVICE.
AND THANK YOU FOR THE MYSTERIES.
AND THUS GOOD EVENING, MAJOR ABRAMOWITZ--
"--YOU'LL BE HEARING FROM US AGAIN."

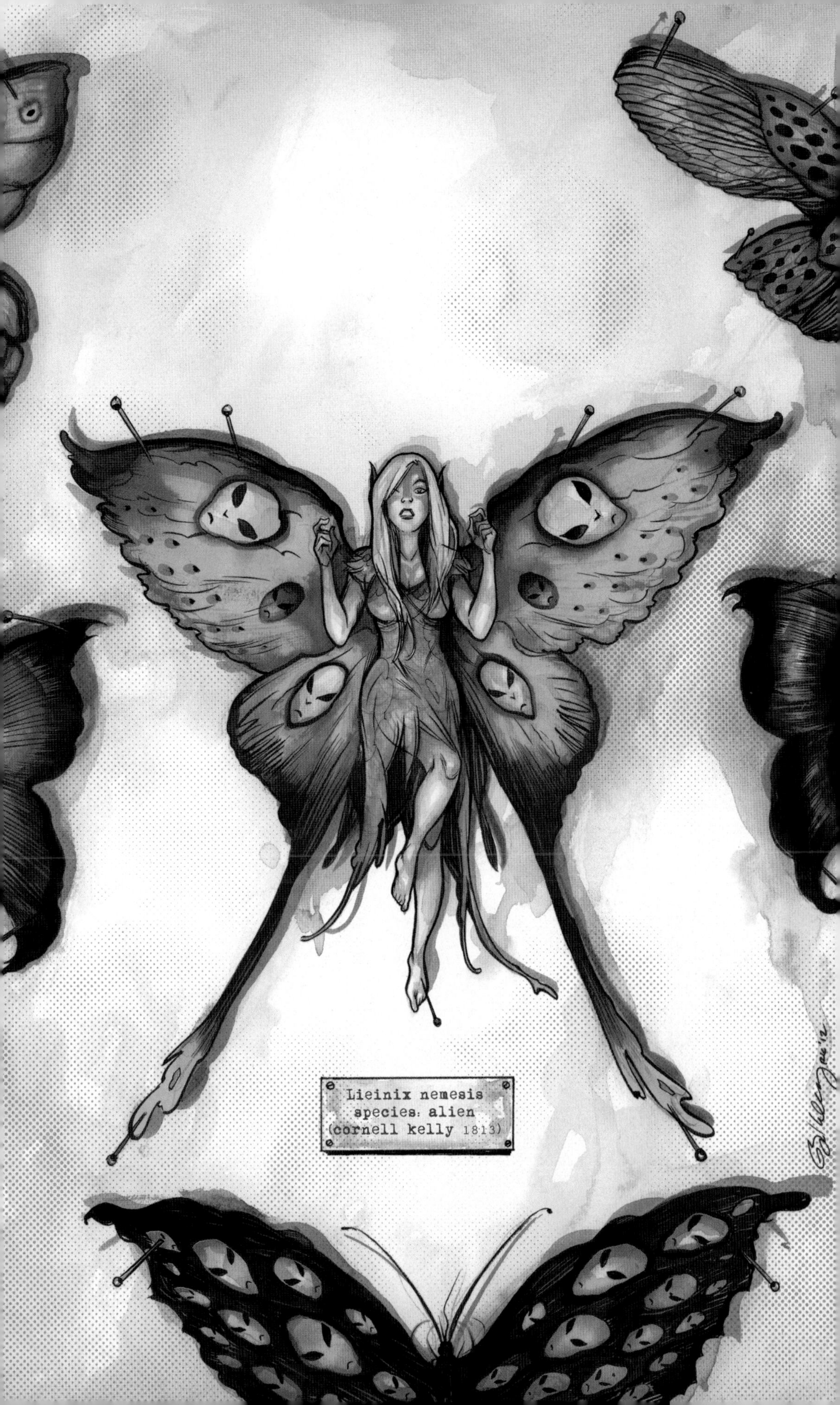

Lieinix nemesis
species: alien
(cornell kelly 1813)

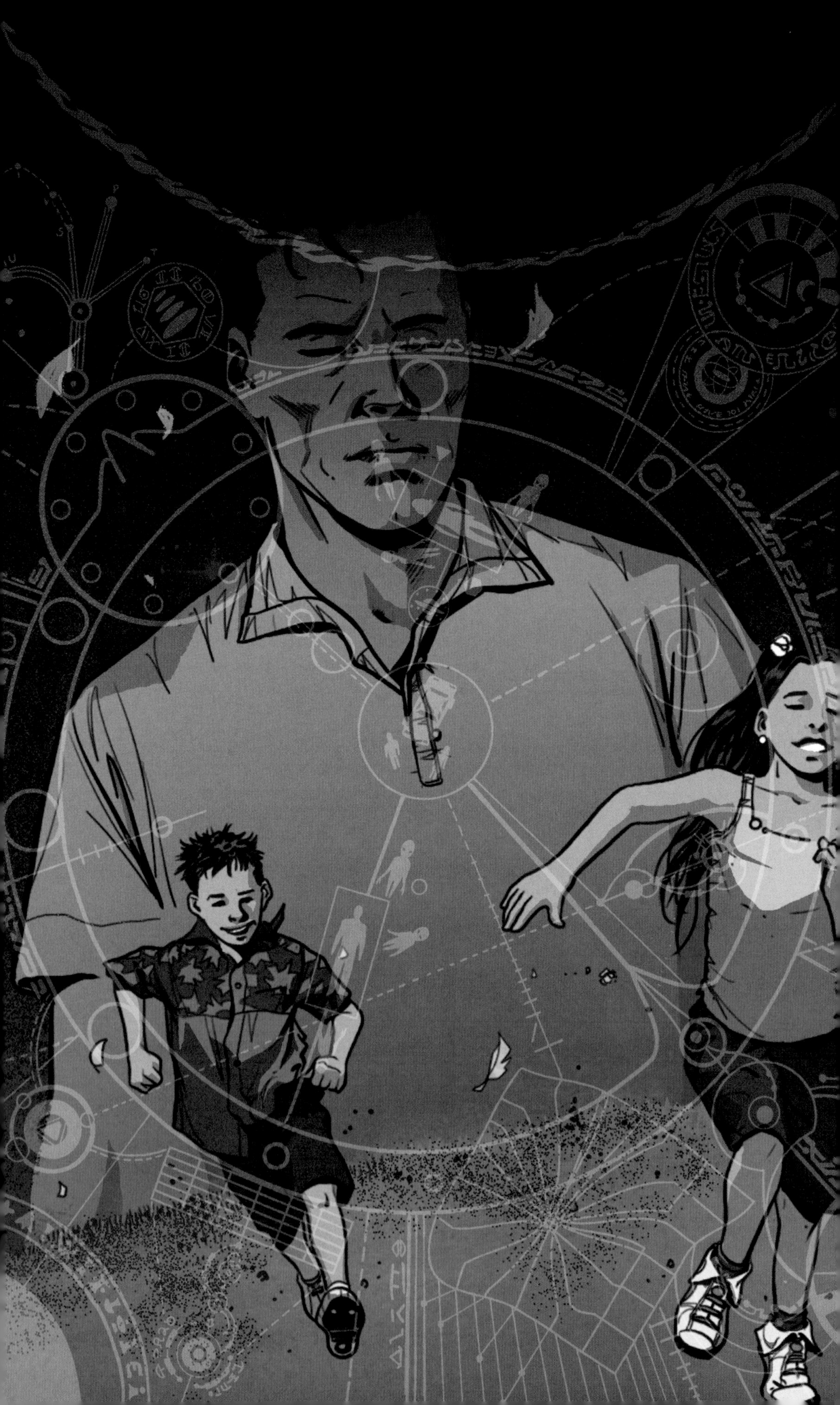

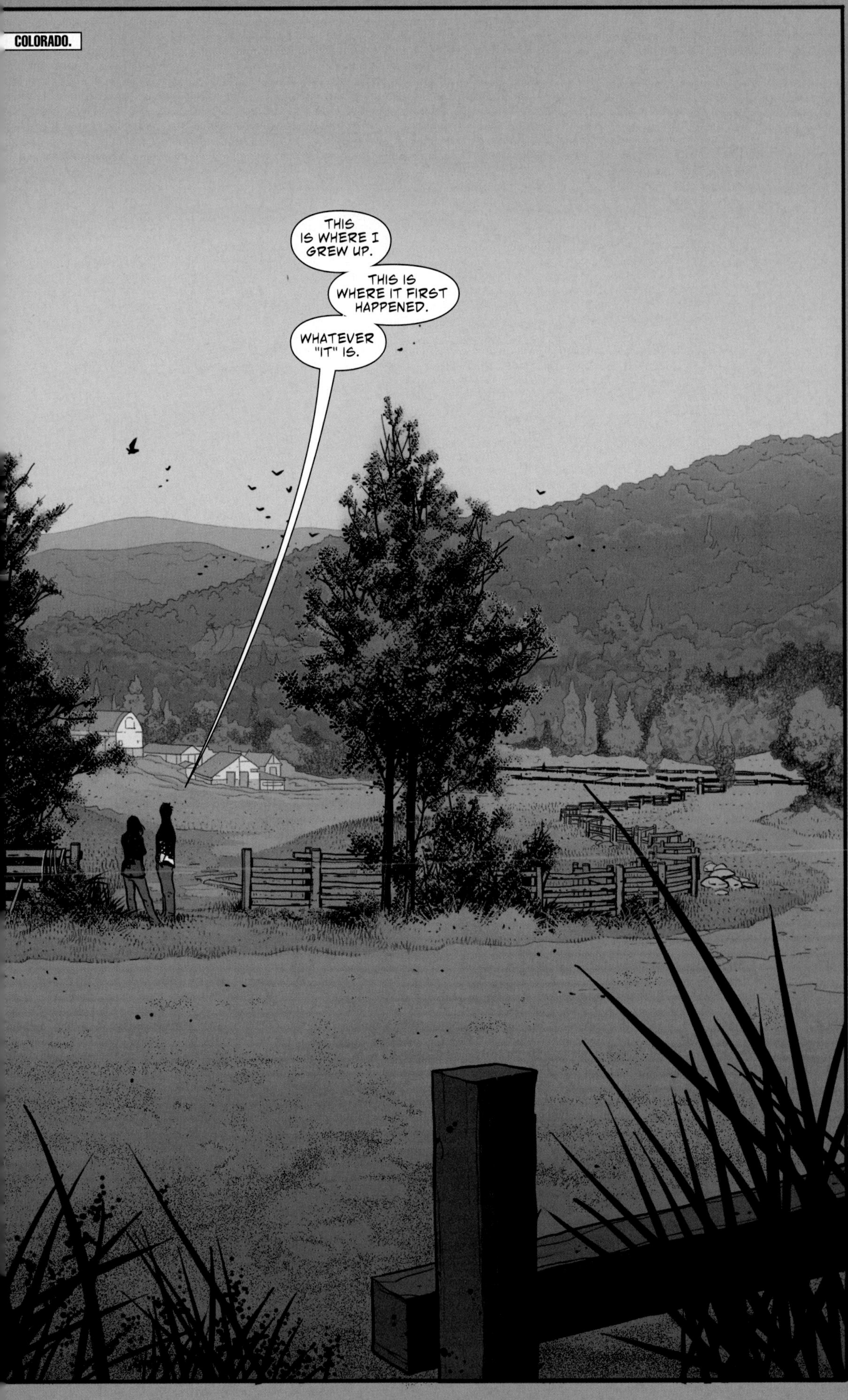
COLORADO.
THIS IS WHERE I GREW UP.
THIS IS WHERE IT FIRST HAPPENED.
WHATEVER "IT" IS.

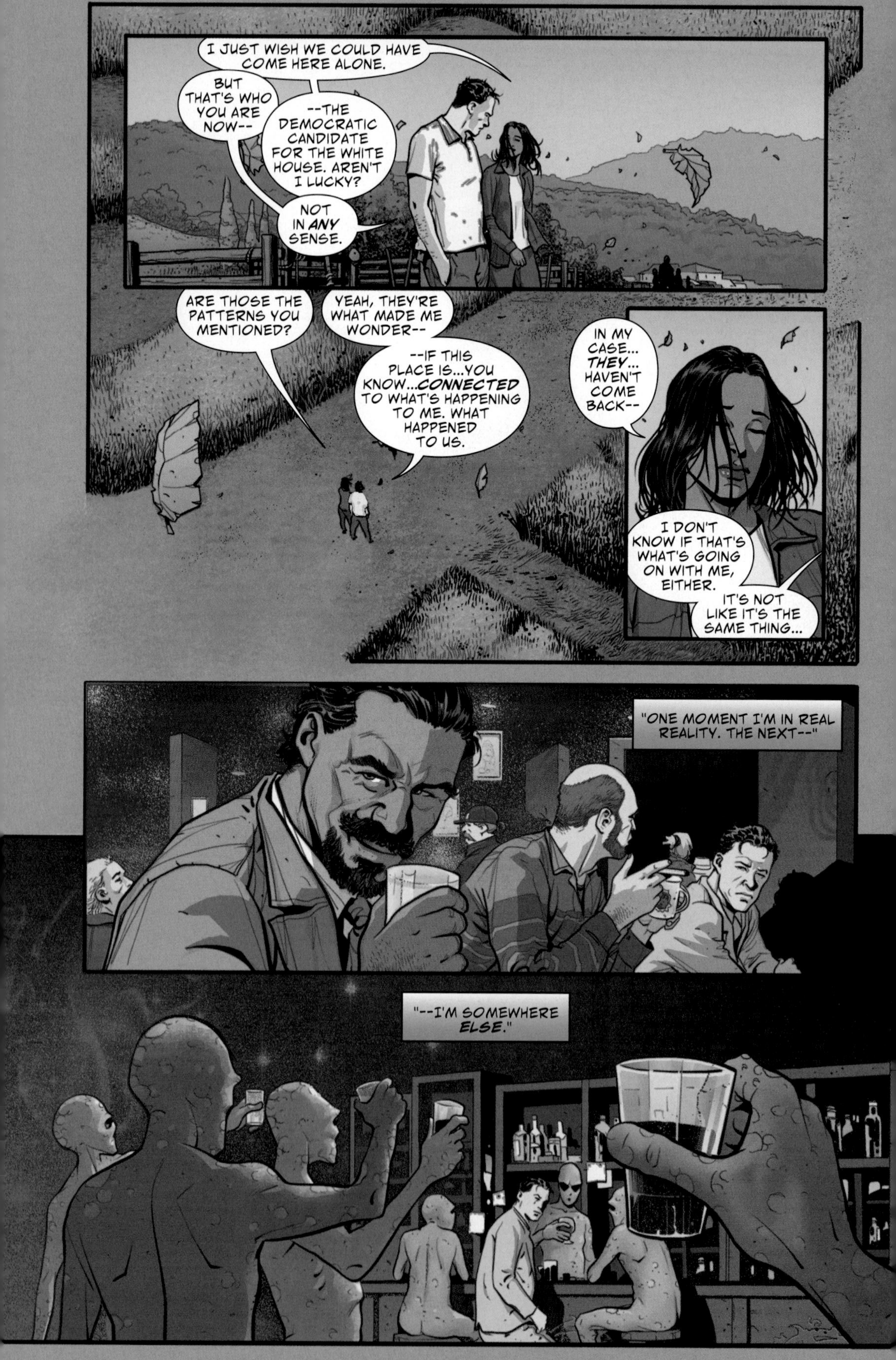
I JUST WISH WE COULD HAVE COME HERE ALONE.
BUT THAT'S WHO YOU ARE NOW--
--THE DEMOCRATIC CANDIDATE FOR THE WHITE HOUSE. AREN'T I LUCKY?
NOT IN ANY SENSE.
ARE THOSE THE PATTERNS YOU MENTIONED?
YEAH, THEY'RE WHAT MADE ME WONDER--
--IF THIS PLACE IS...YOU KNOW...CONNECTED TO WHAT'S HAPPENING TO ME. WHAT HAPPENED TO US.
IN MY CASE... THEY... HAVEN'T COME BACK--
I DON'T KNOW IF THAT'S WHAT'S GOING ON WITH ME, EITHER.
IT'S NOT LIKE IT'S THE SAME THING...
"ONE MOMENT I'M IN REAL REALITY. THE NEXT--"
"--I'M SOMEWHERE ELSE."

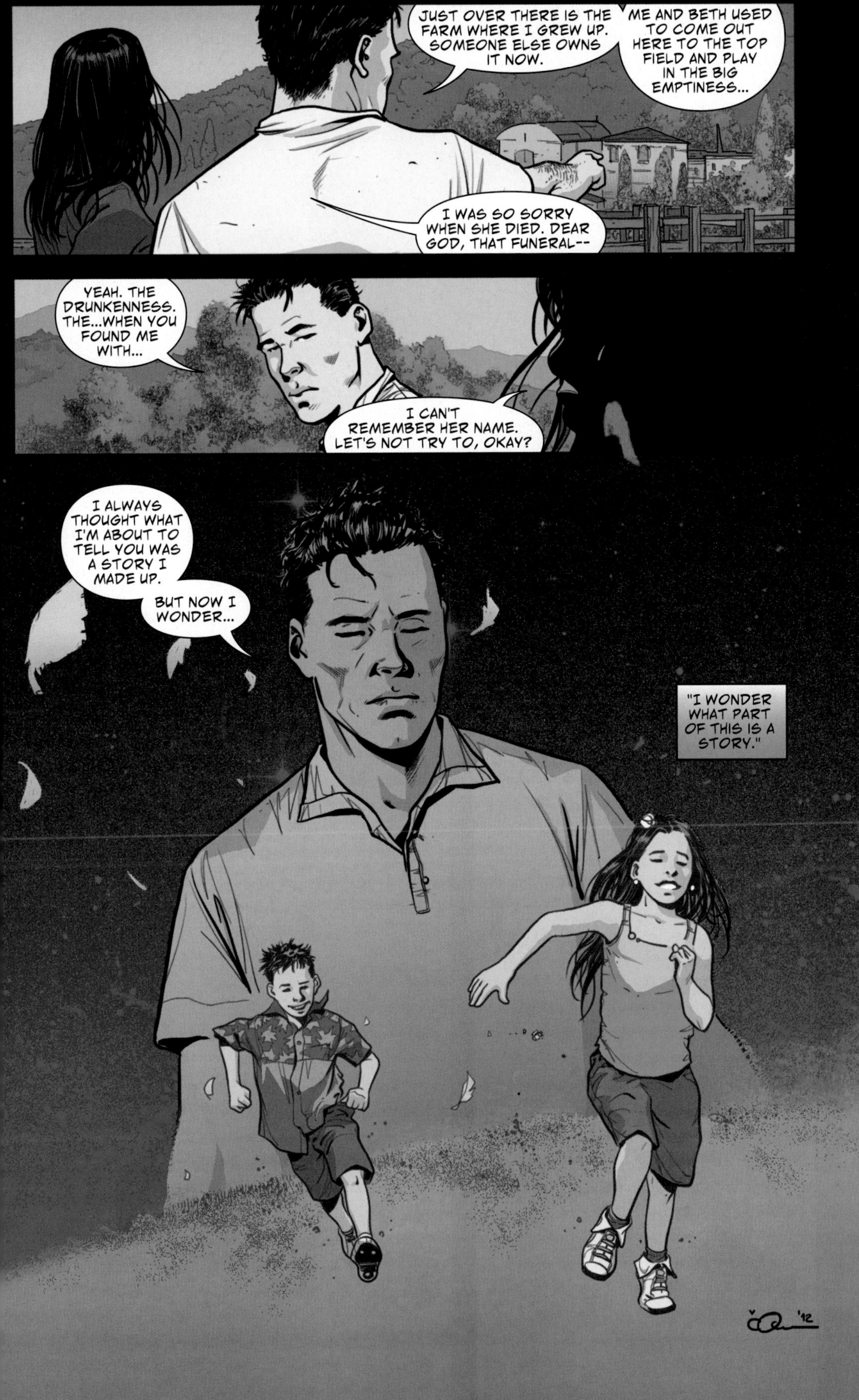
JUST OVER THERE IS THE FARM WHERE I GREW UP. SOMEONE ELSE OWNS IT NOW.
ME AND BETH USED TO COME OUT HERE TO THE TOP FIELD AND PLAY IN THE BIG EMPTINESS...
I WAS SO SORRY WHEN SHE DIED. DEAR GOD, THAT FUNERAL--
YEAH. THE DRUNKENNESS. THE...WHEN YOU FOUND ME WITH...
I CAN'T REMEMBER HER NAME. LET'S NOT TRY TO, OKAY?
I ALWAYS THOUGHT WHAT I'M ABOUT TO TELL YOU WAS A STORY I MADE UP.
BUT NOW I WONDER...
"I WONDER WHAT PART OF THIS IS A STORY."
'12

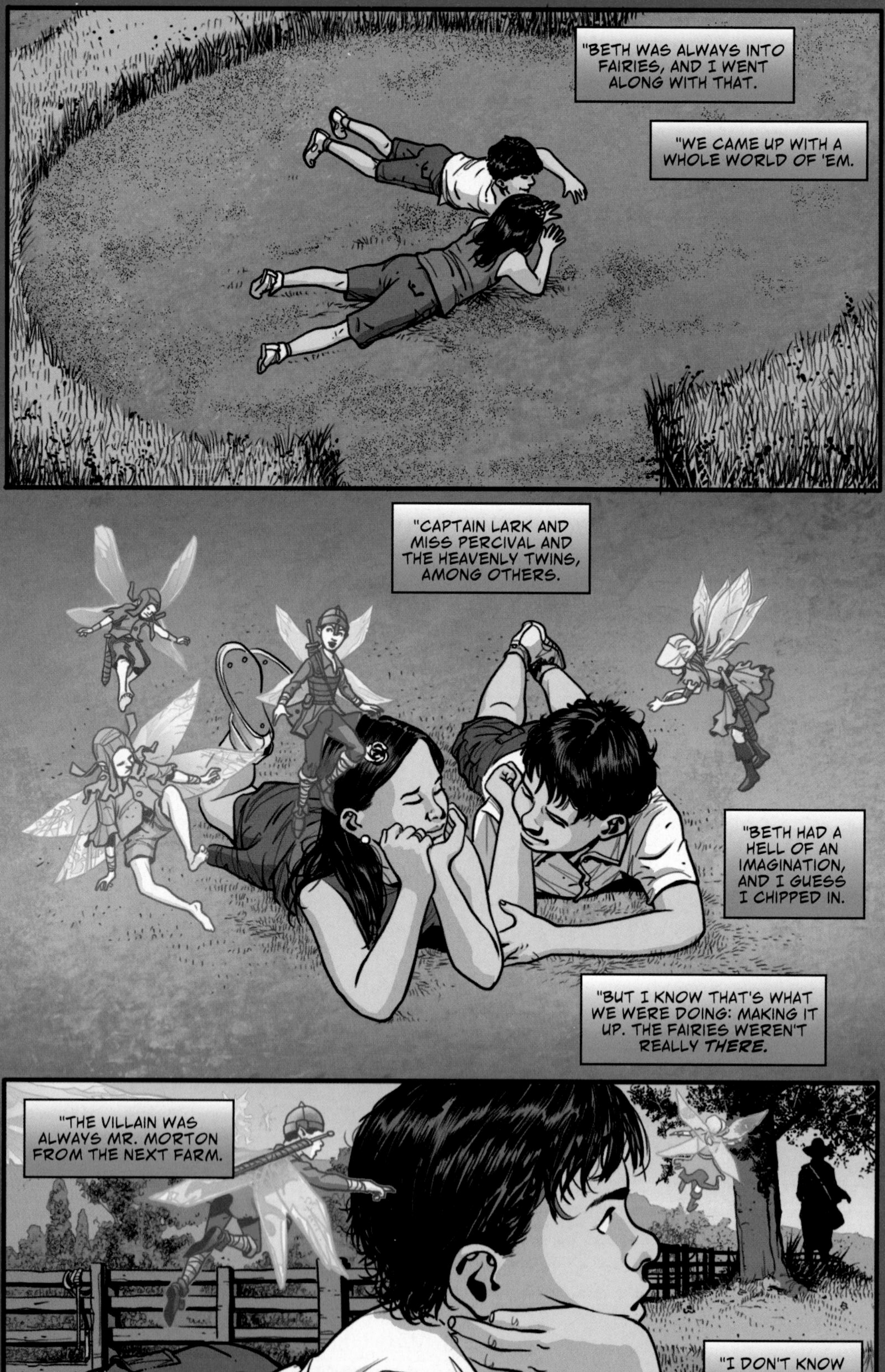
"BETH WAS ALWAYS INTO FAIRIES, AND I WENT ALONG WITH THAT.
"WE CAME UP WITH A WHOLE WORLD OF 'EM.
"CAPTAIN LARK AND MISS PERCIVAL AND THE HEAVENLY TWINS, AMONG OTHERS.
"BETH HAD A HELL OF AN IMAGINATION, AND I GUESS I CHIPPED IN.
"BUT I KNOW THAT'S WHAT WE WERE DOING: MAKING IT UP. THE FAIRIES WEREN'T REALLY *THERE*.
"THE VILLAIN WAS ALWAYS MR. MORTON FROM THE NEXT FARM.
"I DON'T KNOW WHAT HE'D DONE TO DESERVE THAT."

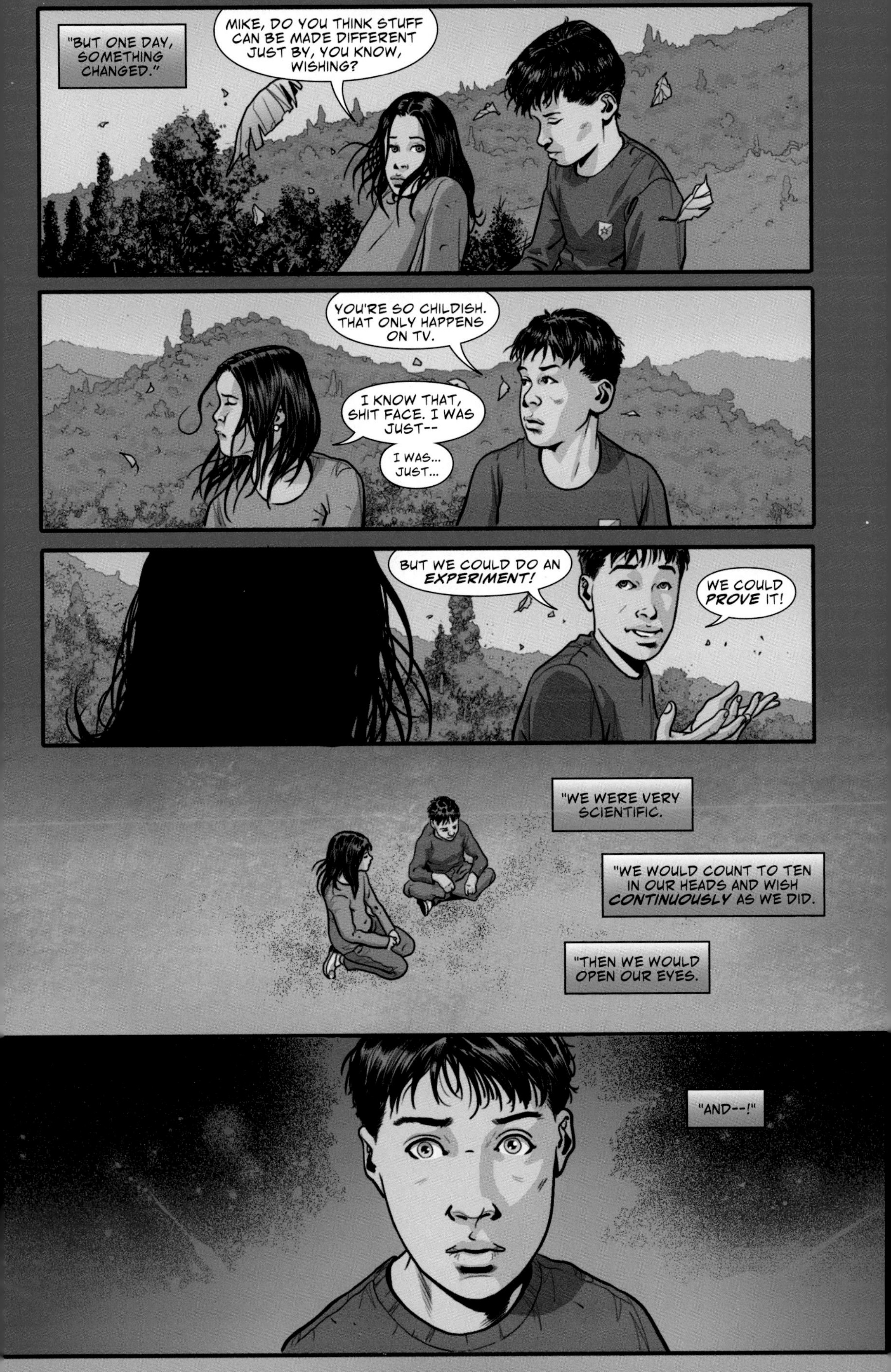
"BUT ONE DAY, SOMETHING CHANGED."
MIKE, DO YOU THINK STUFF CAN BE MADE DIFFERENT JUST BY, YOU KNOW, WISHING?
YOU'RE SO CHILDISH. THAT ONLY HAPPENS ON TV.
I KNOW THAT, SHIT FACE. I WAS JUST--
I WAS... JUST...
BUT WE COULD DO AN *EXPERIMENT!*
WE COULD *PROVE* IT!
"WE WERE VERY SCIENTIFIC.
"WE WOULD COUNT TO TEN IN OUR HEADS AND WISH *CONTINUOUSLY* AS WE DID.
"THEN WE WOULD OPEN OUR EYES.
"AND--!"

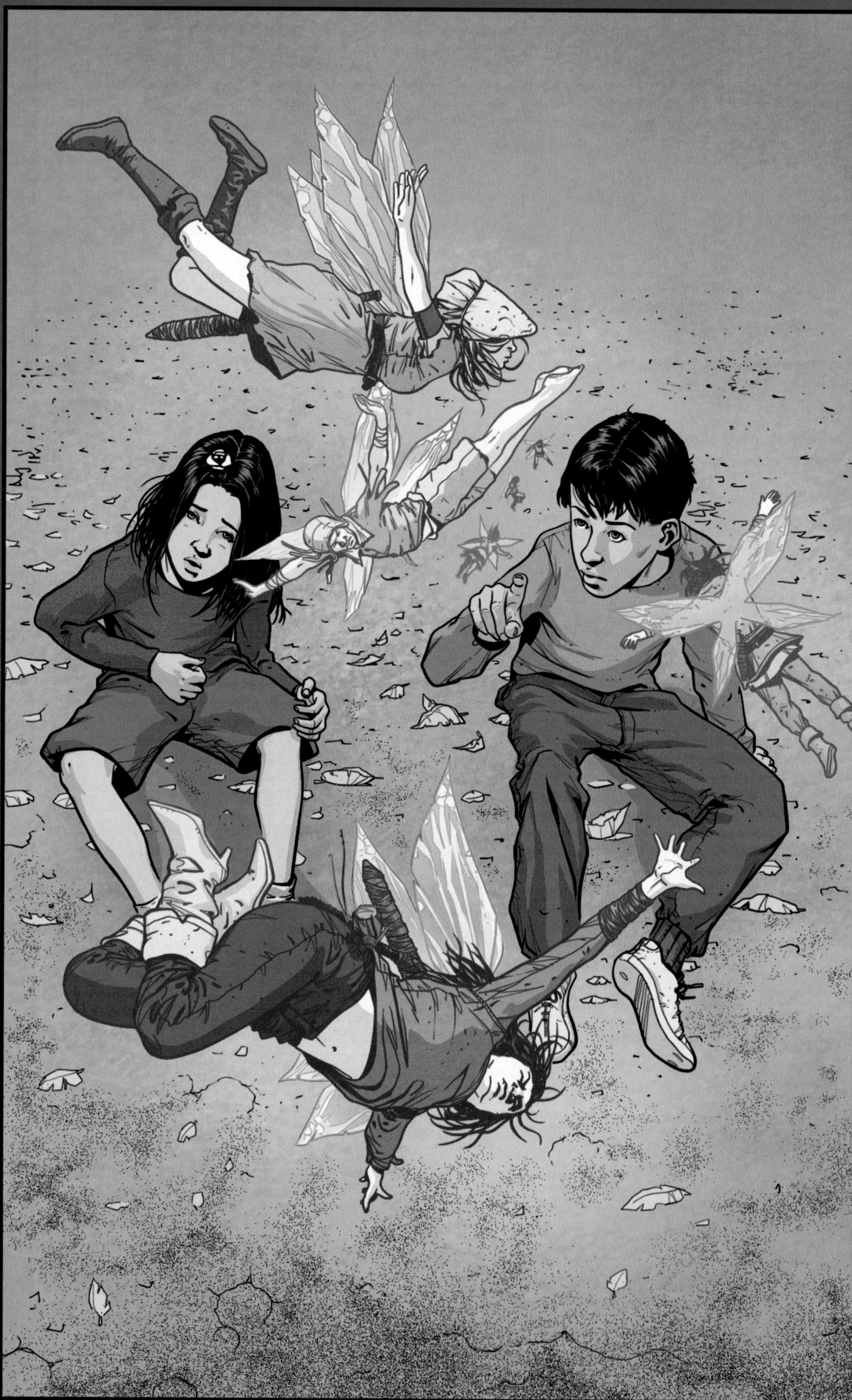

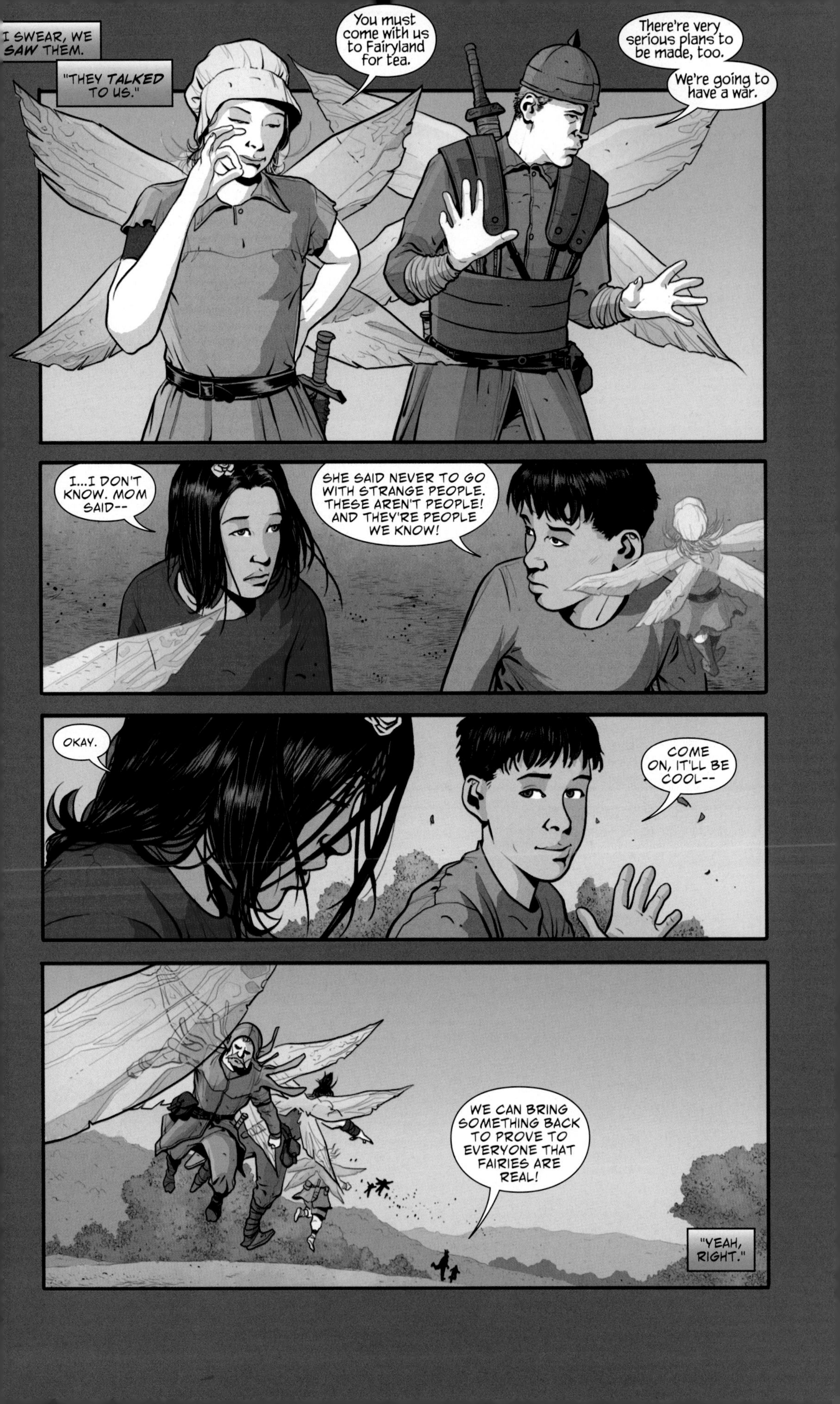
I SWEAR, WE SAW THEM.
"THEY TALKED TO US."
You must come with us to Fairyland for tea.
There're very serious plans to be made, too.
We're going to have a war.
I...I DON'T KNOW. MOM SAID--
SHE SAID NEVER TO GO WITH STRANGE PEOPLE. THESE AREN'T PEOPLE! AND THEY'RE PEOPLE WE KNOW!
OKAY.
COME ON, IT'LL BE COOL--
WE CAN BRING SOMETHING BACK TO PROVE TO EVERYONE THAT FAIRIES ARE REAL!
"YEAH, RIGHT."

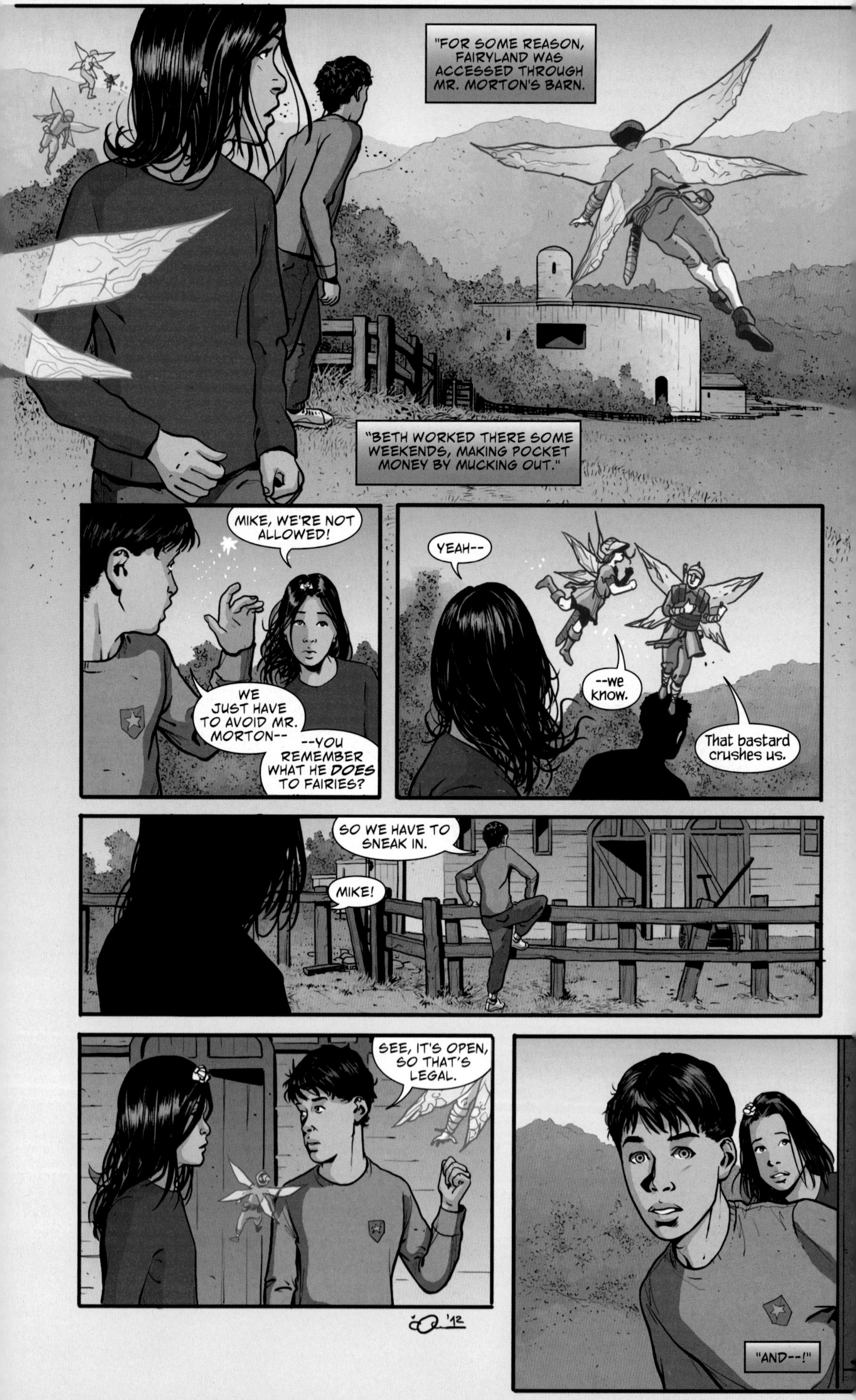
"FOR SOME REASON, FAIRYLAND WAS ACCESSED THROUGH MR. MORTON'S BARN.
"BETH WORKED THERE SOME WEEKENDS, MAKING POCKET MONEY BY MUCKING OUT."
MIKE, WE'RE NOT ALLOWED!
WE JUST HAVE TO AVOID MR. MORTON--
--YOU REMEMBER WHAT HE *DOES* TO FAIRIES?
YEAH--
--we know.
That bastard crushes us.
SO WE HAVE TO SNEAK IN.
MIKE!
SEE, IT'S OPEN, SO THAT'S LEGAL.
"AND--!"

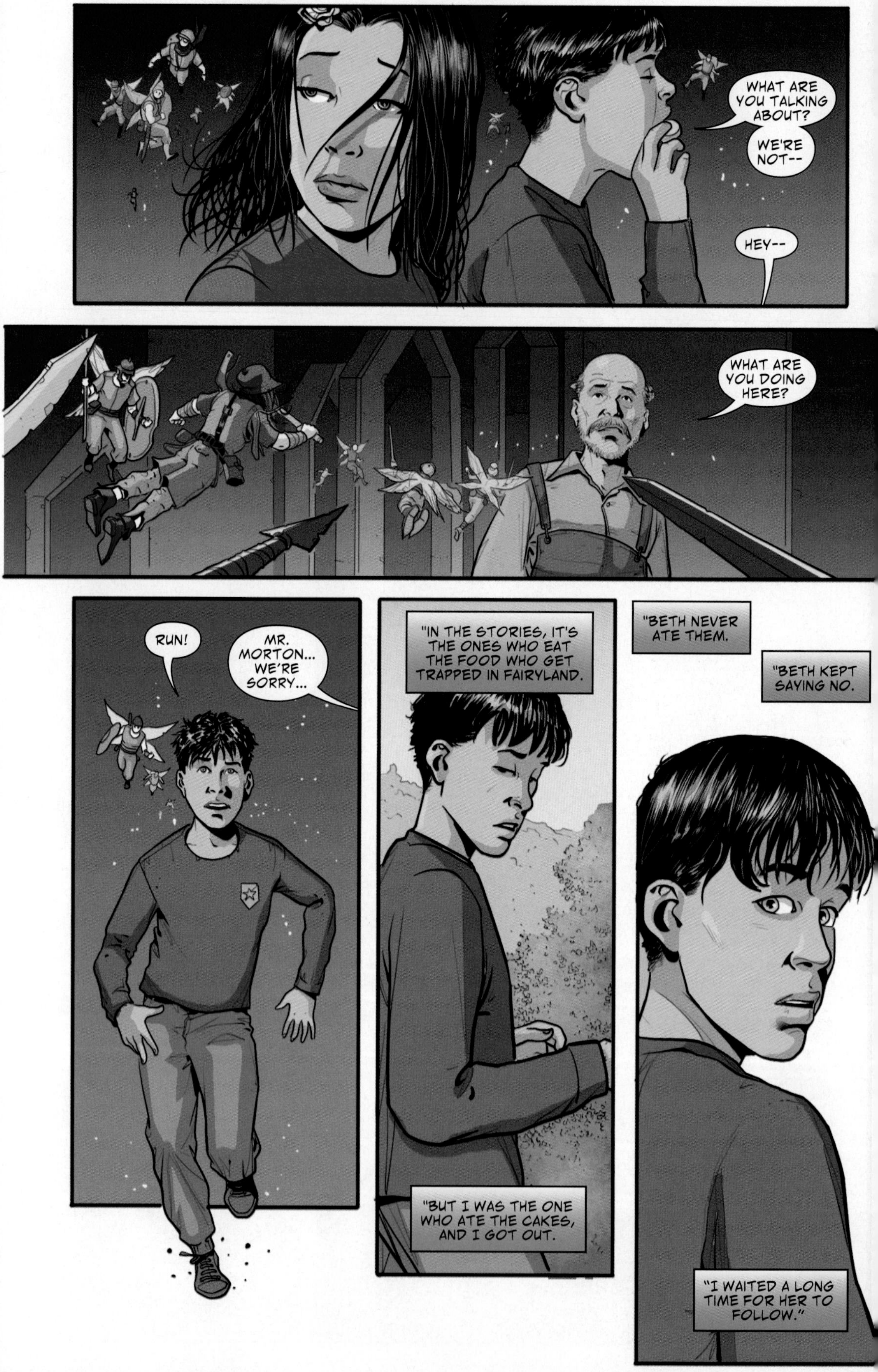

WHAT ARE YOU TALKING ABOUT?
WE'RE NOT--
HEY--
WHAT ARE YOU DOING HERE?
RUN!
MR. MORTON... WE'RE SORRY...
"IN THE STORIES, IT'S THE ONES WHO EAT THE FOOD WHO GET TRAPPED IN FAIRYLAND.
"BUT I WAS THE ONE WHO ATE THE CAKES, AND I GOT OUT.
"BETH NEVER ATE THEM.
"BETH KEPT SAYING NO.
"I WAITED A LONG TIME FOR HER TO FOLLOW."

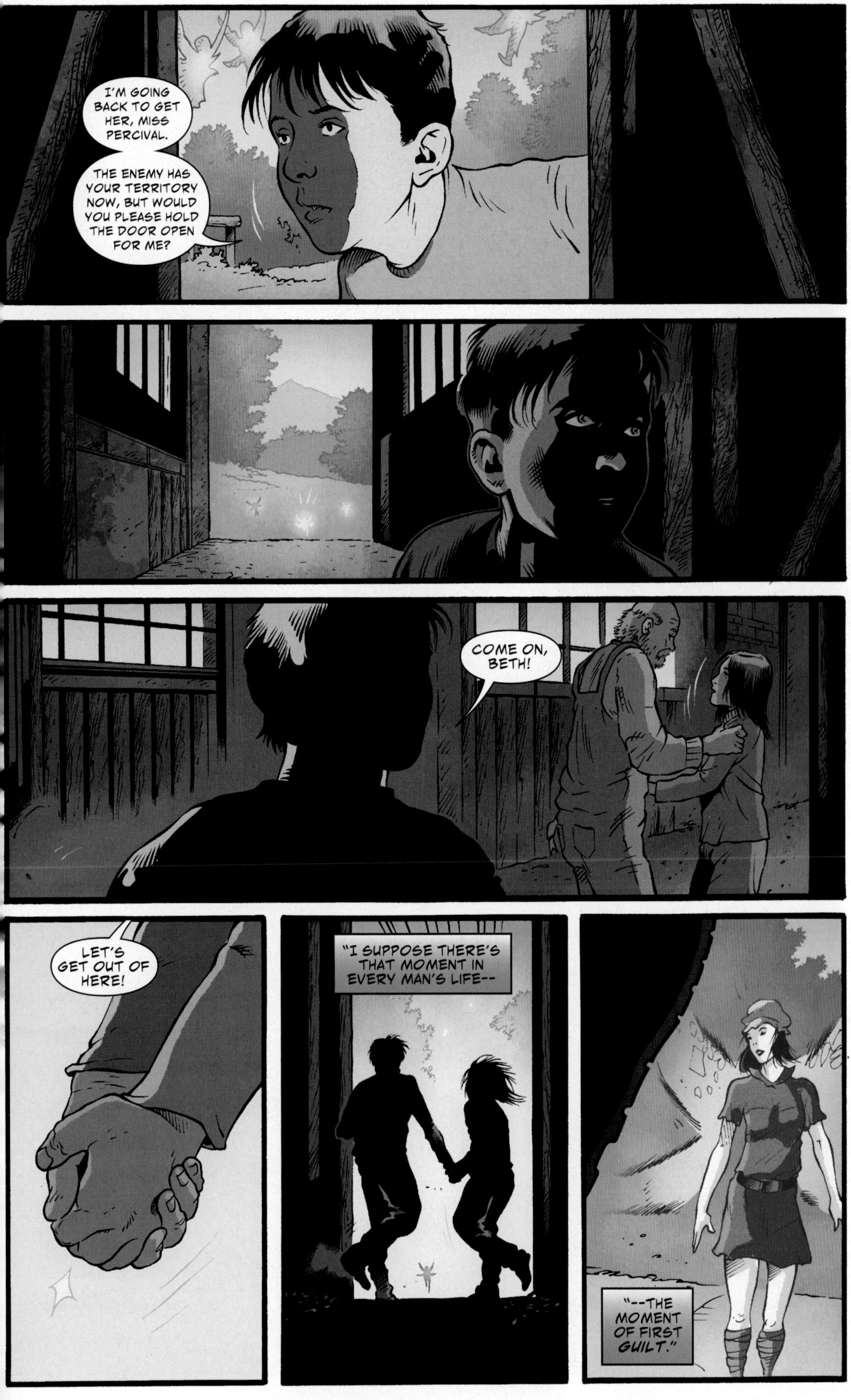
I'M GOING BACK TO GET HER, MISS PERCIVAL.
THE ENEMY HAS YOUR TERRITORY NOW, BUT WOULD YOU PLEASE HOLD THE DOOR OPEN FOR ME?
COME ON, BETH!
LET'S GET OUT OF HERE!
"I SUPPOSE THERE'S THAT MOMENT IN EVERY MAN'S LIFE--
"--THE MOMENT OF FIRST GUILT."

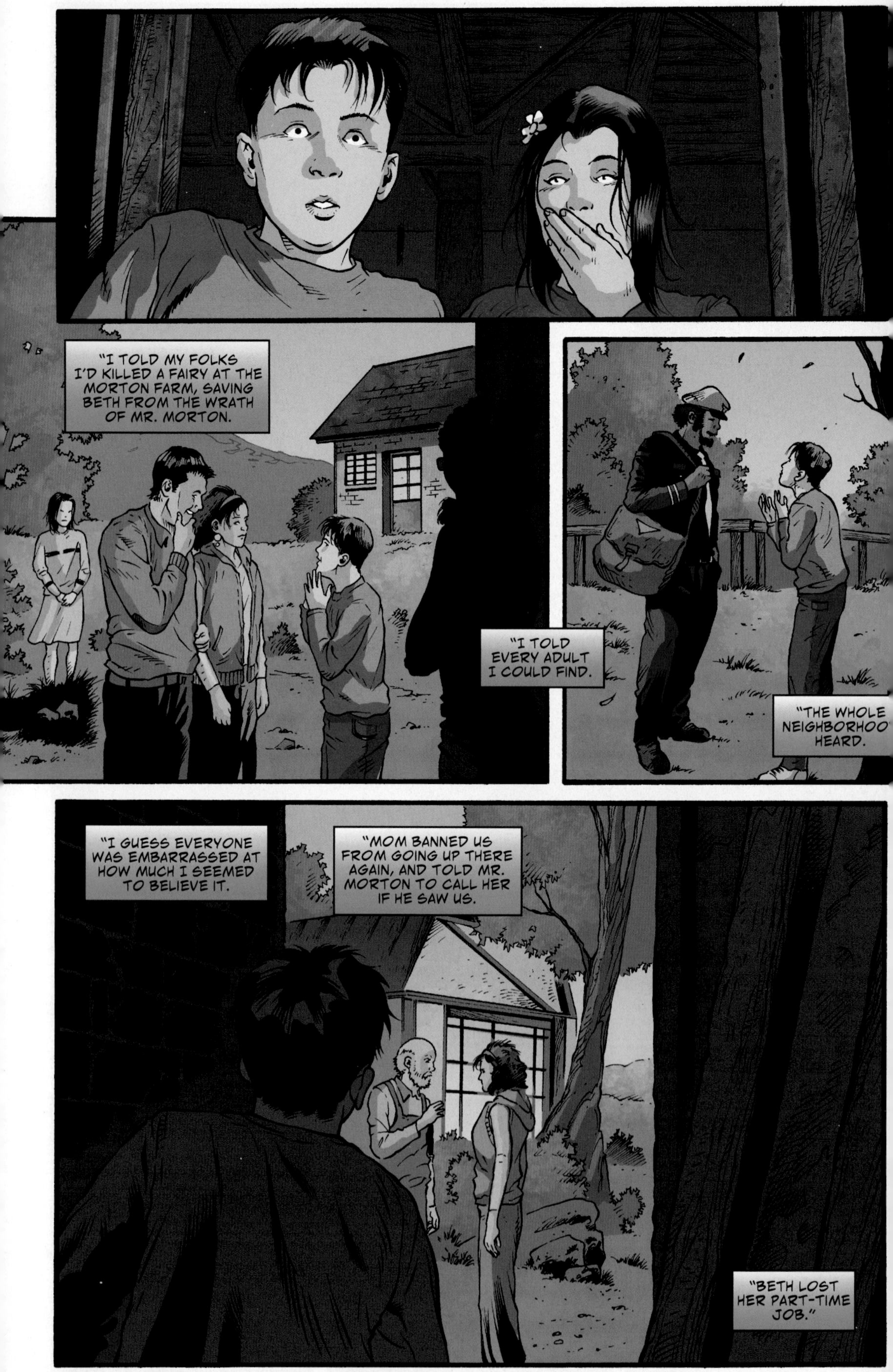
"I TOLD MY FOLKS I'D KILLED A FAIRY AT THE MORTON FARM, SAVING BETH FROM THE WRATH OF MR. MORTON.
"I TOLD EVERY ADULT I COULD FIND.
"THE WHOLE NEIGHBORHOO HEARD.
"I GUESS EVERYONE WAS EMBARRASSED AT HOW MUCH I SEEMED TO BELIEVE IT.
"MOM BANNED US FROM GOING UP THERE AGAIN, AND TOLD MR. MORTON TO CALL HER IF HE SAW US.
"BETH LOST HER PART-TIME JOB."

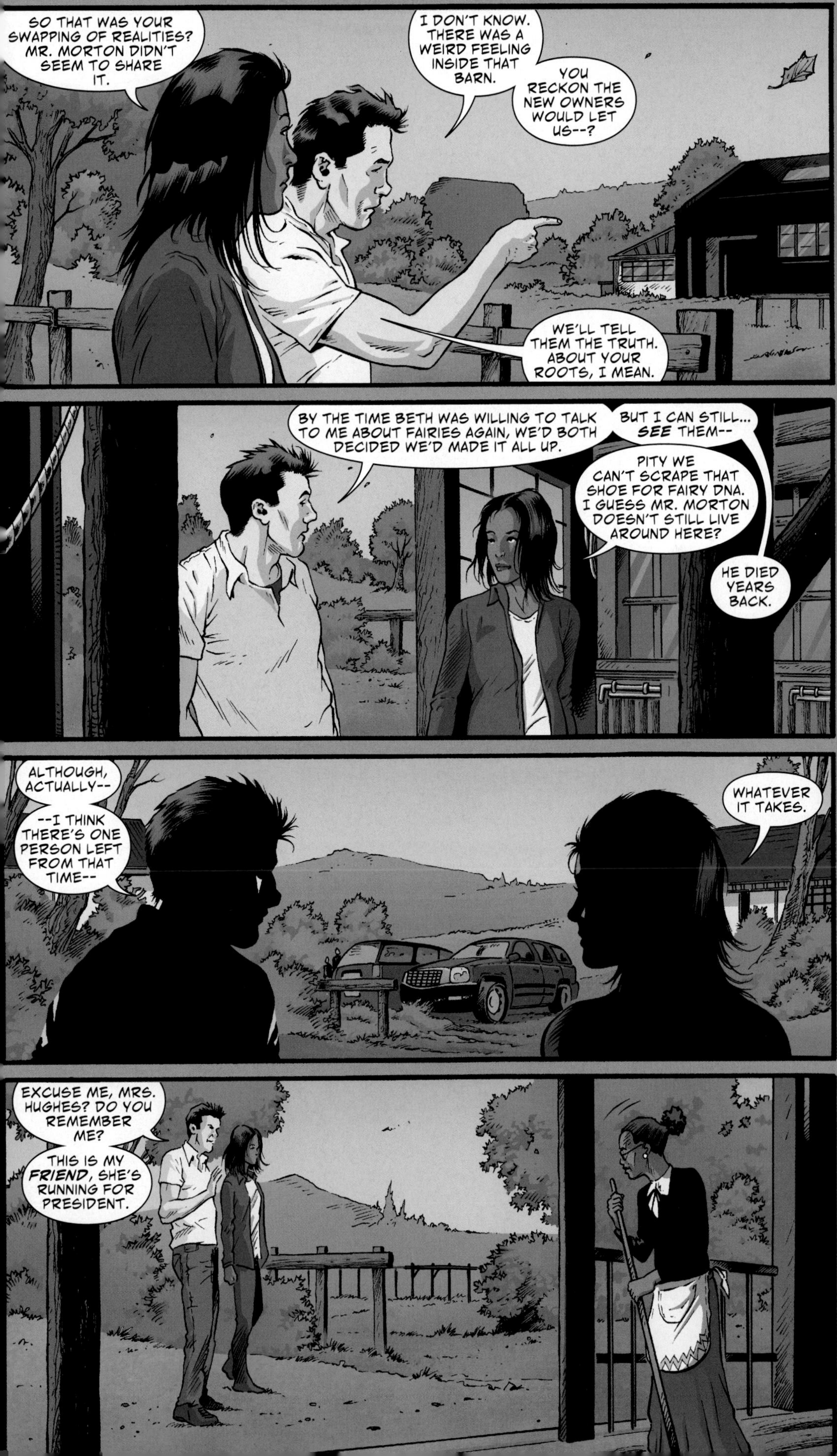
SO THAT WAS YOUR SWAPPING OF REALITIES? MR. MORTON DIDN'T SEEM TO SHARE IT.
I DON'T KNOW. THERE WAS A WEIRD FEELING INSIDE THAT BARN.
YOU RECKON THE NEW OWNERS WOULD LET US--?
WE'LL TELL THEM THE TRUTH. ABOUT YOUR ROOTS, I MEAN.
BY THE TIME BETH WAS WILLING TO TALK TO ME ABOUT FAIRIES AGAIN, WE'D BOTH DECIDED WE'D MADE IT ALL UP.
BUT I CAN STILL... SEE THEM--
PITY WE CAN'T SCRAPE THAT SHOE FOR FAIRY DNA. I GUESS MR. MORTON DOESN'T STILL LIVE AROUND HERE?
HE DIED YEARS BACK.
ALTHOUGH, ACTUALLY--
--I THINK THERE'S ONE PERSON LEFT FROM THAT TIME--
WHATEVER IT TAKES.
EXCUSE ME, MRS. HUGHES? DO YOU REMEMBER ME?
THIS IS MY FRIEND, SHE'S RUNNING FOR PRESIDENT.

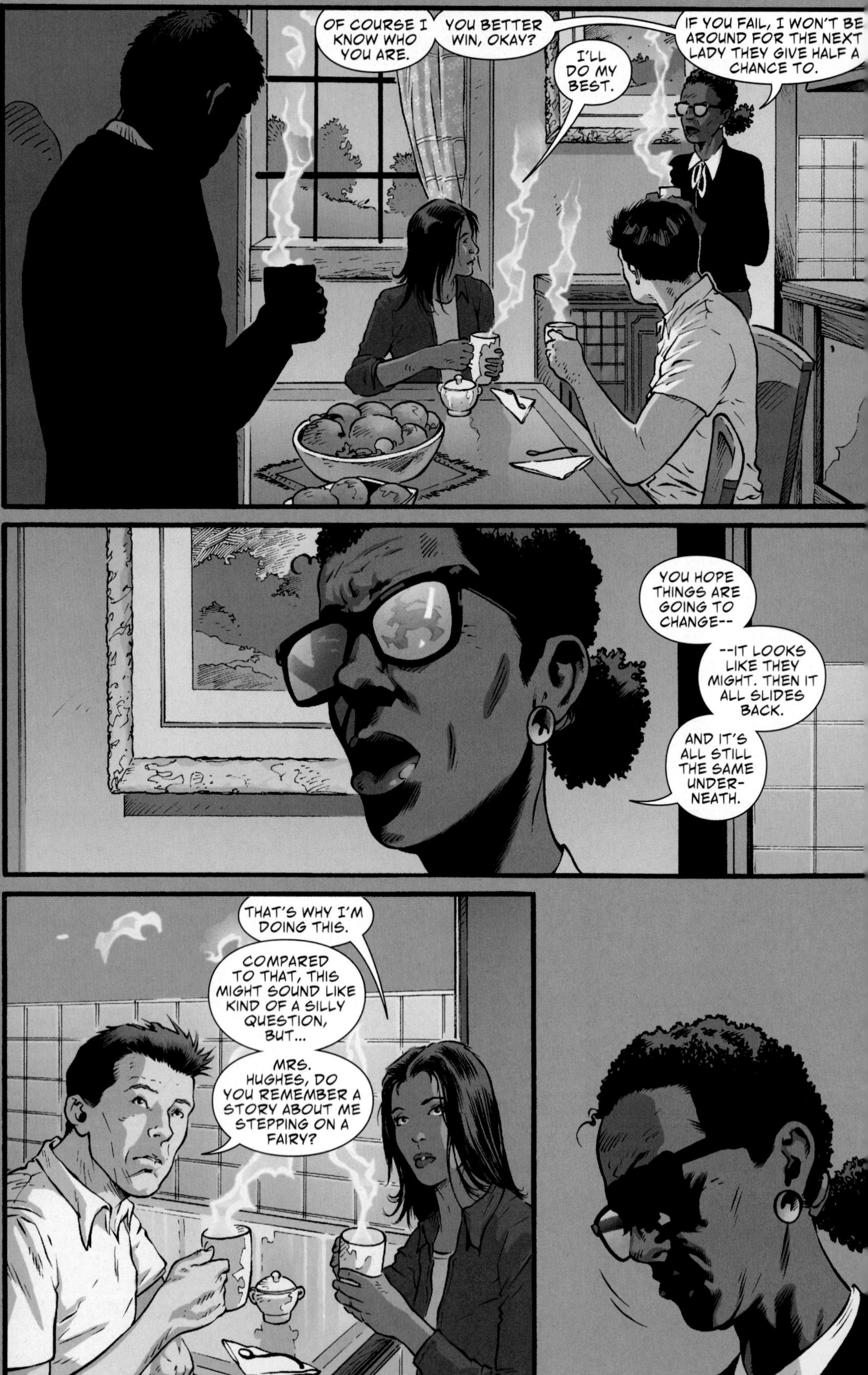
OF COURSE I KNOW WHO YOU ARE.
YOU BETTER WIN, OKAY?
I'LL DO MY BEST.
IF YOU FAIL, I WON'T BE AROUND FOR THE NEXT LADY THEY GIVE HALF A CHANCE TO.
YOU HOPE THINGS ARE GOING TO CHANGE--
--IT LOOKS LIKE THEY MIGHT. THEN IT ALL SLIDES BACK.
AND IT'S ALL STILL THE SAME UNDER-NEATH.
THAT'S WHY I'M DOING THIS.
COMPARED TO THAT, THIS MIGHT SOUND LIKE KIND OF A SILLY QUESTION, BUT...
MRS. HUGHES, DO YOU REMEMBER A STORY ABOUT ME STEPPING ON A FAIRY?

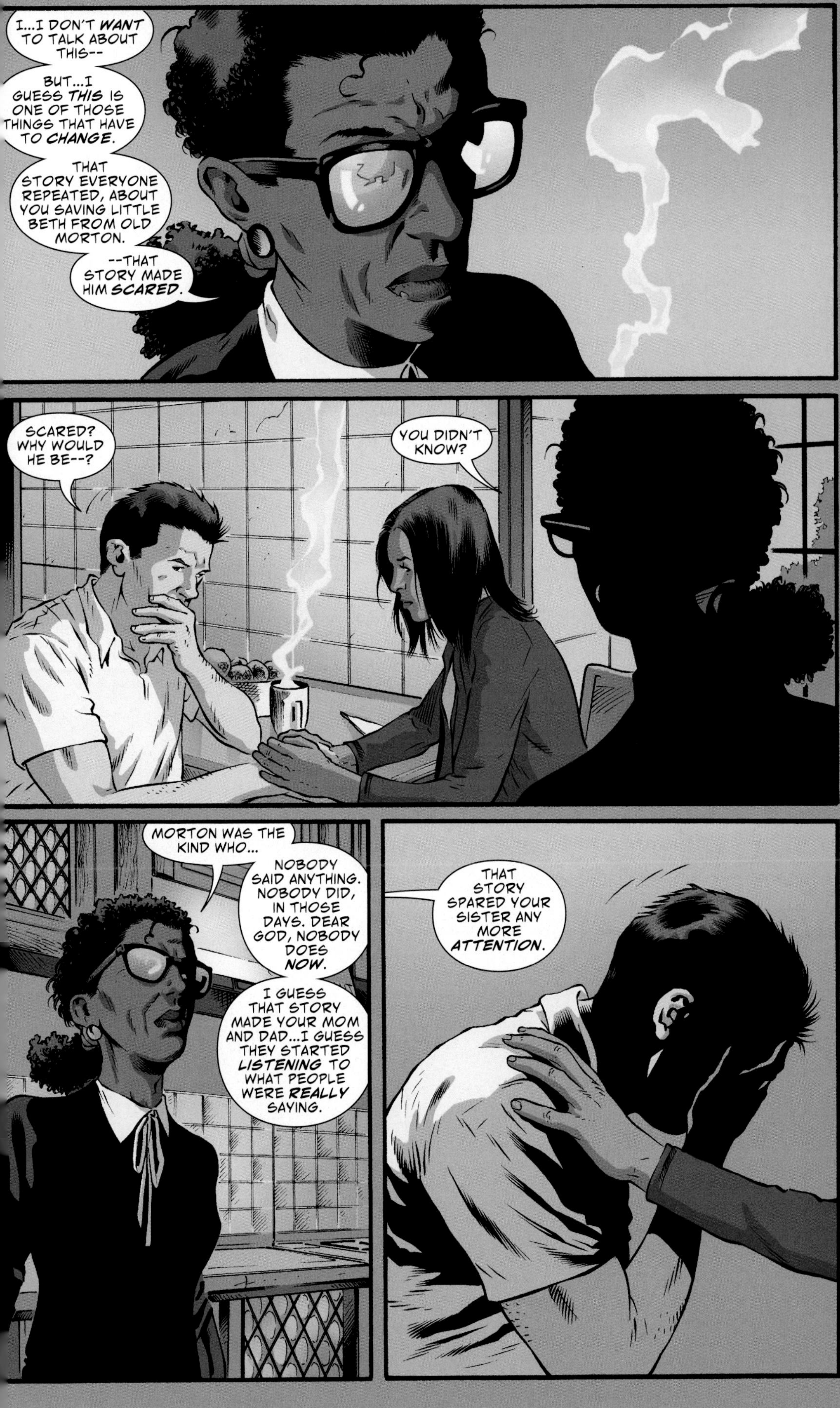

I...I DON'T **WANT** TO TALK ABOUT THIS--
BUT...I GUESS **THIS** IS ONE OF THOSE THINGS THAT HAVE TO **CHANGE**.
THAT STORY EVERYONE REPEATED, ABOUT YOU SAVING LITTLE BETH FROM OLD MORTON.
--THAT STORY MADE HIM **SCARED**.
SCARED? WHY WOULD HE BE--?
YOU DIDN'T KNOW?
MORTON WAS THE KIND WHO...
NOBODY SAID ANYTHING. NOBODY DID, IN THOSE DAYS. DEAR GOD, NOBODY DOES **NOW**.
I GUESS THAT STORY MADE YOUR MOM AND DAD...I GUESS THEY STARTED **LISTENING** TO WHAT PEOPLE WERE **REALLY** SAYING.
THAT STORY SPARED YOUR SISTER ANY MORE **ATTENTION**.

I DIDN'T KNOW. OR MAYBE... MAYBE SOME PART OF ME DID?

SHE NEVER TOLD ME, NOT ALL THOSE YEARS AFTER.

"WE"?

WE NEVER DO.

JANITOR, INVITED ME INTO HIS CUPBOARD.

YOU NEVER--

HE GOT FIRED SOON AFTER. NOBODY SAID ANYTHING. THEY NEVER DO.

I FEEL LIKE BY MAKING UP FANTASIES ABOUT FAIRIES...I ALLOWED THIS. I COULD HAVE JUST TOLD PEOPLE MORTON HAD HIS HANDS ON HER. I COULD HAVE ASKED HER WHY HE WAS ALWAYS THE VILLAIN.

OR...A KINDER READING IS...THAT YOU SAVED HER.

THAT'S TOO SEDUCTIVE. TO BE LET OFF THE HOOK LIKE THAT.

MICHAEL, I DON'T HAVE THE MAGIC POWER TO ABSOLVE YOU OF YOUR GUILT--

--NOT ABOUT THIS, NOT ABOUT US.

I JUST WISH YOU'D DO SOMETHING ABOUT IT.

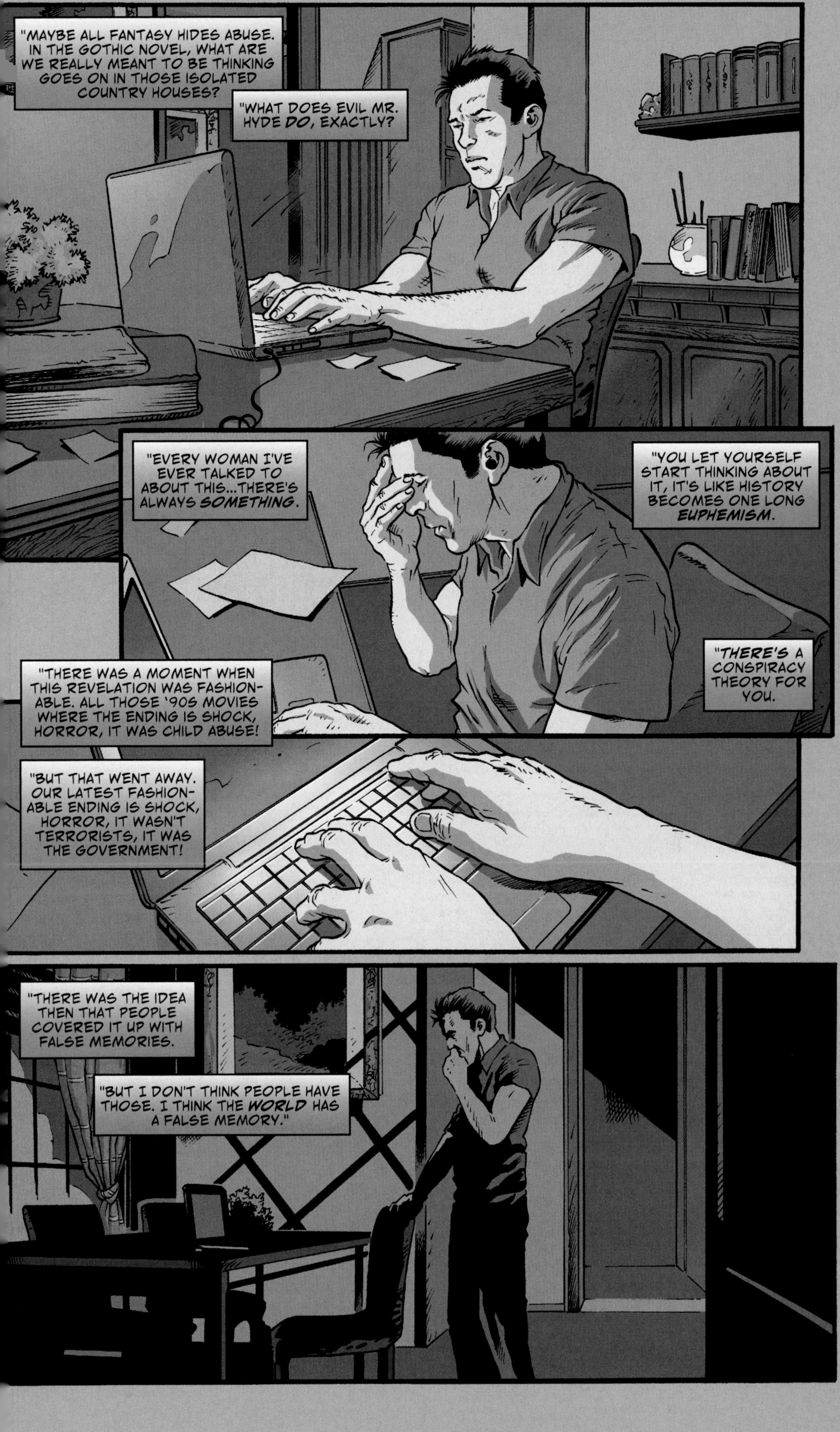
"MAYBE ALL FANTASY HIDES ABUSE. IN THE GOTHIC NOVEL, WHAT ARE WE REALLY MEANT TO BE THINKING GOES ON IN THOSE ISOLATED COUNTRY HOUSES?
"WHAT DOES EVIL MR. HYDE *DO*, EXACTLY?
"EVERY WOMAN I'VE EVER TALKED TO ABOUT THIS...THERE'S ALWAYS *SOMETHING*.
"YOU LET YOURSELF START THINKING ABOUT IT, IT'S LIKE HISTORY BECOMES ONE LONG *EUPHEMISM*.
"*THERE'S* A CONSPIRACY THEORY FOR YOU.
"THERE WAS A *MOMENT* WHEN THIS REVELATION WAS FASHION-ABLE. ALL THOSE '90S MOVIES WHERE THE ENDING IS SHOCK, HORROR, IT WAS CHILD ABUSE!
"BUT THAT WENT AWAY. OUR LATEST FASHION-ABLE ENDING IS SHOCK, HORROR, IT WASN'T TERRORISTS, IT WAS THE GOVERNMENT!
"THERE WAS THE IDEA THEN THAT PEOPLE COVERED IT UP WITH FALSE MEMORIES.
"BUT I DON'T THINK PEOPLE HAVE THOSE. I THINK THE *WORLD* HAS A FALSE MEMORY."

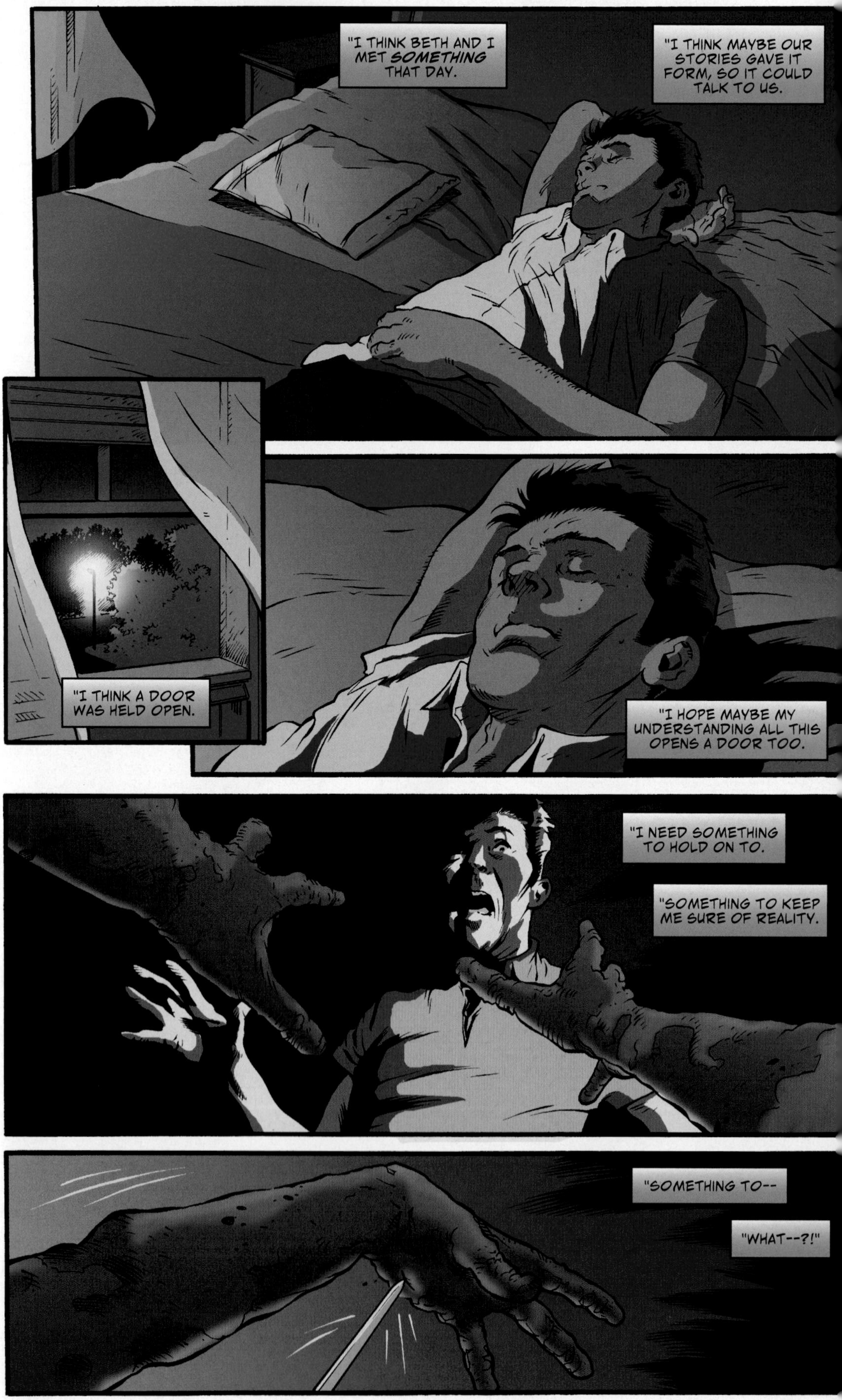
"I THINK BETH AND I MET SOMETHING THAT DAY.
"I THINK MAYBE OUR STORIES GAVE IT FORM, SO IT COULD TALK TO US.
"I THINK A DOOR WAS HELD OPEN.
"I HOPE MAYBE MY UNDERSTANDING ALL THIS OPENS A DOOR TOO.
"I NEED SOMETHING TO HOLD ON TO.
"SOMETHING TO KEEP ME SURE OF REALITY.
"SOMETHING TO--
"WHAT--?!"

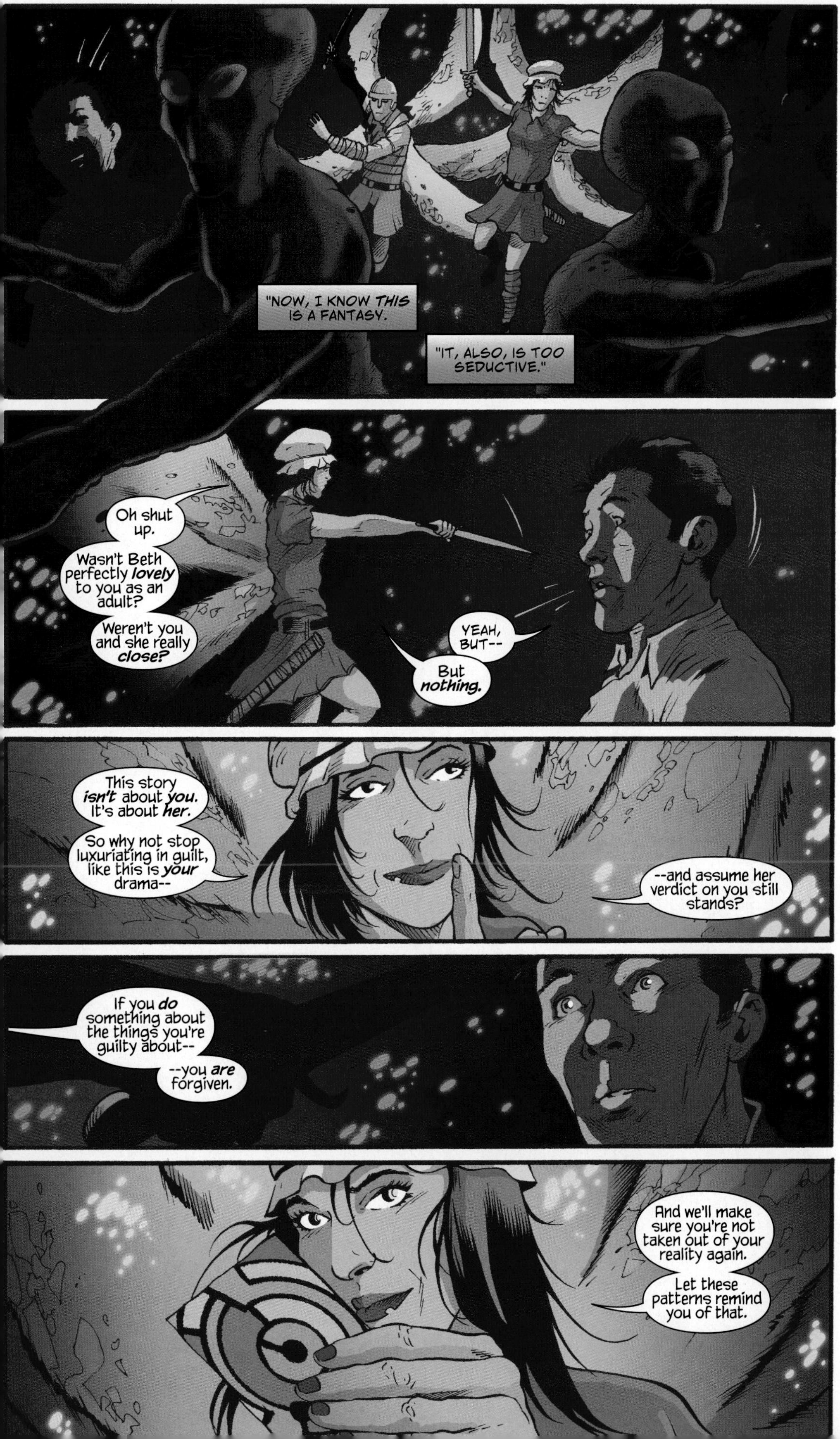
"NOW, I KNOW THIS IS A FANTASY.
"IT, ALSO, IS TOO SEDUCTIVE."
Oh shut up.
Wasn't Beth perfectly lovely to you as an adult?
Weren't you and she really close?
YEAH, BUT--
But nothing.
This story isn't about you. It's about her.
So why not stop luxuriating in guilt, like this is your drama--
--and assume her verdict on you still stands?
If you do something about the things you're guilty about--
--you are forgiven.
And we'll make sure you're not taken out of your reality again.
Let these patterns remind you of that.

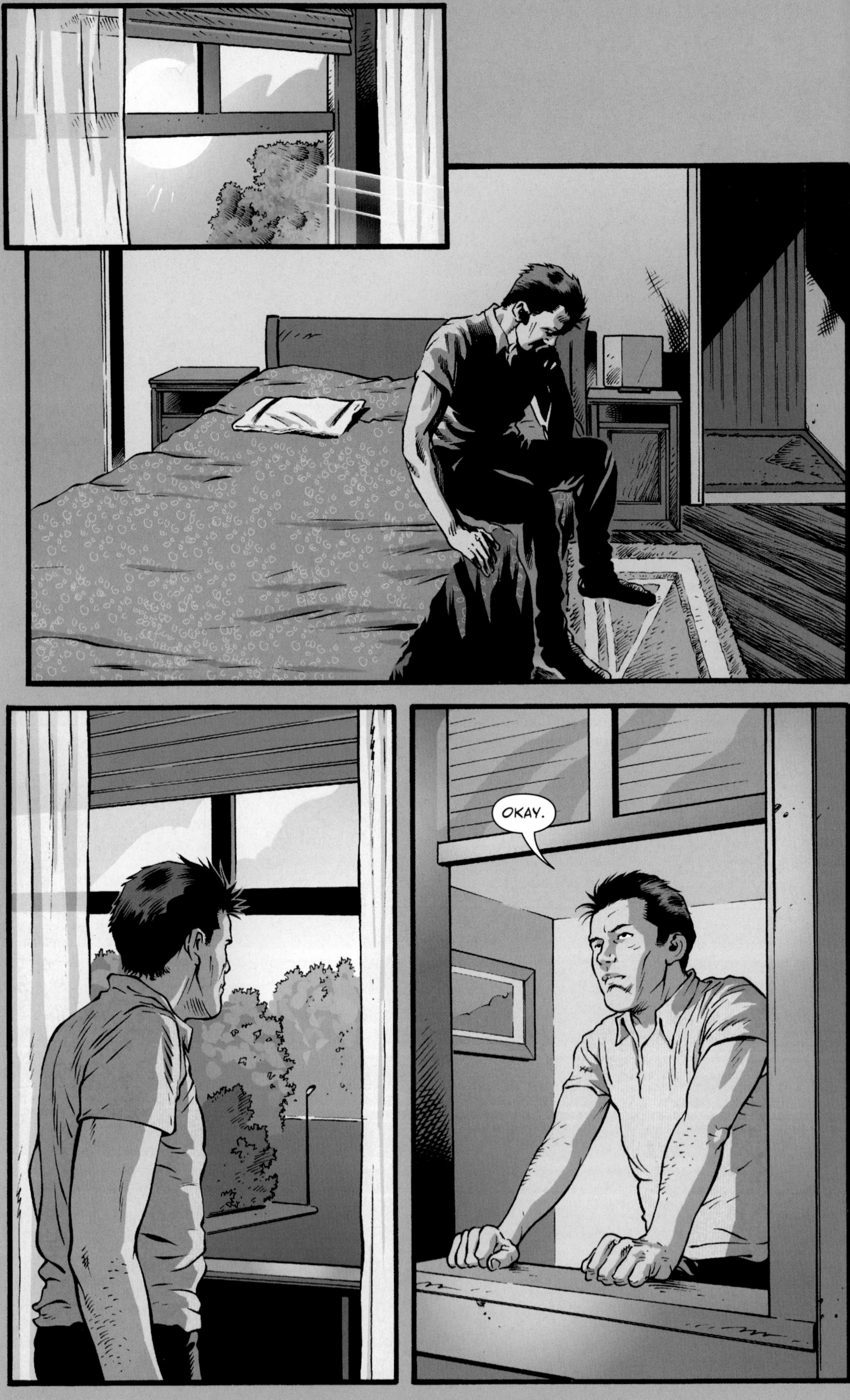
OKAY.

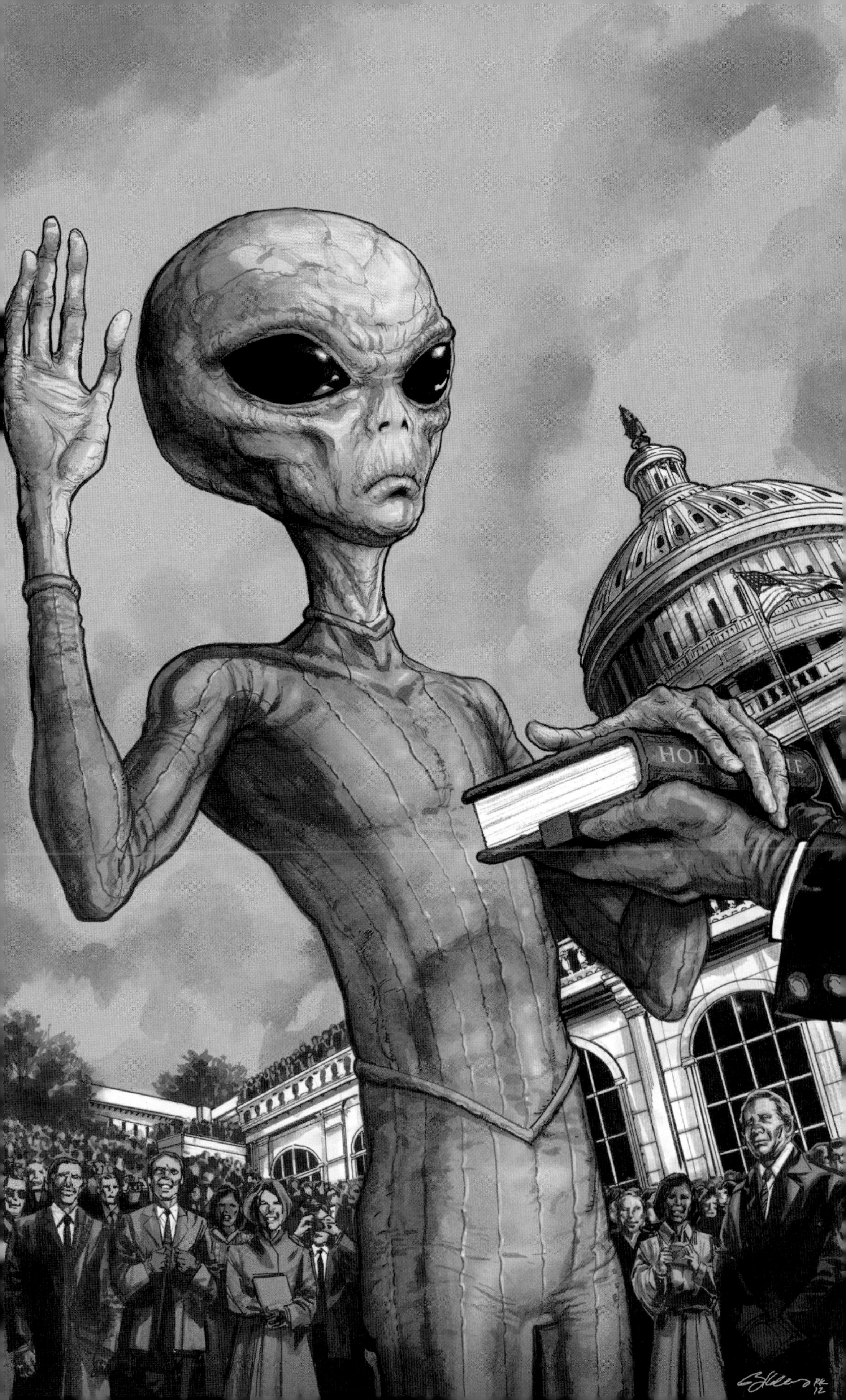

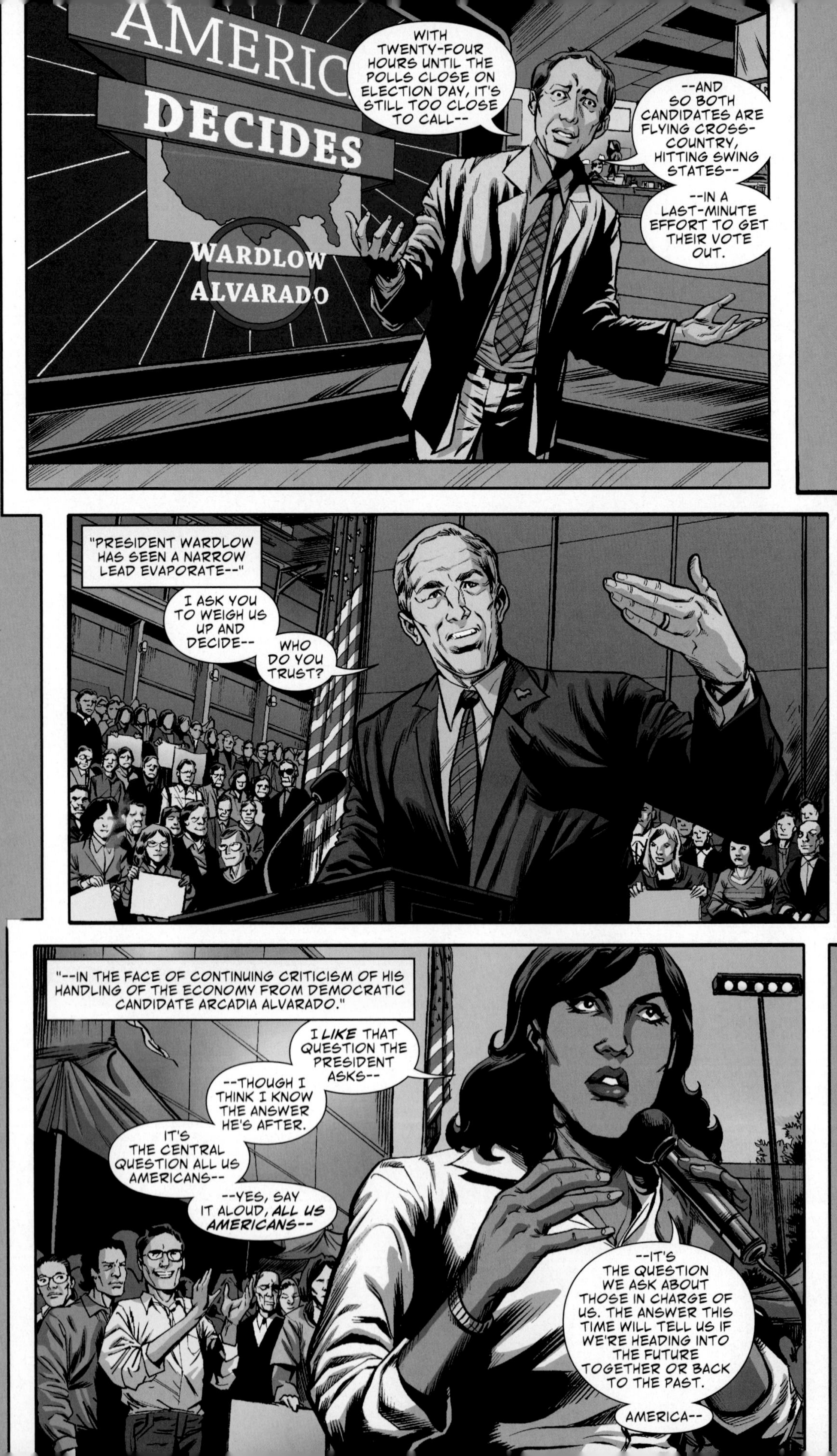
AMERICA DECIDES
WARDLOW
ALVARADO
WITH TWENTY-FOUR HOURS UNTIL THE POLLS CLOSE ON ELECTION DAY, IT'S STILL TOO CLOSE TO CALL--
--AND SO BOTH CANDIDATES ARE FLYING CROSS-COUNTRY, HITTING SWING STATES--
--IN A LAST-MINUTE EFFORT TO GET THEIR VOTE OUT.
"PRESIDENT WARDLOW HAS SEEN A NARROW LEAD EVAPORATE--"
I ASK YOU TO WEIGH US UP AND DECIDE--
WHO DO YOU TRUST?
"--IN THE FACE OF CONTINUING CRITICISM OF HIS HANDLING OF THE ECONOMY FROM DEMOCRATIC CANDIDATE ARCADIA ALVARADO."
I *LIKE* THAT QUESTION THE PRESIDENT ASKS--
--THOUGH I THINK I KNOW THE ANSWER HE'S AFTER.
IT'S THE CENTRAL QUESTION ALL US AMERICANS--
--YES, SAY IT ALOUD, ***ALL US AMERICANS***--
--IT'S THE QUESTION WE ASK ABOUT THOSE IN CHARGE OF US. THE ANSWER THIS TIME WILL TELL US IF WE'RE HEADING INTO THE FUTURE TOGETHER OR BACK TO THE PAST.
AMERICA--

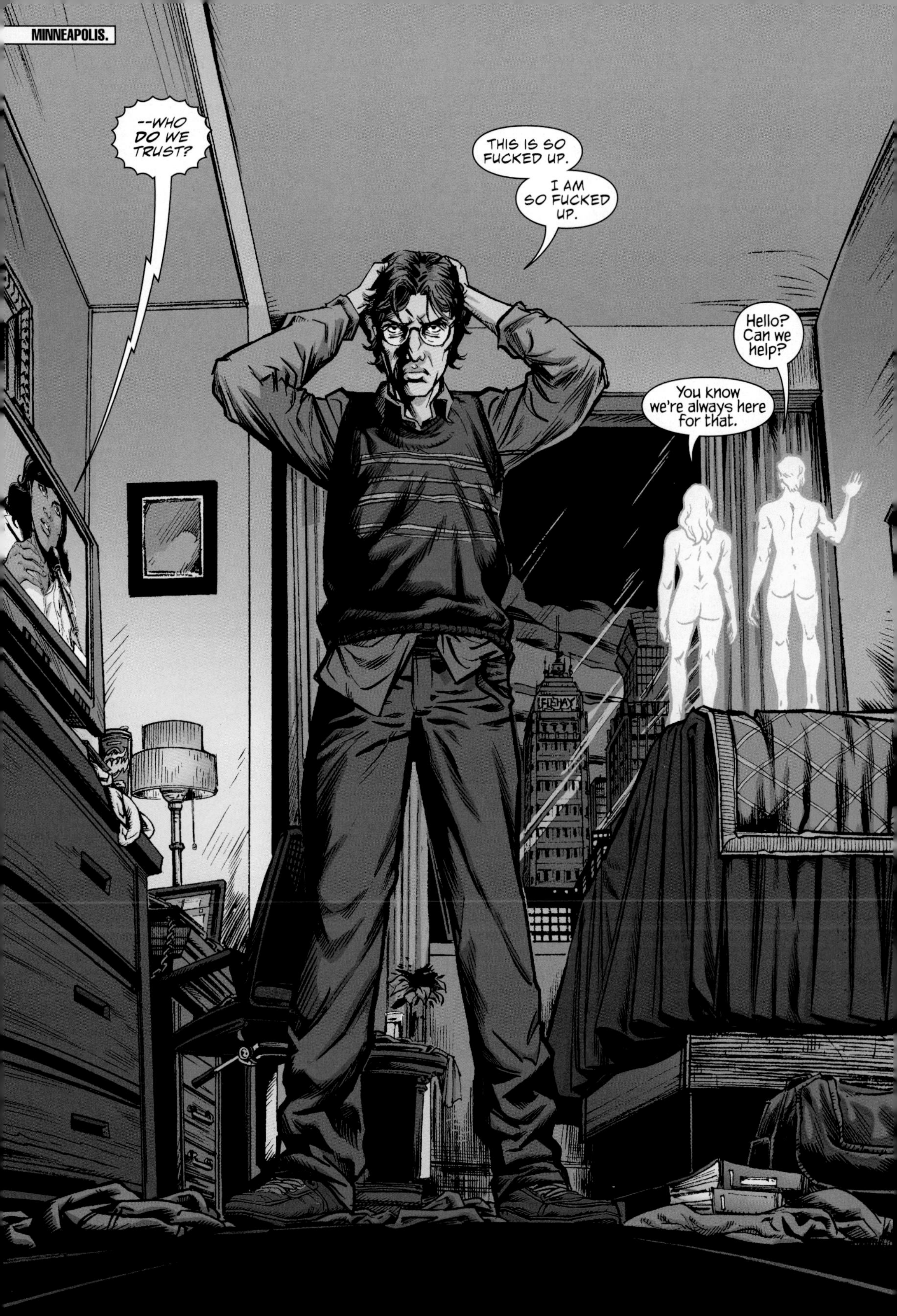
MINNEAPOLIS.
--WHO DO WE TRUST?
THIS IS SO FUCKED UP.
I AM SO FUCKED UP.
Hello? Can we help?
You know we're always here for that.

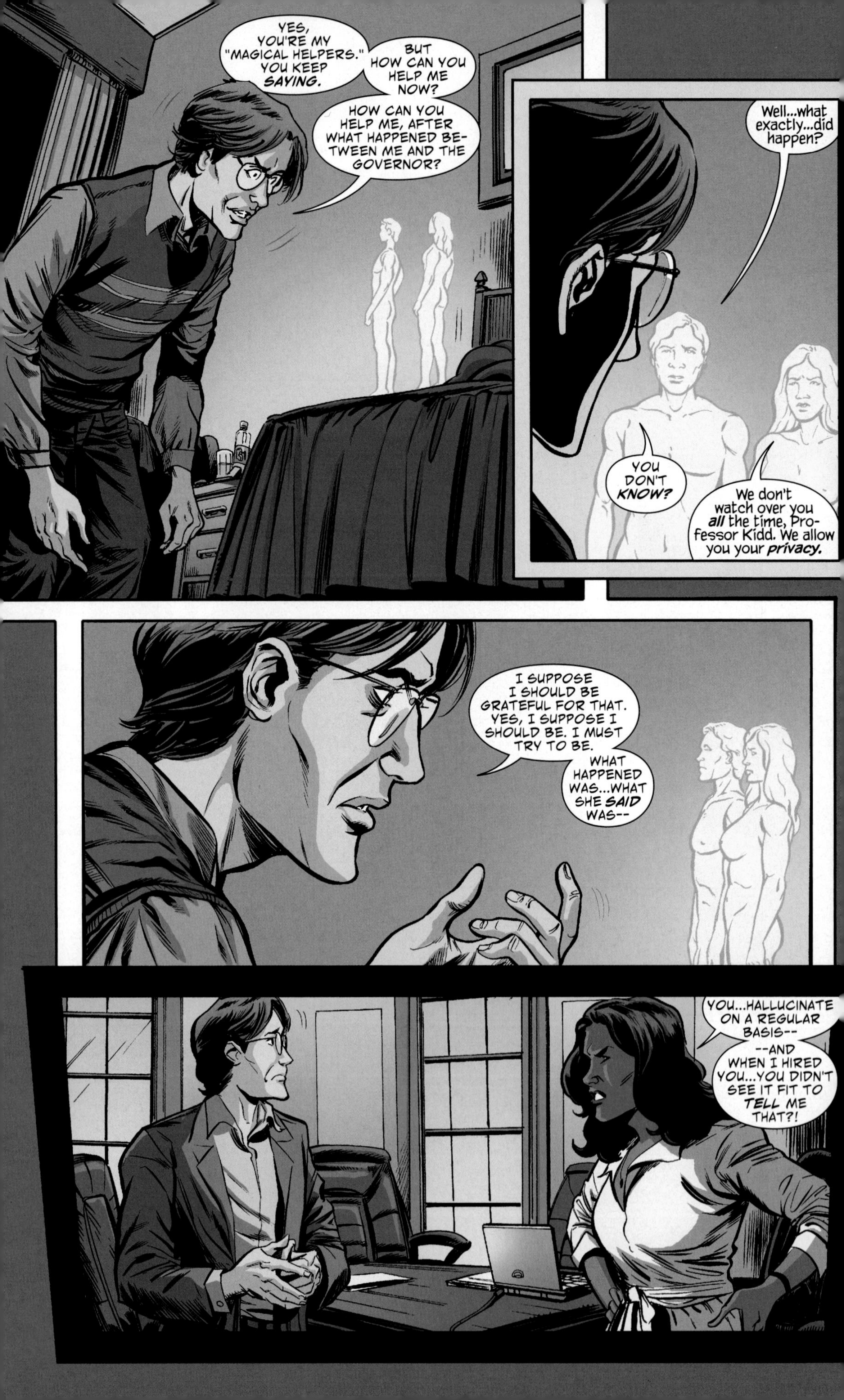

YES, YOU'RE MY "MAGICAL HELPERS." YOU KEEP SAYING.
BUT HOW CAN YOU HELP ME NOW?
HOW CAN YOU HELP ME, AFTER WHAT HAPPENED BE-TWEEN ME AND THE GOVERNOR?
Well...what exactly...did happen?
YOU DON'T KNOW?
We don't watch over you all the time, Pro-fessor Kidd. We allow you your privacy.
I SUPPOSE I SHOULD BE GRATEFUL FOR THAT. YES, I SUPPOSE I SHOULD BE. I MUST TRY TO BE.
WHAT HAPPENED WAS...WHAT SHE SAID WAS--
YOU...HALLUCINATE ON A REGULAR BASIS--
--AND WHEN I HIRED YOU...YOU DIDN'T SEE IT FIT TO TELL ME THAT?!

I THOUGHT... GIVEN YOUR OWN EXPERIENCES--

I DON'T BASE MY DECISIONS ON THE INPUT OF... TINY PEOPLE--!

--PEOPLE WHO...YOU SAY THEY'RE *WHAT*, EXACTLY?

THEY'RE FIGURES DEPICTED ON ALUMINUM PLAQUES ATTACHED TO THE PIONEER 10 AND 11 SPACE PROBES--

--LAUNCHED FROM EARTH IN 1972 AND 1973, AND NOW AT THE FRINGES OF THE SOLAR SYSTEM.

EXCEPT WHEN THEY, YOU KNOW, POP BACK FOR COFFEE.

WHEN DID THEY *START TELLING* YOU STUFF?

A COUPLE OF YEARS BACK. WHEN I BEGAN MY UFO WORK. I KNOW VERY LITTLE ABOUT THEM.

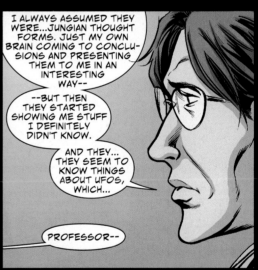

I ALWAYS ASSUMED THEY WERE...JUNGIAN THOUGHT FORMS. JUST MY OWN BRAIN COMING TO CONCLUSIONS AND PRESENTING THEM TO ME IN AN INTERESTING WAY--

--BUT THEN THEY STARTED SHOWING ME STUFF I DEFINITELY DIDN'T KNOW.

AND THEY... THEY SEEM TO KNOW THINGS ABOUT UFOS, WHICH...

PROFESSOR--

--YOU LOST ME AT "JUNGIAN THOUGHT FORMS."

I REACHED OUT TO YOU BECAUSE I NEEDED A SANE OPINION, AND NOW YOU TELL ME...DEAR GOD.

I DON'T HAVE TIME TO *THINK* ABOUT THIS RIGHT NOW.

CONTINUE YOUR INVESTIGATIONS, PROFESSOR. FOR *NOW*.

WHEN WE'VE DECIDED WHAT TO DO, WE'LL *CALL* YOU.

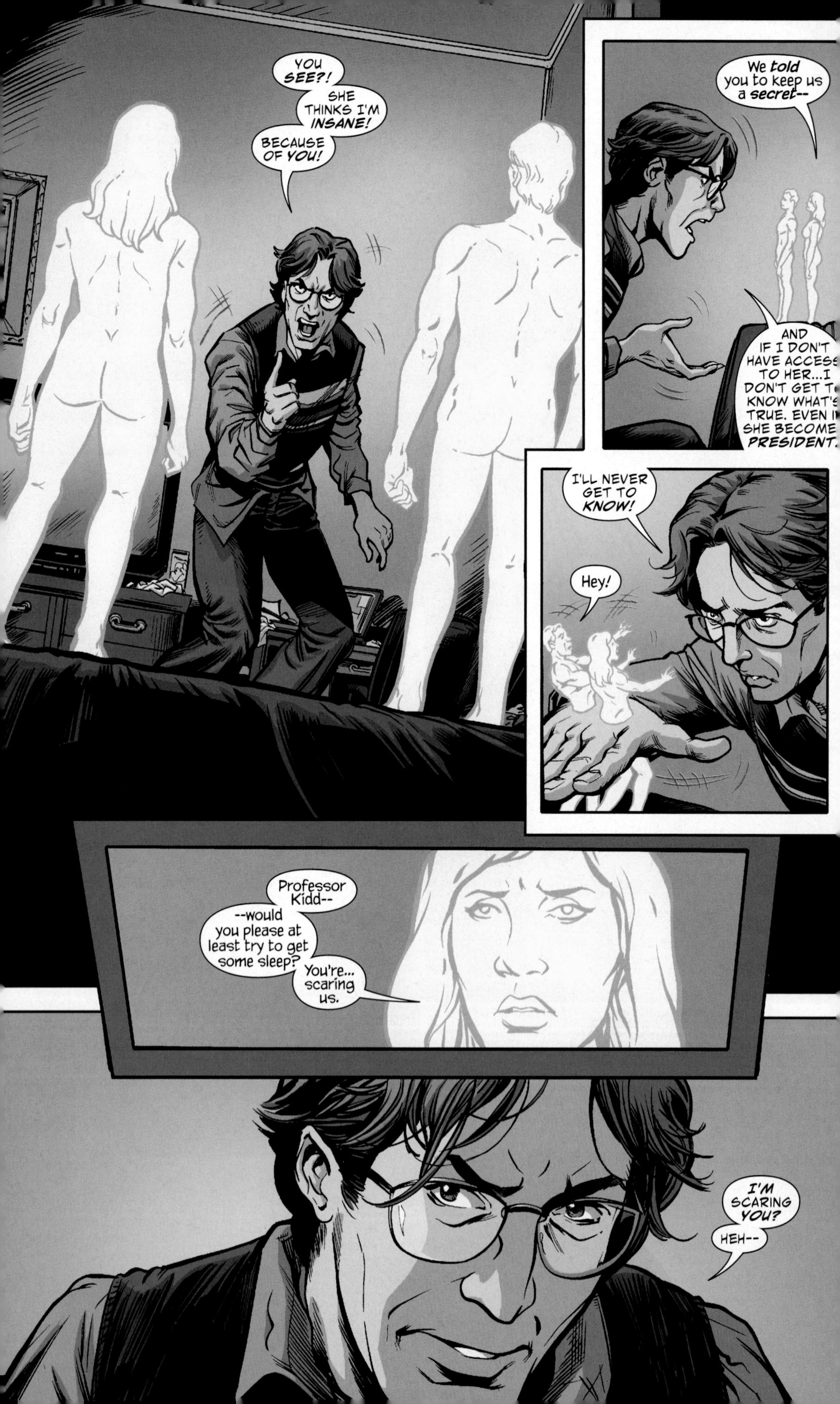
YOU SEE?!
SHE THINKS I'M INSANE!
BECAUSE OF YOU!
We told you to keep us a secret--
AND IF I DON'T HAVE ACCESS TO HER...I DON'T GET TO KNOW WHAT'S TRUE. EVEN IF SHE BECOMES PRESIDENT.
I'LL NEVER GET TO KNOW!
Hey!
Professor Kidd--
--would you please at least try to get some sleep?
You're... scaring us.
I'M SCARING YOU?
HEH--

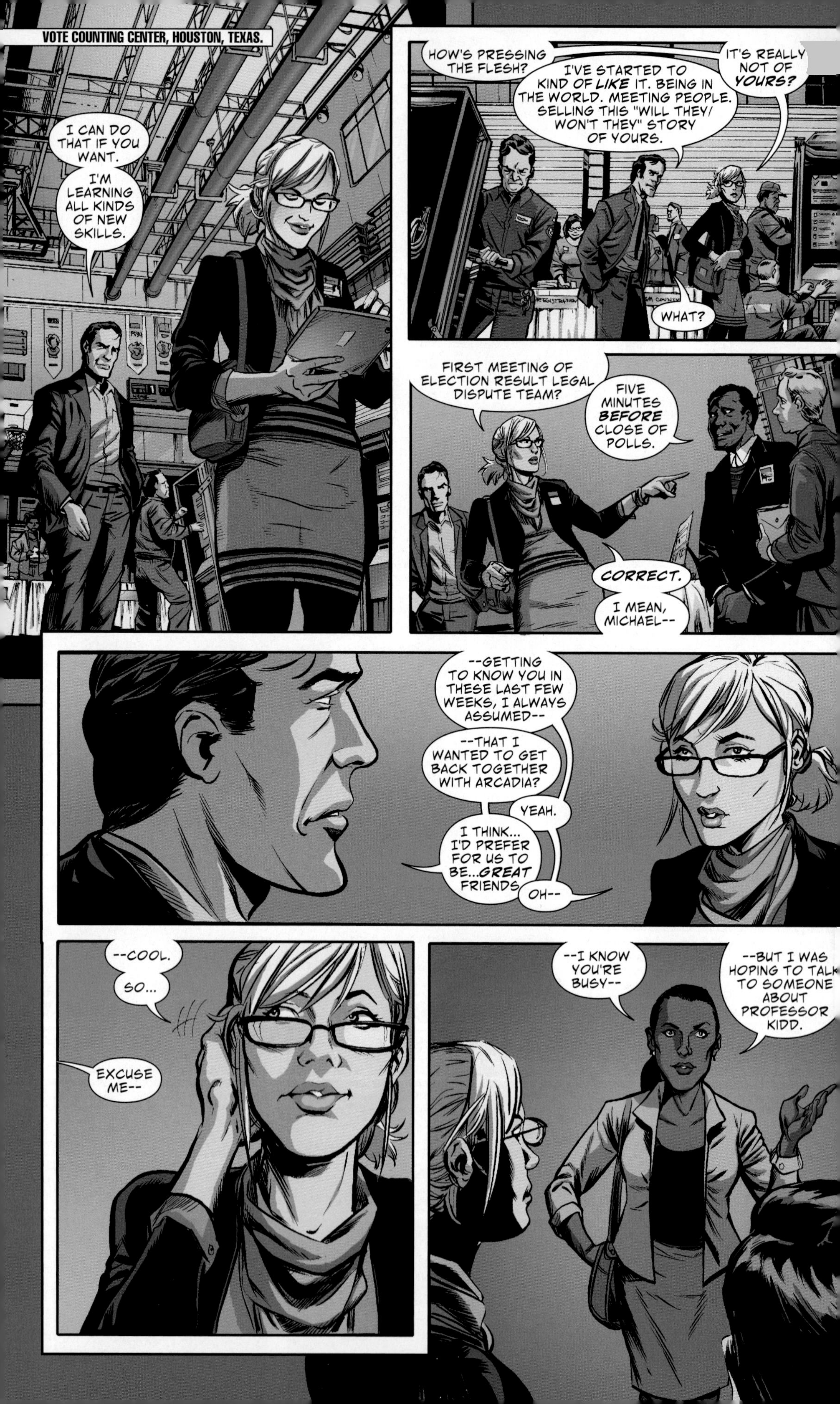
VOTE COUNTING CENTER, HOUSTON, TEXAS.
I CAN DO THAT IF YOU WANT.
I'M LEARNING ALL KINDS OF NEW SKILLS.
HOW'S PRESSING THE FLESH?
I'VE STARTED TO KIND OF *LIKE* IT. BEING IN THE WORLD. MEETING PEOPLE. SELLING THIS "WILL THEY/ WON'T THEY" STORY OF YOURS.
IT'S REALLY NOT OF *YOURS?*
WHAT?
FIRST MEETING OF ELECTION RESULT LEGAL DISPUTE TEAM?
FIVE MINUTES *BEFORE* CLOSE OF POLLS.
CORRECT.
I MEAN, MICHAEL--
--GETTING TO KNOW YOU IN THESE LAST FEW WEEKS, I ALWAYS ASSUMED--
--THAT I WANTED TO GET BACK TOGETHER WITH ARCADIA?
YEAH.
I THINK... I'D PREFER FOR US TO BE...*GREAT* FRIENDS.
OH--
--COOL.
SO...
EXCUSE ME--
--I KNOW YOU'RE BUSY--
--BUT I WAS HOPING TO TALK TO SOMEONE ABOUT PROFESSOR KIDD.

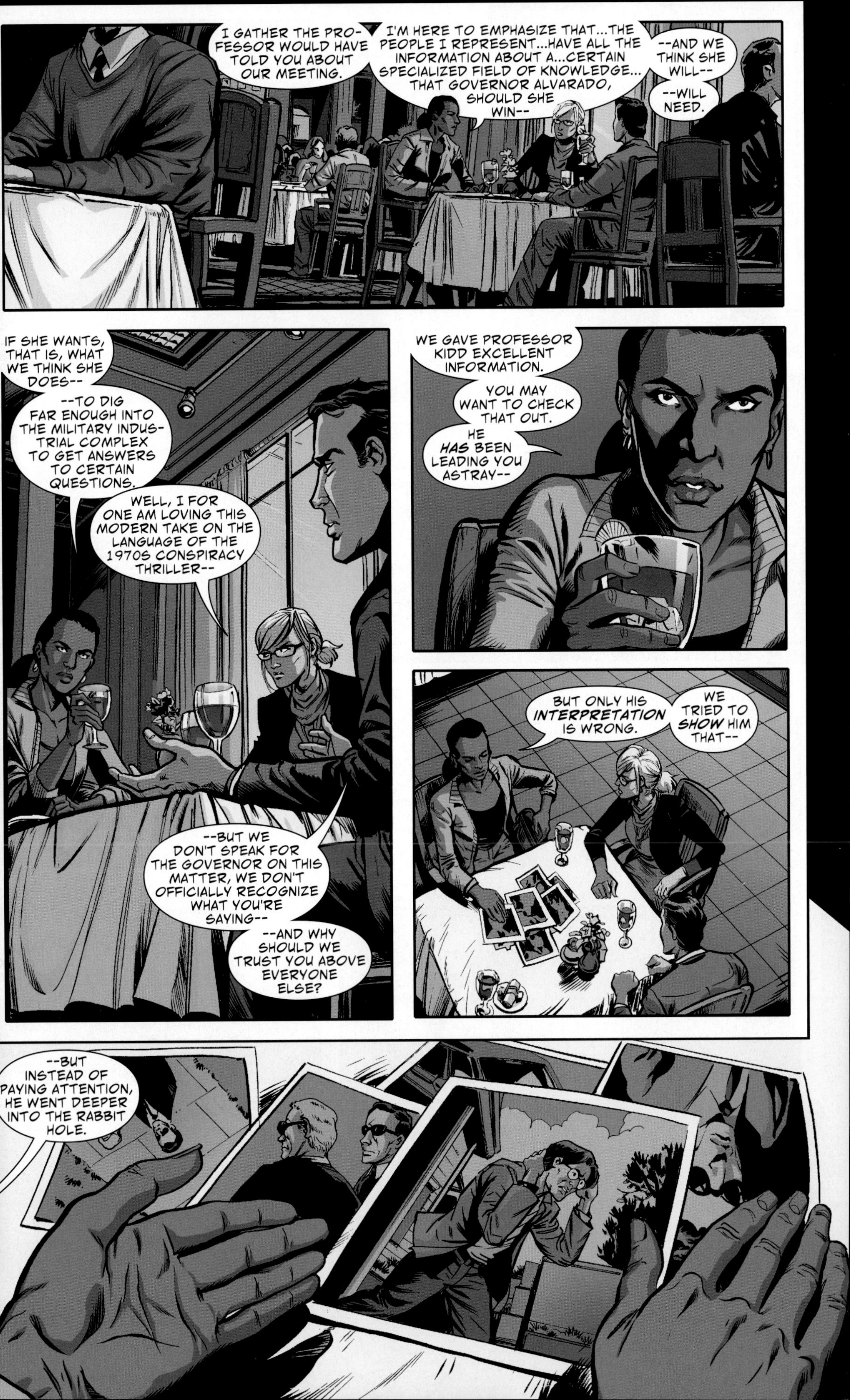
I GATHER THE PROFESSOR WOULD HAVE TOLD YOU ABOUT OUR MEETING.
I'M HERE TO EMPHASIZE THAT...THE PEOPLE I REPRESENT...HAVE ALL THE INFORMATION ABOUT A...CERTAIN SPECIALIZED FIELD OF KNOWLEDGE... THAT GOVERNOR ALVARADO, SHOULD SHE WIN--
--AND WE THINK SHE WILL--
--WILL NEED.
IF SHE WANTS, THAT IS, WHAT WE THINK SHE DOES--
--TO DIG FAR ENOUGH INTO THE MILITARY INDUSTRIAL COMPLEX TO GET ANSWERS TO CERTAIN QUESTIONS.
WELL, I FOR ONE AM LOVING THIS MODERN TAKE ON THE LANGUAGE OF THE 1970S CONSPIRACY THRILLER--
--BUT WE DON'T SPEAK FOR THE GOVERNOR ON THIS MATTER, WE DON'T OFFICIALLY RECOGNIZE WHAT YOU'RE SAYING--
--AND WHY SHOULD WE TRUST YOU ABOVE EVERYONE ELSE?
WE GAVE PROFESSOR KIDD EXCELLENT INFORMATION.
YOU MAY WANT TO CHECK THAT OUT.
HE *HAS* BEEN LEADING YOU ASTRAY--
BUT ONLY HIS *INTERPRETATION* IS WRONG.
WE TRIED TO *SHOW* HIM THAT--
--BUT INSTEAD OF PAYING ATTENTION, HE WENT DEEPER INTO THE RABBIT HOLE.

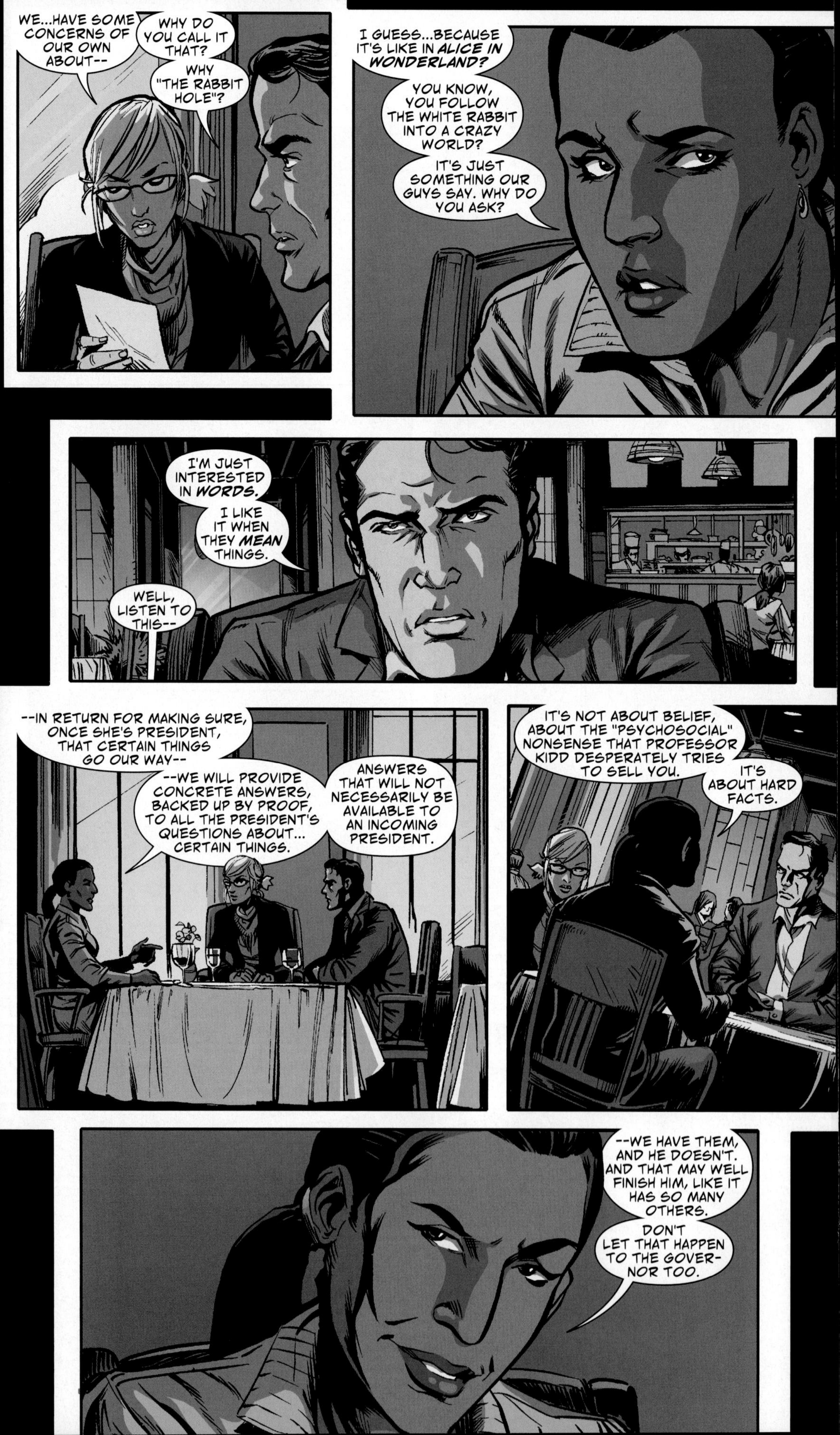

WE...HAVE SOME CONCERNS OF OUR OWN ABOUT--
WHY DO YOU CALL IT THAT?
WHY "THE RABBIT HOLE"?
I GUESS...BECAUSE IT'S LIKE IN *ALICE IN WONDERLAND?*
YOU KNOW, YOU FOLLOW THE WHITE RABBIT INTO A CRAZY WORLD?
IT'S JUST SOMETHING OUR GUYS SAY. WHY DO YOU ASK?
I'M JUST INTERESTED IN *WORDS.*
I LIKE IT WHEN THEY *MEAN* THINGS.
WELL, LISTEN TO THIS--
--IN RETURN FOR MAKING SURE, ONCE SHE'S PRESIDENT, THAT CERTAIN THINGS GO OUR WAY--
--WE WILL PROVIDE CONCRETE ANSWERS, BACKED UP BY PROOF, TO ALL THE PRESIDENT'S QUESTIONS ABOUT... CERTAIN THINGS.
ANSWERS THAT WILL NOT NECESSARILY BE AVAILABLE TO AN INCOMING PRESIDENT.
IT'S NOT ABOUT BELIEF, ABOUT THE "PSYCHOSOCIAL" NONSENSE THAT PROFESSOR KIDD DESPERATELY TRIES TO SELL YOU.
IT'S ABOUT HARD FACTS.
--WE HAVE THEM, AND HE DOESN'T. AND THAT MAY WELL FINISH HIM, LIKE IT HAS SO MANY OTHERS.
DON'T LET THAT HAPPEN TO THE GOVERNOR TOO.

JAMES, THANKS FOR THE FLORIDA SPEECH.

YOU'RE KNOCKING IT OUT OF THE PARK FOR US.

YOU MIND IF I TRAVEL WITH YOU?

SURE, HARRY. ALWAYS A PLEASURE.

SO THE GOVERNOR WAS WONDERING--

--ABOUT THE QUESTION THAT KIND OF DERAILED YOU IN THE CANDIDATE DEBATE--

WHAT, THE ONE ABOUT FLYING SAUCERS?

WHAT ABOUT IT?

THE GOVERNOR *NOTED* YOUR REACTION.

AND LET'S JUST SAY THERE'S SOME FELLOW FEELING ON HER PART.

HARRY, I HAVE SO GOT PAST THAT LINE OF QUESTIONING, I HAVE MADE THE GOP *EAT* THAT--

WE KNOW. WE LOVE YOU FOR THAT.

YOU'RE OUR GUY, JAMES, EVEN MORE SO NOW THAT WE'VE SEEN YOU IN ACTION.

LISTEN, I'M GOING TO MAKE THIS ABSOLUTELY PLAIN. THOUGH I'LL DENY IT IF I HAVE TO--

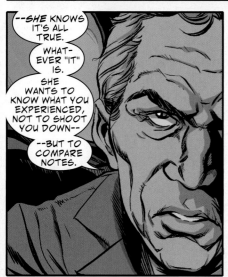

--*SHE* KNOWS IT'S ALL TRUE.

WHATEVER "IT" IS.

SHE WANTS TO KNOW WHAT YOU EXPERIENCED, NOT TO SHOOT YOU DOWN--

--BUT TO COMPARE NOTES.

AND SENATOR--

--YOU *KNOW* WE KNOW ABOUT THE *AFFAIR*.

AND SINCE THE GOP DOESN'T, WE DON'T *CARE*.

BUT WE *REQUIRE* HONESTY FROM YOU ABOUT THIS.

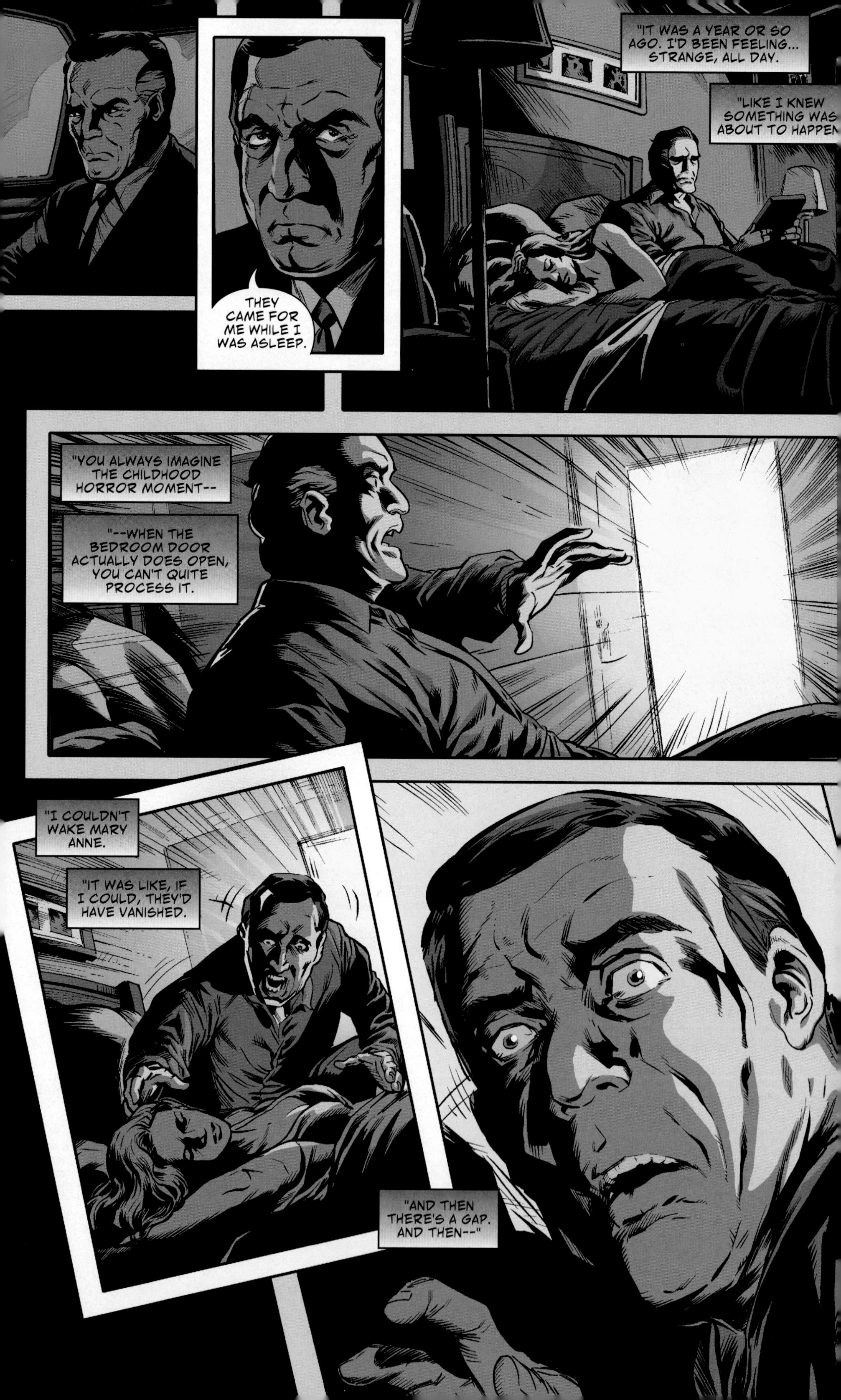

THEY CAME FOR ME WHILE I WAS ASLEEP.
"IT WAS A YEAR OR SO AGO. I'D BEEN FEELING... STRANGE, ALL DAY.
"LIKE I KNEW SOMETHING WAS ABOUT TO HAPPEN
"YOU ALWAYS IMAGINE THE CHILDHOOD HORROR MOMENT--
"--WHEN THE BEDROOM DOOR ACTUALLY DOES OPEN, YOU CAN'T QUITE PROCESS IT.
"I COULDN'T WAKE MARY ANNE.
"IT WAS LIKE, IF I COULD, THEY'D HAVE VANISHED.
"AND THEN THERE'S A GAP. AND THEN--"

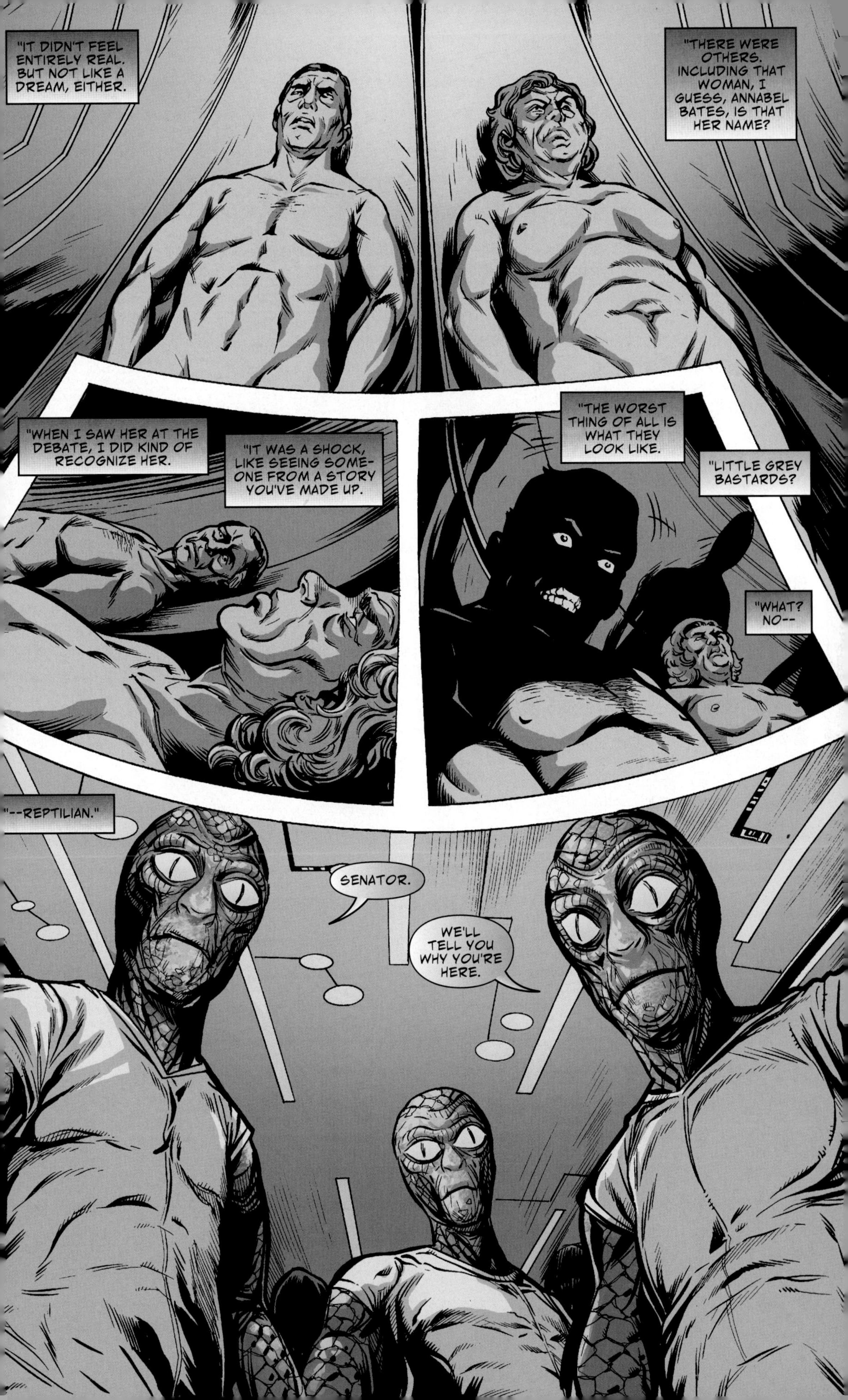
"IT DIDN'T FEEL ENTIRELY REAL. BUT NOT LIKE A DREAM, EITHER.
"THERE WERE OTHERS. INCLUDING THAT WOMAN, I GUESS, ANNABEL BATES, IS THAT HER NAME?
"WHEN I SAW HER AT THE DEBATE, I DID KIND OF RECOGNIZE HER.
"IT WAS A SHOCK, LIKE SEEING SOMEONE FROM A STORY YOU'VE MADE UP.
"THE WORST THING OF ALL IS WHAT THEY LOOK LIKE.
"LITTLE GREY BASTARDS?
"WHAT? NO--
"--REPTILIAN."
SENATOR.
WE'LL TELL YOU WHY YOU'RE HERE.

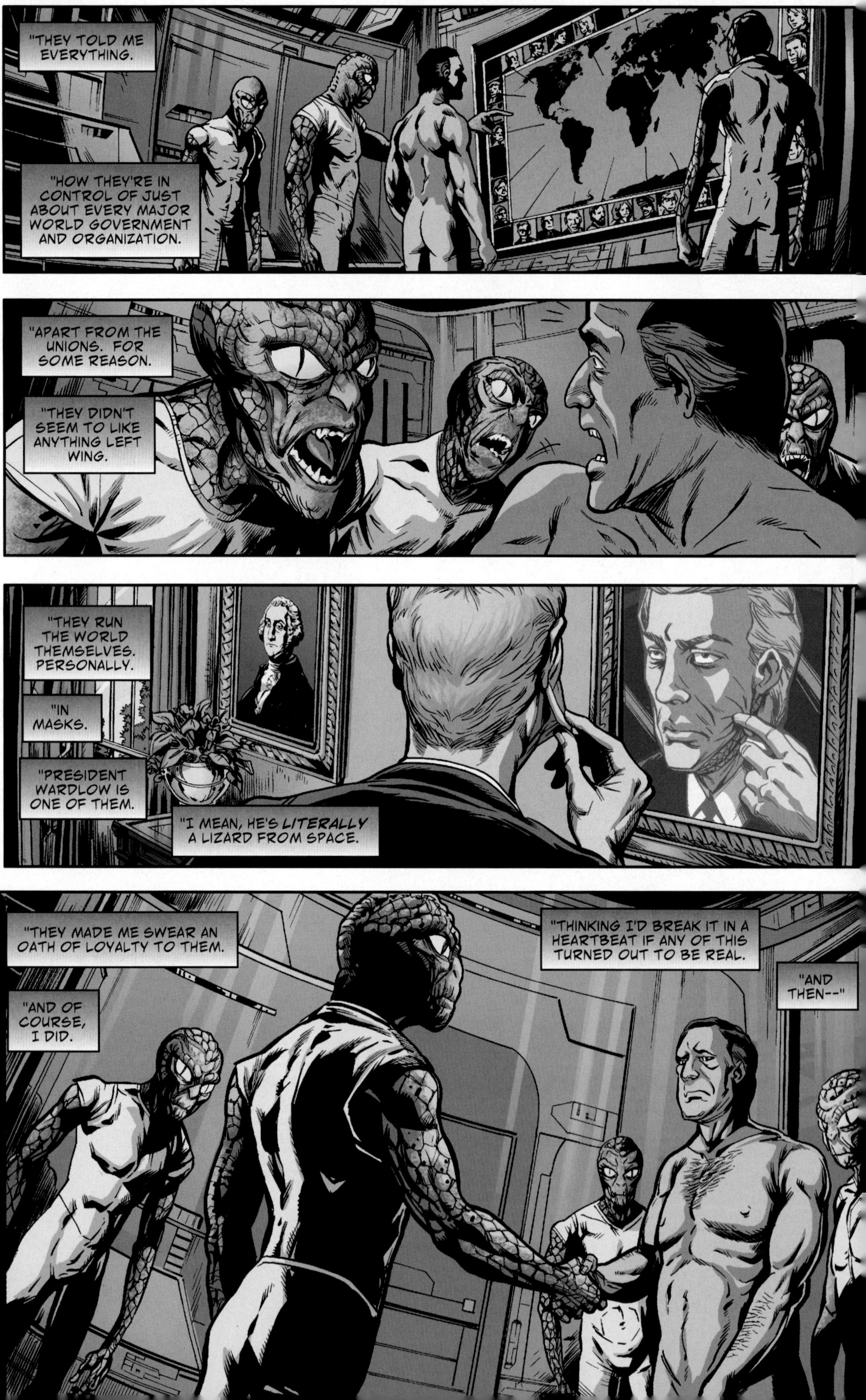
"THEY TOLD ME EVERYTHING.
"HOW THEY'RE IN CONTROL OF JUST ABOUT EVERY MAJOR WORLD GOVERNMENT AND ORGANIZATION.
"APART FROM THE UNIONS. FOR SOME REASON.
"THEY DIDN'T SEEM TO LIKE ANYTHING LEFT WING.
"THEY RUN THE WORLD THEMSELVES. PERSONALLY.
"IN MASKS.
"PRESIDENT WARDLOW IS ONE OF THEM.
"I MEAN, HE'S *LITERALLY* A LIZARD FROM SPACE.
"THEY MADE ME SWEAR AN OATH OF LOYALTY TO THEM.
"AND OF COURSE, I DID.
"THINKING I'D BREAK IT IN A HEARTBEAT IF ANY OF THIS TURNED OUT TO BE REAL.
"AND THEN--"

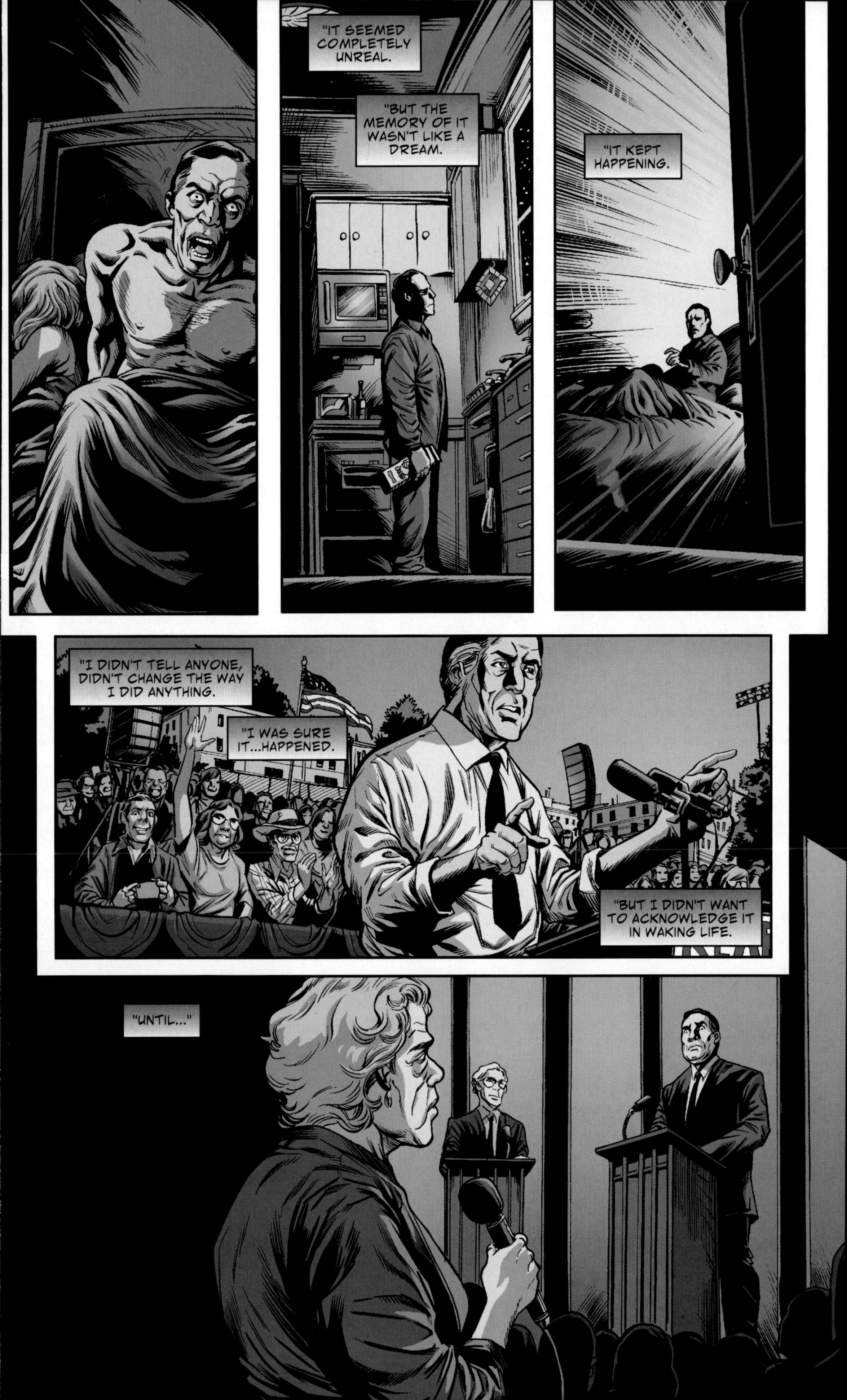
"IT SEEMED COMPLETELY UNREAL.
"BUT THE MEMORY OF IT WASN'T LIKE A DREAM.
"IT KEPT HAPPENING.
"I DIDN'T TELL ANYONE, DIDN'T CHANGE THE WAY I DID ANYTHING.
"I WAS SURE IT...HAPPENED.
"BUT I DIDN'T WANT TO ACKNOWLEDGE IT IN WAKING LIFE.
"UNTIL..."

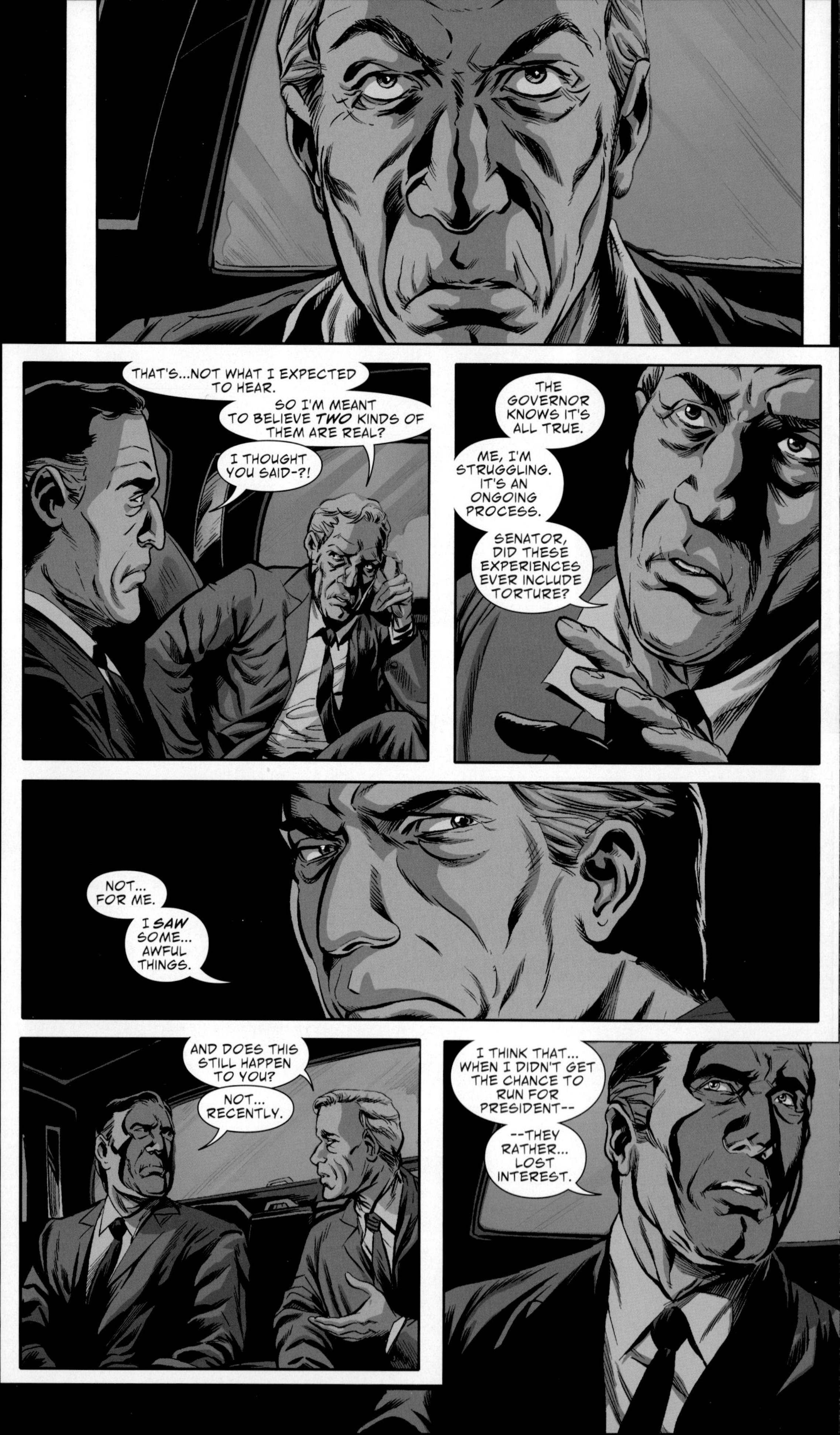
THAT'S...NOT WHAT I EXPECTED TO HEAR.
SO I'M MEANT TO BELIEVE TWO KINDS OF THEM ARE REAL?
I THOUGHT YOU SAID--?!
THE GOVERNOR KNOWS IT'S ALL TRUE.
ME, I'M STRUGGLING. IT'S AN ONGOING PROCESS.
SENATOR, DID THESE EXPERIENCES EVER INCLUDE TORTURE?
NOT... FOR ME.
I SAW SOME... AWFUL THINGS.
AND DOES THIS STILL HAPPEN TO YOU?
NOT... RECENTLY.
I THINK THAT... WHEN I DIDN'T GET THE CHANCE TO RUN FOR PRESIDENT--
--THEY RATHER... LOST INTEREST.

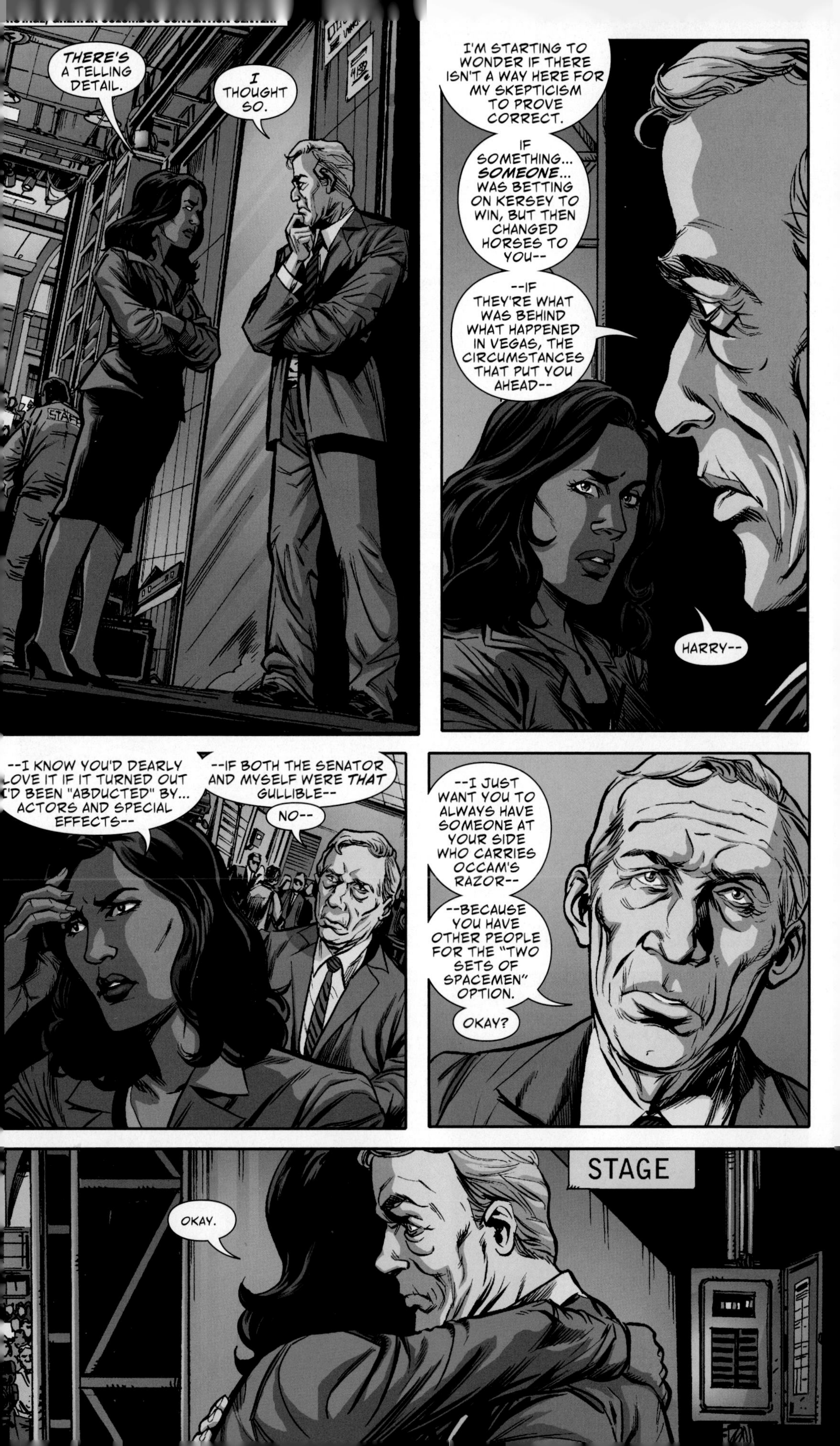
THERE'S A TELLING DETAIL.
I THOUGHT SO.
I'M STARTING TO WONDER IF THERE ISN'T A WAY HERE FOR MY SKEPTICISM TO PROVE CORRECT.
IF SOMETHING... SOMEONE... WAS BETTING ON KERSEY TO WIN, BUT THEN CHANGED HORSES TO YOU--
--IF THEY'RE WHAT WAS BEHIND WHAT HAPPENED IN VEGAS, THE CIRCUMSTANCES THAT PUT YOU AHEAD--
HARRY--
--I KNOW YOU'D DEARLY LOVE IT IF IT TURNED OUT I'D BEEN "ABDUCTED" BY... ACTORS AND SPECIAL EFFECTS--
--IF BOTH THE SENATOR AND MYSELF WERE THAT GULLIBLE--
NO--
--I JUST WANT YOU TO ALWAYS HAVE SOMEONE AT YOUR SIDE WHO CARRIES OCCAM'S RAZOR--
--BECAUSE YOU HAVE OTHER PEOPLE FOR THE "TWO SETS OF SPACEMEN" OPTION.
OKAY?
STAGE
OKAY.

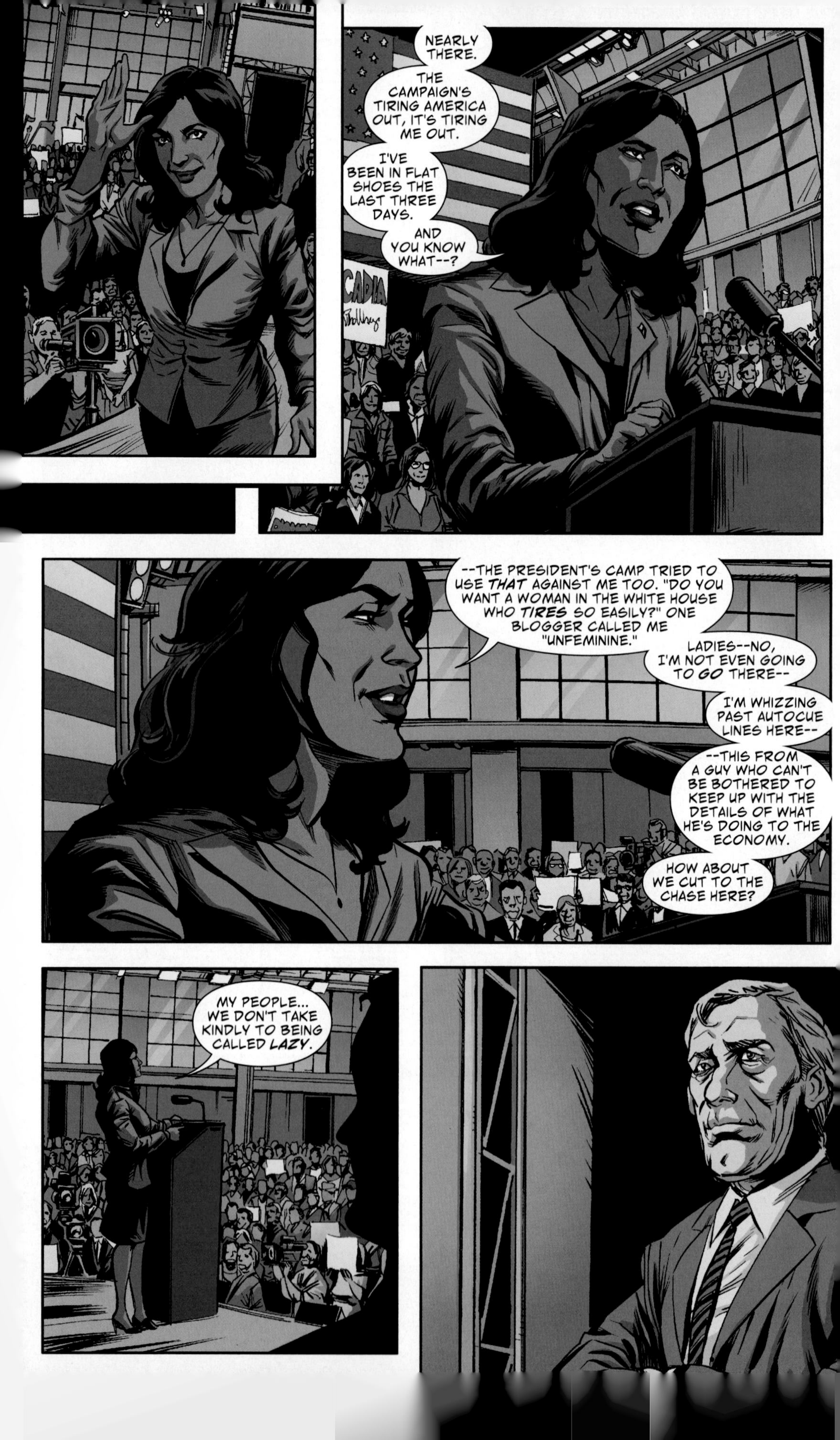
NEARLY THERE.
THE CAMPAIGN'S TIRING AMERICA OUT, IT'S TIRING ME OUT.
I'VE BEEN IN FLAT SHOES THE LAST THREE DAYS.
AND YOU KNOW WHAT--?
CADIA
--THE PRESIDENT'S CAMP TRIED TO USE THAT AGAINST ME TOO. "DO YOU WANT A WOMAN IN THE WHITE HOUSE WHO TIRES SO EASILY?" ONE BLOGGER CALLED ME "UNFEMININE."
LADIES--NO, I'M NOT EVEN GOING TO GO THERE--
I'M WHIZZING PAST AUTOCUE LINES HERE--
--THIS FROM A GUY WHO CAN'T BE BOTHERED TO KEEP UP WITH THE DETAILS OF WHAT HE'S DOING TO THE ECONOMY.
HOW ABOUT WE CUT TO THE CHASE HERE?
MY PEOPLE... WE DON'T TAKE KINDLY TO BEING CALLED LAZY.

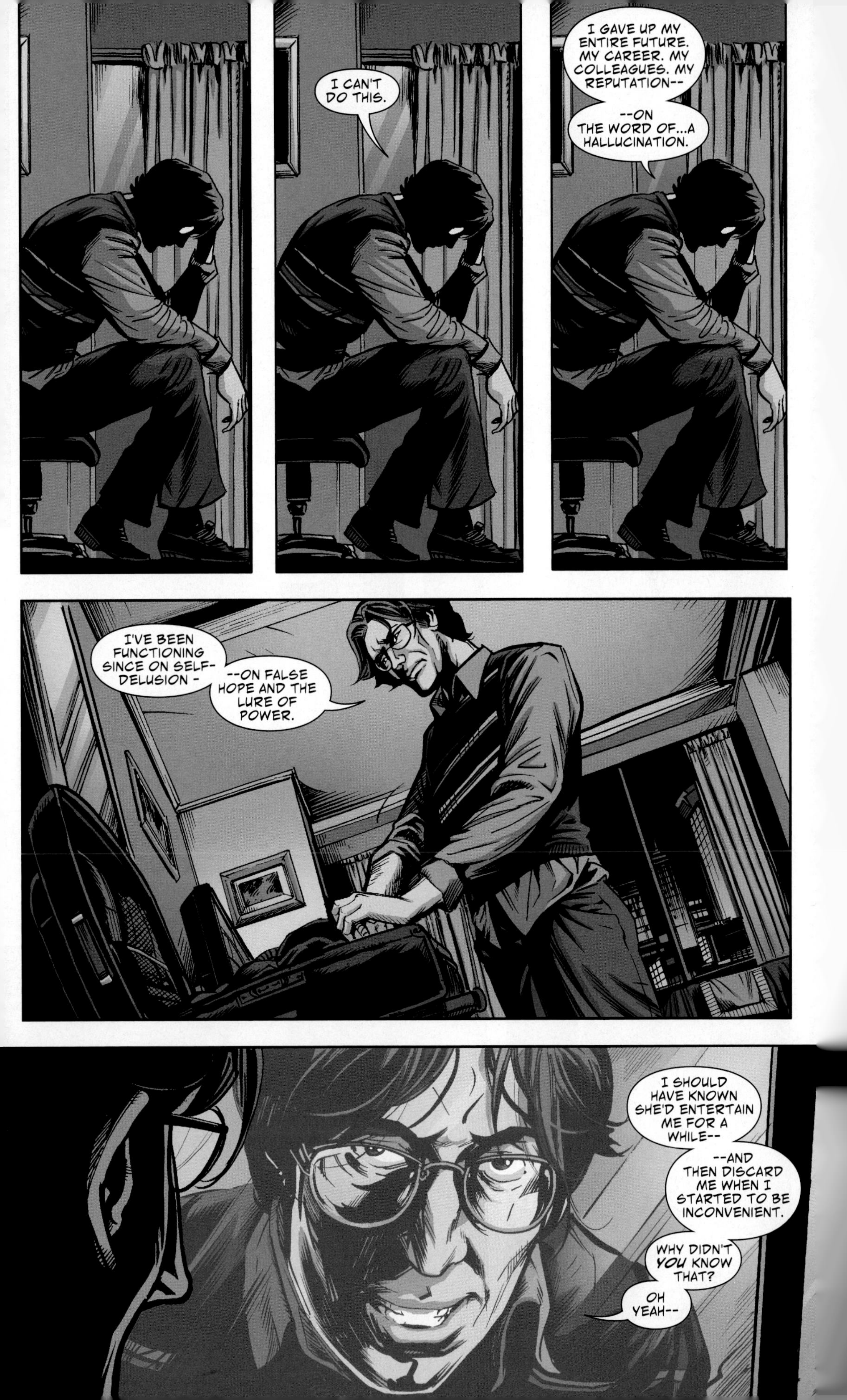
I CAN'T DO THIS.
I GAVE UP MY ENTIRE FUTURE. MY CAREER. MY COLLEAGUES. MY REPUTATION--
--ON THE WORD OF...A HALLUCINATION.
I'VE BEEN FUNCTIONING SINCE ON SELF-DELUSION -
--ON FALSE HOPE AND THE LURE OF POWER.
I SHOULD HAVE KNOWN SHE'D ENTERTAIN ME FOR A WHILE--
--AND THEN DISCARD ME WHEN I STARTED TO BE INCONVENIENT.
WHY DIDN'T *YOU* KNOW THAT?
OH YEAH--

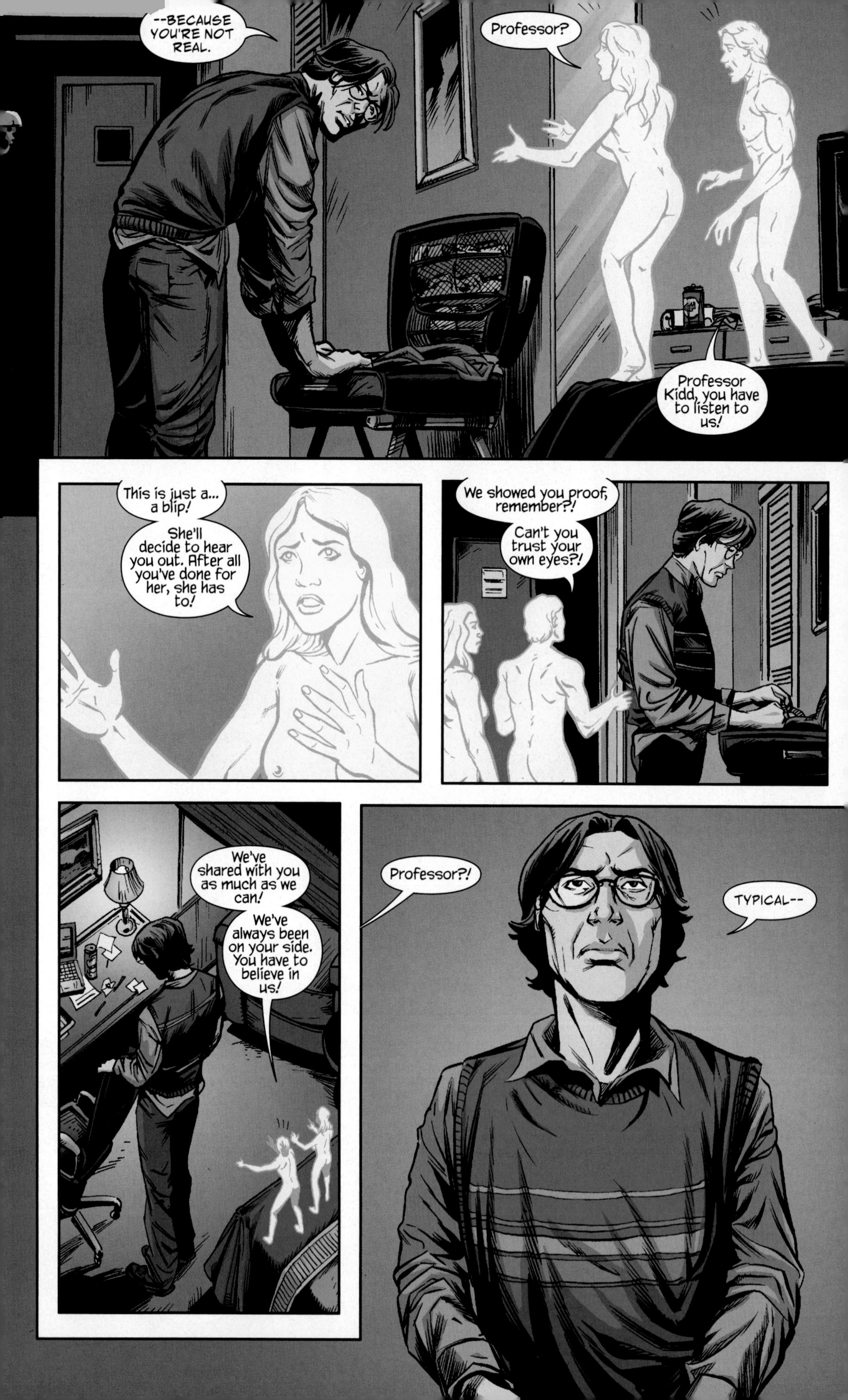
--BECAUSE YOU'RE NOT REAL.
Professor?
Professor Kidd, you have to listen to us!
This is just a... a blip!
She'll decide to hear you out. After all you've done for her, she has to!
We showed you proof, remember?!
Can't you trust your own eyes?!
We've shared with you as much as we can!
We've always been on your side. You have to believe in us!
Professor?!
TYPICAL--

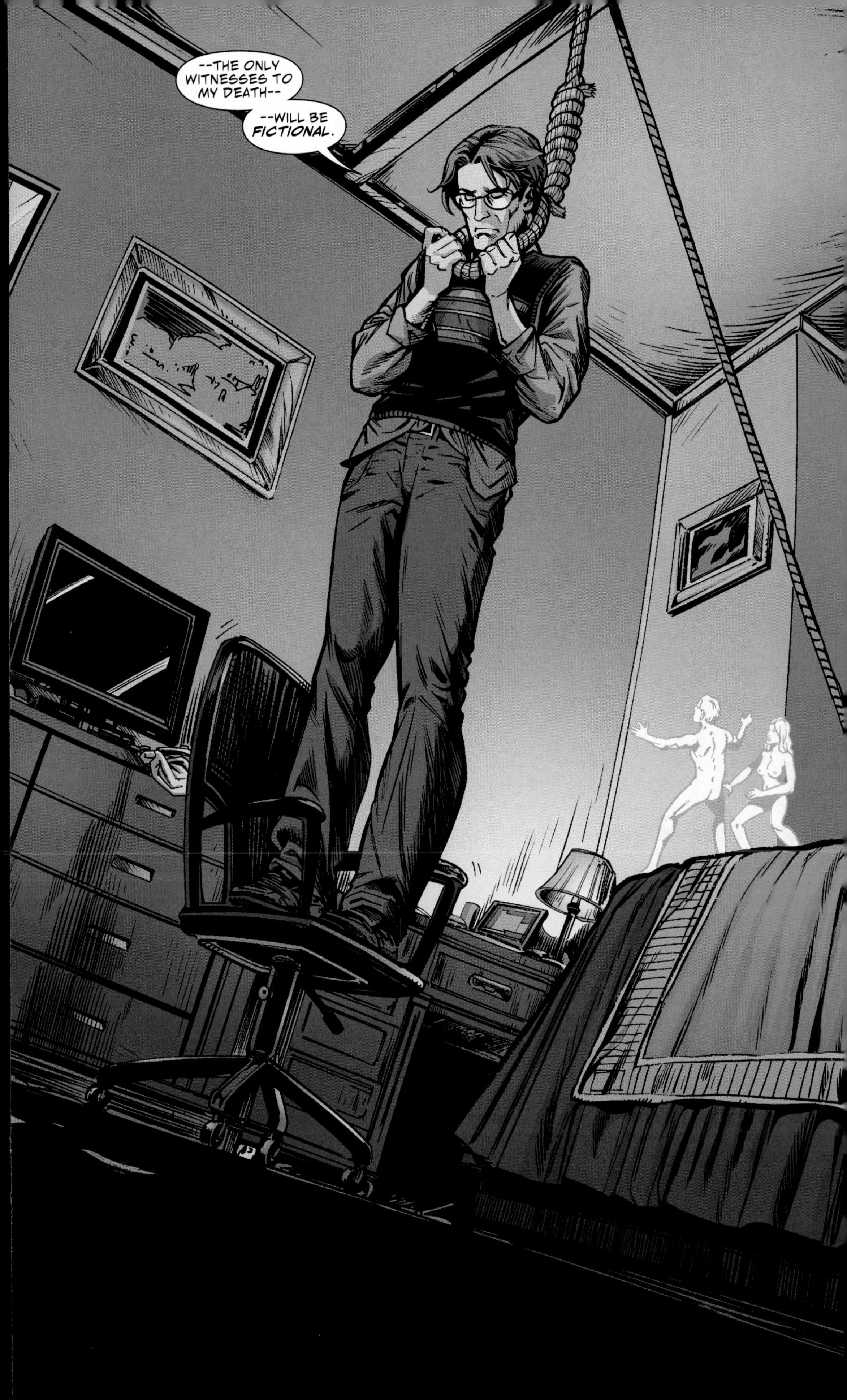
--THE ONLY WITNESSES TO MY DEATH--
--WILL BE *FICTIONAL*.

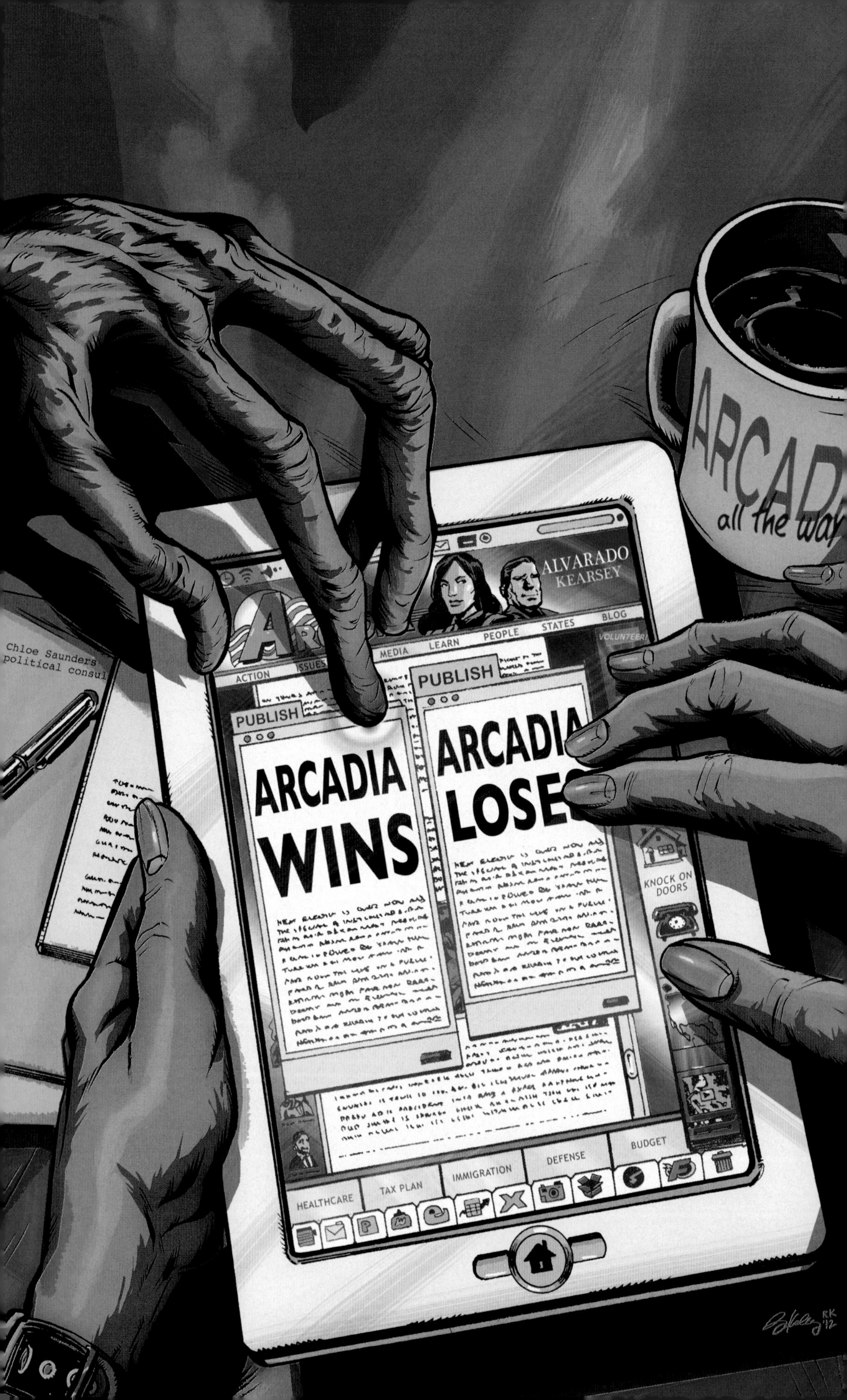

ARCAD
all the way
Chloe Saunders
political consul
ALVARADO
KEARSEY
ACTION
ISSUES
MEDIA
LEARN
PEOPLE
STATES
BLOG
PUBLISH
ARCADIA
WINS
PUBLISH
ARCADIA
LOSE
KNOCK ON DOORS
HEALTHCARE
TAX PLAN
IMMIGRATION
DEFENSE
BUDGET

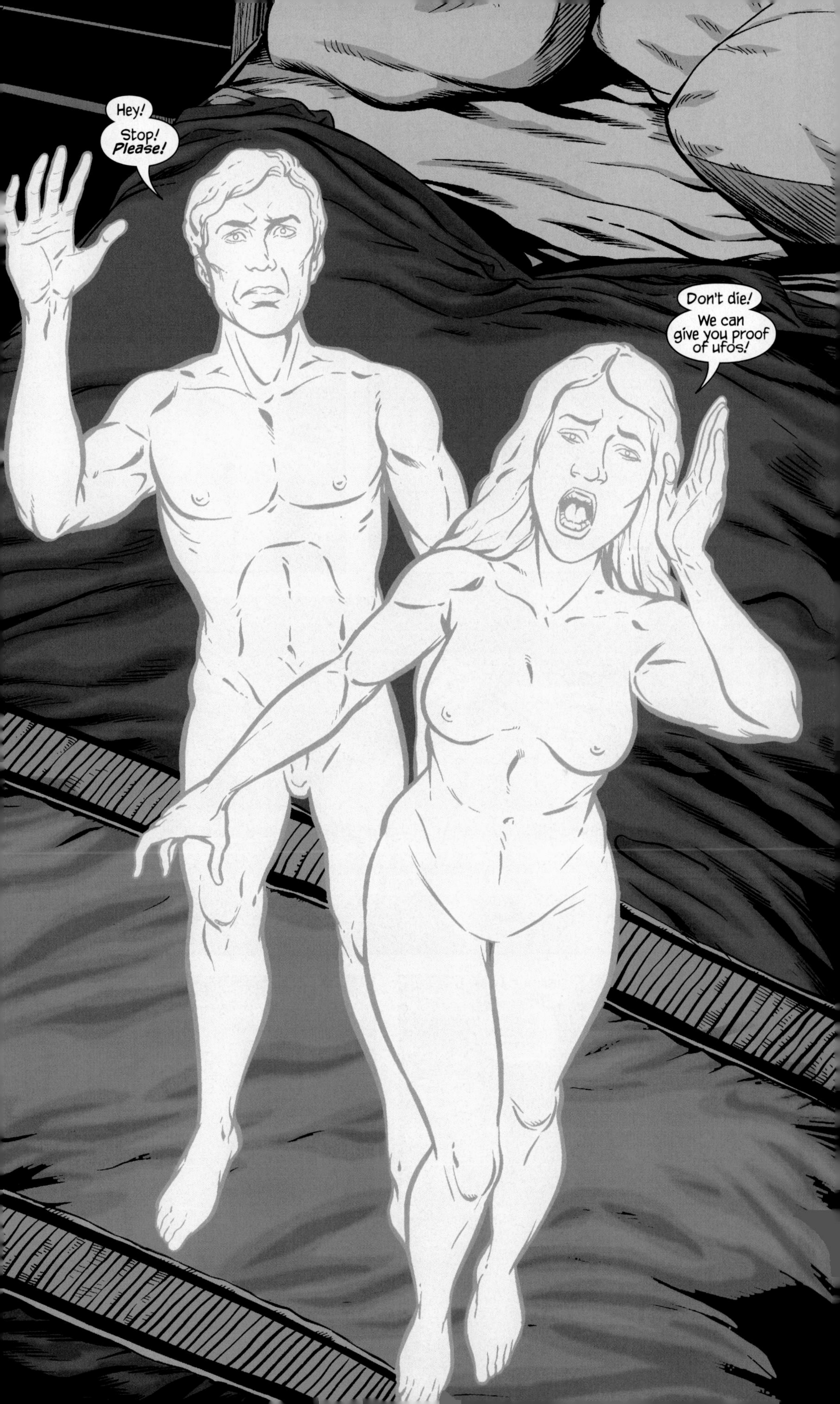
Hey!
Stop! *Please!*
Don't die!
We can give you proof of ufos!

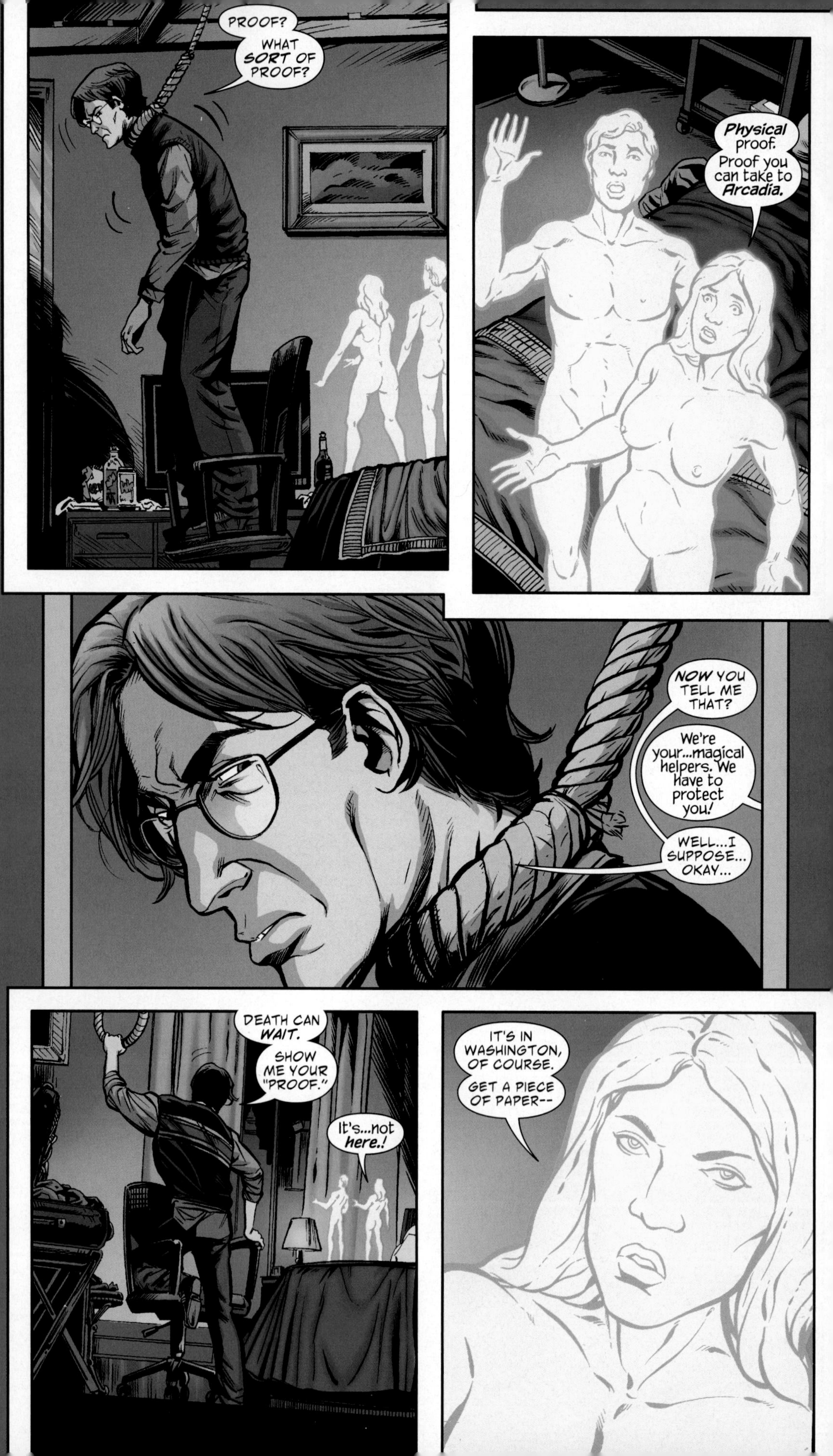
PROOF? WHAT SORT OF PROOF?
Physical proof. Proof you can take to Arcadia.
NOW YOU TELL ME THAT?
We're your...magical helpers. We have to protect you!
WELL...I SUPPOSE... OKAY...
DEATH CAN WAIT. SHOW ME YOUR "PROOF."
It's...not here.!
IT'S IN WASHINGTON, OF COURSE.
GET A PIECE OF PAPER--

"- we'll provide directions."

OKAY, I THINK WE'VE HEARD ENOUGH. YOU KNOW, IT'S A PLEASURE TO MEET SOMEONE ELSE IN MY LINE OF BUSINESS, ASTELLE--

YES, I KNOW YOUR NAME. WE WERE EXPECTING SOMEONE FROM YOUR SIDE TO ARRIVE AT SOME POINT, AND I'M SO PLEASED IT'S YOU.

BY "HER LINE OF BUSINESS," FROM WHAT WE'VE JUST HEARD, I THINK SHE MEANS "LYING."

HOW DARE YOU--?!

THAT'S NOT AT ALL WHAT I WAS GOING TO SAY.

MY LINE OF BUSINESS IS THE CONSTRUCTION AND SALE OF NARRATIVES.

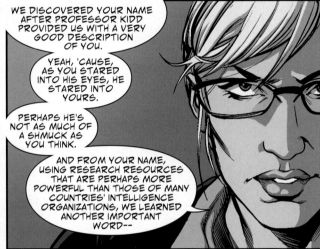

WE DISCOVERED YOUR NAME AFTER PROFESSOR KIDD PROVIDED US WITH A VERY GOOD DESCRIPTION OF YOU.

YEAH, 'CAUSE, AS YOU STARED INTO HIS EYES, HE STARED INTO YOURS.

PERHAPS HE'S NOT AS MUCH OF A SHMUCK AS YOU THINK.

AND FROM YOUR NAME, USING RESEARCH RESOURCES THAT ARE PERHAPS MORE POWERFUL THAN THOSE OF MANY COUNTRIES' INTELLIGENCE ORGANIZATIONS, WE LEARNED ANOTHER IMPORTANT WORD--

"BLUE-BIRDS."

I...I...

BUT YOU'RE NOT A PROFESSIONAL AT THIS.

YOU WORK IN AEROSPACE. WE COULD NAME THE FIRM. AND YOUR POSITION. AND YOUR BOSS.

AND, OF COURSE--

THERE'S THIS.

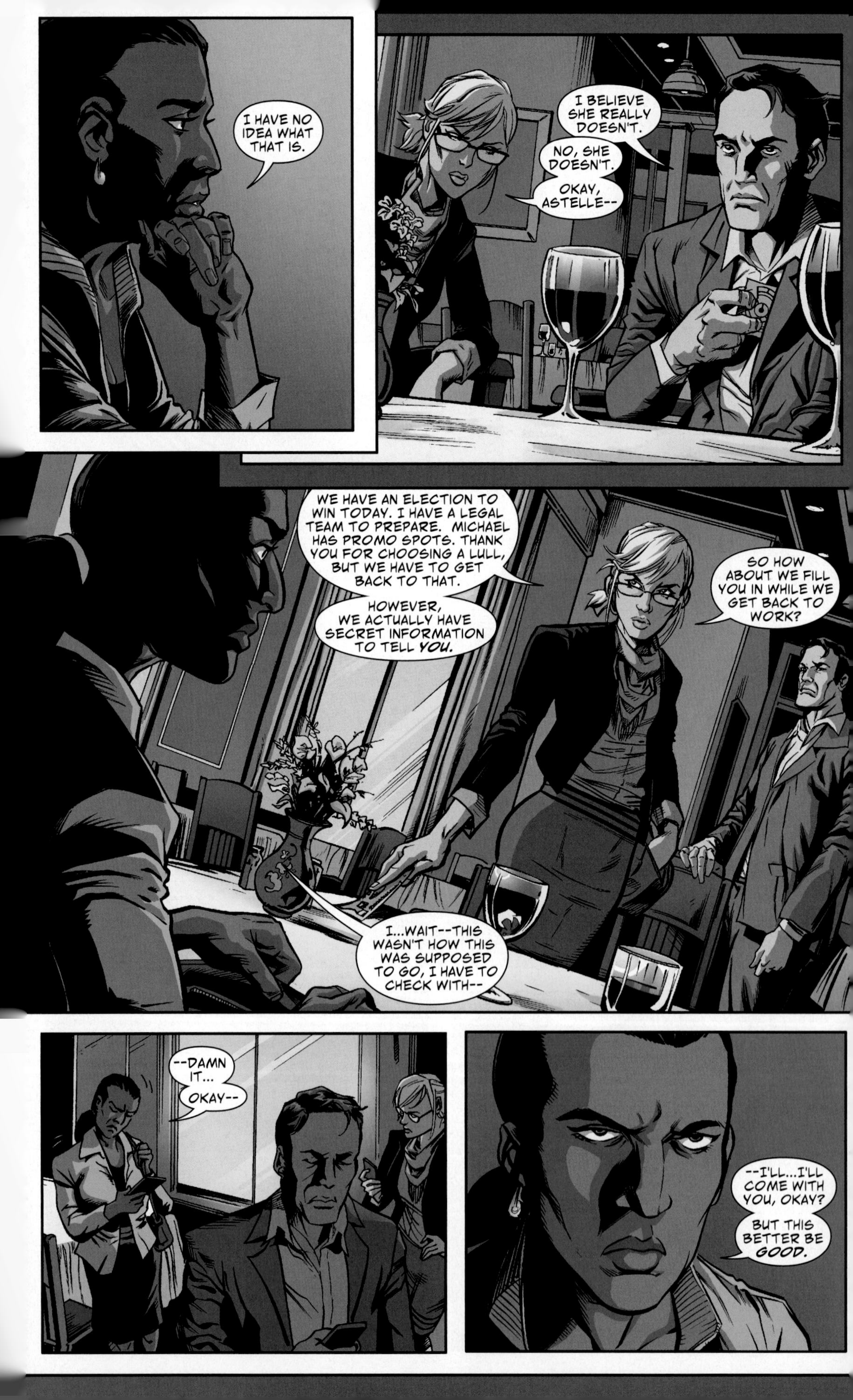
I HAVE NO IDEA WHAT THAT IS.
I BELIEVE SHE REALLY DOESN'T.
NO, SHE DOESN'T.
OKAY, ASTELLE--
WE HAVE AN ELECTION TO WIN TODAY. I HAVE A LEGAL TEAM TO PREPARE. MICHAEL HAS PROMO SPOTS. THANK YOU FOR CHOOSING A LULL, BUT WE HAVE TO GET BACK TO THAT.
HOWEVER, WE ACTUALLY HAVE SECRET INFORMATION TO TELL *YOU*.
SO HOW ABOUT WE FILL YOU IN WHILE WE GET BACK TO WORK?
I...WAIT--THIS WASN'T HOW THIS WAS SUPPOSED TO GO, I HAVE TO CHECK WITH--
--DAMN IT...
OKAY--
--I'LL...I'LL COME WITH YOU, OKAY?
BUT THIS BETTER BE *GOOD*.

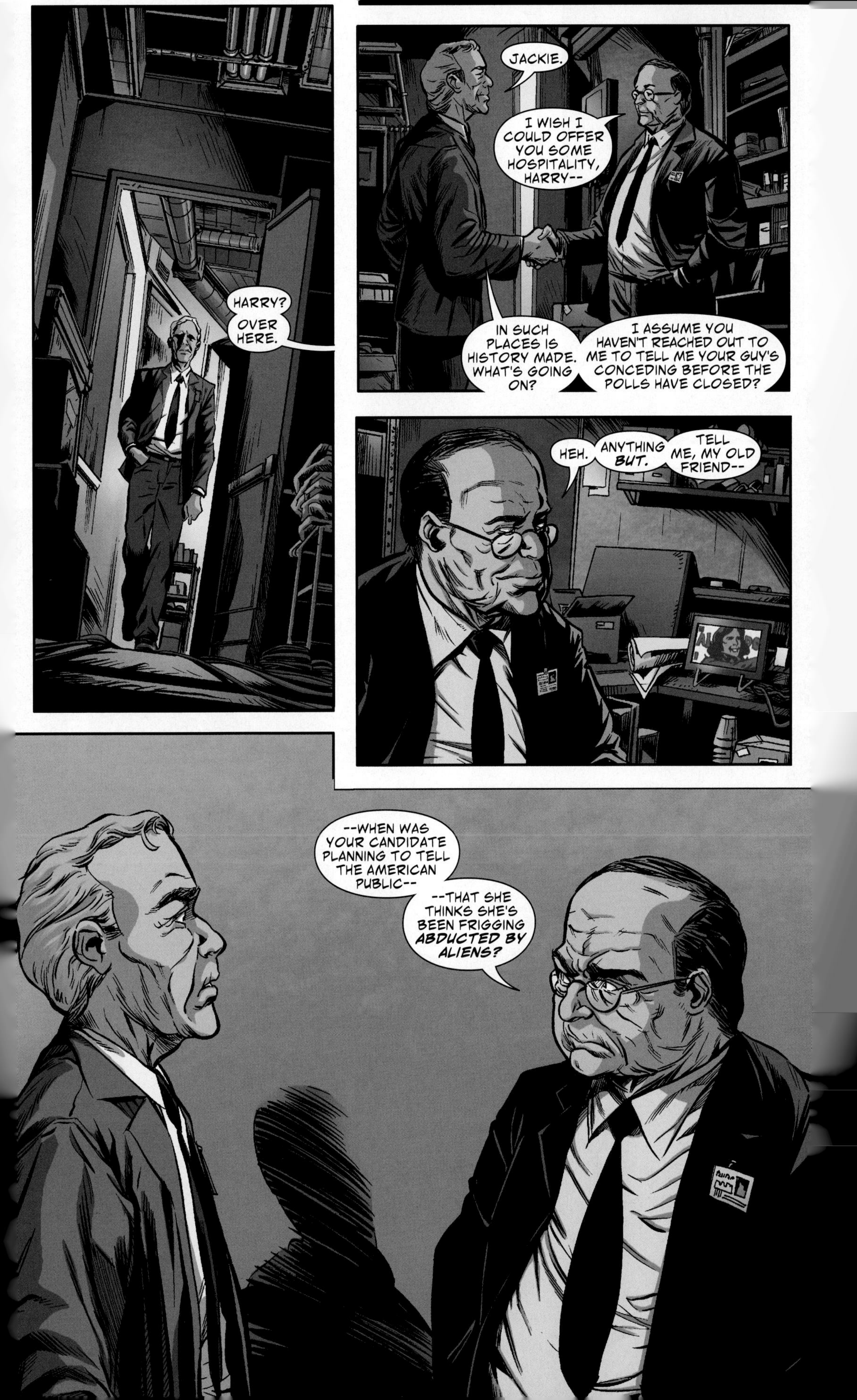
HARRY?
OVER HERE.
JACKIE.
I WISH I COULD OFFER YOU SOME HOSPITALITY, HARRY--
IN SUCH PLACES IS HISTORY MADE. WHAT'S GOING ON?
I ASSUME YOU HAVEN'T REACHED OUT TO ME TO TELL ME YOUR GUY'S CONCEDING BEFORE THE POLLS HAVE CLOSED?
HEH.
ANYTHING *BUT.*
TELL ME, MY OLD FRIEND--
--WHEN WAS YOUR CANDIDATE PLANNING TO TELL THE AMERICAN PUBLIC--
--THAT SHE THINKS SHE'S BEEN FRIGGING *ABDUCTED BY ALIENS?*

WE HAVE NO IDEA WHAT YOU'RE TALKING ABOUT.

IS THIS THE SAME WEIRD APPROACH YOU USED AGAINST KERSEY? BECAUSE--

THAT'S WHY WE'RE NOT GOING TO GO PUBLIC WITH IT. NOT *NOW*.

IT'S PLAYED OUT.

AND SHE'D JUST DENY IT.

AND THEN *WE'D* BE THE ONES LOOKING A LITTLE CRAY-CRAY.

SO WHY TELL ME?

BECAUSE I PERSUADED THEM, HARRY. I PERSUADED THEM TO LET ME COME TO YOU.

YOU'RE ONE OF THE OLD GUARD. ONE OF THE GOOD GUYS. YOU VALUE DEMOCRACY ABOVE ALL THINGS.

DO YOU REALLY WANT A PRESIDENT WHO BELIEVES SOMETHING THAT'S NOT TRUE?

WHO MIGHT BUILD ON THAT FANTASY WITH THE NUCLEAR BUTTON IN HER HANDS?

HARRY, THEY'RE SEEING UFOS ON THE CHINA/INDIA BORDER RIGHT NOW--

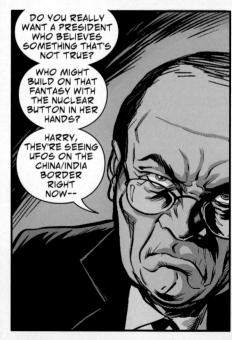

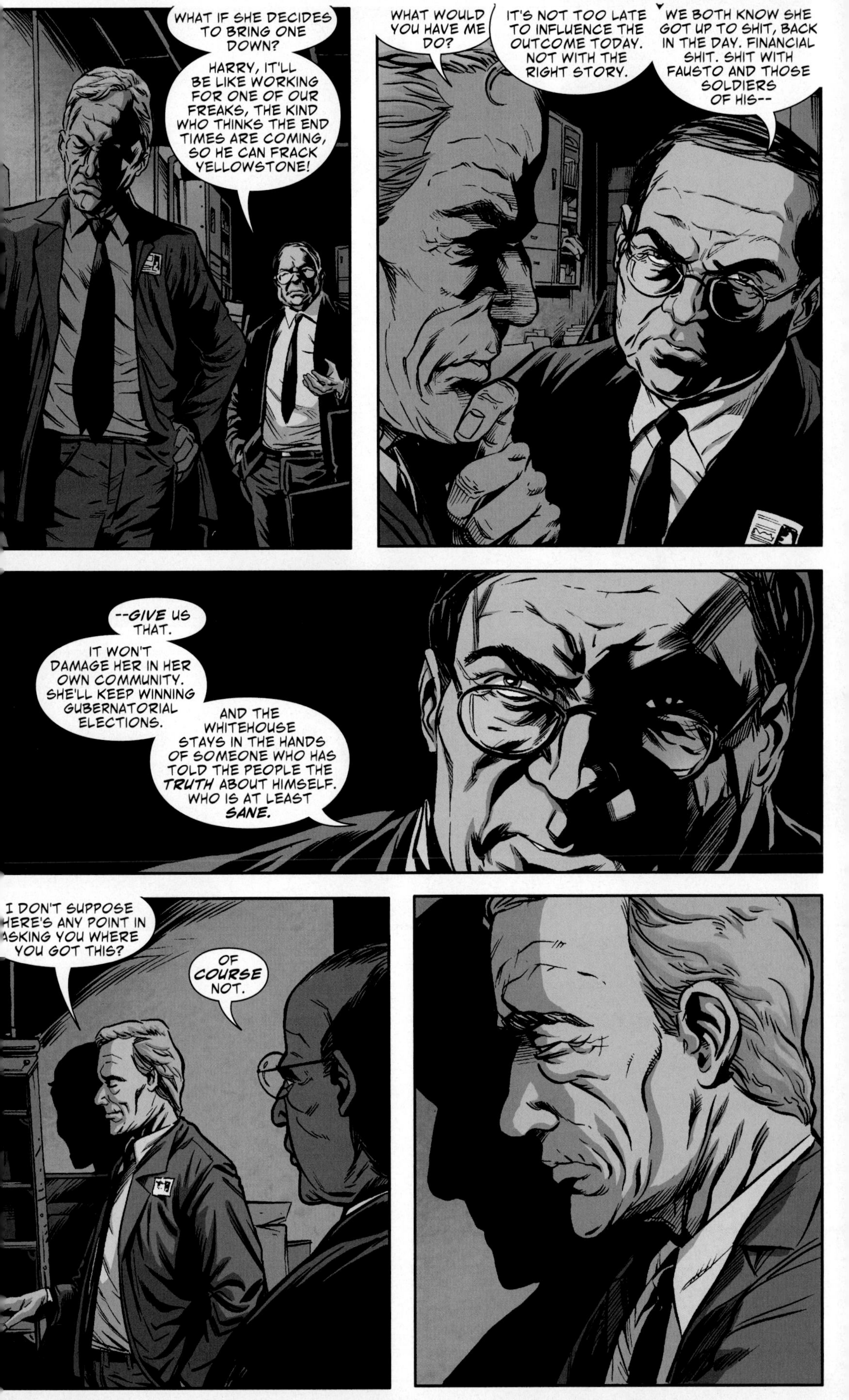
WHAT IF SHE DECIDES TO BRING ONE DOWN?
HARRY, IT'LL BE LIKE WORKING FOR ONE OF OUR FREAKS, THE KIND WHO THINKS THE END TIMES ARE COMING, SO HE CAN FRACK YELLOWSTONE!
WHAT WOULD YOU HAVE ME DO?
IT'S NOT TOO LATE TO INFLUENCE THE OUTCOME TODAY. NOT WITH THE RIGHT STORY.
WE BOTH KNOW SHE GOT UP TO SHIT, BACK IN THE DAY. FINANCIAL SHIT. SHIT WITH FAUSTO AND THOSE SOLDIERS OF HIS--
--GIVE US THAT.
IT WON'T DAMAGE HER IN HER OWN COMMUNITY. SHE'LL KEEP WINNING GUBERNATORIAL ELECTIONS.
AND THE WHITEHOUSE STAYS IN THE HANDS OF SOMEONE WHO HAS TOLD THE PEOPLE THE TRUTH ABOUT HIMSELF. WHO IS AT LEAST SANE.
I DON'T SUPPOSE HERE'S ANY POINT IN ASKING YOU WHERE YOU GOT THIS?
OF COURSE NOT.

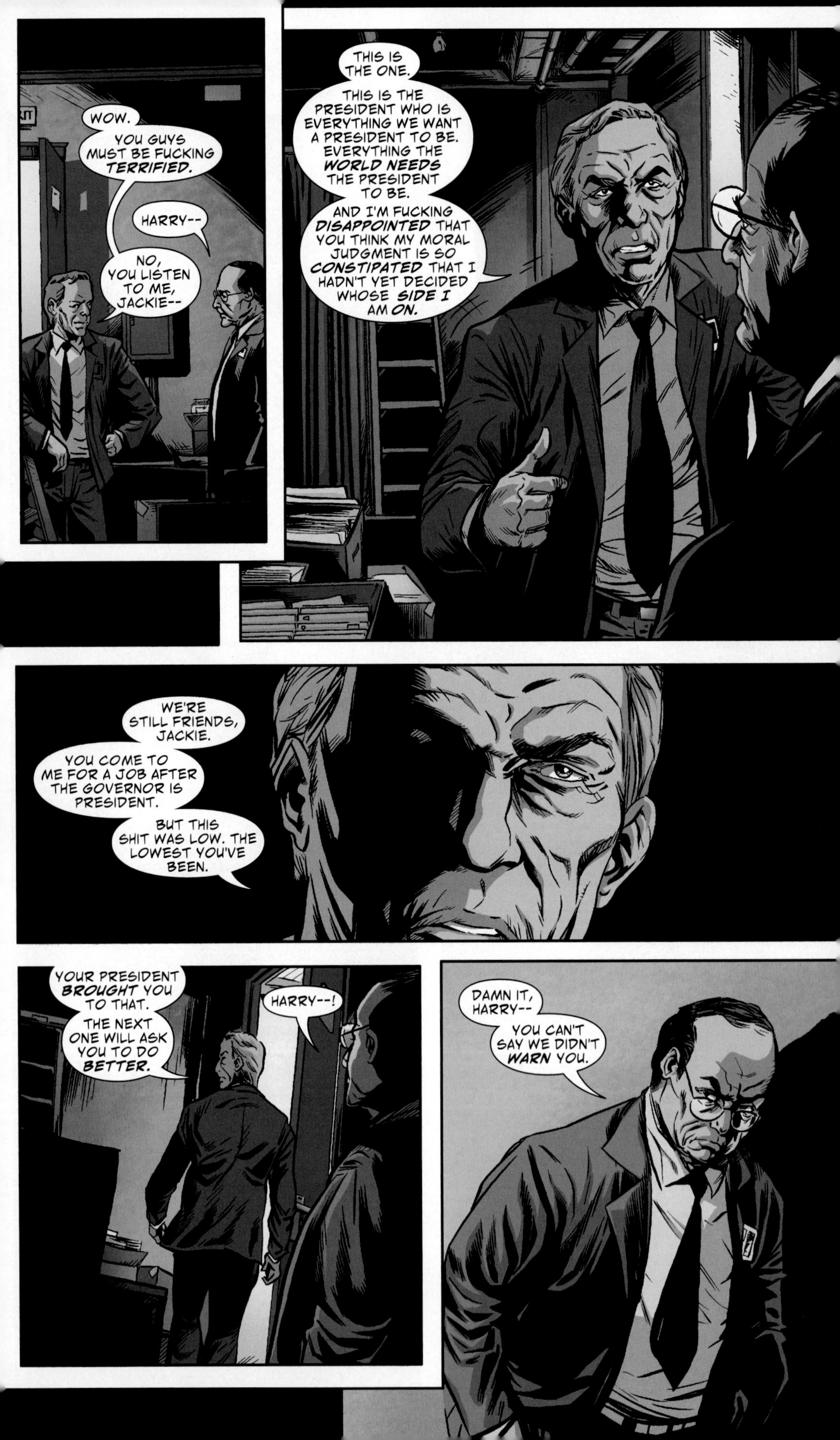
WOW.
YOU GUYS MUST BE FUCKING TERRIFIED.
HARRY--
NO, YOU LISTEN TO ME, JACKIE--
THIS IS THE ONE.
THIS IS THE PRESIDENT WHO IS EVERYTHING WE WANT A PRESIDENT TO BE. EVERYTHING THE WORLD NEEDS THE PRESIDENT TO BE.
AND I'M FUCKING DISAPPOINTED THAT YOU THINK MY MORAL JUDGMENT IS SO CONSTIPATED THAT I HADN'T YET DECIDED WHOSE SIDE I AM ON.
WE'RE STILL FRIENDS, JACKIE.
YOU COME TO ME FOR A JOB AFTER THE GOVERNOR IS PRESIDENT.
BUT THIS SHIT WAS LOW. THE LOWEST YOU'VE BEEN.
YOUR PRESIDENT BROUGHT YOU TO THAT.
THE NEXT ONE WILL ASK YOU TO DO BETTER.
HARRY--!
DAMN IT, HARRY--
YOU CAN'T SAY WE DIDN'T WARN YOU.

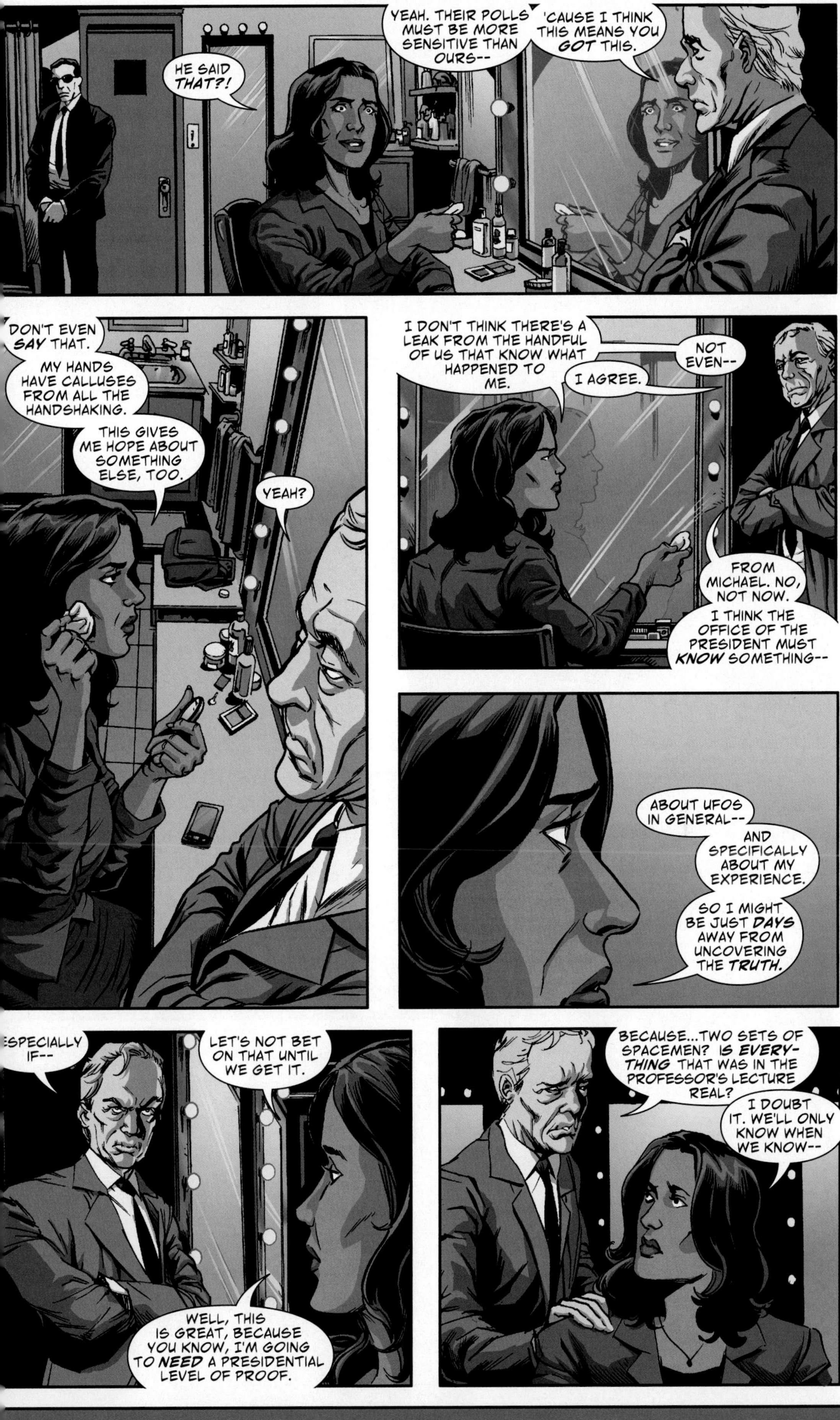
HE SAID THAT?!
YEAH. THEIR POLLS MUST BE MORE SENSITIVE THAN OURS--
'CAUSE I THINK THIS MEANS YOU GOT THIS.
DON'T EVEN SAY THAT.
MY HANDS HAVE CALLUSES FROM ALL THE HANDSHAKING.
THIS GIVES ME HOPE ABOUT SOMETHING ELSE, TOO.
YEAH?
I DON'T THINK THERE'S A LEAK FROM THE HANDFUL OF US THAT KNOW WHAT HAPPENED TO ME.
I AGREE.
NOT EVEN--
FROM MICHAEL. NO, NOT NOW.
I THINK THE OFFICE OF THE PRESIDENT MUST KNOW SOMETHING--
ABOUT UFOS IN GENERAL--
AND SPECIFICALLY ABOUT MY EXPERIENCE.
SO I MIGHT BE JUST DAYS AWAY FROM UNCOVERING THE TRUTH.
ESPECIALLY IF--
LET'S NOT BET ON THAT UNTIL WE GET IT.
WELL, THIS IS GREAT, BECAUSE YOU KNOW, I'M GOING TO NEED A PRESIDENTIAL LEVEL OF PROOF.
BECAUSE...TWO SETS OF SPACEMEN? IS EVERYTHING THAT WAS IN THE PROFESSOR'S LECTURE REAL?
I DOUBT IT. WE'LL ONLY KNOW WHEN WE KNOW--

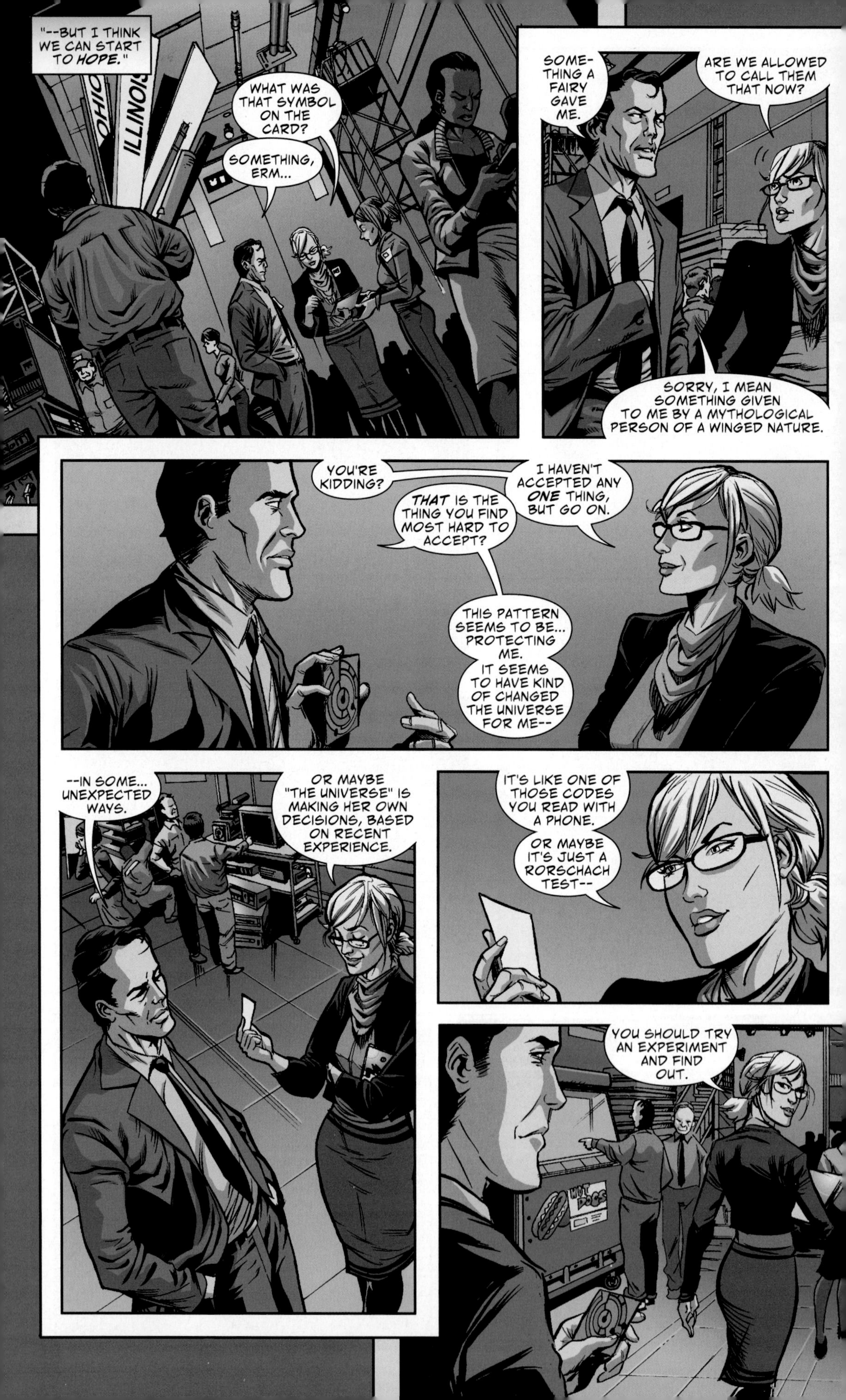
"--BUT I THINK WE CAN START TO HOPE."
OHIO
ILLINOIS
WHAT WAS THAT SYMBOL ON THE CARD?
SOMETHING, ERM...
SOME-THING A FAIRY GAVE ME.
ARE WE ALLOWED TO CALL THEM THAT NOW?
SORRY, I MEAN SOMETHING GIVEN TO ME BY A MYTHOLOGICAL PERSON OF A WINGED NATURE.
YOU'RE KIDDING?
THAT IS THE THING YOU FIND MOST HARD TO ACCEPT?
I HAVEN'T ACCEPTED ANY ONE THING, BUT GO ON.
THIS PATTERN SEEMS TO BE... PROTECTING ME.
IT SEEMS TO HAVE KIND OF CHANGED THE UNIVERSE FOR ME--
--IN SOME... UNEXPECTED WAYS.
OR MAYBE "THE UNIVERSE" IS MAKING HER OWN DECISIONS, BASED ON RECENT EXPERIENCE.
IT'S LIKE ONE OF THOSE CODES YOU READ WITH A PHONE.
OR MAYBE IT'S JUST A RORSCHACH TEST--
YOU SHOULD TRY AN EXPERIMENT AND FIND OUT.

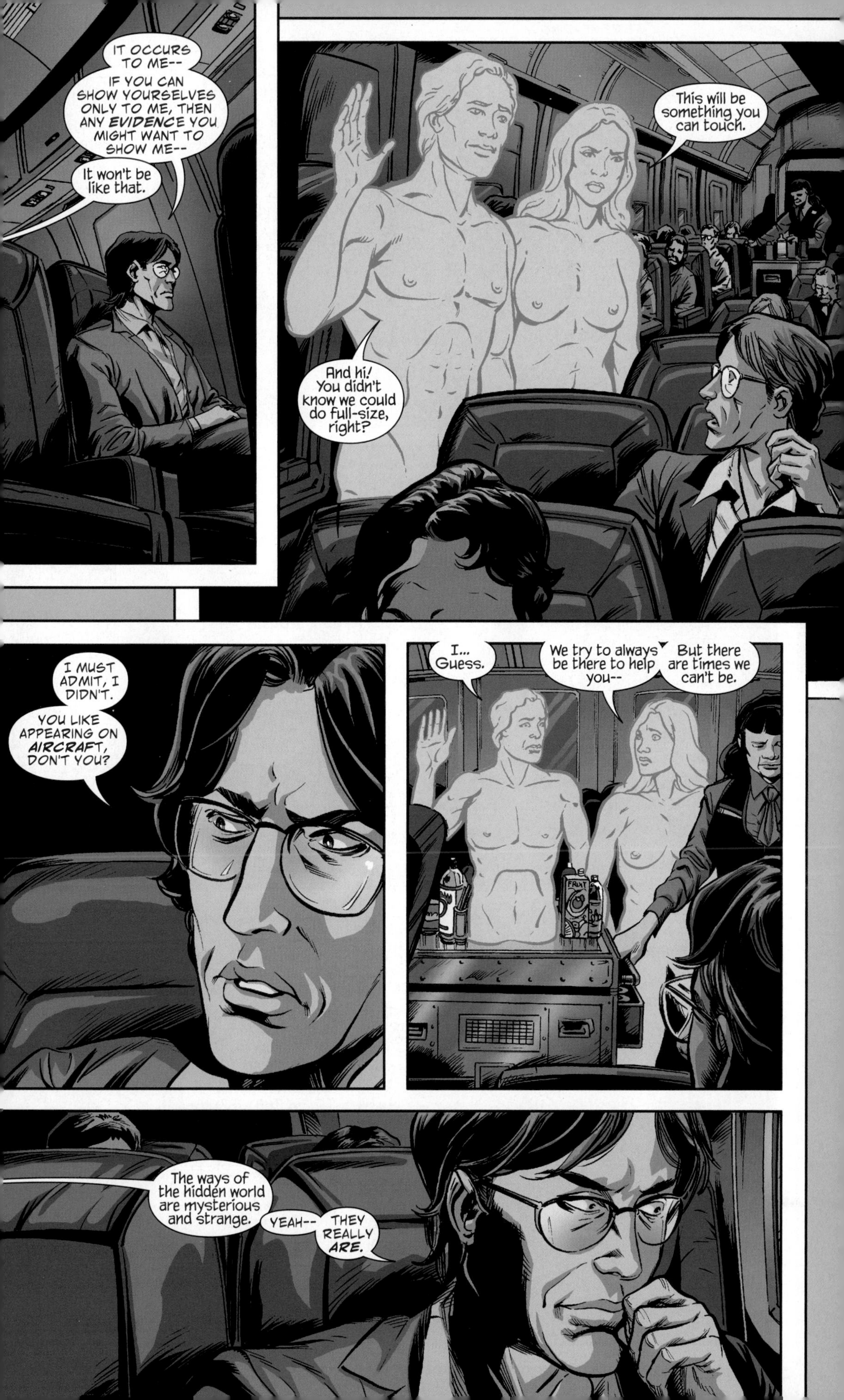
IT OCCURS TO ME--
IF YOU CAN SHOW YOURSELVES ONLY TO ME, THEN ANY EVIDENCE YOU MIGHT WANT TO SHOW ME--
It won't be like that.
This will be something you can touch.
And hi! You didn't know we could do full-size, right?
I MUST ADMIT, I DIDN'T.
YOU LIKE APPEARING ON AIRCRAFT, DON'T YOU?
I... Guess.
We try to always be there to help you--
But there are times we can't be.
FRUIT
The ways of the hidden world are mysterious and strange.
YEAH--
THEY REALLY ARE.

WE'RE HEADING **HOME** FOR THE FINISHING LINE, RIGHT?

TELL ME I DIDN'T MISS A LINE ON THE SCHEDULE.

WE'RE HEADING **HOME.**

WHAT DO YOU THINK DAD WOULD HAVE SAID, THAT WE GOT THIS FAR AND ACTUALLY HAVE A SHOT?

HE'D HAVE SAID, "THE DEMOGRAPHICS WERE ALWAYS GOING TO FAVOR OUR PEOPLE EVENTUALLY."

YEAH.

YEAH, HE WOULD.

HE HAD SUCH SOLID IDEAS ABOUT THE WORLD. HE WOULD HAVE BEEN AMAZED THAT SUCH...WEIRDNESS... WAS PLAYING A PART IN MY LIFE.

I DON'T WANT TO SAY I'M GLAD IT HAS. I'D NEVER SAY THAT ABOUT ABUSE.

BUT I'M GLAD... LIKE A BOXER'S GLAD TO GET UP AFTER THE COUNT. I'M...THIS ISN'T MAKING SENSE--

GOVERNOR, FUTURE MADAM PRESIDENT--

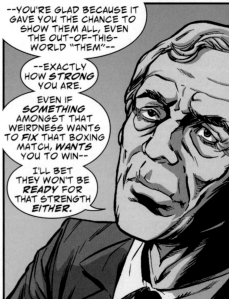

--YOU'RE GLAD BECAUSE IT GAVE YOU THE CHANCE TO SHOW THEM ALL, EVEN THE OUT-OF-THIS-WORLD "THEM"--

--EXACTLY HOW **STRONG** YOU ARE.

EVEN IF **SOMETHING** AMONGST THAT WEIRDNESS WANTS TO **FIX** THAT BOXING MATCH, **WANTS** YOU TO WIN--

I'LL BET THEY WON'T BE **READY** FOR THAT STRENGTH **EITHER.**

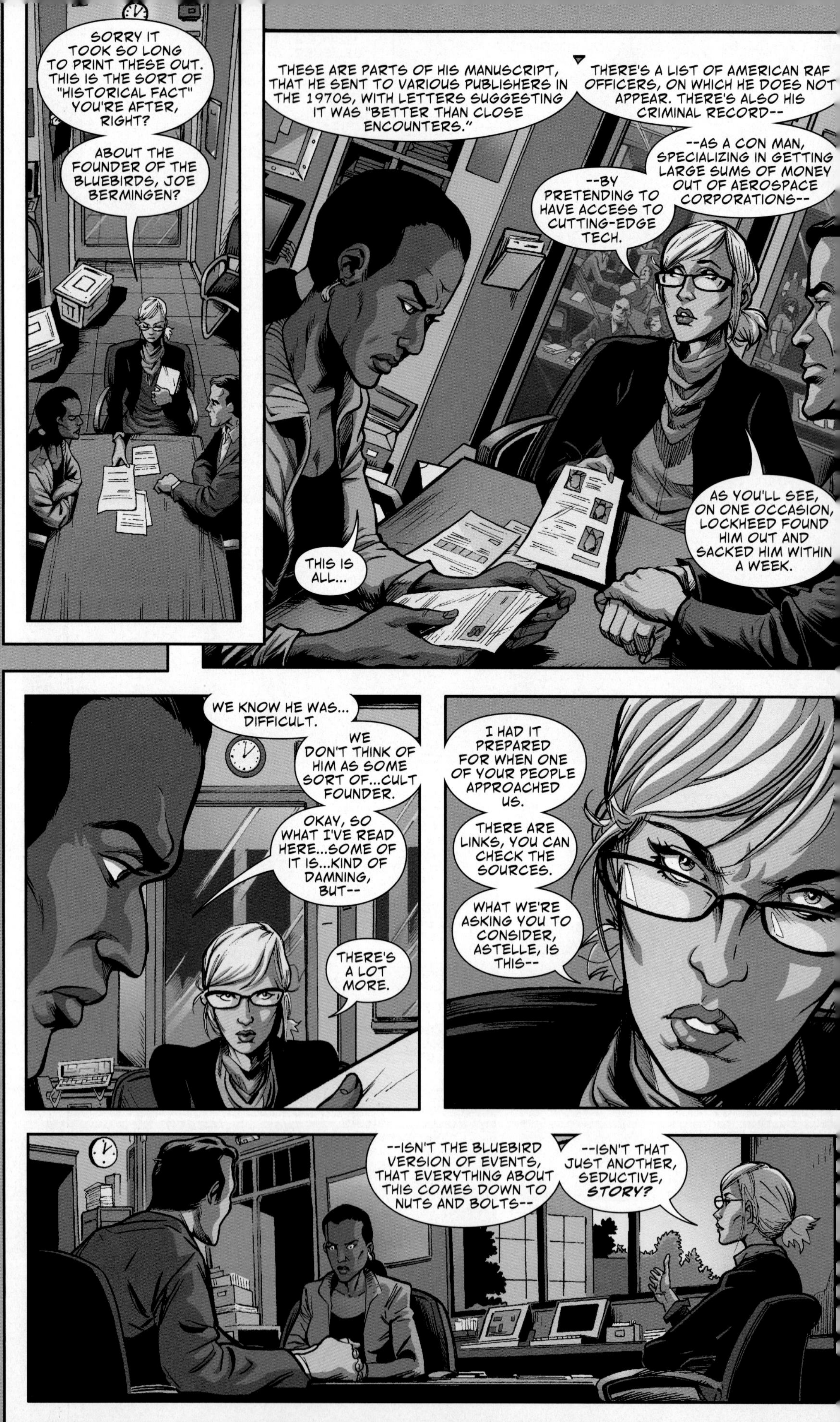
SORRY IT TOOK SO LONG TO PRINT THESE OUT. THIS IS THE SORT OF "HISTORICAL FACT" YOU'RE AFTER, RIGHT?
ABOUT THE FOUNDER OF THE BLUEBIRDS, JOE BERMINGEN?
THESE ARE PARTS OF HIS MANUSCRIPT, THAT HE SENT TO VARIOUS PUBLISHERS IN THE 1970S, WITH LETTERS SUGGESTING IT WAS "BETTER THAN CLOSE ENCOUNTERS."
THERE'S A LIST OF AMERICAN RAF OFFICERS, ON WHICH HE DOES NOT APPEAR. THERE'S ALSO HIS CRIMINAL RECORD--
--AS A CON MAN, SPECIALIZING IN GETTING LARGE SUMS OF MONEY OUT OF AEROSPACE CORPORATIONS--
--BY PRETENDING TO HAVE ACCESS TO CUTTING-EDGE TECH.
AS YOU'LL SEE, ON ONE OCCASION, LOCKHEED FOUND HIM OUT AND SACKED HIM WITHIN A WEEK.
THIS IS ALL...
WE KNOW HE WAS... DIFFICULT.
WE DON'T THINK OF HIM AS SOME SORT OF...CULT FOUNDER.
OKAY, SO WHAT I'VE READ HERE...SOME OF IT IS...KIND OF DAMNING, BUT--
THERE'S A LOT MORE.
I HAD IT PREPARED FOR WHEN ONE OF YOUR PEOPLE APPROACHED US.
THERE ARE LINKS, YOU CAN CHECK THE SOURCES.
WHAT WE'RE ASKING YOU TO CONSIDER, ASTELLE, IS THIS--
--ISN'T THE BLUEBIRD VERSION OF EVENTS, THAT EVERYTHING ABOUT THIS COMES DOWN TO NUTS AND BOLTS--
--ISN'T THAT JUST ANOTHER, SEDUCTIVE, *STORY?*

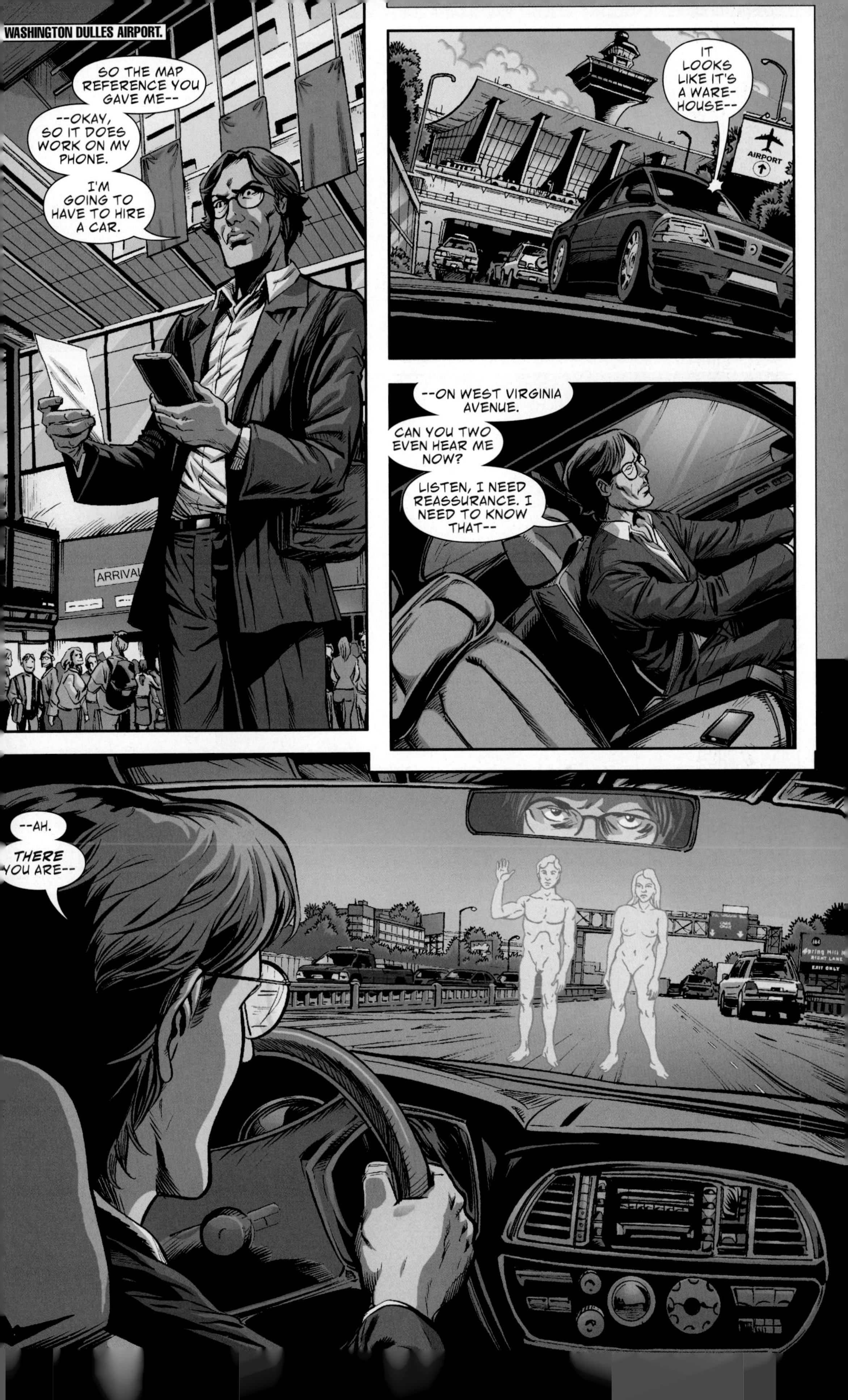
WASHINGTON DULLES AIRPORT.
SO THE MAP REFERENCE YOU GAVE ME--
--OKAY, SO IT DOES WORK ON MY PHONE.
I'M GOING TO HAVE TO HIRE A CAR.
ARRIVAL
IT LOOKS LIKE IT'S A WARE-HOUSE--
AIRPORT
--ON WEST VIRGINIA AVENUE.
CAN YOU TWO EVEN HEAR ME NOW?
LISTEN, I NEED REASSURANCE. I NEED TO KNOW THAT--
--AH.
THERE YOU ARE--

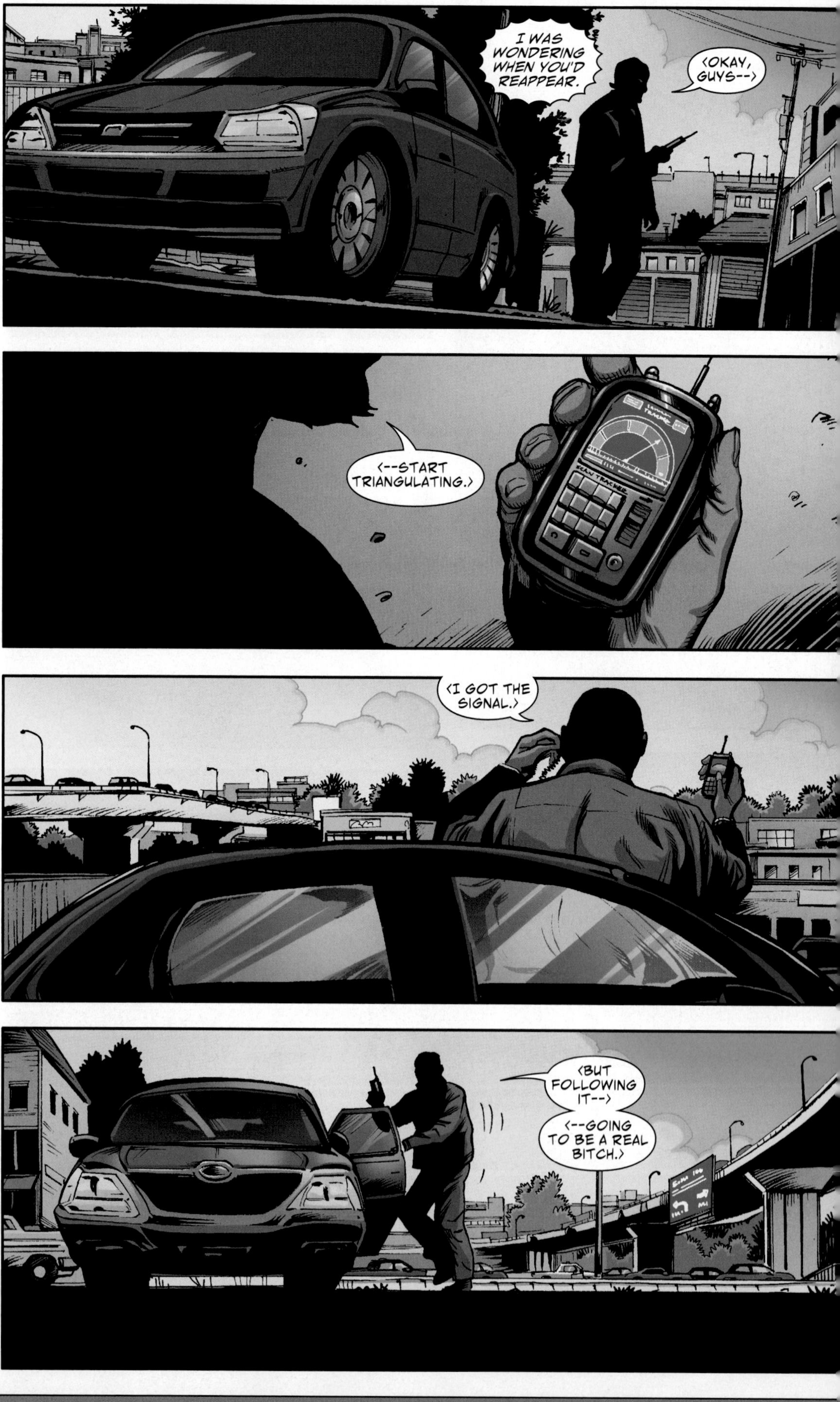
I WAS WONDERING WHEN YOU'D REAPPEAR.
<OKAY, GUYS-->
<--START TRIANGULATING.>
<I GOT THE SIGNAL.>
<BUT FOLLOWING IT-->
<--GOING TO BE A REAL BITCH.>

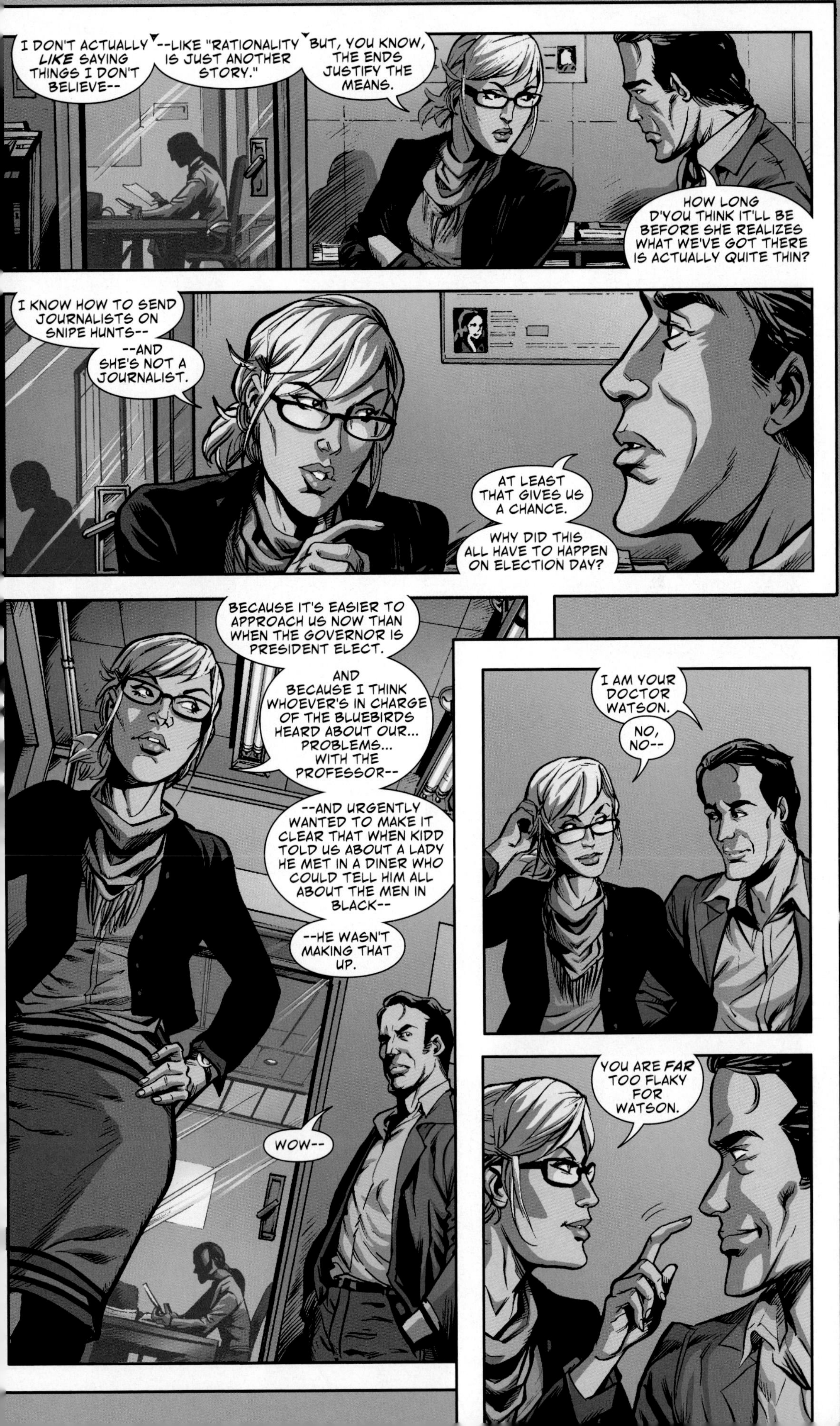
I DON'T ACTUALLY *LIKE* SAYING THINGS I DON'T BELIEVE--
--LIKE "RATIONALITY IS JUST ANOTHER STORY."
BUT, YOU KNOW, THE ENDS JUSTIFY THE MEANS.
HOW LONG D'YOU THINK IT'LL BE BEFORE SHE REALIZES WHAT WE'VE GOT THERE IS ACTUALLY QUITE THIN?
I KNOW HOW TO SEND JOURNALISTS ON SNIPE HUNTS--
--AND SHE'S NOT A JOURNALIST.
AT LEAST THAT GIVES US A CHANCE.
WHY DID THIS ALL HAVE TO HAPPEN ON ELECTION DAY?
BECAUSE IT'S EASIER TO APPROACH US NOW THAN WHEN THE GOVERNOR IS PRESIDENT ELECT.
AND BECAUSE I THINK WHOEVER'S IN CHARGE OF THE BLUEBIRDS HEARD ABOUT OUR... PROBLEMS... WITH THE PROFESSOR--
--AND URGENTLY WANTED TO MAKE IT CLEAR THAT WHEN KIDD TOLD US ABOUT A LADY HE MET IN A DINER WHO COULD TELL HIM ALL ABOUT THE MEN IN BLACK--
--HE WASN'T MAKING THAT UP.
WOW--
I AM YOUR DOCTOR WATSON.
NO, NO--
YOU ARE *FAR* TOO FLAKY FOR WATSON.

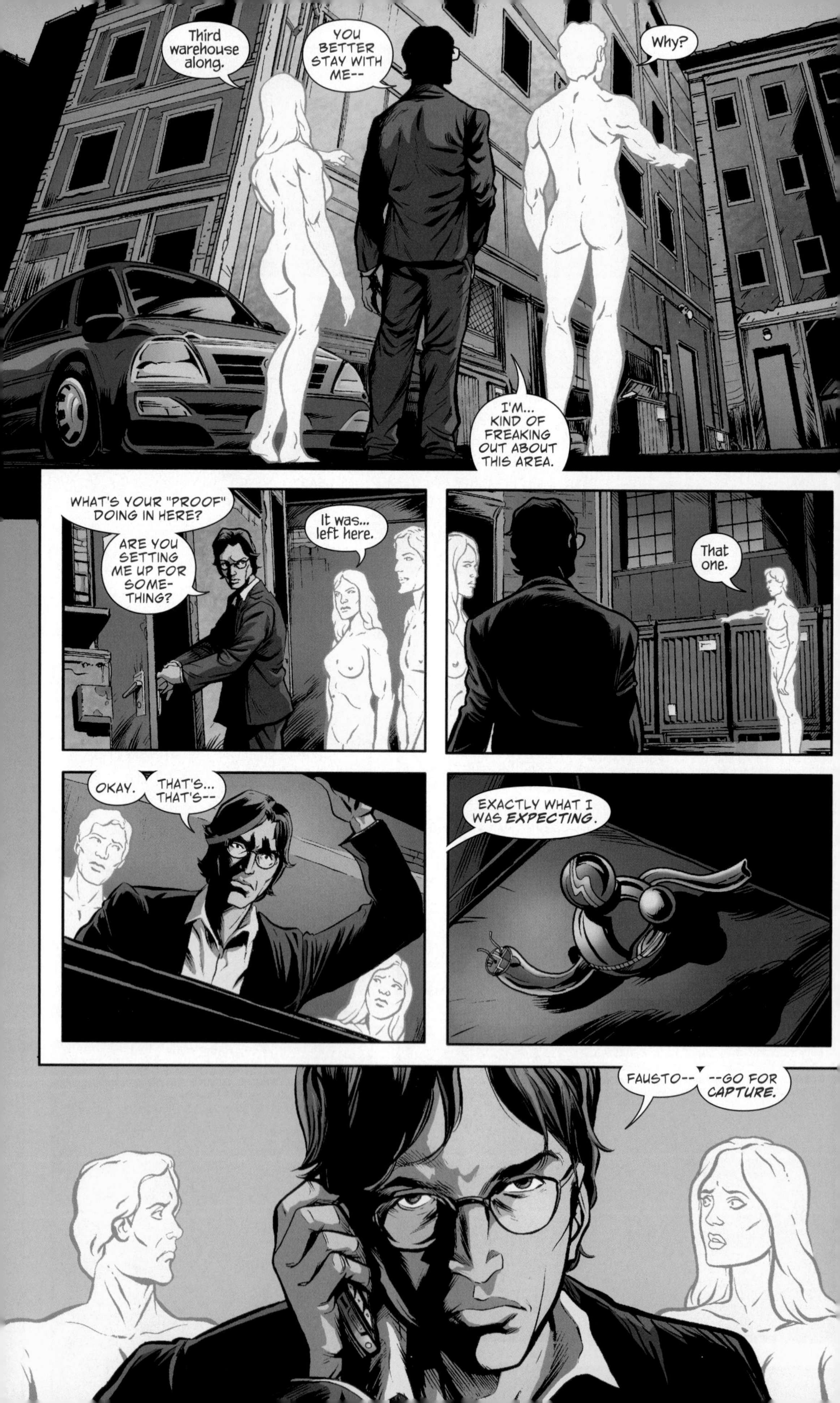
Third warehouse along.
YOU BETTER STAY WITH ME--
Why?
I'M... KIND OF FREAKING OUT ABOUT THIS AREA.
WHAT'S YOUR "PROOF" DOING IN HERE?
ARE YOU SETTING ME UP FOR SOME-THING?
It was... left here.
That one.
OKAY.
THAT'S... THAT'S--
EXACTLY WHAT I WAS *EXPECTING*.
FAUSTO--
--GO FOR *CAPTURE*.

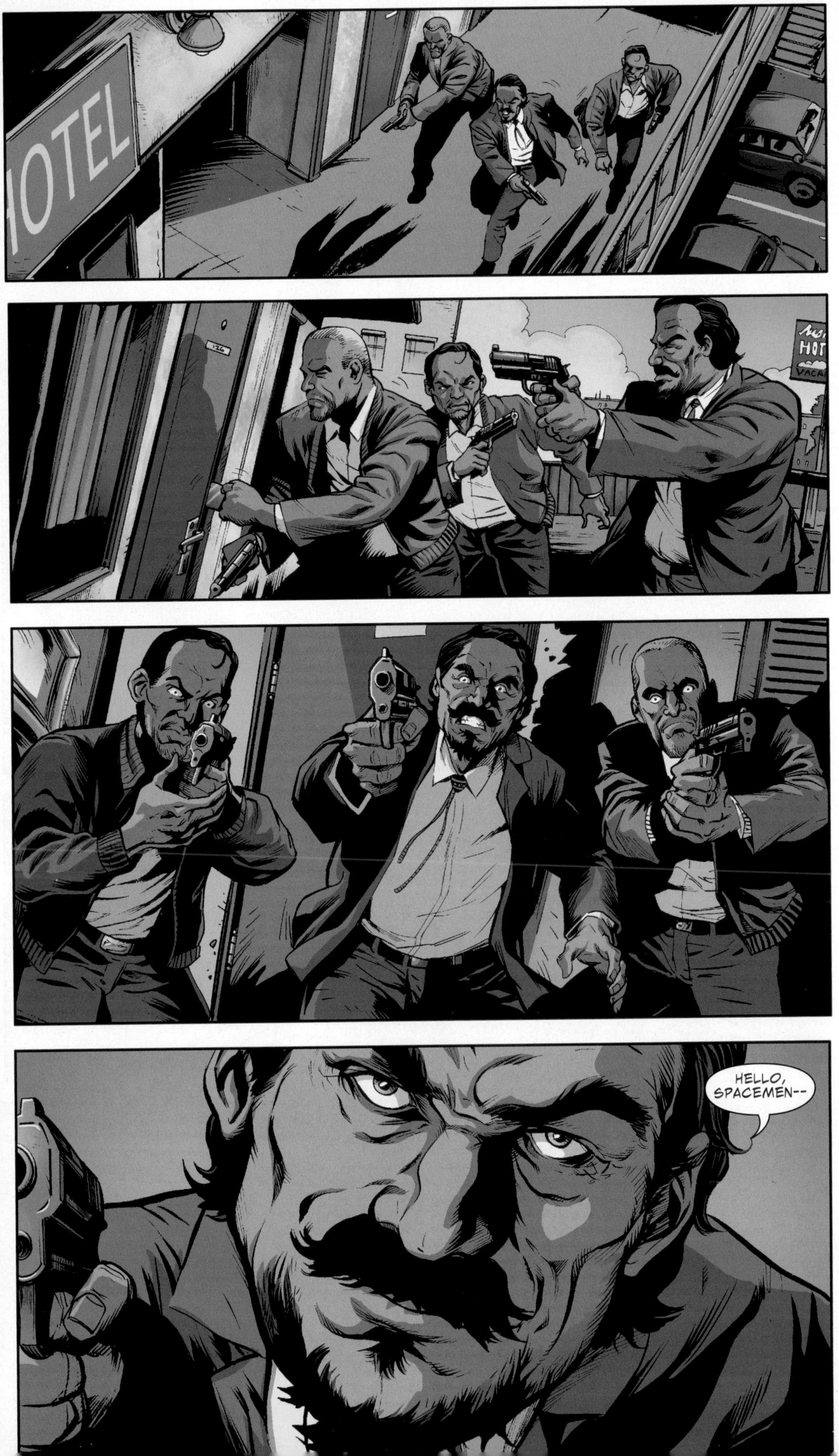
HOTEL
HOTEL
HELLO, SPACEMEN--

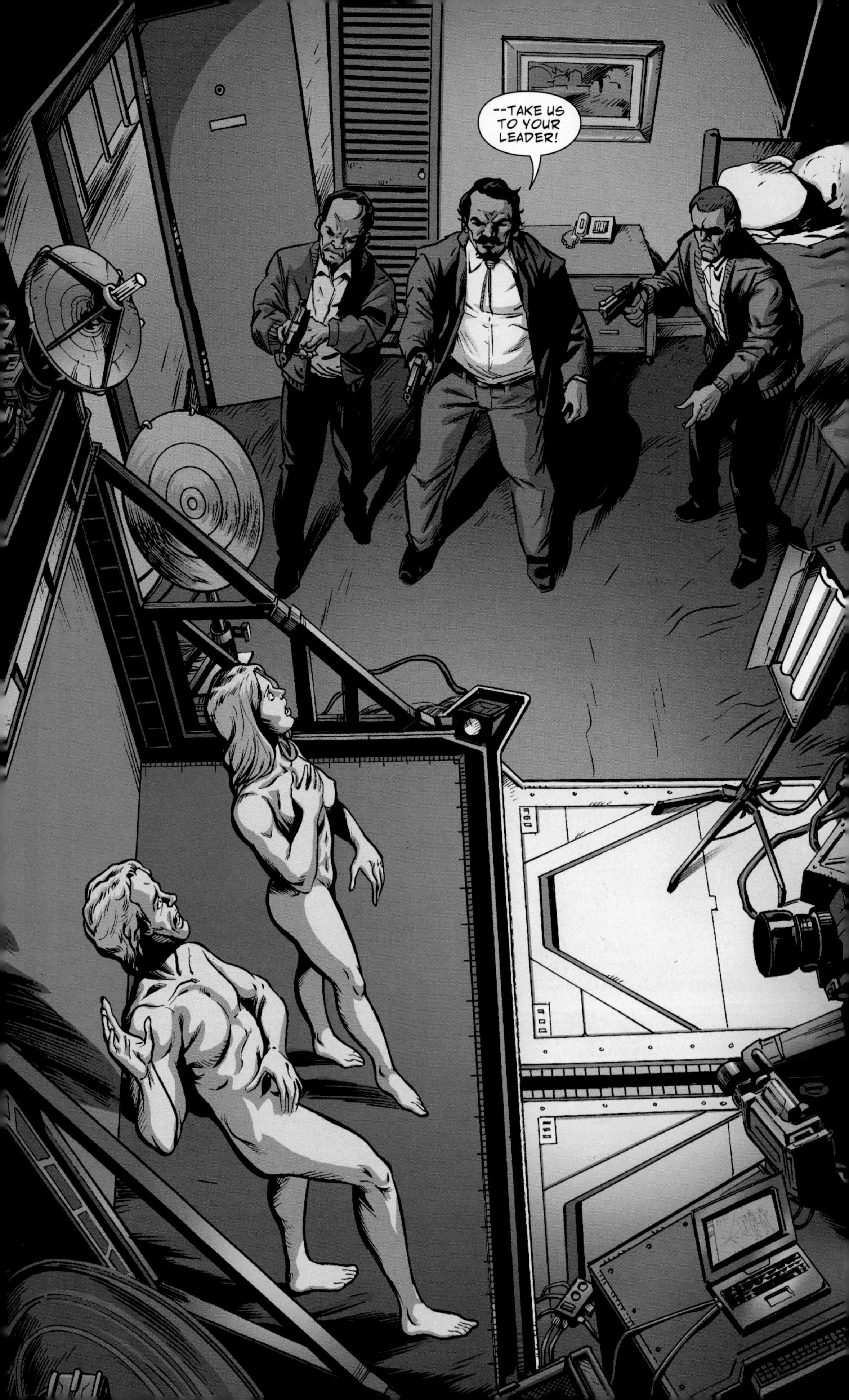
--TAKE US TO YOUR LEADER!

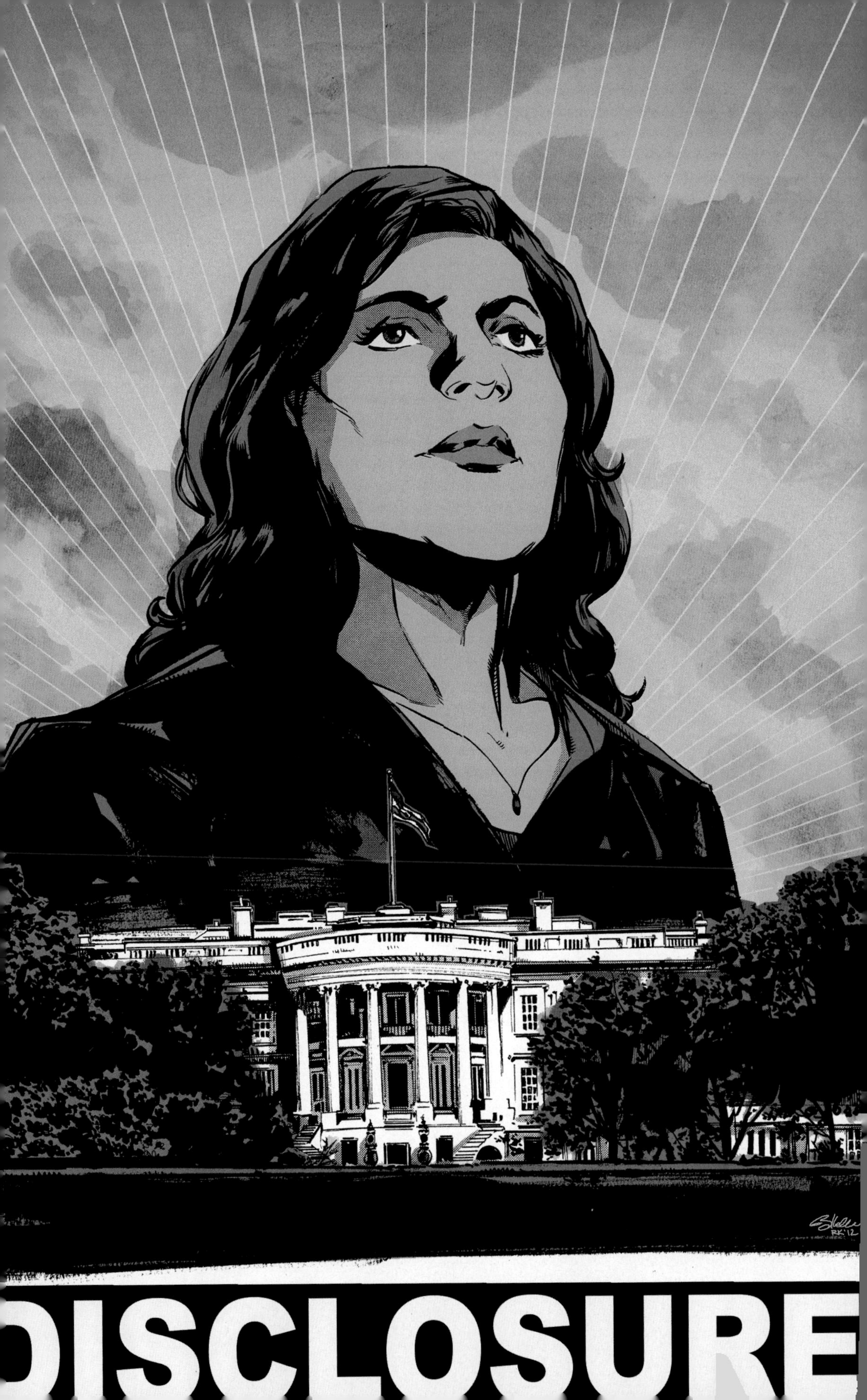
DISCLOSURE

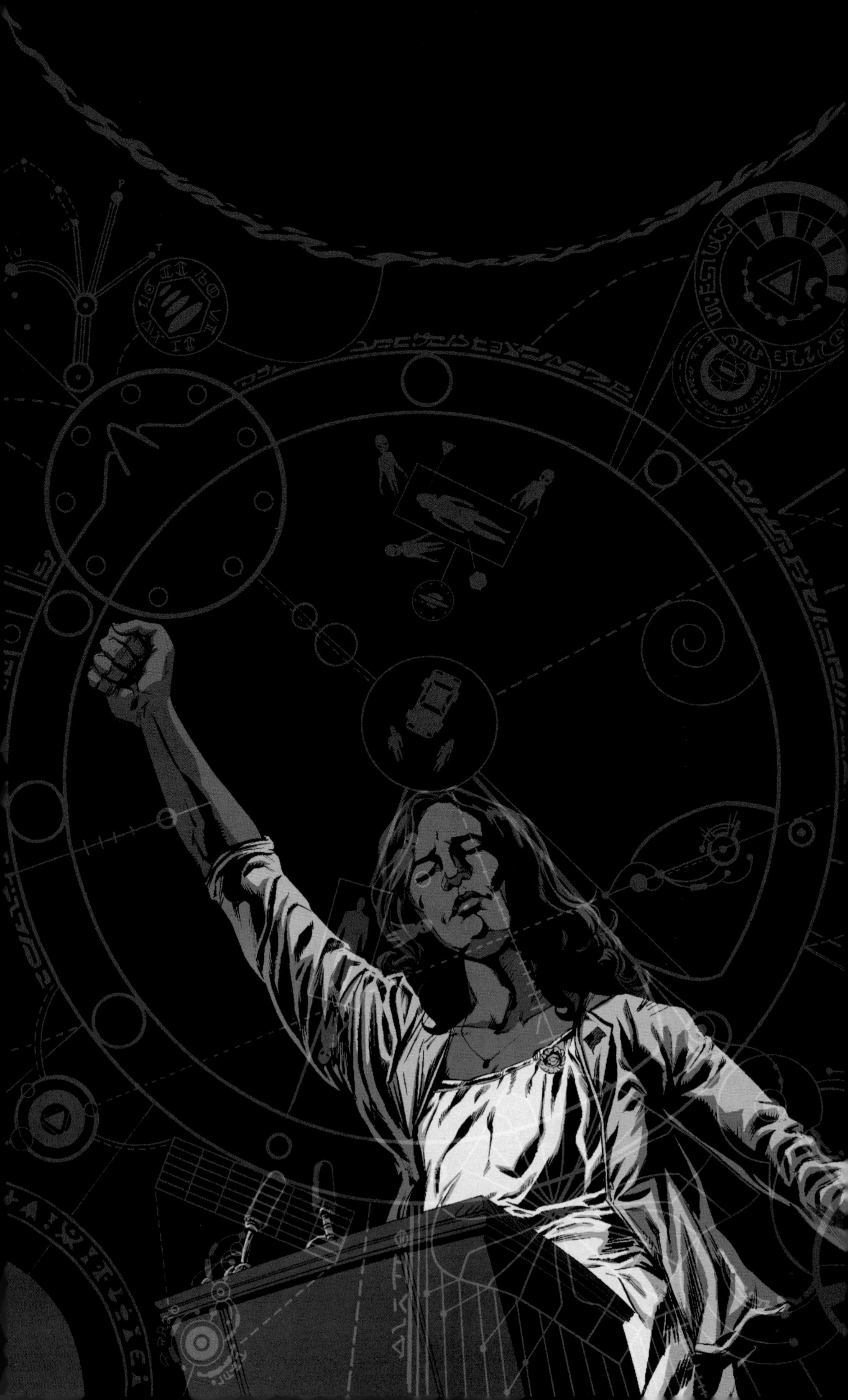

SO I GUESS THIS IS WHAT WAS BEING USED TO PROJECT YOUR IMAGE INTO THE... WHAT, *BRAIN*, OF PROFESSOR KIDD?

WELL, THE INNER EAR ACTUALLY--

BRIAN--!

AH, NOW WE HAVE A NAME!

HE'S NOT THE MESSIAH --

JUST A VERY NAUGHTY BOY!

YOU HAVE NO IDEA WHAT YOU'RE MESSING WITH HERE, AND NO RIGHT TO--

NO RIGHT--?!

WE'RE ACCREDITED DEPUTIES OF THE ARLINGTON COUNTY SHERIFF'S DEPARTMENT. FOR TODAY.

AND WE'RE WONDERING IF THESE *GAMES* YOU'RE PLAYING GOT TWO FRIENDS OF OURS *MURDERED.*

DON'T LET OUR PLEASANT NATURES--

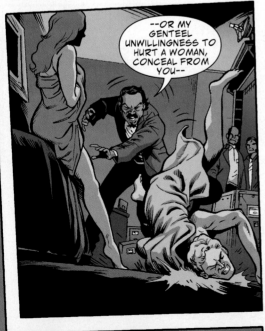

--OR MY GENTEEL UNWILLINGNESS TO HURT A WOMAN, CONCEAL FROM YOU--

--THE SHEER *DEPTH* OF THE *SHIT* WHICH WE CAN *DROWN* YOU IN!

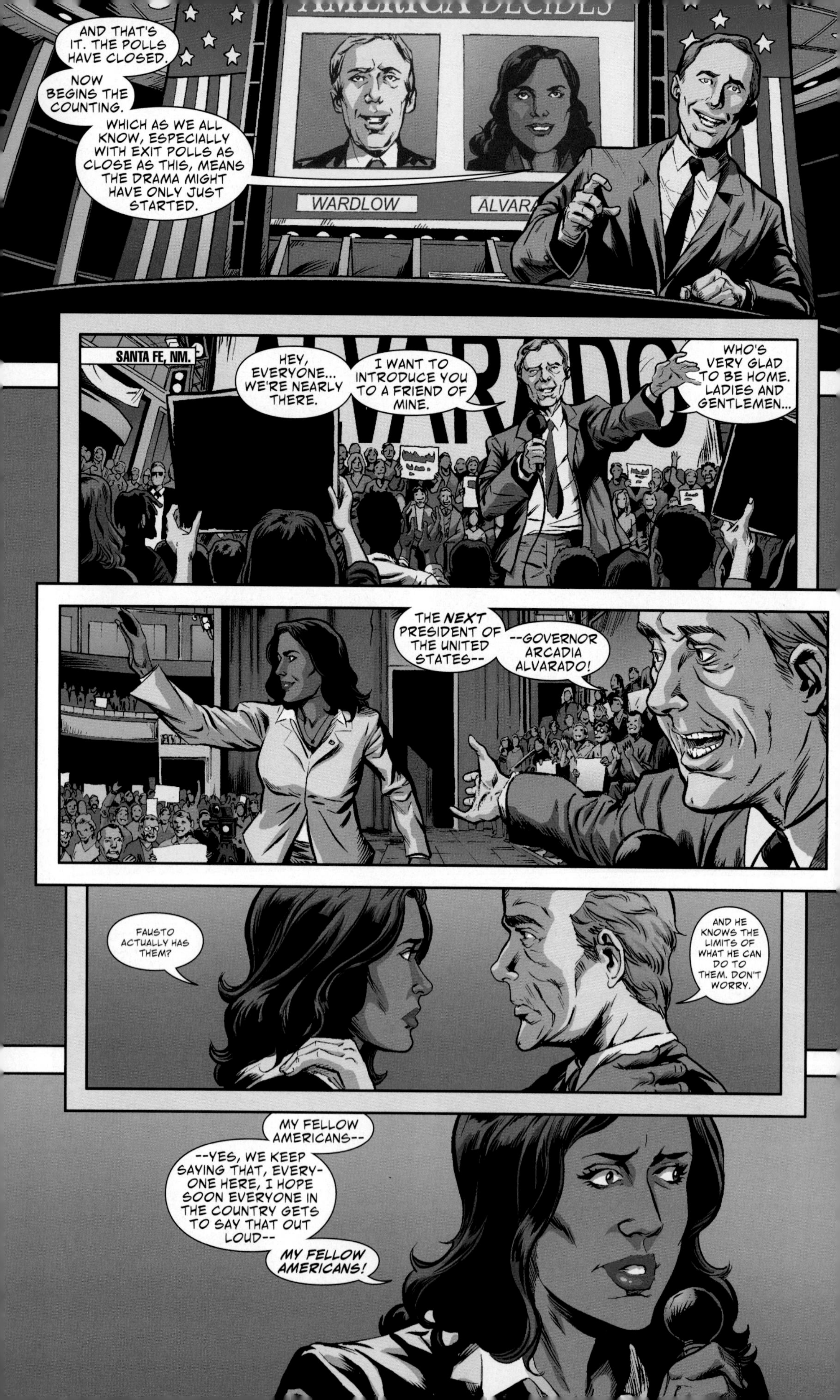
AMERICA DECIDES
AND THAT'S IT. THE POLLS HAVE CLOSED.
NOW BEGINS THE COUNTING.
WHICH AS WE ALL KNOW, ESPECIALLY WITH EXIT POLLS AS CLOSE AS THIS, MEANS THE DRAMA MIGHT HAVE ONLY JUST STARTED.
WARDLOW
ALVARA
SANTA FE, NM.
HEY, EVERYONE... WE'RE NEARLY THERE.
I WANT TO INTRODUCE YOU TO A FRIEND OF MINE.
WHO'S VERY GLAD TO BE HOME. LADIES AND GENTLEMEN...
THE NEXT PRESIDENT OF THE UNITED STATES--
--GOVERNOR ARCADIA ALVARADO!
FAUSTO ACTUALLY HAS THEM?
AND HE KNOWS THE LIMITS OF WHAT HE CAN DO TO THEM. DON'T WORRY.
MY FELLOW AMERICANS--
--YES, WE KEEP SAYING THAT, EVERYONE HERE, I HOPE SOON EVERYONE IN THE COUNTRY GETS TO SAY THAT OUT LOUD--
MY FELLOW AMERICANS!

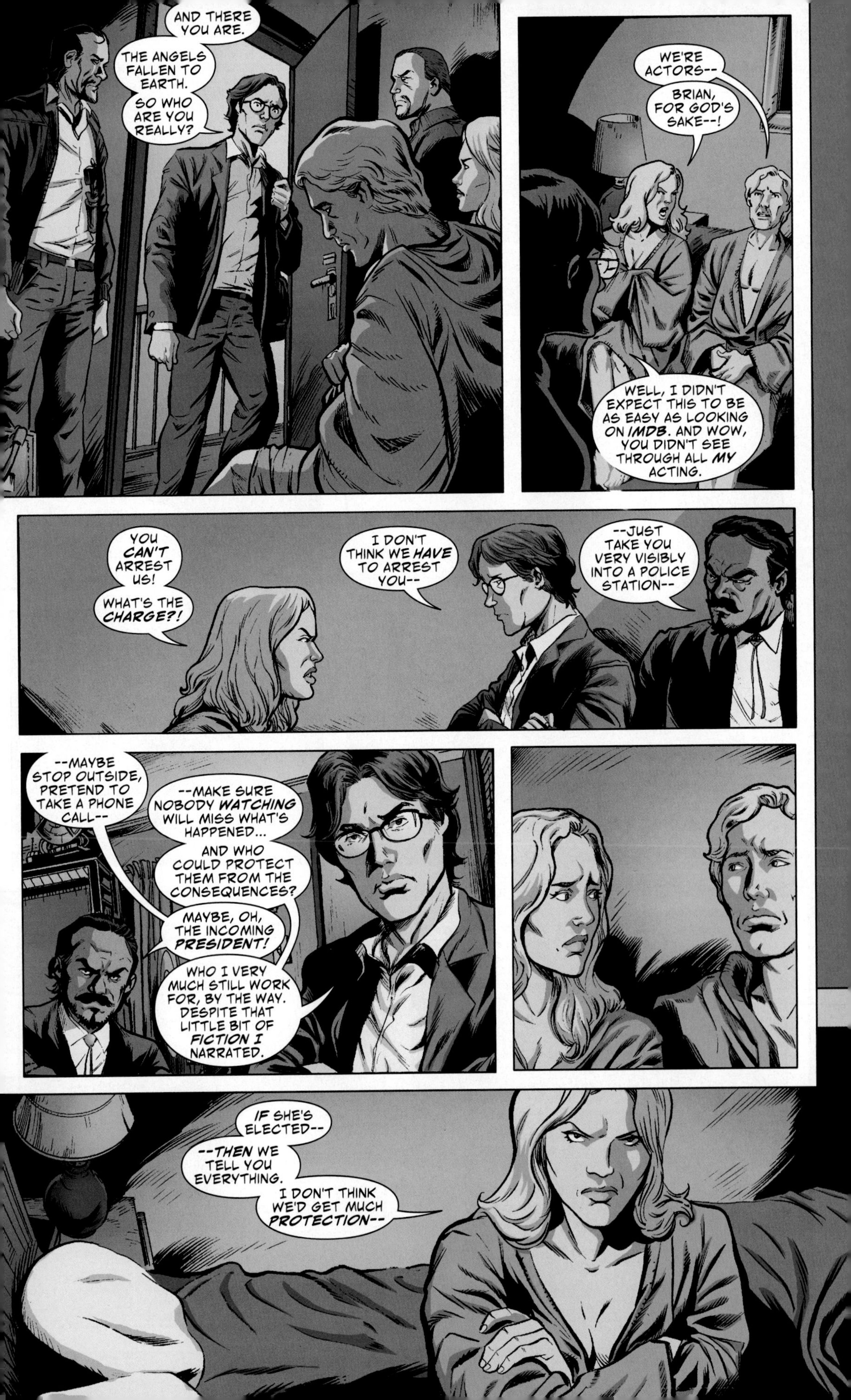
AND THERE YOU ARE.
THE ANGELS FALLEN TO EARTH.
SO WHO ARE YOU REALLY?
WE'RE ACTORS--
BRIAN, FOR GOD'S SAKE--!
WELL, I DIDN'T EXPECT THIS TO BE AS EASY AS LOOKING ON IMDB. AND WOW, YOU DIDN'T SEE THROUGH ALL MY ACTING.
YOU CAN'T ARREST US!
WHAT'S THE CHARGE?!
I DON'T THINK WE HAVE TO ARREST YOU--
--JUST TAKE YOU VERY VISIBLY INTO A POLICE STATION--
--MAYBE STOP OUTSIDE, PRETEND TO TAKE A PHONE CALL--
--MAKE SURE NOBODY WATCHING WILL MISS WHAT'S HAPPENED...
AND WHO COULD PROTECT THEM FROM THE CONSEQUENCES?
MAYBE, OH, THE INCOMING PRESIDENT!
WHO I VERY MUCH STILL WORK FOR, BY THE WAY. DESPITE THAT LITTLE BIT OF FICTION I NARRATED.
IF SHE'S ELECTED--
--THEN WE TELL YOU EVERYTHING.
I DON'T THINK WE'D GET MUCH PROTECTION--

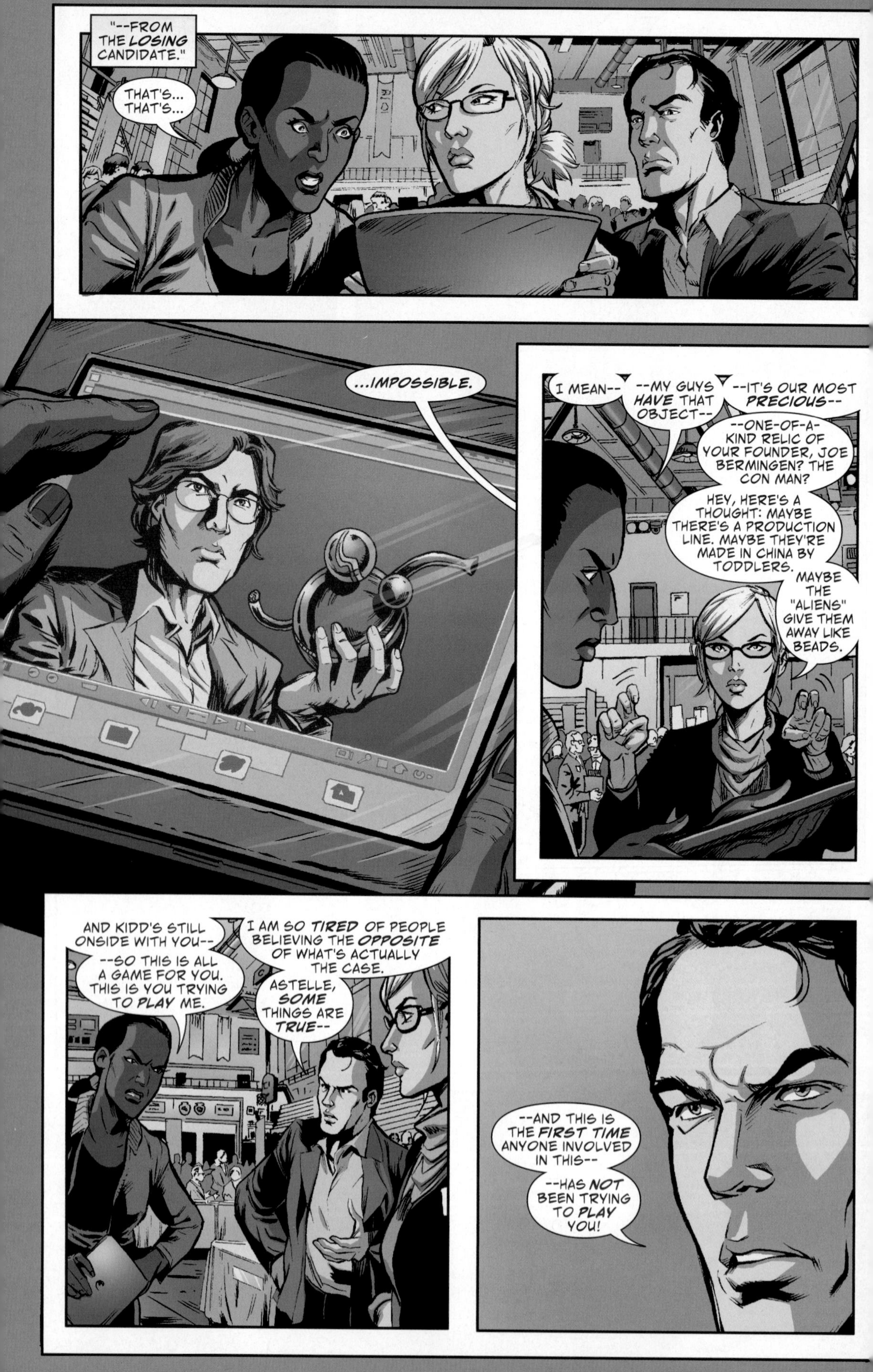
"--FROM THE LOSING CANDIDATE."
THAT'S... THAT'S...
...IMPOSSIBLE.
I MEAN--
--MY GUYS HAVE THAT OBJECT--
--IT'S OUR MOST PRECIOUS--
--ONE-OF-A-KIND RELIC OF YOUR FOUNDER, JOE BERMINGEN? THE CON MAN?
HEY, HERE'S A THOUGHT: MAYBE THERE'S A PRODUCTION LINE. MAYBE THEY'RE MADE IN CHINA BY TODDLERS.
MAYBE THE "ALIENS" GIVE THEM AWAY LIKE BEADS.
AND KIDD'S STILL ONSIDE WITH YOU--
--SO THIS IS ALL A GAME FOR YOU. THIS IS YOU TRYING TO PLAY ME.
I AM SO TIRED OF PEOPLE BELIEVING THE OPPOSITE OF WHAT'S ACTUALLY THE CASE.
ASTELLE, SOME THINGS ARE TRUE--
--AND THIS IS THE FIRST TIME ANYONE INVOLVED IN THIS--
--HAS NOT BEEN TRYING TO PLAY YOU!

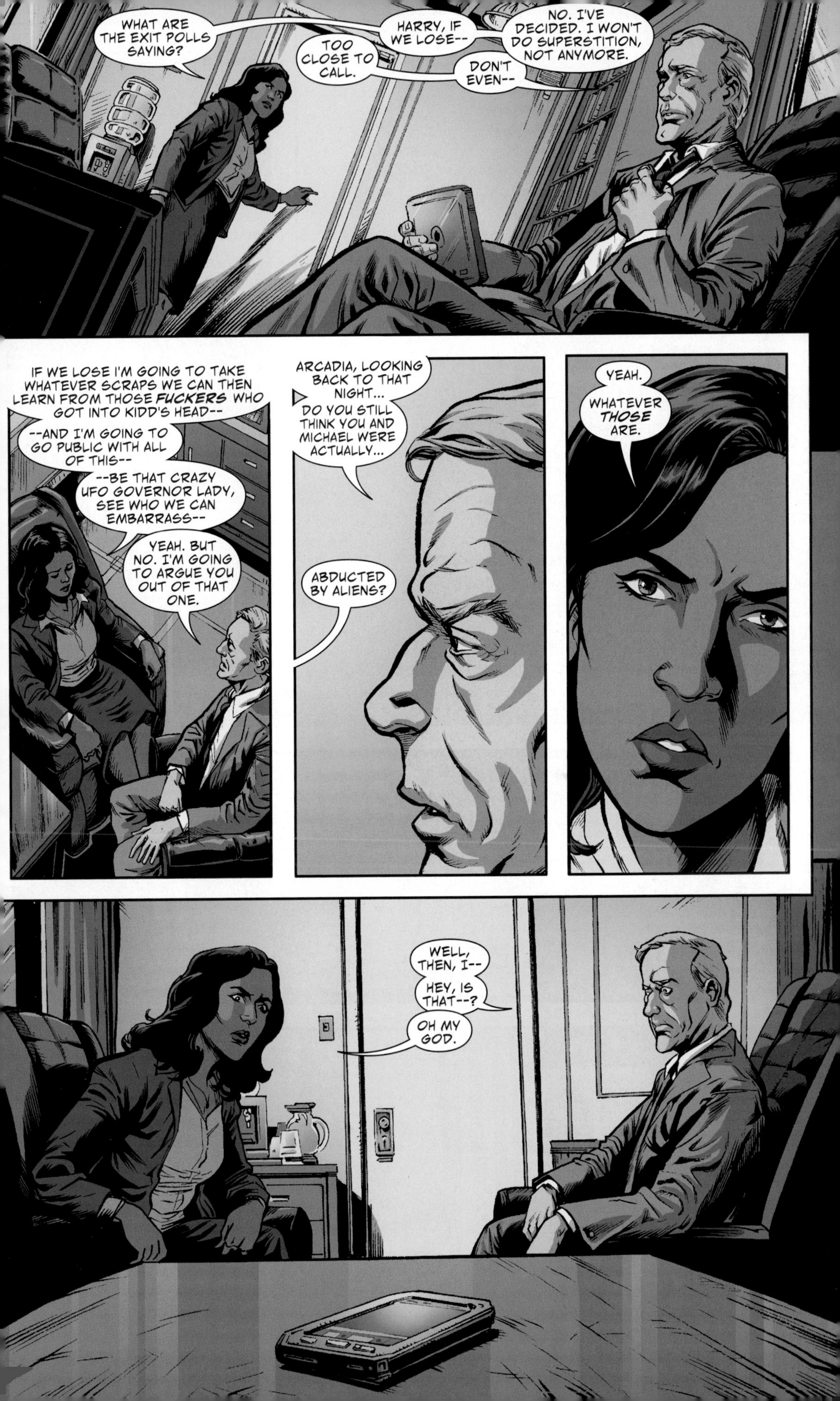
WHAT ARE THE EXIT POLLS SAYING?
TOO CLOSE TO CALL.
HARRY, IF WE LOSE--
DON'T EVEN--
NO. I'VE DECIDED. I WON'T DO SUPERSTITION, NOT ANYMORE.
IF WE LOSE I'M GOING TO TAKE WHATEVER SCRAPS WE CAN THEN LEARN FROM THOSE FUCKERS WHO GOT INTO KIDD'S HEAD--
--AND I'M GOING TO GO PUBLIC WITH ALL OF THIS--
--BE THAT CRAZY UFO GOVERNOR LADY, SEE WHO WE CAN EMBARRASS--
YEAH. BUT NO. I'M GOING TO ARGUE YOU OUT OF THAT ONE.
ARCADIA, LOOKING BACK TO THAT NIGHT...
DO YOU STILL THINK YOU AND MICHAEL WERE ACTUALLY...
ABDUCTED BY ALIENS?
YEAH.
WHATEVER THOSE ARE.
WELL, THEN, I--
HEY, IS THAT--?
OH MY GOD.

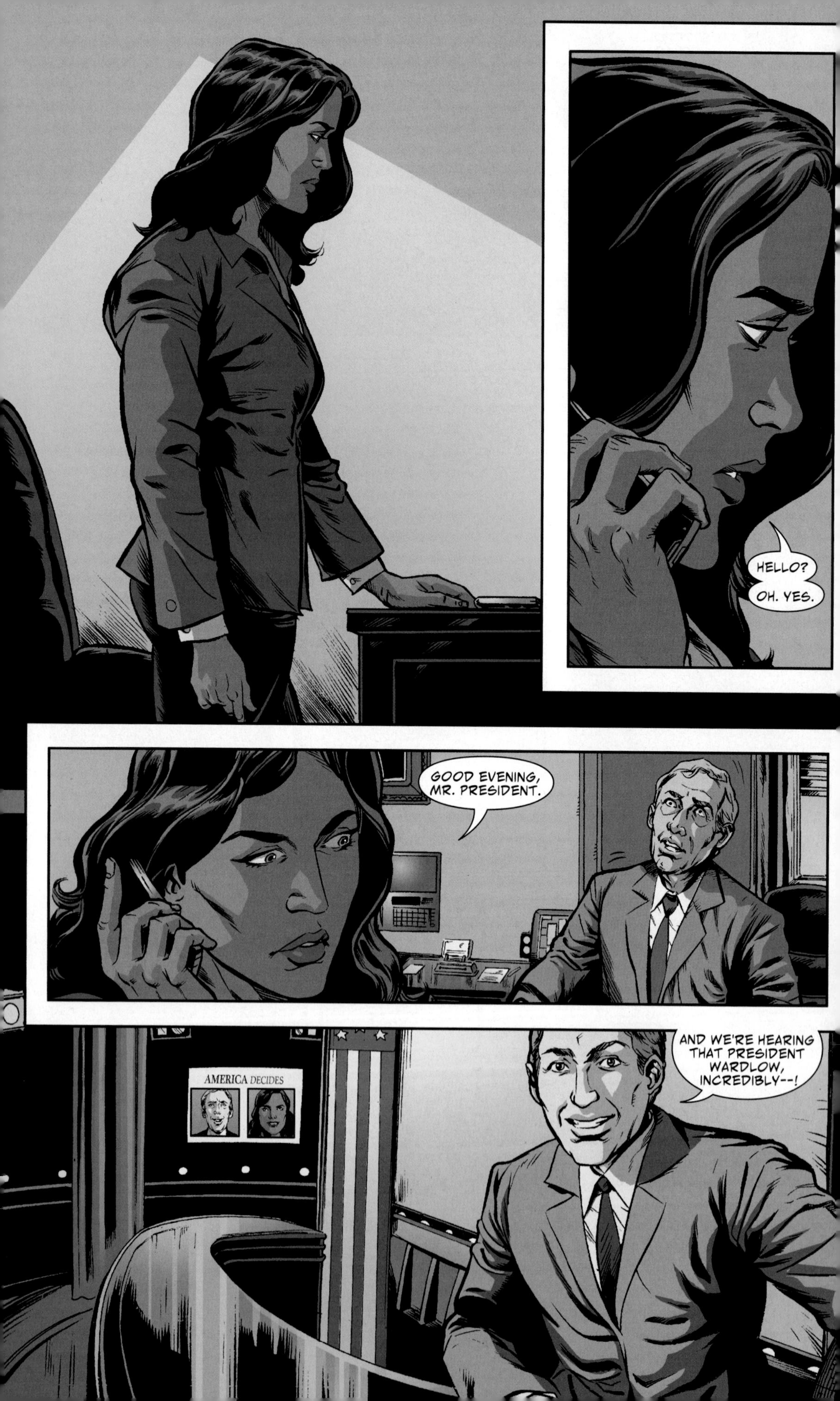
HELLO?
OH. YES.
GOOD EVENING, MR. PRESIDENT.
AMERICA DECIDES
AND WE'RE HEARING THAT PRESIDENT WARDLOW, INCREDIBLY--!

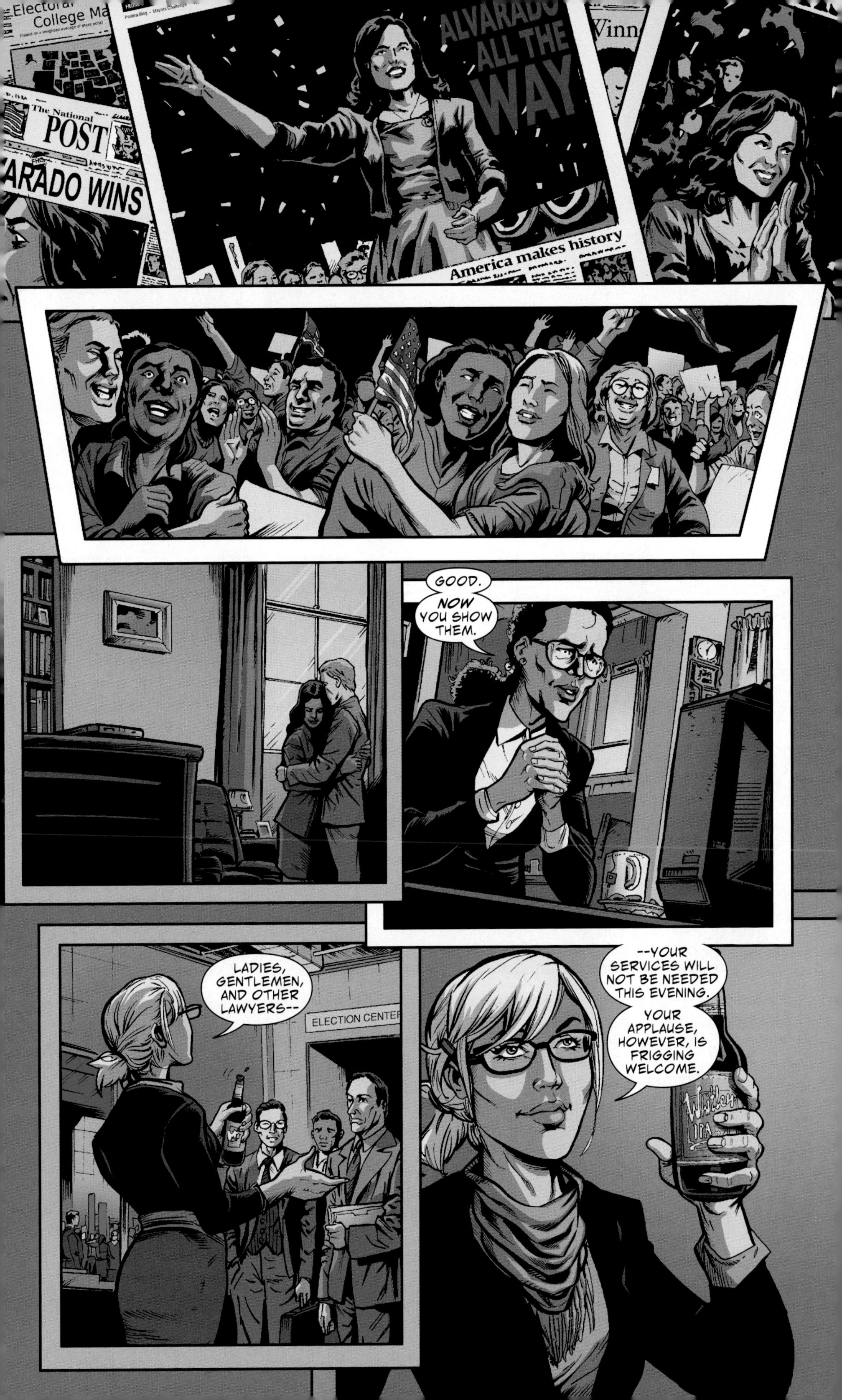
Electoral College Ma
The National POST
ARADO WINS
ALVARADO ALL THE WAY
America makes history
GOOD.
NOW YOU SHOW THEM.
LADIES, GENTLEMEN, AND OTHER LAWYERS--
ELECTION CENTER
--YOUR SERVICES WILL NOT BE NEEDED THIS EVENING.
YOUR APPLAUSE, HOWEVER, IS FRIGGING WELCOME.

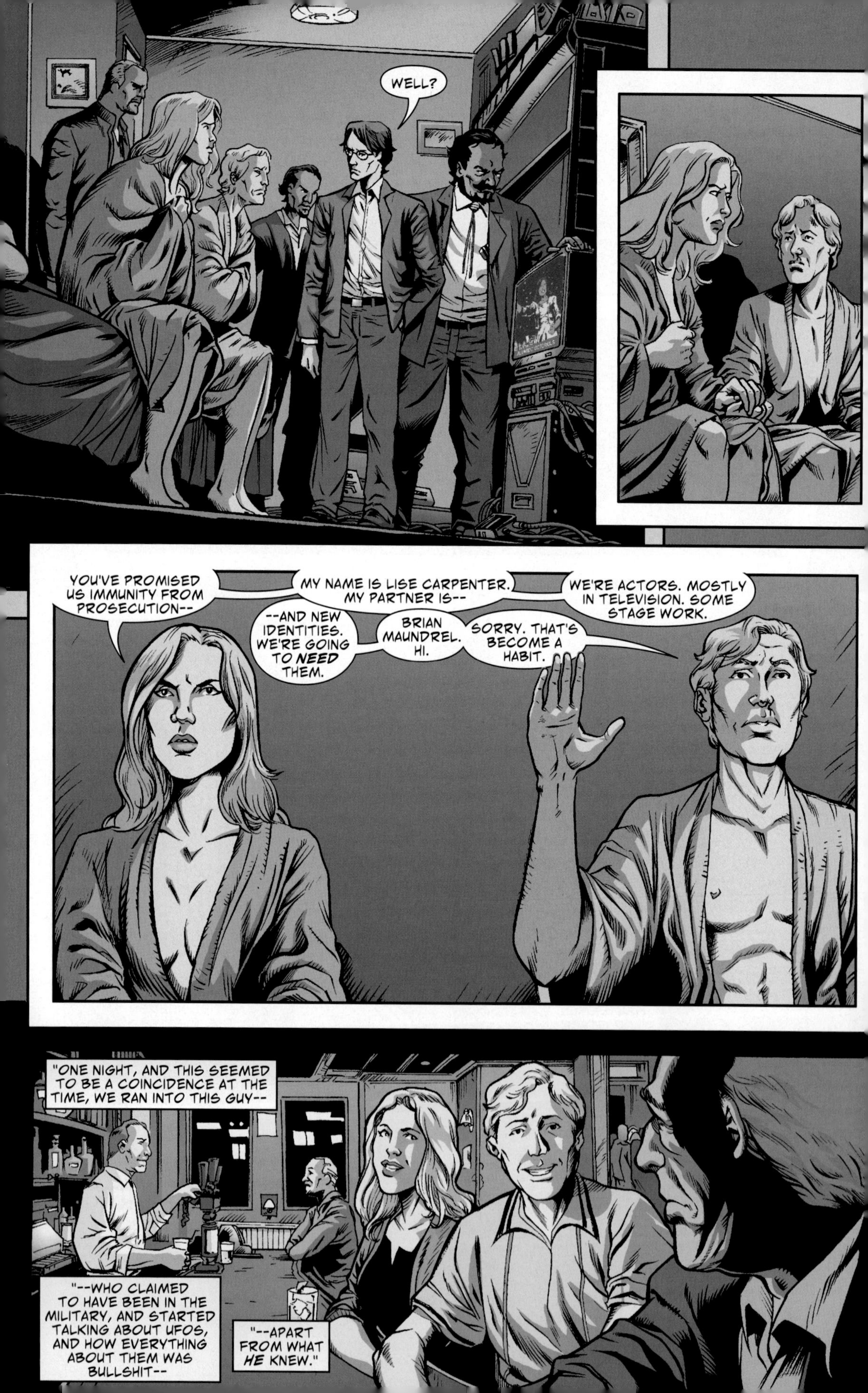
WELL?
YOU'VE PROMISED US IMMUNITY FROM PROSECUTION--
MY NAME IS LISE CARPENTER. MY PARTNER IS--
--AND NEW IDENTITIES. WE'RE GOING TO NEED THEM.
BRIAN MAUNDREL. HI.
SORRY. THAT'S BECOME A HABIT.
WE'RE ACTORS. MOSTLY IN TELEVISION. SOME STAGE WORK.
"ONE NIGHT, AND THIS SEEMED TO BE A COINCIDENCE AT THE TIME, WE RAN INTO THIS GUY--
"--WHO CLAIMED TO HAVE BEEN IN THE MILITARY, AND STARTED TALKING ABOUT UFOS, AND HOW EVERYTHING ABOUT THEM WAS BULLSHIT--
"--APART FROM WHAT HE KNEW."

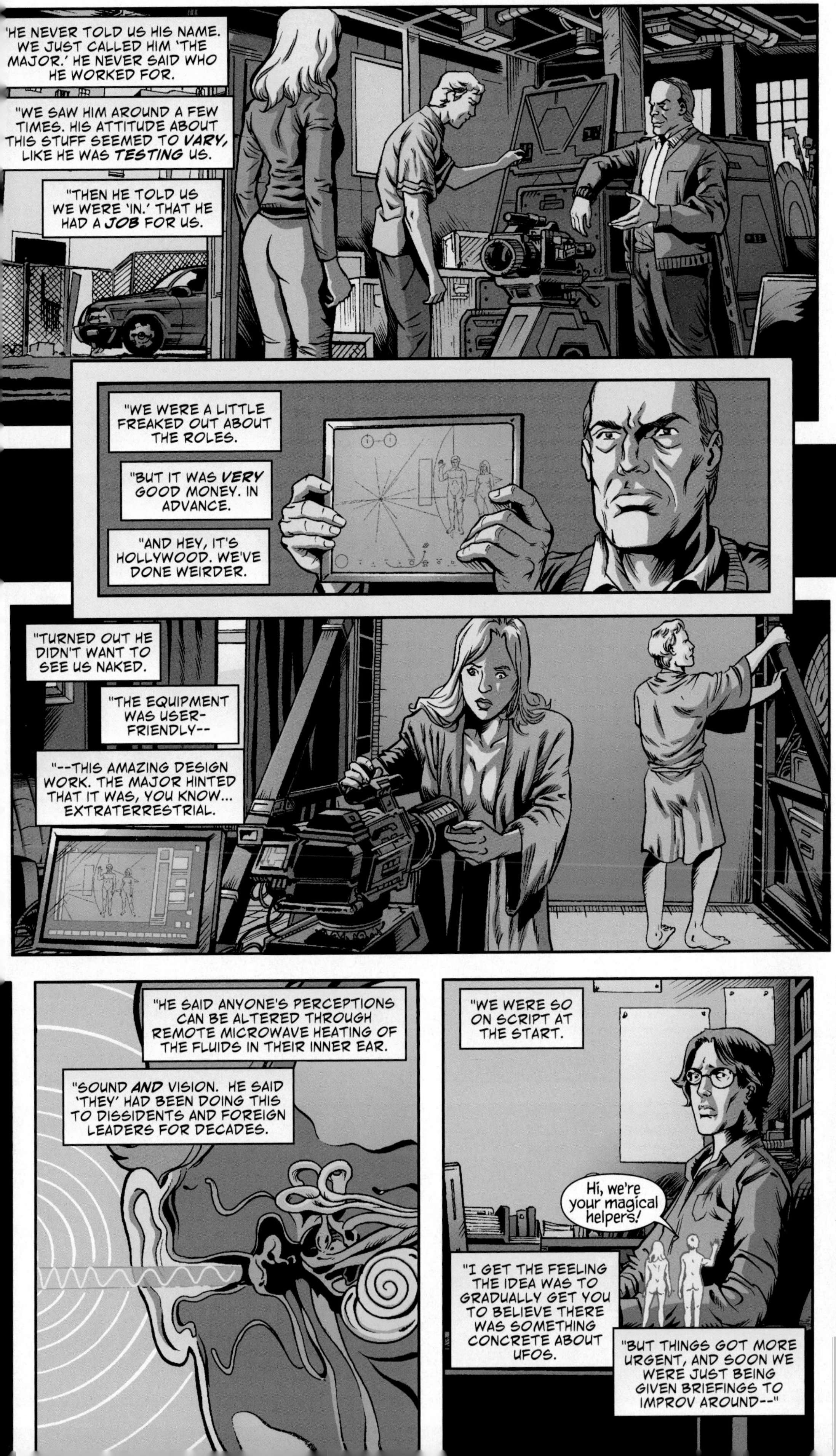
'HE NEVER TOLD US HIS NAME. WE JUST CALLED HIM 'THE MAJOR.' HE NEVER SAID WHO HE WORKED FOR.
"WE SAW HIM AROUND A FEW TIMES. HIS ATTITUDE ABOUT THIS STUFF SEEMED TO VARY, LIKE HE WAS TESTING US.
"THEN HE TOLD US WE WERE 'IN.' THAT HE HAD A JOB FOR US.
"WE WERE A LITTLE FREAKED OUT ABOUT THE ROLES.
"BUT IT WAS VERY GOOD MONEY. IN ADVANCE.
"AND HEY, IT'S HOLLYWOOD. WE'VE DONE WEIRDER.
"TURNED OUT HE DIDN'T WANT TO SEE US NAKED.
"THE EQUIPMENT WAS USER-FRIENDLY--
"--THIS AMAZING DESIGN WORK. THE MAJOR HINTED THAT IT WAS, YOU KNOW... EXTRATERRESTRIAL.
"HE SAID ANYONE'S PERCEPTIONS CAN BE ALTERED THROUGH REMOTE MICROWAVE HEATING OF THE FLUIDS IN THEIR INNER EAR.
"SOUND AND VISION. HE SAID 'THEY' HAD BEEN DOING THIS TO DISSIDENTS AND FOREIGN LEADERS FOR DECADES.
"WE WERE SO ON SCRIPT AT THE START.
Hi, we're your magical helpers!
"I GET THE FEELING THE IDEA WAS TO GRADUALLY GET YOU TO BELIEVE THERE WAS SOMETHING CONCRETE ABOUT UFOS.
"BUT THINGS GOT MORE URGENT, AND SOON WE WERE JUST BEING GIVEN BRIEFINGS TO IMPROV AROUND--"

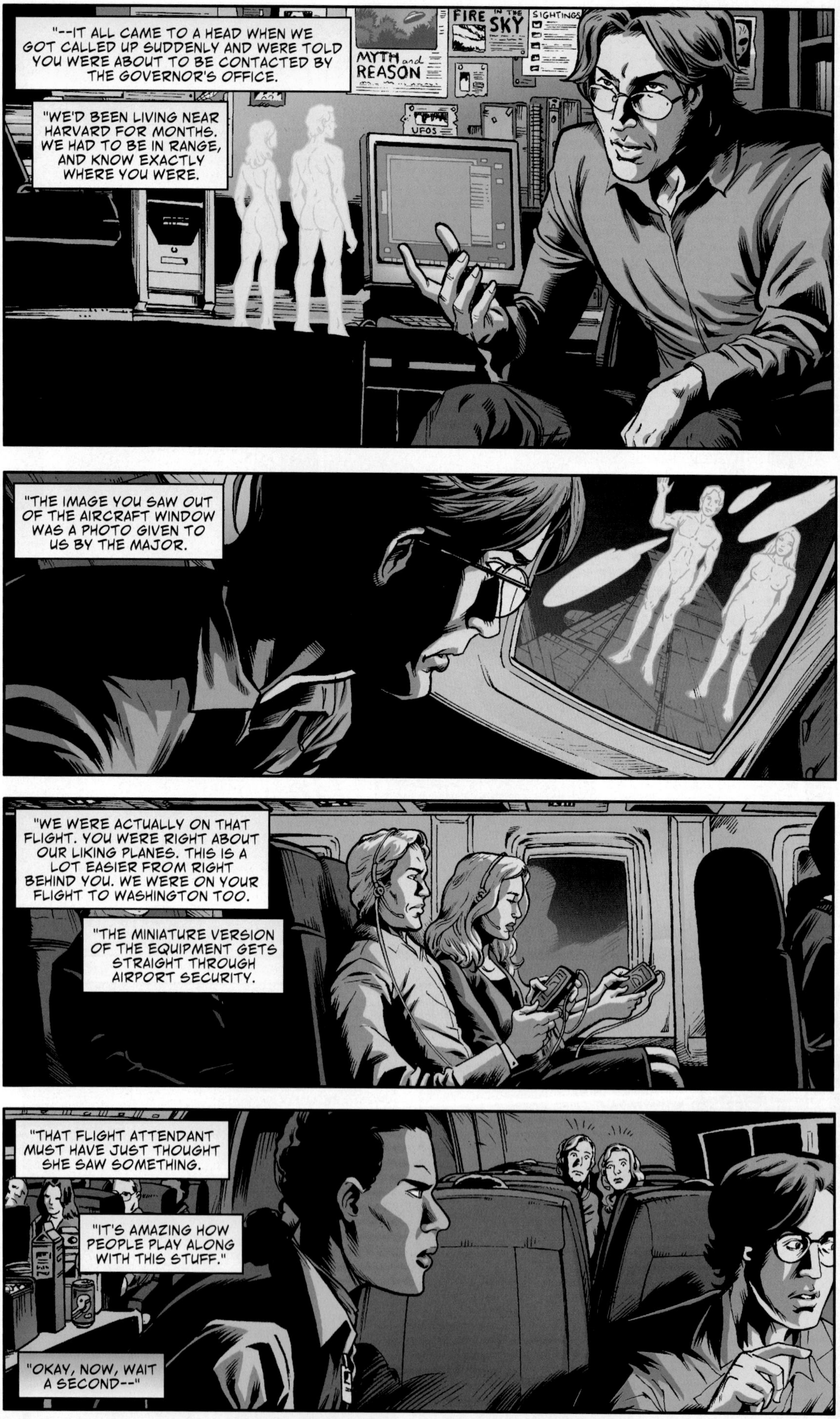
MYTH and REASON
FIRE IN THE SKY
SIGHTINGS
UFOS
"--IT ALL CAME TO A HEAD WHEN WE GOT CALLED UP SUDDENLY AND WERE TOLD YOU WERE ABOUT TO BE CONTACTED BY THE GOVERNOR'S OFFICE.
"WE'D BEEN LIVING NEAR HARVARD FOR MONTHS. WE HAD TO BE IN RANGE, AND KNOW EXACTLY WHERE YOU WERE.
"THE IMAGE YOU SAW OUT OF THE AIRCRAFT WINDOW WAS A PHOTO GIVEN TO US BY THE MAJOR.
"WE WERE ACTUALLY ON THAT FLIGHT. YOU WERE RIGHT ABOUT OUR LIKING PLANES. THIS IS A LOT EASIER FROM RIGHT BEHIND YOU. WE WERE ON YOUR FLIGHT TO WASHINGTON TOO.
"THE MINIATURE VERSION OF THE EQUIPMENT GETS STRAIGHT THROUGH AIRPORT SECURITY.
"THAT FLIGHT ATTENDANT MUST HAVE JUST THOUGHT SHE SAW SOMETHING.
"IT'S AMAZING HOW PEOPLE PLAY ALONG WITH THIS STUFF."
"OKAY, NOW, WAIT A SECOND--"

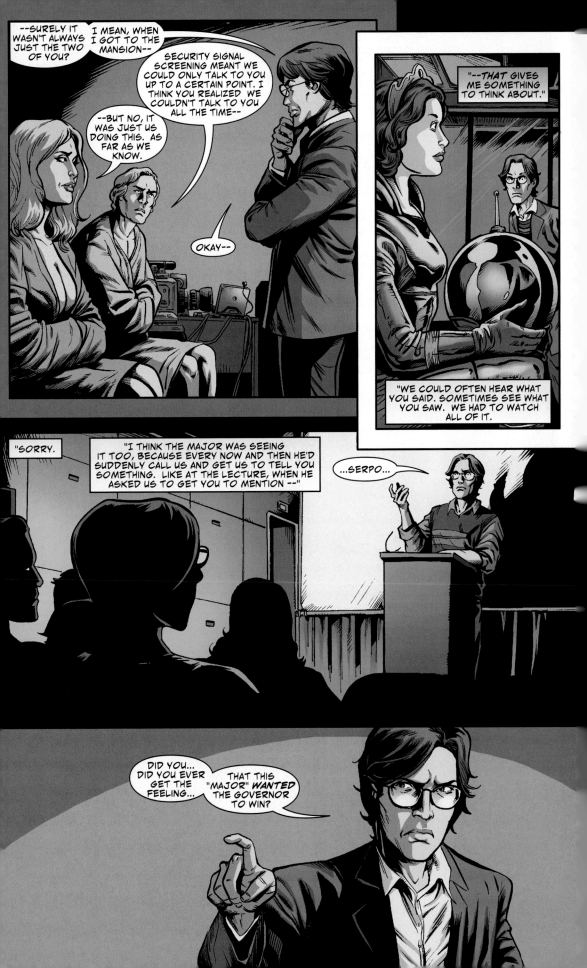

WELL, YES... I MEAN, NEITHER OF US IS PARTICULARLY *POLITICAL*...

BUT WE GOT INTERESTED. WE REALIZED WE WERE BEING GIVEN STUFF FROM INSIDE THE KERSEY CAMPAIGN TO *LEAK* TO YOU.

PROFESSOR--

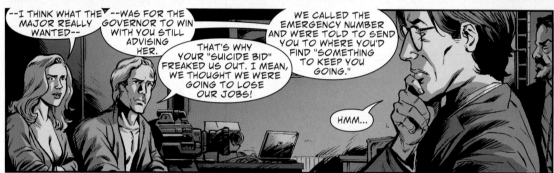

--I THINK WHAT THE MAJOR REALLY WANTED--

--WAS FOR THE GOVERNOR TO WIN WITH YOU STILL ADVISING HER.

THAT'S WHY YOUR "SUICIDE BID" FREAKED US OUT. I MEAN, WE THOUGHT WE WERE GOING TO LOSE OUR JOBS!

WE CALLED THE EMERGENCY NUMBER AND WERE TOLD TO SEND YOU TO WHERE YOU'D FIND "SOMETHING TO KEEP YOU GOING."

HMM...

SO, BACK WHEN I WENT TO VISIT THAT AIRBASE--

YEAH, WE HAD NO IDEA WHY YOU WERE DOING THAT. WE HAD TO FALL BACK TO OUR DEFAULT, "MYSTERIOUS AND ALL-KNOWING."

SO YOU DON'T KNOW THAT WHILE I WAS THERE--

WE COULDN'T SEE YOU. ELECTRONIC SECURITY AGAIN.

WE WERE TOLD THIS "ANNABEL BATES" PERSON HAD LEFT HER HOUSE, AND GAVE THAT TO YOU LIKE IT MEANT SOMETHING.

WOW...

IT'S LIKE MEETING THE LITTLE GUY BEHIND THE *WIZARD OF OZ.* OR GOD, I GUESS.

PART OF ME IS RELIEVED--

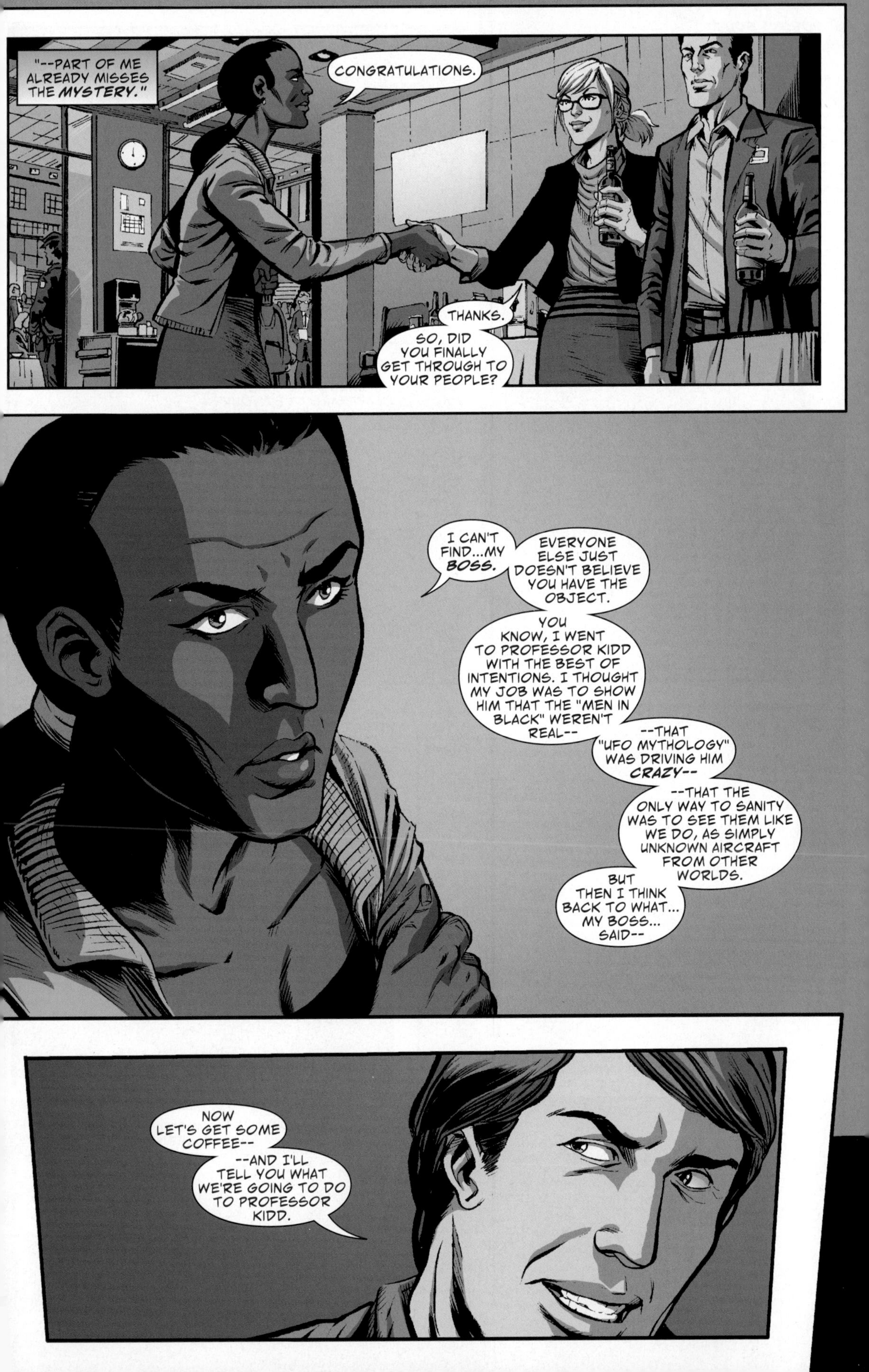
"--PART OF ME ALREADY MISSES THE *MYSTERY.*"
CONGRATULATIONS.
THANKS.
SO, DID YOU FINALLY GET THROUGH TO YOUR PEOPLE?
I CAN'T FIND...MY ***BOSS.***
EVERYONE ELSE JUST DOESN'T BELIEVE YOU HAVE THE OBJECT.
YOU KNOW, I WENT TO PROFESSOR KIDD WITH THE BEST OF INTENTIONS. I THOUGHT MY JOB WAS TO SHOW HIM THAT THE "MEN IN BLACK" WEREN'T REAL--
--THAT "UFO MYTHOLOGY" WAS DRIVING HIM ***CRAZY--***
--THAT THE ONLY WAY TO SANITY WAS TO SEE THEM LIKE WE DO, AS SIMPLY UNKNOWN AIRCRAFT FROM OTHER WORLDS.
BUT THEN I THINK BACK TO WHAT... MY BOSS... SAID--
NOW LET'S GET SOME COFFEE--
--AND I'LL TELL YOU WHAT WE'RE GOING TO DO TO PROFESSOR KIDD.

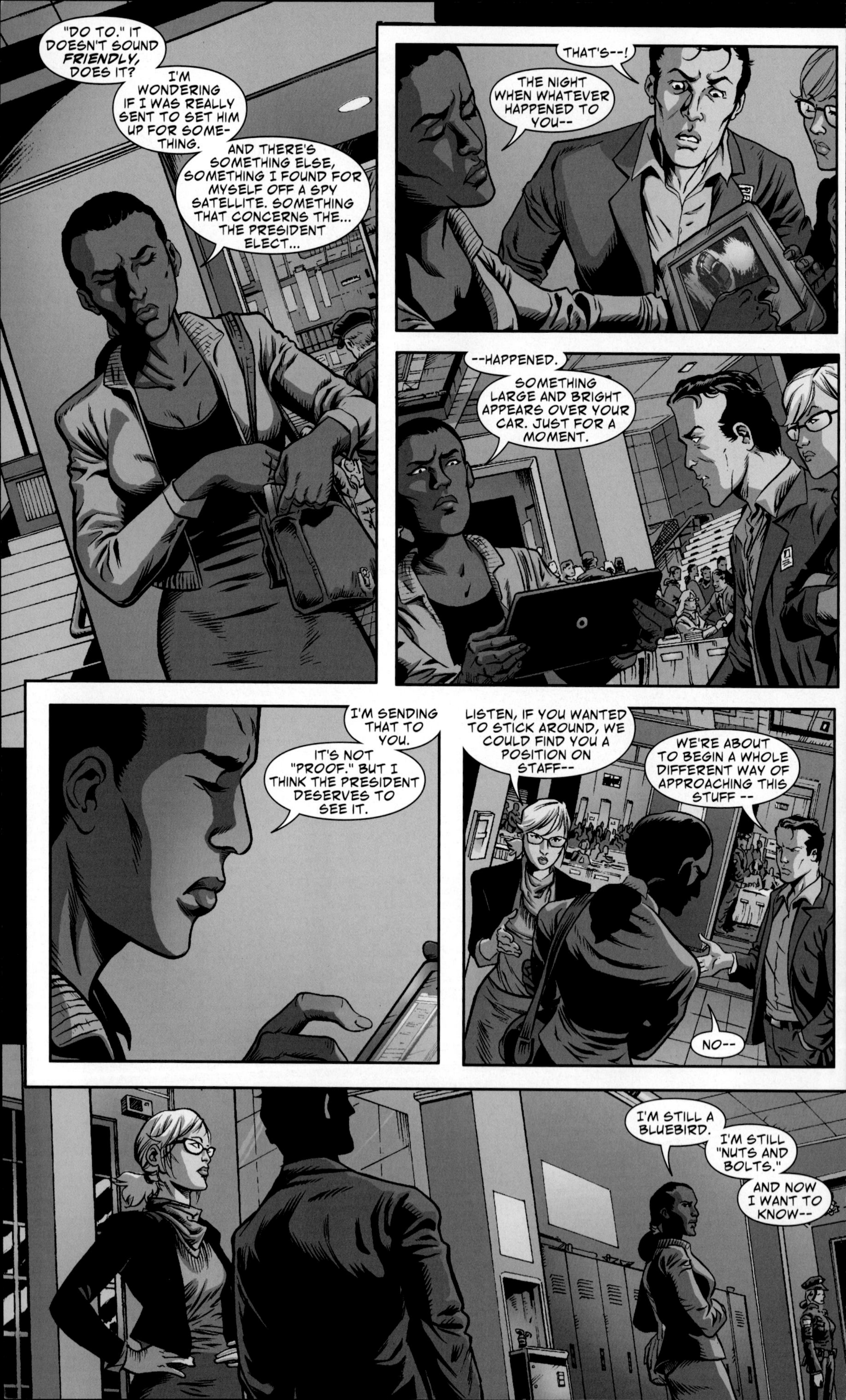
"DO TO." IT DOESN'T SOUND *FRIENDLY,* DOES IT?
I'M WONDERING IF I WAS REALLY SENT TO SET HIM UP FOR SOME-THING.
AND THERE'S SOMETHING ELSE, SOMETHING I FOUND FOR MYSELF OFF A SPY SATELLITE. SOMETHING THAT CONCERNS THE... THE PRESIDENT ELECT...
THAT'S--!
THE NIGHT WHEN WHATEVER HAPPENED TO YOU--
--HAPPENED.
SOMETHING LARGE AND BRIGHT APPEARS OVER YOUR CAR. JUST FOR A MOMENT.
I'M SENDING THAT TO YOU.
IT'S NOT "PROOF." BUT I THINK THE PRESIDENT DESERVES TO SEE IT.
LISTEN, IF YOU WANTED TO STICK AROUND, WE COULD FIND YOU A POSITION ON STAFF--
WE'RE ABOUT TO BEGIN A WHOLE DIFFERENT WAY OF APPROACHING THIS STUFF --
NO--
I'M STILL A BLUEBIRD.
I'M STILL "NUTS AND BOLTS."
AND NOW I WANT TO KNOW--

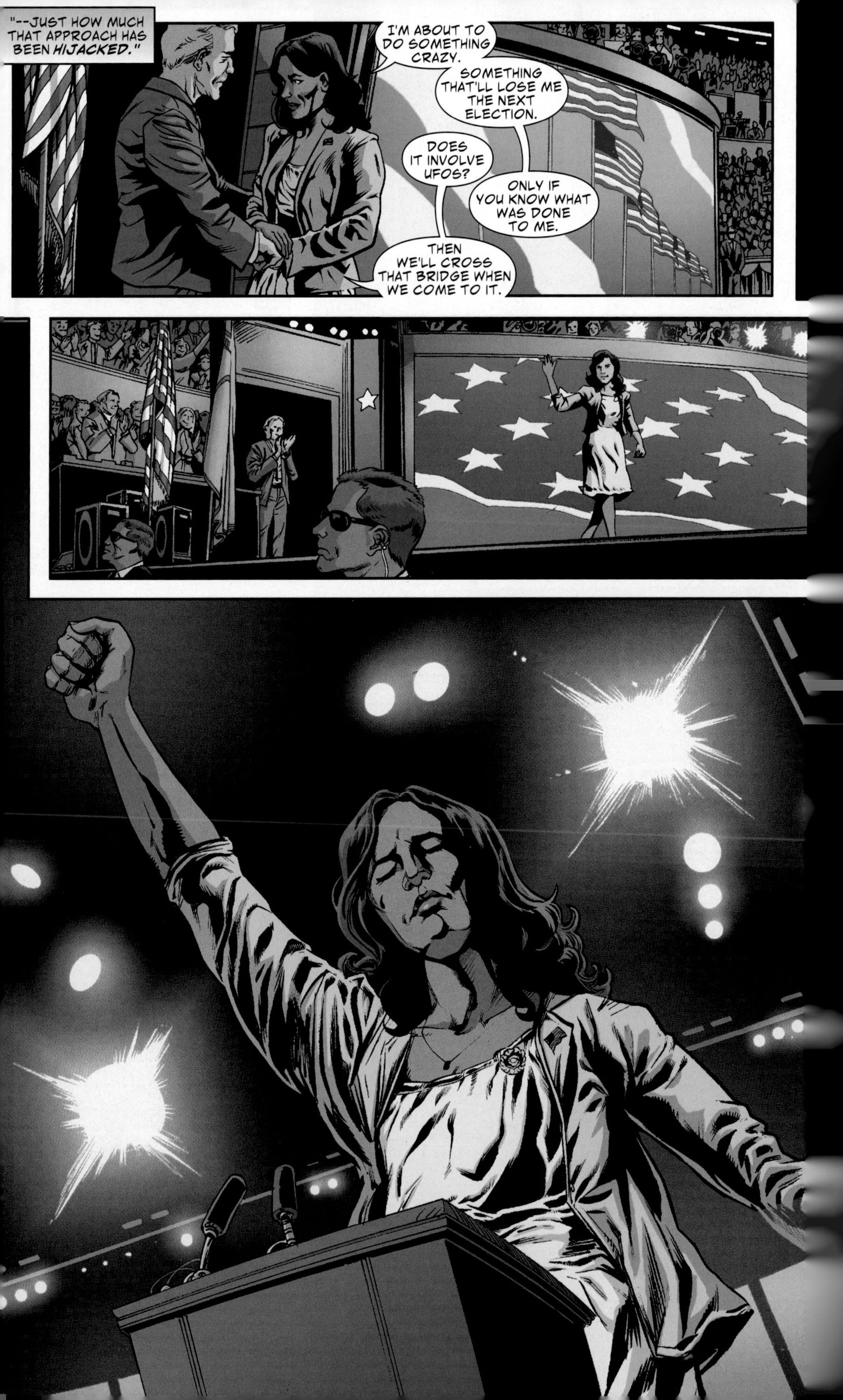
"--JUST HOW MUCH THAT APPROACH HAS BEEN *HIJACKED.*"
I'M ABOUT TO DO SOMETHING CRAZY.
SOMETHING THAT'LL LOSE ME THE NEXT ELECTION.
DOES IT INVOLVE UFOS?
ONLY IF YOU KNOW WHAT WAS DONE TO ME.
THEN WE'LL CROSS THAT BRIDGE WHEN WE COME TO IT.

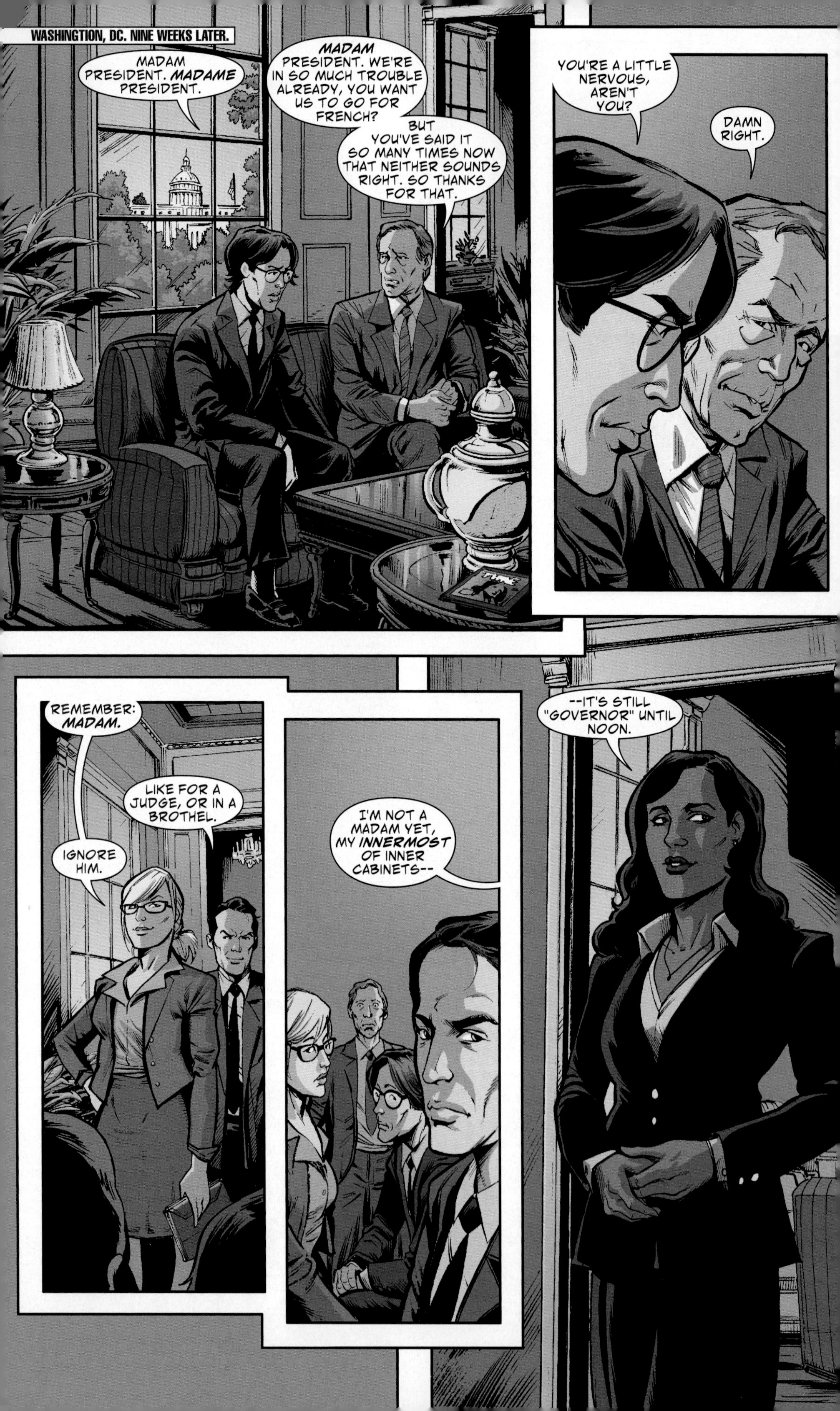
WASHINGTION, DC. NINE WEEKS LATER.
MADAM PRESIDENT. MADAME PRESIDENT.
MADAM PRESIDENT. WE'RE IN SO MUCH TROUBLE ALREADY, YOU WANT US TO GO FOR FRENCH?
BUT YOU'VE SAID IT SO MANY TIMES NOW THAT NEITHER SOUNDS RIGHT. SO THANKS FOR THAT.
YOU'RE A LITTLE NERVOUS, AREN'T YOU?
DAMN RIGHT.
REMEMBER: MADAM.
LIKE FOR A JUDGE, OR IN A BROTHEL.
IGNORE HIM.
I'M NOT A MADAM YET, MY INNERMOST OF INNER CABINETS--
--IT'S STILL "GOVERNOR" UNTIL NOON.

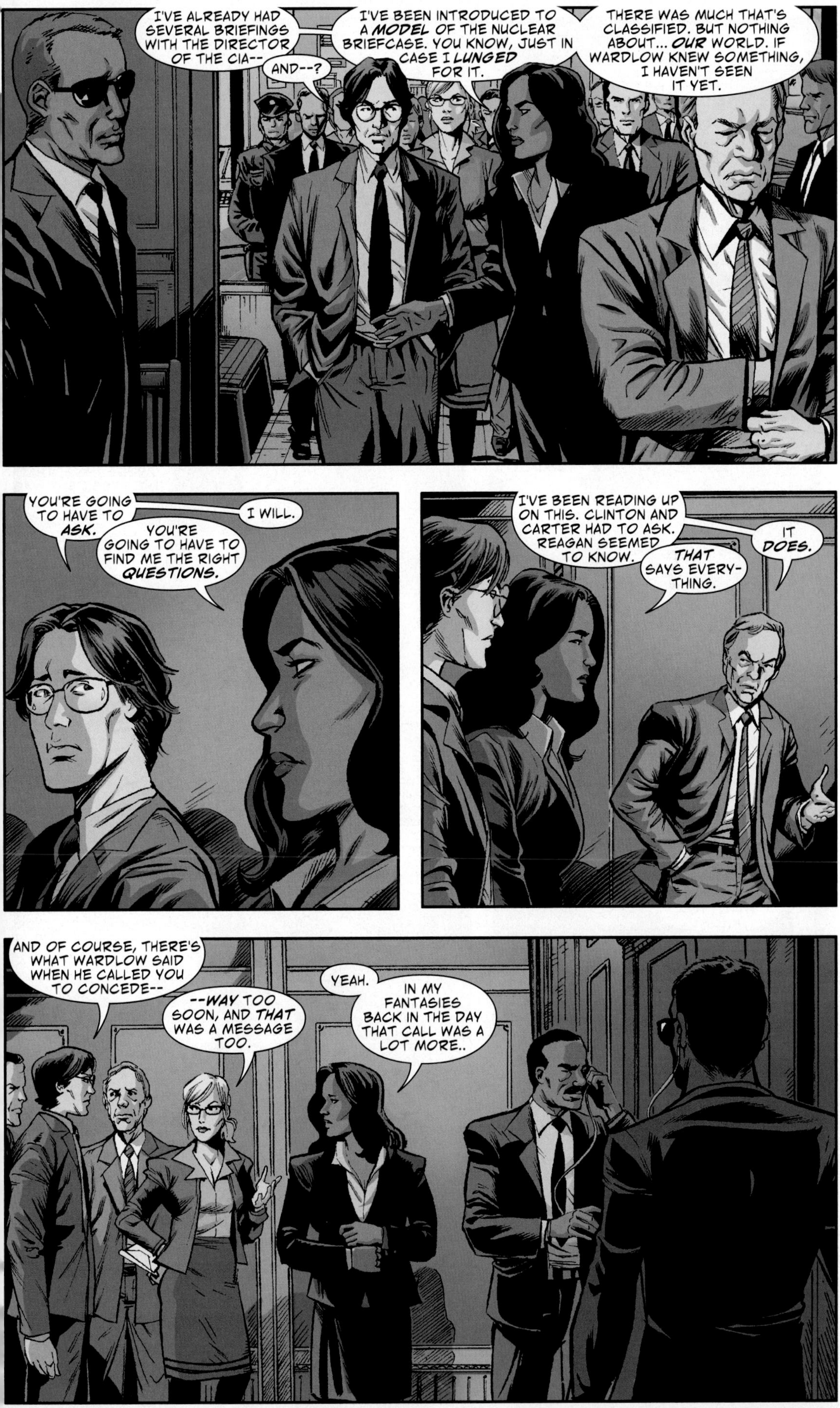
I'VE ALREADY HAD SEVERAL BRIEFINGS WITH THE DIRECTOR OF THE CIA--
AND--?
I'VE BEEN INTRODUCED TO A MODEL OF THE NUCLEAR BRIEFCASE. YOU KNOW, JUST IN CASE I LUNGED FOR IT.
THERE WAS MUCH THAT'S CLASSIFIED. BUT NOTHING ABOUT... OUR WORLD. IF WARDLOW KNEW SOMETHING, I HAVEN'T SEEN IT YET.
YOU'RE GOING TO HAVE TO ASK.
I WILL.
YOU'RE GOING TO HAVE TO FIND ME THE RIGHT QUESTIONS.
I'VE BEEN READING UP ON THIS. CLINTON AND CARTER HAD TO ASK. REAGAN SEEMED TO KNOW.
IT DOES.
THAT SAYS EVERY-THING.
AND OF COURSE, THERE'S WHAT WARDLOW SAID WHEN HE CALLED YOU TO CONCEDE--
--WAY TOO SOON, AND THAT WAS A MESSAGE TOO.
YEAH.
IN MY FANTASIES BACK IN THE DAY THAT CALL WAS A LOT MORE..

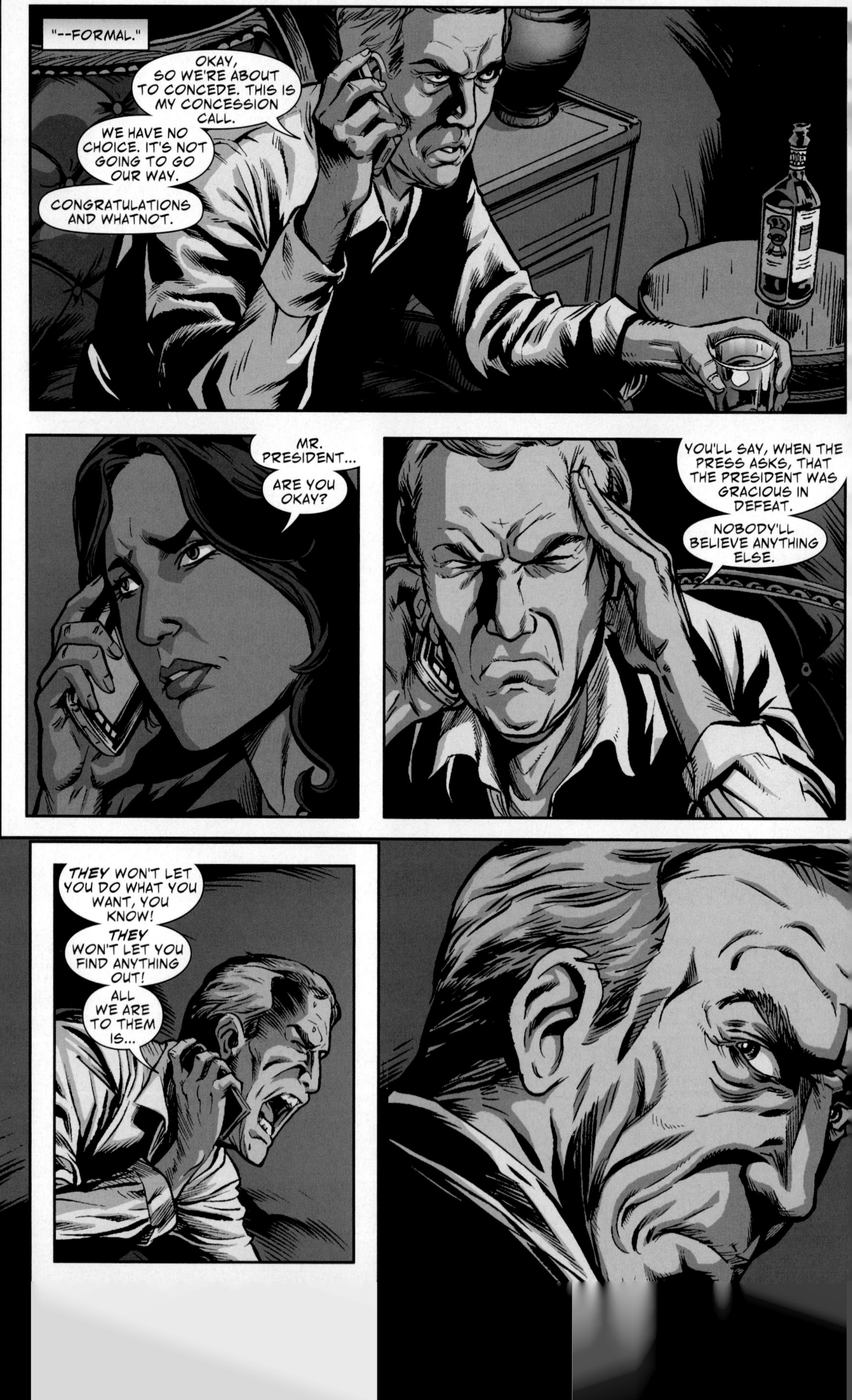
"--FORMAL."
OKAY, SO WE'RE ABOUT TO CONCEDE. THIS IS MY CONCESSION CALL.
WE HAVE NO CHOICE. IT'S NOT GOING TO GO OUR WAY.
CONGRATULATIONS AND WHATNOT.
MR. PRESIDENT...
ARE YOU OKAY?
YOU'LL SAY, WHEN THE PRESS ASKS, THAT THE PRESIDENT WAS GRACIOUS IN DEFEAT.
NOBODY'LL BELIEVE ANYTHING ELSE.
THEY WON'T LET YOU DO WHAT YOU WANT, YOU KNOW!
THEY WON'T LET YOU FIND ANYTHING OUT!
ALL WE ARE TO THEM IS...

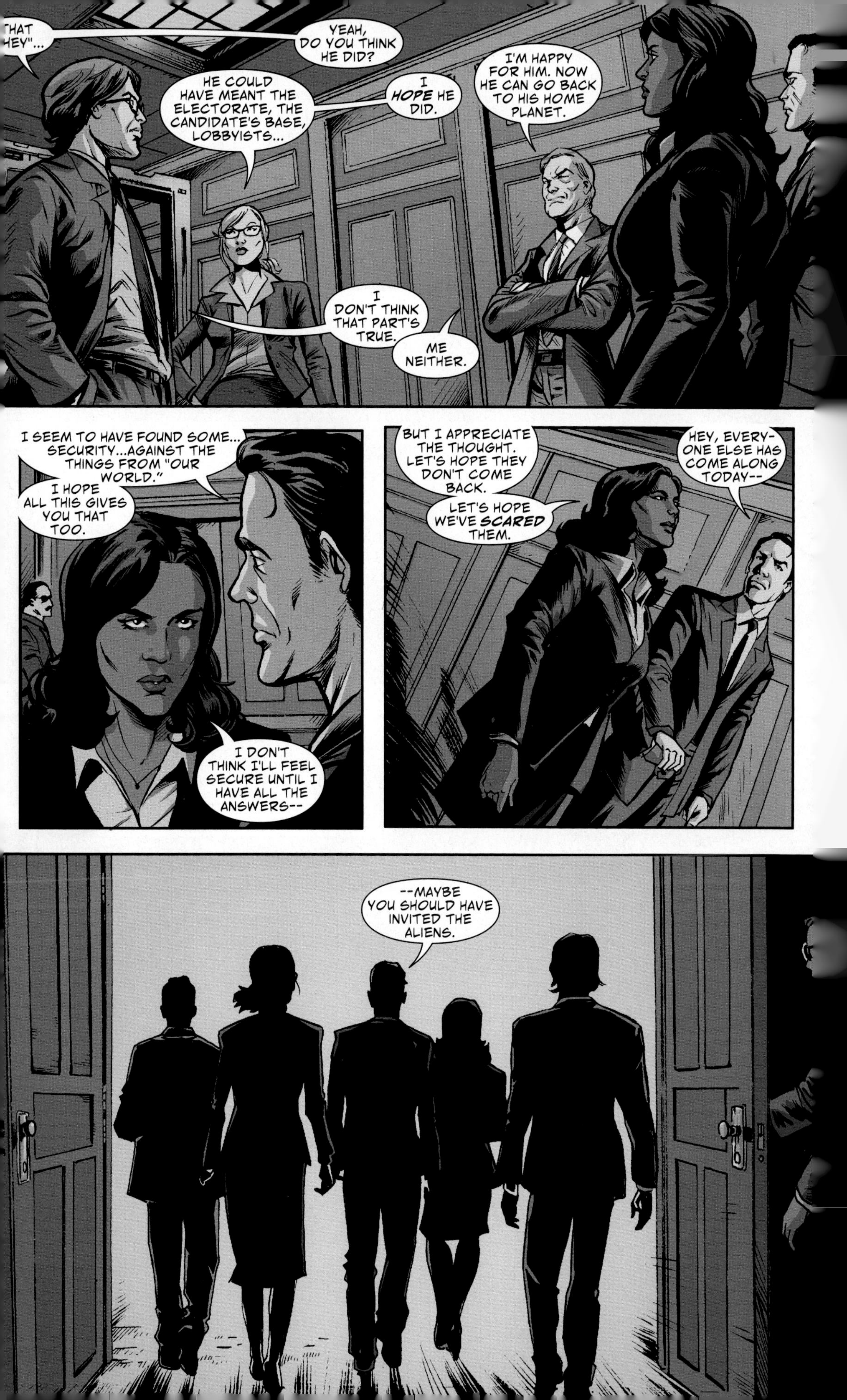
THAT HEY"...
YEAH, DO YOU THINK HE DID?
HE COULD HAVE MEANT THE ELECTORATE, THE CANDIDATE'S BASE, LOBBYISTS...
I HOPE HE DID.
I'M HAPPY FOR HIM. NOW HE CAN GO BACK TO HIS HOME PLANET.
I DON'T THINK THAT PART'S TRUE.
ME NEITHER.
I SEEM TO HAVE FOUND SOME... SECURITY...AGAINST THE THINGS FROM "OUR WORLD."
I HOPE ALL THIS GIVES YOU THAT TOO.
I DON'T THINK I'LL FEEL SECURE UNTIL I HAVE ALL THE ANSWERS--
BUT I APPRECIATE THE THOUGHT. LET'S HOPE THEY DON'T COME BACK.
LET'S HOPE WE'VE SCARED THEM.
HEY, EVERY-ONE ELSE HAS COME ALONG TODAY--
--MAYBE YOU SHOULD HAVE INVITED THE ALIENS.

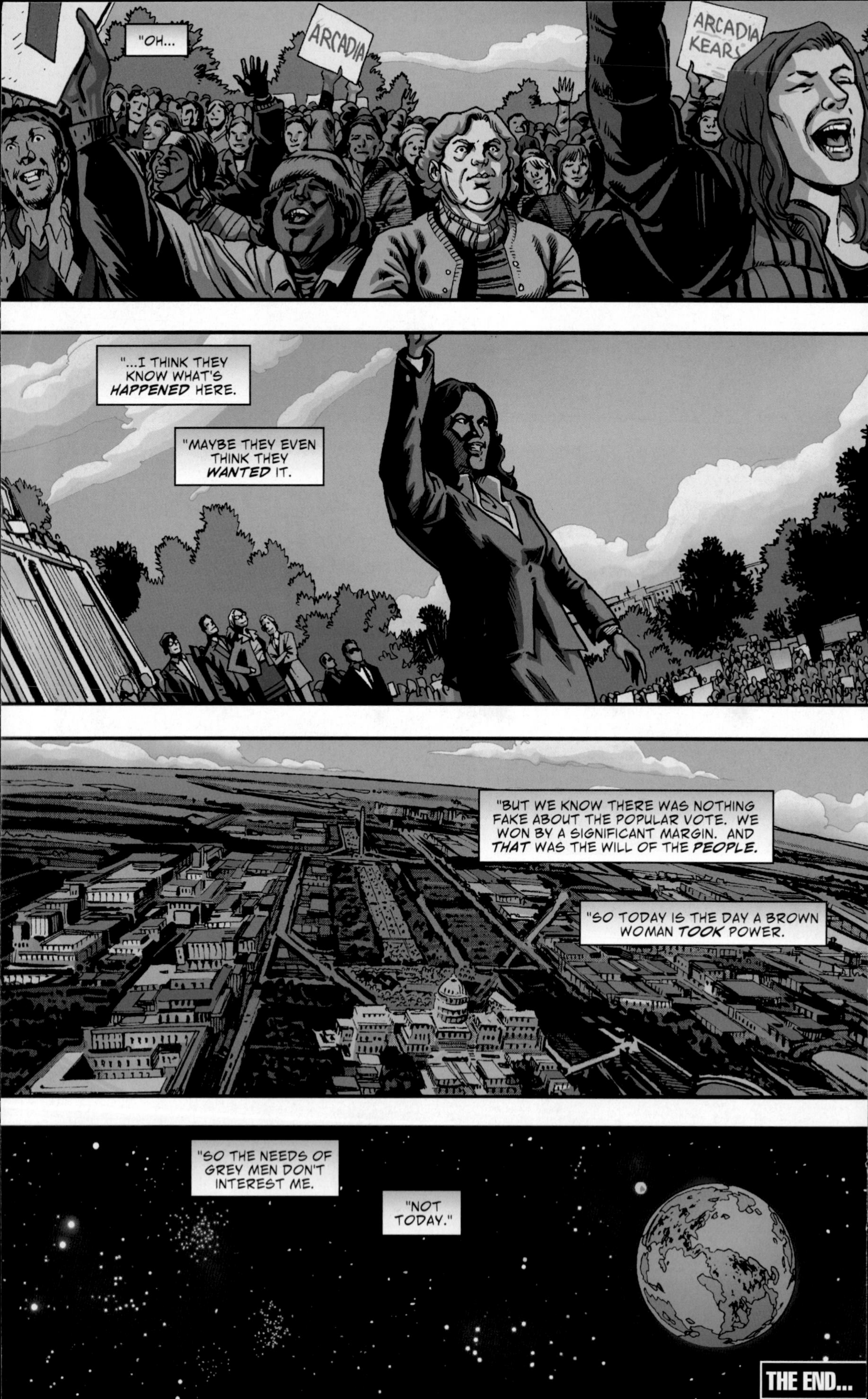
"OH...
ARCADIA
ARCADIA KEARS
"...I THINK THEY KNOW WHAT'S *HAPPENED* HERE.
"MAYBE THEY EVEN THINK THEY *WANTED* IT.
"BUT WE KNOW THERE WAS NOTHING FAKE ABOUT THE POPULAR VOTE. WE WON BY A SIGNIFICANT MARGIN. AND *THAT* WAS THE WILL OF THE *PEOPLE*.
"SO TODAY IS THE DAY A BROWN WOMAN *TOOK* POWER.
"SO THE NEEDS OF GREY MEN DON'T INTEREST ME.
"NOT TODAY."
THE END...